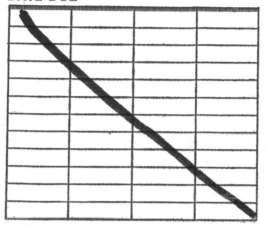

Argentina's Foreign Policy, 1930–1962. Alberto Conil Paz and Gustavo Ferrari.

Italy after Fascism, A Political History, 1943–1965. Giuseppe Mammarella.

The Volunteer Army and Allied Intervention in South Russia, 1917–1921. George A. Brinkley.

Personalities and Policies: Studies in the Formulation of British Foreign Policy in the Twentieth Century. D. C. Watt.

Peru and the United States, 1900–1962. James C. Carey.

Empire by Treaty: Britain and the Middle East in the Twentieth Century. M. A. Fitzsimons.

The USSR and the UN's Economic and Social Activities. Harold Karan Jacobson.

Chile and the United States: 1880–1962. Fredrick B. Pike.

Death in the Forest: The Katyn Forest Massacre. J. K. Zawodny.

East Central Europe and the World: Developments in the Post-Stalin Era. Stephen D. Kertesz, ed.

Soviet Policy Toward International Control of Atomic Energy. Joseph L. Nogee.

Diplomacy in a Changing World. Stephen D. Kertesz and M. A. Fitzsimons, eds.

The Russian Revolution and Religion, 1917–1925. Edited and translated by Boleslaw Szczesniak.

INTERNATIONAL STUDIES OF THE

COMMITTEE ON INTERNATIONAL RELATIONS

UNIVERSITY OF NOTRE DAME

Marx
and the
Western World

Marx
and the
Western World

Edited by NICHOLAS LOBKOWICZ

CONTRIBUTORS
James L. Adams · Helène Carrère d'Encausse · Louis Dupré
Gaston Fessard, S.J. · Iring Fetscher · A. James Gregor
E. V. Il'enkov · Masamichi Inoki · Helio Jaguaribe
George L. Kline · Karel Kosík · George Lichtheim
Nicholas Lobkowicz · Herbert Marcuse · Alfred G. Meyer
Gerhart Niemeyer · Gajo Petrović · Maximilien Rubel
Svetozar Stojanović · Robert C. Tucker · Marx W. Wartofsky
Wlodzimierz Wesolowski

 UNIVERSITY OF NOTRE DAME PRESS
NOTRE DAME—LONDON

Library of Congress Catalog Card Number: 67-12122
Manufactured in the United States of America

PREFACE

Nicholas Lobkowicz

The papers in this volume were presented at an International Symposium held at the University of Notre Dame in April, 1966. The purpose of this Symposium was to draw the attention of the American public to recent developments in the study of Marx and to foster the dialogue, hitherto virtually noncxistent on a scholarly level, between Communist and non-Communist intellectuals.

Until recently many representatives of the "Western World" felt that, in contrast to Plato, Descartes or IIcgel, Marx was a foreign body in the history of occidental culture. In a way, it is easy to understand and even to appreciate this assumption, for powerful political systems, threatening to "bury" the "Western World" in its present form, claim Marx as their greatest authority. Ideas were rejected simply because Marx, viewed as the precursor of Lenin and Stalin, was the first to formulate them explicitly. Ideas and realities of the "socialist" part of the world which can be traced back to Marx's thought were criticized, though under a different name they had long become an integral part of the "Western World." It may even be premature to speak in the past tense; such notions are still very much alive.

There are two main reasons why such conceptions should be banished to the storehouse of narrow-minded and potentially dangerous prejudices. First, it is simply incorrect to say that Marx is a foreign body in the history of Western culture. This is not to say that we necessarily have to consider Marx's contribution as one of the great *positive* achievements of our tradition, but whether we sympathize with Marx's ideas or not, Marx and Marxism are among thé many possible outcomes of centuries of Western thinking and culture. Whoever feels that Marx and the movement which originates from him is a sickness ought to have also the courage to acknowledge that it is an outgrowth of a culture which we usually and perhaps much too easily consider basically sound and healthy.

The other and no less momentous reason why we should give up the notion that Marx is a thinker radically different from Locke or Rousseau or Kant is that this notion makes virtually impossible a meaningful dialogue with representatives of the Communist world. This is not the place to explain that such a dialogue, difficult as it may be, is one of the great tasks of the present. Suffice it to say that true peace is impossible wherever there is no desire to understand each other either as individuals or nations or cultures. This dialogue is still in its beginning; in fact, it hardly has begun at all. Yet it is obvious that it can never outgrow the age of infancy if the "Western World" continues to adhere to the myth that Karl Marx is nothing but a precursor of Stalinist terrorism.

That such notions are historically false has been acknowledged by leading non-Communist Marx scholars for several decades. In particular, the publication of Marx's early philosophical writings in the thirties and their intensive study after the close of World War II have led to a significant reinterpretation and re-evaluation of Marx's thought as a whole. Today many Marx scholars even tend to consider Marx's early thought as much more important than his mature writings—a tendency which Sidney Hook in a number of recent articles has rightly described as questionable. Yet whatever may be the relevance of Marx's early thought for the understanding of his mature views, there can be no doubt that the publication and discussion of Marx's early philosophical speculations significantly contributed to a "reoccidentalization" of Marx in the minds of a number of Western scholars. Unfortunately, however, these insights of a few have remained all but unnoticed by the great public; this is particularly the case in the United States where the first study concerned with the "early Marx" was published as late as 1961.

Until a few years ago the Western interest in the philosophy of the young Marx and thus also in the "humanistic" aspects of Marx's thought as a whole was regarded by most Communist scholars as a bourgeois misunderstanding if not willful prevarication. Only recently have Communist authors become interested in Marx the philosopher and have noticed that there is a deep gap between Engels' or Lenin's allegedly scientific ideology and Marx's early "humanism." But once this topic ceased to be a taboo in the Communist world as well, there inevitably emerged a desire and basic willingness to exchange one's views and to initiate a dialogue. Communist scholars have acknowledged that they had something to learn from their non-Communist colleagues, and non-Communist authors have become increasingly hesitant to reject a Marxist interpretation solely on the grounds that its author is a Communist.

To situate Marx in the tradition of which he is a part and to contribute to the dialogue, my proposal suggested to the participants to try to clarify four questions:

    a) Which elements of Marx's original thought have become an integral part of the "Western" tradition and why?

    b) Which elements of Marx's original thought did not become part of "Western" thought, though perhaps they might have contributed to it?

    c) Which elements of Marx's thought have been neglected by Communists and why?

    d) How much of Western criticism of Communism, adequately understood, may turn out to be an implicit criticism of the Western World and its tradition?

As the reader of this volume will observe, only a few of the participants chose to give a direct answer to any of these four questions. Most preferred detailed and patient analyses which, as the Symposium went on, made one increasingly aware of the fact that such questions are little more than leitmotifs permitting one to see Marx in a new light. Consequently I feel unable to present in this preface anything resembling a clear-cut conclusion reached by the contributors.

Rather, the present volume should be considered the beginning of an endeavor which all of us felt should continue at Notre Dame and elsewhere. It will be the task of future historians to puzzle about the problem why it was that precisely in the early 1960's, at a time when the cries and echoes of the "cold war" still had not subsided, a peculiar détente began to emerge in the mind of intellectuals who hitherto had considered themselves militant activists of inimical camps—a détente which future historians hopefully might be able to record as one of the first signs of a more peaceful and human era.

There are many developments which historians will have to take into account: the death of Stalin and the ensuing de-escalation of political terrorism in one part of the world; the election of Pope John XXIII, a man with a truly unique charisma, to be a spiritual leader in the other part; the fact that both parts had to cope with an infinite number of technological, economic and sociological problems which, simply because they are the burden implicit in advanced industrialization, do not halt before a Curtain or Wall; and an increasing desire among all men to lay aside ideological differences in order to co-operate in the immense task of achieving a truly human existence for each and every man. In all probability the said historian will not ascribe too great an importance to what intellectuals said and "did." He will be well aware of the fact that history is seldom influenced by what scholars and university professors think, particularly since so many among them tended to be decades behind their time. Perhaps, however, he will be able to note that the intellectuals added their share by beginning to recognize and later to teach their fellow men that much of what one had fought and deplored in others was in fact a hidden dimension and potentiality of one's own past and present. In any case, this was the spirit of the Symposium: to contribute the intellectual's small share to peace and a better world by exchanging views, removing misunderstandings and, in general, trying to understand each other.

In addition this volume gathers together an immense amount of learning and scholarship that even by itself is certainly of value. For the Notre Dame Symposium was not only one of the very first symposia held in the West which brought together "socialist" and "capitalist" scholars to discuss major *weltanschauliche* issues. It was also the first truly international meeting concerned with the ideas of Karl Marx. It is no exaggeration to say that this volume contains the results and conclusions of some of the most prominent Marx specialists of the mid-twentieth century.

Two of the papers, namely, the second one by Professor Rubel and my own, were not presented at the Symposium. Two of the contributors were unable to attend our meeting and their papers, mimeographed in advance, were distributed among the participants: Professor George Lichtheim had to return to England earlier than we had anticipated and Professor E. V. Il'enkov was hospitalized. The Symposium was sponsored by the Committee on International Relations of the University of Notre Dame. I should like to use this occasion to thank Professor Stephen Kertesz, Chairman of the Committee, for his encouragement and help during the many months which I devoted to preparing both the symposium and this volume.

My thanks also go to Mrs. Anne Kozak of the University Press for the many hours of patient work which she devoted to the final editing of the papers.

CONTENTS

ABBREVIATIONS

As unfortunately there does not exist a complete edition of Marx's writings in English and moreover several of the papers in this volume originally referred to various translations into foreign languages, the editor has supplied all references to Marx's and Engels' writings with references to the standard German editions. In addition, he has added references to English translations whenever possible; wherever such a reference is missing, no English translation existed.

It may be added that a reference to an English translation does not always mean that the author is using this translation. Several authors preferred directly to translate from the German original in which case the reference indicates only the corresponding passage in an available translation.

All of Marx's and Engels' writings prior to *The German Ideology* were quoted according to

MEGA   Karl Marx-Friedrich Engels, *Historisch-kritische Gesamt-ausgabe*, ed. by D. Rjazanov and (since 1932) V. Adoratskij, Frankfurt a.M. (since 1932: Berlin) 1927 ff. ABBREVI-ATED: *MEGA*, followed by part, volume, section if applicable (*Halbband*), page.

All other writings by Marx and Engels were quoted according to

MEW   Karl Marx-Friedrich Engels, *Werke*, Dietz Verlag Berlin 1961 ff. ABBREVIATED: *MEW*, followed by volume and page. It should be noted that this edition still is not complete; two or three volumes containing Marx's and Engels' later letters are still to appear. When referring to letters still not contained in this edition, no reference to a German text was given.

As it seems little known in the United States, we did not refer to the edition Karl Marx, *Frühe Schriften*, ed. by H.-J. Lieber and P. Furth, Darmstadt 1962 ff., even though this edition contains a number of valuable corrections of the text in *MEGA* and *MEW*.

Part I:
The Foundations

1: ON THE INTERPRETATION OF
MARX'S THOUGHT
George Lichtheim

I

A consideration of the phenomenon called "Marxism" has an obvious starting point in Marx's own reflections on the subject of intellectual systematizations. According to him, they were either "scientific" (in which case they entered into the general inheritance of mankind) or "ideological," and then fundamentally irrelevant, for every ideology necessarily misconceived the real world of which science (*Wissenschaft*) was the theoretical reflection. Yet it is a truism that in some respects Marxism itself has acquired an ideological function. How has this transmutation come about, and what does it tell us about the theoretical breakthrough which Marx effected and which his followers for many years regarded as a guarantee against the revival of "ideological" thinking within the movement he has helped to create?

Regarded from the Marxian viewpoint, which is that of the "union of theory and practice," the transformation of a revolutionary *theory* into the *ideology* of a post-revolutionary, or pseudo-revolutionary, movement is a familiar phenomenon. In modern European history—to go back no further—it has furnished a theme for historical and sociological reflections at least since the aftermath of the French Revolution. Indeed there is a sense in which Marx's own thought (like that of Comte and others) took this experience as its starting point. In the subsequent socialist critique of liberalism, the latter's association with the fortunes of the newly triumphant bourgeoisie furnished a topic not only for Marxist thought, but it also enabled Marx to draw the conclusion that the "emancipation of the working class" had been placed upon the historical agenda by the very success of the liberal bourgeoisie in creating the new world of industrial capitalism.

In so far as "Marxism," during the later nineteenth century, differed from other socialist schools, it signified just this: the conviction that the "proletarian revolution" was *a historical necessity*. If then we are obliged to note that the universal aims of the Marxist school and the actual tendencies of the empirical workers' movement have become discontinuous, we shall have to characterize Marxism and the "ideology" of that movement during a relatively brief historical phase which now appears to be closed. The phase itself was linked to the climax of the "bourgeois revolution" in those European countries where the labor movement stood in the forefront of the political struggle for democracy, at the same time that it groped for a socialist theory of the coming post-bourgeois order. Historically Marxism fulfilled itself when it brought about the upheaval of 1917–1918 in Central and Eastern Europe. Its subsequent evolution into the ideology of the world Communist movement, for all the latter's evident political significance, has added little to its theoretical content. Moreover as far as Soviet Marxism and its various derivations are concerned, the original "union of theory and practice" has now fallen apart.

This approach to the subject is not arbitrary but follows from the logic of the original Marxian conception of the *practical* function of *theory*. It was not part of Marx's intention to found yet another political movement or another "school of thought." Rather his prime purpose as a socialist was to articulate the practical requirements of the labor movement in its struggle for emancipation. His theoretical work was intended as a "guide to action." If it has ceased to serve as such, one may only conclude that the actual course of events had diverged from the theoretical model which Marx had extrapolated from the political struggles of the nineteenth century. In fact it is today generally agreed among Western socialists that the model is inappropriate to the post-bourgeois industrial society in which we live, while its relevance to the belated revolutions in backward pre-industrial societies is purchased at the cost of growing divergence between the utopian aims and the actual practices of the Communist movement. From a different viewpoint the situation may be summed up by saying that while the bourgeois revolution is over in the West, the proletarian revolution has turned out to be an impossibility: at any rate in the form in which Marx conceived it in the last century, for the notion of such a revolution giving rise to a classless society has now acquired a distinctly utopian ring. Conversely the association of socialism with some form of technocracy—understood as the key role of a new social stratum in part drawn from the industrial working class which continues to occupy a subordinate function—has turned out to be much closer than the Marxist school had expected. In short, the "union of theory and practice" has dissolved because the working class has not in fact performed the historic role assigned to it in Marx's theory and because the gradual socialization of the economic sphere in advanced industrial society has become parallel with the emergence of a new type of social stratification. On both counts, the "revisionist" interpretation of Marxism—originally a response to the cleavage between the doctrine and the actual practice of a reformist labor movement—has resulted in the evolution of a distinctively "post-Marxian" form of socialist theorizing while the full doctrinal content of the original systematization is only retained, in a debased and caricatured form, in the so-called "world view" of Marxism-Leninism: itself the ideology of a totalitarian state-party which has long cut its connections with the democratic labor movement. While the Leninist variant continues to have operational value for the Communist movement—notably in societies where that movement has taken over the traditional functions of the bourgeois revolution—the classical Marxian position has been undercut by the development of Western society. In this sense, Marxism (like liberalism) has become "historical." Marx's current academic status as a major thinker in the familiar succession from Helgel (or indeed from Descartes-Hobbes-Spinoza) is simply another manifestation of this state of affairs.[1]

II

While the interrelation of theory and practice is crucial for the evaluation of Marx—far more so than for Comte who never specified an historical agent for the transition to the "positive stage"—it does not by itself supply a criterion for judging the permanent value of Marx's theorizing in the domains of philosophy, history, sociology or eco-

[1] Cf. *inter alia* the treatment of the subject in *Karl Marx—Selected Writings in Sociology and Social Philosophy*, ed. by T. B. Bottomore and M. Rubel, London 1956, and the recent spate of editions of Marx's early writings. Historically, the interpretation of Marxism as the theory of a revolutionary movement which has now come to an end, goes back to the writings of Karl Korsch; cf. in particular his *Karl Marx*, London-New York 1963.

nomics. In principle there is no reason why his theoretical discoveries should not survive the termination of the attempt to construct a "world view" which would at the same time serve as the instrument of a revolutionary movement. This consideration is reinforced by the further thought that the systematization was after all undertaken by others—principally by Engels, Kautsky, Plekhanov and Lenin—and that Marx cannot be held responsible for their departures from his original purpose, which was primarily critical. While this is true, the history of Marxism as an intellectual and political phenomenon is itself a topic of major importance, irrespective of Marx's personal intentions. Moreover it is arguable that both the "orthodox" codification undertaken by Engels and the various subsequent "revisions" have their source in Marx's own ambiguities as a thinker.

As far as Engels is concerned, the prime difficulty arises paradoxically from his life-long association with Marx. This, combined with his editorial and exegetical labors after Marx's death, conferred a privileged status upon his own writings even where his private interests diverged from those of Marx, e.g. in his increasing absorption in problems peculiar to the natural sciences. While Engels was scrupulous in emphasizing his secondary role in the evolution of their common viewpoint,[2] he allowed it to be understood that the "materialist" metaphysics developed in such writings as the Anti-Dühring was in some sense the philosophical counterpart of Marx's own investigations into history and economics. Indeed his very modesty was a factor in causing his quasi-philosophical writings to be accepted as the joint legacy of Marx and himself. The long-run consequences were all the more serious in that Engels, unlike Marx, lacked proper training in philosophy and had no secure hold upon any part of the philosophical tradition, except for the Hegelian system, of which he virtually remained a life-long prisoner. The "dialectical" materialism, or monism, advanced in the Anti-Dühring and in the essays on natural philosophy published in 1925 under the title Dialectics of Nature, has only the remotest connection with Marx's own viewpoint, though it is a biographical fact of some importance that Marx raised no objection to Engels' exposition of the theme in the Anti-Dühring. The reasons for this seeming indifference must remain a matter for conjecture. What cannot be doubted is that it was Engels who was responsible for the subsequent interpretation of "Marxism" as a unified

[2] Cf. in particular his letter to F. Mehring of July 14, 1893, and the preface to the English edition of The Condition of the Working Class in England.

system of thought destined to take the place of Hegelianism and indeed of classical German philosophy in general. That it did so only for German Social-Democracy, and only for one generation, is likewise an historical factum. The subsequent emergence of Soviet Marxism was mediated by Plekhanov and Lenin and differs in some respects from Engels' version (e.g. in the injection of even larger doses of Hegelianism) notably in the introduction by Lenin of a species of voluntarism which had more in common with Bergson and Nietzsche than with Engels' own rather deterministic manner of treating historical topics. In this sense Leninism has to be regarded as a "revision" of the orthodox Marxism of Engels, Plekhanov and Kautsky.

The whole development has obvious political, as well as intellectual, significance. I have dealt with it at some length elsewhere and must here confine myself to the observation that Soviet Marxism is to be understood as a monistic system *sui generis*, rooted in Engels' interpretation of Marx but likewise linked to the pre-Marxian traditions of the Russian revolutionary intelligentsia. Unlike "orthodox" Marxism, which in Central Europe functioned for at least one generation as the "integrative ideology" of a genuine workers' movement, Soviet Marxism was a pure intelligentsia creation, wholly divorced from the concerns of the working class. Its unconscious role has been to equip the Soviet intelligentsia (notably the technical intelligentsia) with a cohesive world view adequate to its task in promoting the industrialization and modernization of a backward country. Of the subsequent dissemination and vulgarization of this ideology in China and elsewhere, it is unnecessary to speak.[3]

In the light of what was said above about the transformation of Marxism from a revolutionary critique of bourgeois society into the systematic ideology of a non-revolutionary, or post-revolutionary, labor movement in Western Europe and elsewhere, this contrasting,

[3] It is impossible here to document the links in the historical chain leading from Engels to Lenin and beyond, but reference should be made to Plekhanov's essay "Zu Hegels sechzigstem Todestag," originally published in *Neue Zeit*, November 1891, and reprinted in G. Plekhanov, *Selected Philosophical Works*, Moscow 1961, vol. I, p. 455 ff. Lenin's contribution to the "philosophical" debate in his *Materialism and Empiriocriticism* (1909) is well known, as is his belated discovery of Hegel; cf. his *Philosophical Notebooks* of 1914–1916, now reprinted in vol. 38 of the *Collected Works*. The embarrassment caused to his editors by the evident incompatibility of the rather simple-minded epistemological realism expounded in the earlier work with the more "dialectical" approach of the *Notebooks* is among the minor charms of Soviet philosophical theorizing.

though parallel, development in the Soviet orbit presents itself as additional confirmation of our thesis. The latter assigns to Marxism a particular historical status not dissimilar from that of liberalism: another universal creed which has evolved from the philosophical assumptions and hypotheses of the eighteenth-century Enlightenment. The universalist content is, however, differently distributed. Liberalism was from the start markedly reluctant to disclose its social origins and sympathies whereas Marxism came into being as the self-proclaimed doctrine of a revolutionary class movement. The humanist approach was retained in both cases, but whereas liberal philosophy in principle denies any logical relation between the social origin of a doctrine and its ethico-political content, Marxism approached the problem by designating the proletariat as the "universal" class and itself as the theoretical expression of the latter's struggle for emancipation: conceived as synonymous with mankind's effort to raise itself to a higher level. Hence although for contemporary liberalism the unsolved problem resides in the unacknowledged social content of its supposedly universal doctrine, the difficulty for Marxism arises from the failure of the proletariat to fulfill the role assigned to it in the original "critical theory" of 1843–1848 as formulated in Marx's early writings and in the *Communist Manifesto*. Since liberalism cannot shake off the death-grip of "classical," i.e. bourgeois, economics—for which the market economy remains the center of reference—Marxism (at any rate in its Communist form) is confronted with the awkward dissonance between its universal aims and the actual record of the class upon whose political maturity the promised deliverance from exploitation and alienation depends. There is the further difference that the Marxian "wager" on the proletariat represents an "existential" option (at any rate for intellectuals stemming from another class), whereas liberalism—at least in principle—claims to be in tune with the commonsense outlook of educated "public opinion." This divergence leads back to a consideration of the philosophical issues inherent in the original codification of "orthodox Marxism."

III

Marx's early theoretical standpoint, as set out in the *Holy Family* (1845) and the *German Ideology* (1845–1846), was a development of French eighteenth-century materialism, minus its Cartesian physics and the related epistemological problem in which he took no interest. The basic orientation of this materialism was practical, and its application to social life led in the direction of socialism, once it was admitted that between man and his environment there was an interaction which left room for a conscious effort to remodel his existence. As Marx put it in the *Holy Family*, "If man is shaped by his surroundings, his surroundings must be made human. If man is social by nature he will develop his true nature only in society. . . ."[4] Materialism or naturalism (the terms are employed interchangeably by Marx) is the foundation of communism. This conclusion follows *necessarily*, once it is grasped that the material conditions of human existence can and must be altered if man is to reach his full stature. Materialism is revolutionary because when applied to society it discloses what the idealist hypostatization of "spirit" obscures: that man's history is a constant struggle with his material environment, a struggle in which man's "nature" is formed and re-formed. The historicity of human nature, which is a necessary consequence of this anthropological naturalism, raises the question as to what criterion we possess for judging the activities of men in their effort to subdue the nonhuman environment: an effort mediated by social intercourse with other men, since it is only in and through society that men become conscious of themselves.[5]

The answer Marx gives is open to criticism on the grounds of circularity, since it amounts to saying that man's "nature" is constituted by his *Praxis*, i.e., his capacity for constituting a man-made world around him. However this may be, it is plain that for Marx the only "nature" that enters into consideration is man's own plus his surroundings which he transforms by his "practical activity." The external world, as it exists in and for itself, is irrelevant to a materialism that approaches history with a view toward establishing what men have made of themselves. It is doubly irrelevant because, on the Marxian assumption, the world is never simply "given" to consciousness, any more than man himself is the passive receptacle of sense impressions. An external environment, true knowledge of which is possible,

---

[4] *MEGA*, I, 3, p. 307 ff.; cf. K. Marx-F. Engels, *The Holy Family*, Moscow.

[5] "Language, like consciousness, . . . arises . . . from the necessity of intercourse with other men. . . . Hence consciousness from the very start is a social product and remains one as long as men exist at all," *MEGA*, I, 5, 19; cf. K. Marx-F. Engels, *The German Ideology*, New York 1960, p. 19.

is a fantasy in abstraction from man's active role in molding the object of perception. The only world we know is the one we have constituted—that which appears in our experience. The "subjective" nature of this experience is checked by its social character which in turn is rooted in the permanent constitutents of man as a "species being" (*Gattungswesen*) who "comes to himself" in society. There is, in the strict sense, no epistemological problem for Marx. The dialectics of perception and natural environment cannot, in his view, be compressed into a formula, for "reason" is itself historical and its interaction with nature is just what appears in history. Man has before him a "historical nature," and his own "natural history" culminates in his conscious attempt to reshape the world of which he forms a part.

The notion that this anthropological naturalism is anchored in a general theory of the universe finds no support in Marx's own writings. There is no logical link between Marx's conception and the "dialectical materialism" of Engels and Plekhanov, any more than there is a necessary connection between Marx's pragmatic view of conscious mental activity as an aspect of *Praxis* and the epistemological realism of Lenin. Indeed in the latter case there is positive incongruity. Perception as a mirror-image of an external reality which acts upon the mind through physical stimuli has no place in Marx's theory of consciousness. The copy theory of perception set out in *Materialism and Empiriocriticism* (apart from being inadequate and self-contradictory in the way Lenin presents it) is incompatible with the Marxian standpoint. Its formulation arose from the accidental problem of working out a new theoretical basis for the natural sciences—a problem in which Marx had taken no interest. It also involved a divergence from Engel's approach, since materialism for Engels was not the same as epistemological realism. In Engels' quasi-Hegelian discussion of this theme, "matter" conserved some of the attributes of a primary substance which was somehow involved in the constitution of the universe. The difference between idealism and materialism was seen by Engels to lie in the former's claim to the ontological pre-eminence of mind or spirit whereas natural science was supposed by him to have established the materiality of the world in an absolute or ultimate sense. The resulting medley of metaphysical materialism and Hegelian dialectics (first described as "dialectical materialism" by Plekhanov) was conserved by Lenin, but his own theory of cognition—which was what mattered to him—was not strictly speaking dependent on it.

Matter as an absolute substance, or constitutive element of the universe, is not required for a doctrine which merely postulates that the mind is able to arrive at universally true conclusions about the external world given to the senses. Lenin's standpoint in fact is compatible with any approach which retains the ontological priority of the external world (however constituted) over the reflecting mind. Belief in the existence of an objective reality is not peculiar to materialists. It is, moreover, only very tenuously connected with the doctrine of nature's ontological primacy over spirit which Lenin had inherited from Engels and which was important to him as a defense against "fideism."

The whole confusion becomes comprehensible only when it is borne in mind that the transformation of Marx's own naturalism into a metaphysical materialism was a practical necessity for Engels and his followers without being a logical one. It was required to turn "Marxism" into a coherent *Weltanschauung*, first for the German labor movement and later for the Soviet intelligentsia. As such it has continued to function, notwithstanding its philosophical inadequacies, but it has also suffered the fate of other systematizations undertaken for non-scientific reasons. At the same time it has paradoxically served to weaken the appeal of Marx's own historical materialism, since the latter was supposedly derived from a metaphysical doctrine of the universe—or an indefensible theory of cognitive perception—with which in reality it had no connection whatever.

IV

To grasp the full extent of this intellectual disaster it is necessary to see what Marx intended when he applied his realistic mode of thought to the understanding of history. The doctrine sketched out in his early writings (notably in the first section of the *German Ideology*) and subsequently given a succinct formulation in the well-known Preface to the 1859 *Critique of Political Economy* was "materialist" in that it broke with the traditional "idealist" procedure wherein ordinary material history was treated as the unfolding of principles laid up in the speculative heavens. The primary datum for Marx was the "real life-process" in which men are engaged, the "production and reproduction of material existence," as he put it on some occasions. In this context, the so-called higher cultural activities appeared as the "ideological reflex" of the primary process whereby men organize their relationship to nature and to each other. Whatever may be said in criticism of this approach, it is quite independent of any metaphysical assumptions about the ontological priority of an absolute substance called "matter," though for evident psychological reasons it was easy to slide from "historical" to "philosophical" materialism. Even so, the grounding of the former in the latter does not necessarily entail the further step of suggesting that human history is set in motion and kept going by a "dialectical" process of contradiction within the "material basis." Such a conclusion follows neither from the materialist principle nor from the quasi-Hegelian picture Marx drew in the 1859 Preface where he referred briefly to the succession of stages from "Asiatic society," via Antiquity and the Middle Ages, to the modern (European) epoch. Marx's own historical research (notably in the *Grundrisse* of 1857–1858) stressed the radical discontinuity of these "historical formations." It is by no means the case that the emergence of European feudalism from the wreck of ancient society was treated by him as a matter of logical necessity. Even in relation to the rise of capitalism he was careful to specify the unique historical preconditions which made possible the "unfolding" of the new mode of production. The notion of a dialectical "law" linking primitive communism via slavery, feudalism and capitalism with the mature communism of the future was once more the contribution of Engels who in this as in other matters bore witness to the unshakeable hold of Hegel's philosophy upon his own cast of mind.

The reverse side of this medal is the ambiguous relationship of Marx and Engels to Comte and of Marxism to Positivism. The point has occasionally been made[6] that in dealing with the rise of the "historical school" in nineteenth-century Europe, one has to go back to the intermingling of Hegelian and Comtean strands in the 1830's— mediated in some cases by writers who had actually studied under both Comte and Hegel.[7] It is also arguable that Marx may have been more deeply influenced by Comte than he was himself aware since some of Saint-Simon's later writings are now known to have been in

---

[6] E.g. by F. A. Hayek, in *The Counter-Revolution of Science*, Glencoe 1955, especially p. 191 ff.

[7] *Ibid.*, p. 193.

part drafted by his then secretary. However this may be, it is undeniable that the general effect of Engels' popularization of Marx ran parallel to the more direct influence of Positivism properly so called. With only a slight exaggeration it may be said that "Marxism" (as interpreted by Engels) eventually came to do for Central and Eastern Europe what Positivism had done for the West: It acquainted the public with a manner of viewing the world which was "materialist" and "scientific," in the precise sense which these terms possessed for writers who believed in extending to history and society the methods of natural sciences. While Marx had taken some tentative steps in this direction, it was Engels who committed German Socialism wholeheartedly to the new viewpoint.

At first sight it is not apparent why a Hegelian training in philosophy should predispose anyone in favor of the Comtean approach, which in some respects stands at the opposite pole. Moreover Marx owed more to the French materialists than did Engels; consequently there appears to be a certain paradox in the notion that the fusion of Hegelian and Comtean modes of thought was mediated by Engels. It must, however, be born in mind that the *Philosophie Positive* had two aspects. In so far as it stressed the purely empirical character of science and dispensed with metaphysical explanations, it belonged to the tradition of the Enlightenment in its specifically French "materialist" form (which was the only one Marx took seriously). Where it aimed at a universal history of mankind, its influence ran parallel to that of Hegelianism. Now the peculiarity of Marx's "historical materialism" is that it combines universalism and empiricism. For Marx (e.g. in the Preface to the 1859 work) the historical process has an internal logic, but investigation into the actual sequence of socioeconomic formations is a matter for empirical research. The link between the two levels of generality is to be found in the interaction between technology ("forces of production") and society ("relations of production"). This interaction, however, is not uniform, i.e. not of such a kind that the historical outcome can be predicted in each case with reference to a general law abstracted from the principle of interaction. Unlike Hegel, Marx does not treat history as the unfolding of a metaphysical substance and unlike Comte, he does not claim to be in possession of an operational key which will unlock every door. Even the statement that "mankind always sets for itself only such tasks as it can solve"[8] is simply an extrapolation from the empirically observable circumstance that in every sphere of life (including that of art) problems and solutions have a way of emerging jointly. A formulation of this kind is at once too general and too flexible to be termed a "law." It is a working hypothesis to be confirmed or refuted by historical experience. Similarly the statement that socialism grows "necessarily" out of capitalism is simply a way of saying that economic conflict poses an institutional problem to which socialism supplies the only rational answer. Whether one accepts or rejects this, Marx is not here laying down a "law," let alone a universal law. On his general assumptions about history, the failure to solve this particular problem (or any other) remained an open possibility. In such a case there would doubtless be regress, perhaps even a catastrophe. The "relentless onward march of civilization" is a Comtean, not a Marxian, postulate. If the second generation of his followers understood Marx to have expounded a kind of universal optimism, they thoroughly misunderstood the meaning and temper of his message.[9]

In relation to bourgeois society the Marxian approach may be summarized by saying that this formation contains within itself the germs of a higher form of social organization. Whether these latent possibilities are utilized, depends upon historical circumstances which have to be investigated in their concreteness. One cannot deduce from a general law of social evolution the alleged necessity for one type of society to give birth to a more developed one—otherwise it would be incomprehensible why classical Antiquity regressed and made room for a primitive type of feudalism instead of evolving to a higher level. In fact Marx held that the collapse had been brought about by the institution of slavery, which was both the basis of that particular civilization and the organic limit of its further development.[10] In principle the same might happen again. If Marx makes the assumption that the industrial working class is the potential bearer of a higher form of social organization, he is saying no more than that no other class appears capable of transcending the *status quo*. What might be called the existential commitment of Marxism to the labor movement follows from this assumption. Like every commitment it carries with

[8] *MEW*, XIII, 9; cf. K. Marx-F. Engels, *Selected Works*, Moscow 1951, vol. I, p. 363.
[9] On this point cf. Korsch, *op. cit.*, p. 51 ff.
[10] *Grundrisse der Kritik der politischen Ökonomie*, Berlin 1953, p. 380 ff.

it the implied possibility of failure. Were it otherwise, there would be no sense in speaking of "tasks" confronting the movement: it would be enough to lay down a "law" of evolution in the Comtean or Spencerian manner. Belief in an evolutionary "law" determining the procession of historical stages was not only the mark of "orthodox" Marxism as formulated by Kautsky and Plekhanov under the influence of Spencer and other evolutionists but was also the mark of Engels whose synthesis of Hegelian and Comtean modes of thought made possible this fateful misunderstanding.

V

In justice to all concerned it has to be borne in mind that Marxism and Positivism did have in common their descent from the Saint-Simonian school. It was in the latter that the notion of history as a developmental process subject to "invariable laws" was first adumbrated in confused fashion, later to be given a more adequate formulation by Comte and Marx. The justification for treating these two very disproportionately gifted thinkers under the same heading arises from the evident circumstance that their contemporaries were affected by them in roughly similar ways. In general it might be said that Marx did for the Germans—notably for German sociology and the "historical school" (Schmoller, Weber, Sombart, Troeltsch and so on)—what Comte had earlier done for Durkheim and his school in France. And this assimilation of Comtean and Marxian modes of thought into the canon of academic sociology was evidently rendered possible by their commitment to the idea of history as the special mode of societal evolution. In saying this, one is simply stating the obvious, although on occasion this does no harm. It was Saint-Simon who had first declared that the proper business of social science is the discovery of laws of development governing the course of human history. To say that Marx, no less than Comte, remained true to this perspective is simply to say that he remained faithful to his intellectual origins (which in this case antedated the Hegelianism of his student days since we know that he had come across Saint-Simonism while still a schoolboy). That human history forms a whole—in Hegelian terms a "concrete totality"—was a certainty he never surrendered. There is the same attachment to the original vision in his oft-repeated statement that knowledge of the "laws" underlying historical development will enable society to lessen the "birthpangs" inseparable from the growth of a new social formation. Insight into the regularities of history is, by a seeming paradox, seen as a means of controlling the future course of development.

In all these respects Comte and Marx appeared to be saying the same thing, and it was this similarity which led so many Positivists to describe themselves as Marxists: notably in France, where indeed this identification became a factor in the evolution of the Socialist movement. Yet the differences are as important as the similarities. Comte's sociology dispensed with the notion of class conflict which for Marx was the central motor of historical progress. The Comtean view of society not only posited the latter as the basic reality—over against the state on the one hand, and the individual on the other—but also elevated it to a plane where the "science of society" was seen to consist in the elucidation of an harmonious interdependence of all the parts. From the Marxian viewpoint this is sheer fantasy, a willful disregard of the reality of conflict whereby alone social progress takes place. In the subsequent evolution of the two systems this difference in approach translated itself *inter alia* into the conflicting doctrines of Russian Populism (heavily impregnated by Comte) and its Marxist rival. There is a sense in which the defeat of *Narodnichestvo* represented the victory of the Marxian over the Comtean school. The Russian Marxists were aware of this situation, and down to Lenin's polemics in the 1890's the need to differentiate themselves from the Positivist belief in the organic unity of society played an important role in the development of their thinking.[11]

The last-mentioned consideration, however, also serves to define the historical context within which the Marxian doctrine could expect to play a role in the formation of a revolutionary movement. When in the 1880's some former Populists turned from *Narodnichestvo* to Marxism, they did so because they found in Marx a convincing statement of the thesis that the economic process would "slowly but unavoidably undermine the old regime," so that the Russian proletariat, "in an historical development proceeding just as inexorably as the development of capitalism itself," would thereby be enabled to

[11] Cf. *inter alia* Plekhanov's writings of the 1880's (now reproduced in vol. I of his *Selected Works*.) See also Ryazanov's preface to the 1929 German edition of Plekhanov's *Fundamental Problems of Marxism* (1908).

"deal the deathblow to Russian absolutism."[12] In other words, what they found was a *theory of the bourgeois revolution*. The latter being a "necessary" process—in the sense that the political "superstructure" was bound, sooner or later, to be transformed by the autonomous evolution of the socioeconomic realm—it was possible to interpret Marx's doctrine in a determinist sense. In *Das Kapital* Marx had done so himself, to the extent that he had treated the "unfolding" of the new mode of production—once it had come into being—as a process independent of the conscious desires and illusions of its individual "agents." Hence the link between the "materialist conception of history" and the notion of "ideology" as "false consciousness." What his contemporaries (and the first generation of his followers) failed to see was that the entire construction was strictly appropriate only to the evolution of bourgeois society, which in Western Europe was coming to an end, while in Russia the "bourgeois revolution" was about to be carried through by a movement hostile to the traditional aims of the middle class. Marxism as a theory of the bourgeois revolution was destined to celebrate its triumph on Russian soil at the very moment when it began to falter in the post-bourgeois environment of Western industrial society. This discontinuity was later to be mirrored in the cleavage between the determinist character of "orthodox Marxism" and the voluntarist strain which came to the fore in the theory and practice of the Communist movement. The latter, faced with the evident exhaustion of the revolutionary impulse which had accompanied the great economic gearshift of the nineteenth century, was increasingly obliged to seek fresh sources of popular spontaneity in areas of the world not yet subjected to industrialism (whether capitalist or socialist). At the theoretical level, the uncomprehended necessity to find a substitute for the revolutionary proletariat of early capitalism—an aspect of the bourgeois revolution, for it is only the latter that rouses the working class to political consciousness—found its expression in the doctrine of the vanguard: an elite which substitutes itself for the class it is supposed to represent. This development signifies the dissolution of the Marxian "union of theory and practice": a union originally built upon the faith that the working class *as such* can and will emancipate itself, and the whole of mankind, from political and economic bondage.

[12] Cf. Plekhanov's pamphlet *Socialism and the Political Struggle* (1883).

2: THE YOUNG AND THE OLD MARX

Iring Fetscher

I. INTRODUCTION TO THE PROBLEM

In the old European social democratic parties, Karl Marx was honored as a great economist, as the writer of *Das Kapital*, a book intended to prove the inevitable decline of the capitalistic system with scientific rigor. In the perspective of Lenin's interpretation of Marxism and the activities of the Communist International, Marx appeared to be first of all a political thinker who taught the working class to create its own organization as a basis for the seizure of political power. Under this perspective, the "Critique of the Gotha Programme" was praised as one of Marx's most important contributions. However in the development of the Communist *Weltanschauung* of the Socialist and of Communist parties, Friedrich Engels and even Joseph Dietzgen were far more significant and influential than Marx himself.

In part this view results because the young Marx, that is, Marx the *philosopher*, was almost unknown and absolutely neglected until the publications of Karl Korsch and Georg Lukács in 1923. The early writings of Marx, known to some experts, were held to be brilliant but not genuinely Marxist, and as such they were at best believed to be significant for our evaluation of the genesis, not for the understanding, of Marx's mature works. In this respect, the words with which Mehring in his 1918 biography of Marx ended the chapter on his early writings are characteristic of the then prevailing appreciation of the young Marx:

> Thus in shadowy contours we observe an outline of socialist society beginning to form. In the *Deutsch-Französische Jahrbücher*, Marx is still ploughing the philosophic field, but in the furrows turned over by his critical ploughshare the first shoots of the materialist conception of history began to sprout, and under the warm sun of French civilization they soon began to flower.[1]

[1] Franz Mehring, *Karl Marx, The Story of His Life*, Ann Arbor 1962, p. 73.

Consequently the philosophical writings of Marx were understood as the first steps toward a scientific method of historical materialism that obviously was not considered to be a philosophy, and thus Marx's early writings were inevitably considered "immature" whereas even the publications of a socialist as theoretically feeble as Kautsky were taken to be far-reaching applications of the supposedly scientific method inaugurated by Marx.

Karl Korsch and Georg Lukács had grown up in an entirely different intellectual climate. They not only knew the neo-Kantian theory of knowledge but also Hegel's philosophy; moreover Lukács was familiar with the problems of the differentiation between the natural sciences on the one side and the humanities and the social sciences on the other through his early contacts with such outstanding representatives of neo-Kantianism as Emil Lask and Max Weber. The logic of inquiry within these disciplines could no longer be conceived of as a universally applicable theory, and consequently difference between causal and/or functional analysis on the one hand and the interpretation of cultural phenomena in their complete totality (*Sinnverstehen*) on the other was, from now on, held to be fundamental. Wilhelm Dilthey, no less than Max Weber, belonged to the great inspiring masters. Consequently Lukács and Korsch, illuminated by the ideas of this most recent epoch of the history of German philosophy and with the intention of helping the revolutionary consciousness to an adequate and deeper understanding of its own contemporary status, went back to Hegel and the young Marx although they did and could not know all early writings of Marx of that time.

The reproaches against Lukács and Korsch from the side of the social democratic and Communist orthodox writers were raised as a defense. Not only was the older interpretations of Marx's theory as an economic theory threatened, so also was a general method of historical investigation. Lukács and Korsch insinuated that Marx had cast the problems of the bourgeois philosophy into a more adequate mould with deeper understanding than could have been achieved by the bourgeois philosophers themselves and on a new basis which definitely opened a way for final solution. To the ideologues of the social democratic and Communist parties, it still appeared necessary to emphasize the radical difference between the bourgeois and the proletarian revolution, on the one hand, and the two *Weltanschauungen*, on the other hand. Lukács, and later on Max Horkheimer, Walter Benjamin,

Herbert Marcuse and Theodor Adorno even thought that to stress the continuity of the bourgeois and the revolutionary movements was most important because of the fact that the German and Italian bourgeoisie were in the age of fascism about to betray the ideals of their own past. They endeavored to show to the bourgeois intellectuals the gulf between the liberal principles and humanitarian aspirations of the early bourgeoisie and the meaning and scope of the modern barbarianism which grew out, as they thought, of the antagonism of contemporary capitalist society and led to fascism.

Both the dangers of fascism and the reappraisal of Hegel's philosophy led to a new interpretation of Marx's early writings. Humanism, a genuine constituent of Marx's early works, could no longer be taken for granted. It was negated in practice and disavowed in theory by the fascist movements as well as Stalinism. Thus the time was obviously ripe to win the young Marx as an ally in the fight against these forms of rising barbarism.

This in turn necessitated reappraisal of Hegel's philosophy. Therefore the authors just mentioned set out to fight against the myth of Hegel as the Prussian state philosopher. They took up an issue with which Marx and Engels had already dealt but which had again become accentuated by the mystification of Hegel in works like those of Kuno Fischer and other authors of imperial Germany.

While the representatives of positivist neoliberalism denounced Hegel (and with him Rousseau and other modern philosophers of democracy), these authors emphasized the perspicacity with which Hegel had anticipated the pitfalls and inconsistencies of the liberal society and its elementary dynamics and with which he already had seen through the liberal formulation of the rights of man.

The interpretation of Marx's early writings, of course, depended to a great extent on the evaluation of the bourgeois philosophical tradition. Whereas Lukács and Korsch interpreted Marx's intentions as an attempt to solve by a radical theory and revolutionary *praxis* the problems with which the bourgeois philosophy could not come to grips, Marx was, according to the doctrines of Social Democrats and Communists, the founder of a scientific proletarian *Weltanschauung* that they contrasted emphatically with the *Weltanschauung* of the bourgeoisie. Because both political movements, Social Democracy and Communism, intended to create their own *Weltanschauung*—each of course with a specific character—they had to stress the difference between Hegel and the young Marx on the one hand and the old Marx on the other; and consequently, both had to de-emphasize Marx's early writings. To the ideologues of Stalinism, the discussion of and the references to the young Marx were inexpedient because Marx in his early writings spoke of the proletarian revolution and socialism as a means for the realization of a genuinely human society and not as absolute and dogmatic standards. The new Soviet society, labeled socialist by its own ideologues, was threatened to be exposed to criticism based on the characteristics Marx attributed to a truly "human society." This conception obviously and definitely stood, among other things, in sharp contrast to the conception of the state and law as it was propagated by the Stalinist orthodox writers as by many others.

In the light of the motives I have just mentioned, which functioned as an impediment to the incorporation of the young Marx into the theories and doctrines of the labor movement, the rather late and first publication of the important parts of his early writings, above all the *Philosophic and Economic Manuscripts* and the *German Ideology* (both first published in 1932), was less relevant. One should not forget that some of the early writings, like Marx's contribution to the *Deutsch-Französische Jahrbücher* were previously known and that leading social democrats were well informed about Marx's literary bequest without pressing for publication. Not until recently were there signs of a reappraisal of the young Marx in the "socialist" states —a reappraisal which was triggered, however, as Adam Schaff once remarked by the intensive research and studies of Western scholars. Moreover it seems to me that the achieved status of the Soviet society and the perspectives of as well as the planning for a transition to a "real" Communist society nowadays also favor a frank confrontation with the young Marx. The disparity between contemporary socialist states and Marx's conception of a real human society can be more easily described today as the distance between the socialist phase and the terminal Communist stage of the transition. This now sounds more credible than at an early stage of the movement originated by Marx; at that time this transition was still so far removed in time that the distance between socialism and Communism would have been considered only as a contrast.

Undoubtedly we should also consider the fact that the misery in which the working class had to live for decades in capitalist societies was, by and large, done away with by the development of modern techniques and by the political and social interventions of the state, so that the more subtle and more critical arguments of the young Marx were welcomed in those countries as an enrichment to the polemical arsenal of the Communist parties.

II. THE MEANING OF MARX'S EARLY WRITINGS FOR AN INTERPRETATION OF THE CRITIQUE OF POLITICAL ECONOMY

The historical distance which separates the present from the political, social and economic problems characteristic of Marx's time has grown so great that we are at least able to come to grips with his critical theory *as a whole*. I do not think that this is due to its obsolescence or outdatedness. Rather I believe that Marx's theory was worn out by the various kinds of interpretation which were placed on parts, rather than on the whole, of his theoretical framework. Consequently it seems to me that, as a consequence, the appreciation of the whole of Marx's writings was best and most successfully provided in those cases where individual critical scholars—without a close party affiliation and, therefore, without any total allegiance to an ideological body of doctrine—turned to Marx. The insight, by the way, that independence from organization and parties is an indispensable precondition for any genuinely scientific work was reiterated many times by Engels, for example, in a letter to August Bebel (April 1, 1891) where he wrote: "You, within the party, need the socialist science and this science cannot prosper without liberty."

The grasping of the meaning of Marx's theory as a whole with all of its complexities and problems has been impeded, among other things, by the fact that his method was reduced to "historical materialism" and that historical materialism was conceived of as a particular case of the application of so-called "dialectical materialism." The mere inclusion of Marx's critical theory into a comprehensive and allegedly scientific *Weltanschauung* made an adequate understanding of all its complexities impossible. Isolated elements of Marx's theory were integrated into the system of a supposedly global materialistic *Weltanschauung* at the very time that Marxist intellectuals were integrated into a hierarchically structured party machine which became more petrified the further the time of revolutionary transition was left behind and the more the movement changed into a new system of domination. Adam Schaff vaguely alluded to these contingencies when he wrote that the epoch of the personality cult had prevented many intellectuals from adequately appreciating Marx's early writings.

*   *   *

After these introductory remarks, let me get down to the substance of the problem and allow me to first state a thesis which I shall try to prove during the remainder of my paper. As in the works of most great thinkers, one unique and central issue can be traced through the whole of Marx's work, i.e., in his scientific investigations and his instructions for praxis, one fundamental problem was uppermost during all his lifetime. The central problem is the question: how did it happen that the bourgeois revolution did not achieve its proclaimed aims, and why, despite formally legalized freedoms, individuals came, in the course of the division of labor and modern market mechanism, to be dominated by social processes which prevailed behind their backs and prevented everybody from achieving a status of humanity which could have been realized in the light of the wealth of the society that already existed?

Marx's central and most important insight was that this new dependence was not the consequence of the bad intentions of individuals or of a particular social group, but rather the inevitable implication of a specific socioeconomic structure. More specifically his task consisted, first, in the identification of a social class, which more than any other had to be interested in the transformation of this economic structure; secondly, in furnishing an irrefutable proof that the dynamics of the contemporary society made this transformation increasingly easier even if one supposed that the minorities possessing interests in the perpetuation of the prevailing order would resist any reorganization of society. The smaller the privileged class, the greater is its interest in the concealment of the real social conditions and the less valid is the "bourgeois economics" which, in its "heroic" early phase, had even once advanced a rudimentary critique of political economy on which Marx could build up his own theory.

With these remarks I am trying to indicate the possibility of an interpretation that encompasses Marx's writings as a whole; up to this time the inherent unity of his work has not been proved. I intend to do this by discussing the critical categories that Marx developed in the *Philosophic and Economic Manuscripts* and in his notebook of the midforties and by showing that these categories are still the basis of the critique of political economy in *Grundrisse der Kritik der Politischen Ökonomie* (1857–1858) as well as in *Das Kapital* (1867) and were never disavowed by the old Marx.

In other words I intend to show that an interpretation of the early writings not only helps us to recognize the motives which led Marx to write a critique of political economy (*Das Kapital*) but also, in addition, that the critique of political economy implicitly and, in part, even explicitly, still contains that same critique of alienation and reification which was the very topic of his early writings.

A. ALIENATION AND REIFICATION IN THE WORKS OF 1844

The manuscripts of 1844 had, by and large, been planned as a critique of political economy. In his introduction Marx wrote that he wanted to publish successively brochures containing his critiques of law, ethics, politics and so forth and that he intended finally to approach the whole subject once again in a separate work.[2]

The starting point in this first attempt at a critique of political economy was the critical study of the "political economy" to which Marx was led mainly by Engels' "Outlines." As for the method to be used, Marx referred here (as in the introduction to his "Critique of the Hegelian Philosophy of Right") to Ludwig Feuerbach; moreover an explicit reference to Hegel's *Phenomenology of Mind* evidences an influence which can be traced even to the point of the manuscripts' whole literal formulations.

"Critique of political economy" at this time and later always meant first a critique of the capitalist economy accepted as absolutely rational by bourgeois economists and secondly, a critique of the corresponding theoretical self-consciousness. In Marx's mind, this critique did not first of all and exclusively lead to a moral condemnation in the name of some absolute ethical norms. Rather it was intended as proof of the deficiencies of the capitalist and all preceding modes of production, measured against and based on the standards of a truly human society, which had now objectively become possible because of the

---

[2] *MEGA*, I, 3, 33; cf. Karl Marx, *Philosophic and Economic Manuscripts.*, trans. by M. Milligan, Moscow 1961, p. 15.

scientific and technological knowledge and wealth that the most developed nations had secured. Marx praised the historical achievements of capitalism for its superiority over all preceding modes of production and to a corresponding extent criticized its limitations, the obstruction of further human progress.

The early writings stress the limitations, the repressions, the inhumanity and the shortcomings of capitalism much more than any appreciation of its achievements, it is true. But it would be completely wrong to insinuate that in 1844 Marx radically and a-historically condemned capitalism. As the main deficiency of the theoretical self-consciousness of the bourgeoisie Marx considered its inability to grasp that capitalism was a phenomenon that had grown out of history and, consequently, was a relative and surmountable mode of production.

> Political economy starts from the fact of private property but it does not explain it to us. It conceives the *material* process of private property in abstract and general terms . . . which then, serve it as laws. It does not *comprehend* these laws. . . .[3]

That is to say, the bourgeois political economy did not understand that these allegedly *natural* laws grew out of specific *social* relations of both production and property and that these "laws" only reflect human relationships which constituted themselves as quasi-objective and independent patterns, vis á vis and opposite to the interacting individuals.

In the manuscripts of 1844 Marx searched "for the essential connection between private property, avarice, the separation of labour, capital and landed property, exchange and competition, value and the devaluation of man, i.e., *between this whole alienation and the money-system*."[4] In this context, "money economy" stands as a metaphor for capitalism in which products (and even individuals) are degraded to the category of pure commodities, the value of which is totally distinct and finds its most complete expression in money (and its more and more abstract forms to the very credit system). As you may remember, Marx begins his discussion with the famous description of alienated labor, and he proceeds in four steps; moreover he refers to the same phenomena under various perspectives.

---

[3] *MEGA*, I, 3, 81; cf. trans., p. 67.
[4] *Ibid.*, 82; cf. trans., p. 68.

1. *The alienation of the laborer from the product of his activities* leads to a consolidation of the product as an independant power; as a result this means that:

> The worker becomes all the poorer the more wealth he produces and the more his production increases in power and range. The worker becomes an ever cheaper commodity the more goods he creates. The *devaluation* of the human world increases in direct relation with the *increase in value* of the world of things.[5]

Hegel's conception of the humanization of man through a creative transformation of nature by work stands behind this description. Unlike the animal, man must become what he can be through labor. As an entity with only potential faculties, he can only come to self-consciousness and to a conscious relationship with all other men through an objectification of his powers. But this process, which is the more evident the more perfect man's domination over nature becomes, leads to alienation as soon as the objects created by man stand "alien and hostile," or in opposition to its creators and as soon as the objects are subject to their own patterns of behavior and "coldly" disregard the hopes, wishes and aspirations of the individuals.

2. The alienation of the worker from his product, from the perspective of the working class, appears as an *alienation of the productive and creative activity itself.* Alienated labor cannot be understood as a proper articulation of one's faculties but as forced labor conceived simply as a means for sheer subsistence. Labor, therefore, does not live up to Marx's requirements; it is not "the satisfaction [of a genuine human] need but only a *means* to satisfy needs external to it [namely labor]." Since labor is not a pleasurable activity but rather one of self-sacrifice and "self-castigation," all human behavior consequently becomes perverted.[6]

At this point Marx's arguments become moral and normative, but he nevertheless considers the standards of his critical appreciation as part of a *historical* analysis and as the *expression of the anticipation of future possibilities,* definitely not as a *Wesensschau* of allegedly eternal and moral norms.

> From all this, it can be seen that man (the worker) feels himself to be freely active only in his animal functions—eating, drinking and

[5] *Ibid.,* 83; cf. trans., p. 69.
[6] *Ibid.,* 86; cf. trans., p. 72.

procreating, or at most also in his dwelling and personal adornment—
while in his human functions he is reduced to an animal. The animal
becomes human and the human becomes animal. Eating, drinking and
procreating are, of course, also genuinely human functions. But, considered in abstraction from the sphere of all other human activity and
turned into final and sole ends, they are animal.[7]

If a man's productive activities are nothing other than forced labor
necessary for subsistence and for that reason external to him, his interests shift entirely to those animal functions (mentioned by Marx); or
as we would rather say today, all of his aspirations become absorbed
in his wish for further consumption, made possible and imposed on
him by modern economy. Moreover this consumption has become
more senseless in the same degree that his productive work has
become more spiritless.

3. As alienation from his productive activity effected through indirect coercion, or other-directedness, and not on his own initiative and
responsibility, the worker becomes *alienated from his species*. To con-
strue man's animal functions as his proper ones means a loss of
humanity itself. "Free conscious activity is the species-character of
human beings," and "productive life is species-life."[8] *Only man* can
fail to realize his real potentialities. His privileged status *vis à vis* the
animal, which consists in his faculty to turn external nature into his
"inorganic body," is converted into a serious disadvantage, because
through alienation he is deprived of this "inorganic body."

4. The immediate consequence of this alienation of the worker
from his species-life (and of humanity) means the "*alienation of man
from other men*" which can most impressively be inferred from the
relation between the sexes.

This broad description of alienation can hardly be found in the later
works of Marx. But we can assume that he did not question it later
and that it is consonant with the brief hints in the Grundrisse (1857–
1858) and in Das Kapital (1867). In contrast to these later works,
Marx in 1844 had only a vague idea about the abolition of alienation;
in any case he did not then relate the revolutionary *praxis* to the self-
antagonism of the capitalistic mode of production as directly as he
did in later works. In 1844 his argumentation was as follows: the
alienated relation to the labor-product mediately produces the power

[7] *Ibid.*
[8] *Ibid.*, 88; cf. trans., p. 75.

of one person over others, just as religious alienation produces the power of a heavenly being over its believers. Private property no longer appears as the basis, but as the product and consequence of alienated labor, "just as the gods originally were not the source but the effect of the illusion of man"[9] only much later on this relation becomes an interrelation.

*   *   *

Marx believed that the solution to the problem could be found by putting the question in a different way. No longer did he seek the origin of private property but rather "the relation of *alienated labor* to the evolution of humanity":

> If one speaks of *private property*, one thinks of dealing with something outside man. Speaking of labour, one immediately deals with man. To state the problem in this way includes its solution.[10]

The abolition of an alienated society can only be carried out by the workers, for the "non-worker" it appears only as a state (*Zustand*) of alienation, whereas by the worker himself it is experienced as an "*activity* [Tätigkeit] of alienation."[11] By his alienated mode of production, the worker simultaneously produces himself and his opposite; he becomes a commodity, but as a "self-conscious and self-active commodity"[12] he obtains the basis for abolishing the entire world of commodities. Marx interprets this insight (following Engels) as a consequence of the evolution of economic theories from mercantilism to the physiocrats and the bourgeois political economy to the final socialist criticism. This theoretical development runs parallel to the development of civil society. By 1844 Marx knew that the victory of capitalism over all precapitalistic modes of production was a precondition for the abolition of all alienation.

Marx separated the theories of the *Aufhebung* of alienated society into two or three logically successive forms: into a first form of Communism, which meant only the generalization of private property into Communist property. This leads to *crude Communism*. There

---

[9] *Ibid.*, 92; cf. trans., p. 80.
[10] *Ibid.*, 93; cf. trans., p. 82.
[11] *Ibid.*, 94; cf. trans., p. 80.
[12] *Ibid.*, 98; cf. trans., p. 85.

is no connection between this way of abolishing private property and the real appropriation of alienated reality. On the contrary all people would be reduced, according to this notion, to the unnatural simplicity of poor people without needs and wants. "Community [in this case] is only a community of labor and equality of salary paid out by the Communist capital, the community as the universal capitalist."[13] The obvious indication of this kind of brute Communism which Marx understood as a primitive generalization of private property is the *Weibergemeinschaft*, the community of women. This Communism is inhuman, not because it destroys capitalism but because it makes capitalism broader, more radical and more absolute. *It does not transcend capitalistic society but even lags behind some of the more progressive aspects of private property.* Nevertheless Marx thought at this time that at least from the theoretical point of view this kind of Communism was a stage through which one necessarily had to pass.

The second type of Communism, Marx considered, is of a political nature, democratic or despotic. It too remains imperfect and "affected by private property, i.e., the alienation of man."

In its third form alone, "Communism means the positive transcendence of private property and consequently, *a genuine appropriation of the human essence* by and for man." By this Marx meant a society in which all people can freely employ all their manifold and differentiated faculties in order to be able to appropriate their products in the free and many-sided way of "total men." In it, the mere possession of goods no longer prohibits the many-sided and more differentiated forms of appropriating humanized nature. The refined eye, ear and emotions of all are now able to appropriate the past and present achievements of the human creativity.[14]

A complete description of this unalienated society was furnished by Marx in his *Exzerpthefte*, the notebooks written during this period, where he tried to show how in such a society the productive activities of free individuals are correlated, and how these activities reflect the human species, and not an alien, objectified and reified world. In it, there would be no more greed, competition, profit-making, cheating, fraud and exploitation; rather all relationships would be

---

[13] *Ibid.*, 112; cf. trans., p. 100.
[14] *Ibid.*, 114 ff.; cf. trans., p. 102 ff.

in harmony, and an atmosphere of love would be initiated by free consciousness so that all of man's activities would enrich man.[15]

B. The Concept of Alienation and Reification as Elaborated in the "Grundrisse der Kritik der politischen Ökonomie" (1857–1858)

Since the publication of the Grundrisse,[16] which were edited in Moscow in 1939 and 1941, it is easier than before to prove the continuity of Marx's thought. These manuscripts date back to the time when Marx prepared the Kritik der politischen Ökonomie, published in June, 1859, and of which the first volume of Das Kapital is but an enlarged and revised version. In the Grundrisse, Marx pondered problems and topics he had dealt with in his early writings and made use of the results of his more recent economic studies.

The historical process which led to an extreme alienation of individuals from their social relationships is described here in a more precise way than in 1844. In the money system, the intercourse of individuals with that entire society of which they are a part became completely objectified. Money has become an alien power to them. The individual "carries his social power and his relationship to society in his pocket." Thus "the activity and the product of activity is the exchange-value, i.e., a universal in which all individuality and particularity is negated and extinguished."[17] The difference between modern and precapitalistic societies is to be found in the fact that the social character of their productive activity, the participation of the individual in the social production process and the social character of the product today appear alien and contradictory to individuals. On the surface, no relations of personal dependency exist; rather all individuals appear as free; but in reality, everybody is totally subject to alien objective laws (fremde Sachgesetzlichkeit) that result from blind social and economic processes. More than ever before, Marx emphasizes, however, at the same time the progressive and necessary character of these social relationships. He contrasts them to the restricted and limited relationships in previous modes of society (for example,

[15] MEGA, I, 3, 544 ff.
[16] Karl Marx, Grundrisse der Kritik der politischen Ökonomie (Rohentwurf), Berlin 1953.
[17] Ibid., p. 75.

to the patriarchal modes of antiquity and the Middle Ages). He welcomes the dissolution of small-group subsistence economies and the development of the worldwide division of labor and the successive exchange of goods in the market as processes through which productivity is enlarged.

> The exchange as mediated through exchange value and money presupposes mutually dependent producers and simultaneously the absolute isolation of their private interests and a division of social labour, the unity and mutual complementarity of which must exist as a quasi-natural relation outside the individuals and independently of them. The pressure upon each other of general demand and supply mediates the connection of mutually indifferent individuals.[18]

This corresponds very closely to the description of the systems of wants and needs and of the *"Not- und Verstandesstaat"* depicted by Hegel, which allegedly constitutes itself—without the knowledge and will of the individuals—through Adam Smith's "invisible hand." Marx blamed the indifference of people for each other and the impossibility of facing up to their relationship to society; but he clearly saw that the new mode of production was superior to all previous ones and that it simultaneously tended to destroy all genuine social relations, that it isolated the producers (and consumers) and that despite its immense wealth it impoverished people in both literal and figurative senses, i.e., that the increasing specialization of skills and abilities prevented the individual from realizing all of his powers.

Everybody must convert his product (his activity) into an exchange value, into "money," because only in this, and in no other form, is to be found social power and indispensable power over others. From this fact one realizes that "people produce only for society and in society" and that on the other hand their production is not immediately social and not associatively organized. This means that everybody has to sell his product in order that he may take it over in the form of money as an objectification of the social character of his own production. In money, the individual producer acquires, though in alienated form, a part of social productivity; in money he appropriates in alienated form, without knowing it, part of the community. In as much as the division of labor extends over the whole world and leads to a world market (with a world-wide currency), the intercourse

---

[18] *Ibid.*, p. 76.

of individuals becomes universal. But at the same time, as a result of these interrelations, the dependence of individuals becomes more and more radical; thus, Marx could see in this status the transitory conditions leading to a new form of society and economy.[19]

Moreover we must remember that Marx launched his polemics against any *romantic* glorification of "natural" precapitalistic relations with their local, functional, social and personal restrictions. *He definitely preferred the world-wide interconnections of the participants of the capitalist world market.* But Marx considered them as transitory and as a necessary precondition to the future subordination of all social relations to the control of associatively organized producers, because he did not conceive any status as something occurring naturally, but as a product of historical *praxis.* Any status had been hitherto achieved in history without being consciously sought for. The present situation constitutes the precondition of a future society in which man, as a whole being, will be a real possibility. Man will no longer be a product of nature but a product of history. In a word, this means *that the total emancipation of man presupposes his total alienation.*

Armed with this historical insight, Marx thought it equally ridiculous to long for the "original plentitude" of primitive social relations or to hold fast to the human emptiness that marks the present. However his essential point was that the *bourgeois consciousness could not overcome the undialectical contrast of romantic aspirations and cynical acceptance of both a rich and an impoverished present.*[20] These contrasts comprise its being, and will, consequently, remain with it to its end.

However progress toward a universal capitalistic mode of production does not appear only as a necessary precondition for the universal promotion of productive capacities; rather it leads to the final point where all personal relations are broken and subjected to the universal basis of new social interrelationships. As soon as most individuals are dominated by "material conditions" or by socially objectified interrelations, and not by other individuals, then the task for mankind is obvious: *to bring these interrelations under mankind's common control and so to break through the course of history, where until now*

---

[19] *Ibid.,* p. 80.
[20] *Ibid.,* p. 80 ff.

power elites have been circulating without ever facing up to the root cause of dependence and repression. Surely, as Marx stresses, "individuals are now dominated by abstractions whereas they previously depended on each other," but these abstractions finally bring forth the preconditions on which also all previous modes of domination rested. Throughout history, the dependence of "slaves" on their "masters," has not resulted from the will of the dominating classes but can be explained only by the *primitive modes of production* and the necessities of those limited social conditions (which required specific organizations, as for instance, special military provisions). Whereas in previous stages of history the objective conditions appeared as personal, "in the modern world the personal relations are clearly seen as the pure expression of the modes of production and exchange." In the possibility of such an insight, Marx saw another important advantage of capitalist society.

As I have already intimated, Marx in the *Grundrisse* elaborated on the notion with which he first dealt in the *Philosophic and Economic Manuscripts*—the notion that "world history is nothing but the producing of man by man's work." More than in the early writings, the positive meaning of the capitalistic mode of production is stressed, but the lines of argumentation are by and large the same as before.

C. The Fetish Character of the Commodities and the Concept of the Destruction of Alienation in DAS KAPITAL

In *Das Kapital*, capitalist society is conceived of as a dialectical totality in which antagonisms, since they tend to transcend present social conditions, are necessary. As with any totality, the parts reflect the whole and every part is governed by the same principles as the whole. What characterizes capitalistic society is the commodity character it attributes to everything. In the societies of Marx's time this process of converting all things into commodities had not yet come to an end, but Marx thought that he could foresee that the process would closely follow this model. The dialectical reconstruction of social entities, which is only possible in so far as societies are truly governed by dialectical processes, does not construct the whole from its parts but presupposes that the parts can only be understood as parts of the whole. This means that the explication cannot properly begin until the analysis has been brought to its end.

In the beginning of *Das Kapital* Marx deals with "the Commodity." Everyone in a capitalistic society is familiar with commodities, but Marx wants to understand them in their historical genesis and becoming and in their structure. In his study of the commodity character of products, his analyses from his early writings are taken for granted.

In the chapter mentioned, Marx analyzes commodity according to four steps: 1) the double character of the commodity is reflected upon; it represents use-value and value. As use-value, it possesses specific qualities; as a value, it has no quality but represents a mere quantity. 2) This character of the product is traced back to labor's own twin qualities, which arise with its division. On the one side, the workers produce particular work (*besondere Arbeit*); on the other, as a result of their general work (*allgemeine Arbeit*), they produce exchange-values. What Marx does is to probe backward from the fixed being to the activities from which it results. 3) Marx shows, historically, how the value-form had developed from the simple and accidental to the money-form until in the money economy the absolute split of use-value from exchange-value has become clearly evident. Now all products of human activities represent only money-equivalents and the general work of society is only able to recognize itself in reification. 4) Marx analyzes the fetish-character of the commodity and its mysteries.

> The mystery of the form of commodity consists in the fact that for individuals it reflects the social character of their own work, as objective qualities of the products of labor themselves, as *social* natural qualities of these things (*gesellschaftliche Natureigenschaften*) and, consequently, that it mirrors the social relations of the producers to the total work as a social relationship among objects existing outside them.[21]

The commodity character of a product of human activity consists in the phenomenon that this product possesses a value which can be abstractly expressed in money and therefore becomes interchangeable with other products. This quality of exchange and interchangeability appears as a quality of the object itself, a quality which is due to its being a part of the general (world) market, to the laws of which this commodity is subject. In reality, however, these reified relations of things reflect social relations of the producers and the owners of the

---

[21] *MEW*, XXIII, 86; cf. Karl Marx, *Capital*, Moscow 1954 ff., vol. I, p. 72.

means of production. "It is only the determinate social relation of individuals which takes the chimerical shape of a relation of objects."[22] This phenomenon, that an entity resulting from the activities of individuals comes to dominate their life, can only be analyzed according to the way Feuerbach saw the relationship between God and man.

> To find an analogy, we have to take refuge in the nebulous sphere of the religious world. Here the products of our imagination appear as independent, intelligent and autonomous figures related to man. The same is true in the world of commodities with the products of man's work. This I call the *fetishism* which is attached to the labour-products as soon as they are produced as commodities and which is by consequence, inseparable from the production of commodities.[23]

As soon as people relate themselves to their objects as to a fetish, they begin to attribute some qualities to this dead object which in reality stem from their own life, the power and impotence of their own social relations, for example. In other words, the magic power attributed to the fetish is only real in so far as belief in it makes possible the success of the tribe. But erroneously, this success is attributed to the fetish and not to the organized power of the tribe, just as the interchangeability of the commodity is believed due to the character of the products and not to the division of labor and the market mechanisms. There is a dearth of conscious organization of production in both cases. What Marx calls in this context *fetishism*, he described in his early writings as *alienation*.

Let me quote one more sentence: "Its own social movement possesses for them (the producers of commodities) the form of a movement of objects, which they are controlled by rather than controlling."[24] That the fetishism of commodities, i.e., the mysticism of the commodity world, is only the specific expression of the capitalist mode of production is proved by Marx in his examples of Robinson and of the medieval mode of production. In both of these cases, the measure of labor is regulated by the individual and social needs of specific use-values, i.e., the social character of production is presupposed, whereas in the commodity-producing society the social character of the production of independently producing private workers

---

[22] *Ibid.*
[23] *Ibid.*
[24] *Ibid.*, 89; cf. trans., p. 75.

is constituted in the process of circulation—and there only in alien-ated form. In the Middle Ages "the social conditions of individuals appeared in their works as their own personal conditions and were not concealed as the social conditions of objects."[25] *The relations were transparent and not mystified.*

However as we have already seen in his manuscripts of 1857, Marx rejects any romantic glorification of these older modes of production. The commodity-producing society with its alienation is obviously necessary as one transitory stage which lays the material groundwork for a new society. In *Das Kapital* Marx compared this new society to an "association of free people" (a term which he borrowed from Max Stirner and which he mocked many times in other contexts).

> In so far as such an association works with socialized means of produc-tion and the individuals consciously organize their individual powers to a social power . . . then all determinations of Robinson's mode of production are reiterated . . . , but now socially, no longer individually.[26]

The product of such an organized productive activity would im-mediately be social, and one part of it could remain social and be employed as means of production, whereas other parts could be dis-tributed for the sake of individual consumption. Marx does not reflect in detail on the mode of distribution but considers it dependent on the level of the producers' development. It might be organized along the socialist line of proportional distribution according to the amount of work performed by individuals or along communist lines according to genuine individual needs.

If one looks only at the chapter on the fetish character of commod-ity, one might believe that Marx expected the *Aufhebung* of aliena-tion to be achieved solely through the common control of production based on the division of labor and that he no longer challenged the principle of the division of labor itself. One could insinuate that Marx considered it sufficient that the sum of all individual labor forces become one social labor force, a situation which could be consonant with maintenance of division of labor. But Marx unmistakably stresses the necessity to overcome the division of labor. His argument in chap-ter 13 of the first volume of *Das Kapital*—it is true—is based on the revolutionary character of technology and not on the individuals'

[25] *Ibid.*, 91; cf. trans., p. 77.
[26] *Ibid.*, 92; cf. trans., p. 78.

needs to employ their own potentialities, but eventually it leads to
the same conclusion as the early writings:

> If change of special work is carried through rather like some overwhelm-
> ing natural law, and with the blindly destructive effects of a natural law
> which finds obstacles everywhere, then large industry because of its
> catastrophes must make it a life and death matter to accept both the
> change of jobs and the greatest possible *individuality of the worker as a*
> *general social law of production, and to adapt the social conditions to*
> *the worker's normal realization.* It becomes a question of life and death
> to replace the monstrosity of a poor labour population—a reserve held
> for disposition to meet the varying exploitation needs of capital with
> the disposal of man for varied jobs; the partial individual (*Teilindi-*
> *viduum*), the bearer of a partial social function, by the *totally developed*
> *individual,* for whom many social functions constitute successive modes
> of activity.[27]

The "total man," whom Marx postulated in his early writings as
a contrast-image to the impoverished one-sided, cripple individual
who really existed, is here conceived as a necessity to which the capitalist mode of production itself is pushed. This is one of the many
observations by which Marx showed himself far ahead of his time, for
not until recently was there a widely shared opinion that modern
modes of production require a most comprehensive training of the
laborer to allow him to adapt himself to the ever-changing requirements of industrial production.

III. SOME FINAL REMARKS

Nobody would deny that the style and the ambiance did change in
Marx's writings. There is indeed a difference between the sober explication in *Das Kapital* with its emphasis on theoretical vigor and
empirical detail and the critical and moralistically sounding analyses
of 1844. But there remains *one fundamental topic* which is the starting as well as the ending point: *the quest to transcend capitalist soci-*
ety toward a more human, free and satisfactory society. There is no
warrant for the conclusion that the old Marx buried the hopes of his
youth and abandoned the fulfillment of his aims. His later writings
can only be adequately understood in the light of his first writings. If
later, the "how" of this transformation and its empirical chances of

---

[27] *Ibid.,* 511 ff.; cf. trans., p. 487. Our italics.

realization were stressed more strongly than the necessity of the "that" (of which Marx remained too deeply convinced to need stressing), this should not be mistaken for an escape into a general philosophy of history or an exclusive concentration on the analytical restructuring of the modes of the capitalist economy. His intentions, throughout his life, were directed towards a "*critique* of the political economy" and this means the practical critique of capitalist society as much as it does its theoretical conception in the doctrines of the bourgeois economists. Marx did not bring forth a new proletarian economic theory to stand beside the classical bourgeois theories. And the widespread notion of an "economic theory for the proletariat" sometimes sanctioned by Marx and Engels themselves, is, by and large, misleading.

In *Das Kapital* Marx's reflections centered around a critique of those alienated social relations he had already criticized in 1844. If Marx (and particularly Engels later on), were not always conscious of the continuity of this critical approach, this would not amount to a serious objection against my interpretation. *Das Kapital* remains a fragment, and being bound to the galley of his journalistic writings, plagued by illness and lack of genuine enthusiasm, overwhelmed by organizational duties, Marx was no longer able to ponder his work and treat it as a whole. His successors had already begun during his life time to pick out pieces of his theoretical reflections which they found expedient for their political and organizational aims. The story of the interpretation of his work was, as in all cases of great thinkers, a story of misinterpretations.

COMMENT

Marx W. Wartofsky

Fetscher's thesis is overwhelmingly correct: the old Marx is not a rejection nor even a revision of the young "moral" or "humanist" Marx. Nor does the later economic analysis abandon the dialectical character of the earlier writings. Rather, as Fetscher shows, the concepts of alienation and objectification which are central to the so-called "humanist" writings are central also to the critique of political economy in *Das Kapital*. Further the so-called economic alienation exemplified in the fetishism of commodities is not simply an "economic" matter but remains still that human self-alienation which Marx discusses in his early works.

What then is the difference, if any, between the young and the old Marx? In his *Theses on Feuerbach*, Marx suggests that whereas Feuerbach speaks of an abstract humanity, of "human essence," the need is to address oneself instead to the concrete, "sensuous-practical" life of man. In the *German Ideology*, this practical life is described as rooted in the two-fold activity of the production of the needs of daily existence and the production of men—i.e. human reproduction and all that this entails in the way of family and social organization. Perhaps the difference between "young" and "old" is no more than the difference between the earlier programmatic statements and the elaboration and fulfillment of this program in the mature works; for in a clear sense, the analysis of capitalist production and exchange is the elaborated critique of "sensuous-practical" human activity in its concrete form, in commodity production. One might conclude that the early Marx remained relatively abstract and programmatic in his formulations and that the older Marx was therefore more concrete in applying these formulations to the existing historical conditions. But this will not do, for it perpetuates a positivist myth: that the "humanism" of the early Marx is poetic and metaphorical and thus "abstract" and that "concreteness" is reserved to hard-headed economic analysis. However there may just as well be a humanism which is "concrete," as there may be an economic analysis which is "abstract" (in the sense in which both Marx and Hegel understood these terms). Moreover it seems a perverse and narrow "dialectic" which insists that the young and the old Marx are dichotomous because they are different, as if the integrity and continuity of Marx's philosophical framework could have been preserved only if he had spent the rest of his life endlessly repeating what he had said in his earliest works. On such a perverse view, Marx's *development*, in the sense that his later works are transformations of earlier ideas, is taken to be evidence that his later work is opposed to, or even contradictory to, his earlier work. A profounder view of the integrity of Marx's views from "young" to "old" is to see in Marx the fundamental continuity of certain root-concepts—in particular, the central ones of alienation and objectification.

As Fetscher points out perspicuously, the integrity and continuity of Marx's philosophical views can be seen in the concept of commodity (*Ware*) in *Das Kapital*. Here the process of alienation (which Hegel had examined in the *Phänomenologie des Geistes*, and Feuerbach in *Das Wesen des Christenthums*, as a process of alienation in *consciousness*) is given its materialistic interpretation as having its ground in the practical alienation of one's life activity in production—i.e. in the transformation of labor into labor-power, as being itself an estranged (*entfremdete*) object, as an exchange-value.

Here the clue to Marx's epistemology is clear. The deeper thesis, which underlies both the earlier and the later writings, is that consciousness arises out of and is shaped by *praxis*, or dialectically speaking, that consciousness is itself the transformation or *Aufhebung* of *praxis* from sheer blind activity to activity directed upon an object. But this *Vergegenständlichung* or objectification of one's own *praxis* requires that this *praxis* becomes an object of consciousness, that its immediacy in sheer activity be overcome. This is not simply a matter of reflex-awareness, nor is the representation of *praxis* a matter of passive mirroring. The *praxis* can be represented as objective only if in fact it has become an object, separated from the subjective activity of man; that is, the condition for the objectification of *praxis* is the alienation of the object of this activity from the activity itself, the representation of the self's activity under the form of an "other," set over against the self. The self which represents this *praxis* as an alienated being, in its "mystical" or "imaginary" or "phantasmagorial" form has not yet achieved conscious—i.e. rational—domination over its own *praxis*.

Fetscher is doubly right in using the Leibnizian analogy of the monad in this context: the self, as "monad," mirrors the social character of the commodity in the isolated object, the economic "quantum"; and at the same time, the social character of the commodity mirrors the totality of social relations of production which constitute the self as a social being. As Feuerbach sought the character of human essence in its projected form in religious consciousness, so Marx seeks the character of man's practical nature under the concrete conditions of commodity-production in its projected form in the commodity itself. If the commodity were indeed the ultimate "unit" of Marx's analysis, it would not be a fetish. And if Marx had obliged the critics by leaving out such residues of dialectics as "the fetishism of commodities," then one could have comfortably settled down with Marx as another classical economist. But Marx's analysis in *Das Kapital* is at the same time political economy *and* philosophical anthropology. The analysis of the commodity is for him a fundamental means whereby to analyze the abstract "human" nature in its concrete historical-social form. Thus, in this sense, Marx's later work is the continuation of his earlier work, indeed the answer to and the elaboration of Feuerbach's analysis of "human essence." Commodity-analysis thus evidences the human in revealing the character of that *praxis* which is hidden in the commodity-as-fetish and in the production relations of capitalism. Marx's ostensibly "economic" analysis is no more and no less than the disalienation of the concept of *praxis*, and in this sense it remains phenomenological and anthropological analysis as well.

The shibboleth that Marx deals simply with "economic man," i.e. with an abstraction fashioned for purposes of economic analysis, is the least literate of the current illiteracies concerning Marxism. We should add this to Fetscher's account of the perversions which abstract "organizational" or "political" consequences on the one hand or simply "historical" ones on the other. Fetscher shows in his paper that each of these is a perversive abstraction of that integral social human being, that "whole" which is retained in Marx's view. It should be added that the "economist" abstraction of Marx is no less vicious than these others; Marx has no philosophical consistency on the grounds of reducing Marx's political economy to some abstracted version of economic analysis and then contrasting this with an equally abstracted early "humanism." This misses the whole point of Marx's development: that political economy is, in effect, applied anthropology and that Marx seeks in the *fact* of abstracted economic man the sources of this abstraction, of this alienation of man's integral *praxis* in the form of simply "economic" activity. The mode of analysis is empirical here as it is in Marx's analysis of real value, for example. There is no transcendental access to human nature by way of establishing some human essence in thought; rather, it is in the examination of concrete practice that knowledge of man's nature is to be achieved. (In the same way, for example, Marx sees the analysis of the real value of commodities as depending, in the first instance, on the analysis of concrete relations among commodities in the marketplace—i.e. their exchange-values and the relation of this exchange-value to cost of production.)

The "whole man" for Marx is therefore not simply the "economic man," but the man whom "economic man" hides from view and represses as long as production, circulation and exchange are such that commodities remain "objects" beyond humanly conscious—i.e. rational—control. Dialectically, the achievement of such control requires such an "objectification" as its condition, not simply out of some conative *Drang* of consciousness for an object of consciousness—this is after all Marx's criticism of Feuerbach's "passive" or "abstract" version of alienation—but rather out of the needs of conscious practice itself, in meeting the needs of existence. In short, commodity production has to be fully objectified before the possibility of dominating it can appear. In this sense too Fetscher rightly assesses Marx's non-and-anti-romantic view of capitalist development. Capitalism is not simply a morally repugnant fall from grace, but it is the necessary stage for the development of that socialized production which provides the basis for the transformation of production relations from those between non-human "objects" into I-Thou relations.

Marx sought this transformation not in the realm of a change of heart or of feeling—though he did not deny that it could take place there as well. The reason was that he sought a fundamental social transformation, not simply an individual one. One may love one's wife and children, one's friends or one's fellow human beings in Kant's sense of treating them as ends and not as means only. However Marx argued that the possibility of a radical transformation of human relations of this sort lay not in the marginal relations *outside* the fundamental human *praxis* of producing the means of existence and providing for the continuity of the species but rather in the heart of this *praxis* itself, i.e., in the relations of production. What Feuerbach set forth as the essence of humanity—the recognition of one's species character, of oneself as member of a species, as a human being among human beings—Marx developed as the recognition of one's species-character in the concrete, i.e. in socialized production, mirrored in alienated form in the commodity and to be disalienated in the achievement of the socialization of production-relations. Since the objectification of this social character of production is achieved most fully in capitalist commodity production, then (in this dialectical sense) capitalist production lays the foundations for real humanism, but it does so only in alienated form, in commodity-relations, in the "cash-nexus" between man and man. For Marx, however, the disalienation depends not simply on the "recognition" of the social nature of commodity production. Contrary to the "critical critics" with whom Marx and Engels battled in *The Holy Family* and in *The German Ideology*, Marx saw this "recognition" not as simply an intellectual or "rational" domination of the sociality of production in theory, but rather as the embodiment of this theoretical understanding in the practice of a socialist society. If disalienation were to be achieved simply by enlightenment, then the Marxian millenium should have arrived with the publication of *Das Kapital*. Marx insists instead on a "recognition" *in praxi*—i.e. in the transformation of the contradiction between private ownership of the means of production and the social nature of commodity-production, or in Marx's terms, between the forces of production and the production relations; this transformation constitutes, in effect, "real" as opposed to "theoretical" socialism.

It remains a fact of present-day life in socialist societies that the simple economic transformation may be a necessary but not a sufficient condition for the achievement of "real humanity." But more than this, neither Marx nor Engels ever claimed. The ascription to them of simple-minded "economic determinist" or "epiphenomenalist" doctrines in terms of which changes in economic organization are simply "reflected" in human, conscious relations completely vulgarizes Marx's and Engels' views of the relations between being and consciousness. A critical consciousness,

one which does not merely mirror passively but which is itself active in
changing human practice, is thus not simply a reflex of an abstracted
"economic man." Rather, it is itself the achievement of an enlightened
praxis which can no more remain at mere "awareness" of socialized
production, in the passive sense, than Marx's thought could remain simply
at a passive "awareness" of capitalist production and exchange.

An enlightened *praxis* demands criticism in order to achieve full self-
conscious awareness; it demands therefore the full release of critical human
faculties. "Marxist orthodoxy" is thus a contradiction in terms and could
come to be embodied only in what one may call an alienated Marxism,
one whose essence, in critical *praxis*, has become petrified in the fossil-form
of ritual and dogma and has in effect been turned upon itself. Every one
of the forms of "abstract" Marxism, which Fetscher so clearly describes,
runs the risk of such fossilization, no matter how "concretely" it represents itself, in terms of action, or of practical embodiment in state and
organization. Such abstractive misinterpretations, it seems to me, lie in
two directions, represented by adherence to either a "young" or an "old"
Marx. For the revelation of Marx as an abstract humanist is as much a
misconstrual as the depiction of him as having somehow gotten over this
humanism or of retaining it only as a left-over or residual romanticism of
the early Feuerbachian years.

3: DID THE PROLETARIAT NEED MARX AND DID MARXISM HELP THE PROLETARIAT?[1]

Maximilien Rubel

I

1. The state of permanent crisis which characterizes our century has provoked many thinkers to rethink completely traditional philosophical conceptions and moral values. Among the doctrines that pretend to give coherent and definitive answers to the problems which this re-evaluation implies, Marxist ideology occupies an important place. To what extent are the defenders of this doctrine justified? The answer is made difficult by the existence within this school of several currents of thought, each of which claims to be the "true" Marxism in opposition to "false" Marxisms.

2. In recent years there have been several attempts to shed new light on all the controversies raised by these conflicts. It necessitates going back to the "sources" in order to grasp the thought of Marx and of Engels, ordinarily considered as forming a single body of doctrine.

---

[1] The original wording of the subject I was supposed to deal with read in a slightly different way: "Did the proletariat need Marxism, and did Marxism help the proletariat?" I must confess that I was in a state of great perplexity in contemplating the problems involved in these questions. And even after having asked Professor Lobkowicz for a change in the wording of my subject in substituting, in the first question for Marxism the name of Marx, I felt some embarrassment; not because it seemed difficult to answer the two questions. Rather the reason for my perplexity was simply this: I had the immediate conviction that the questions were *unscientific* and that in dealing with them I would have to express mainly judgments relating not to facts but to *values*. But I understood soon that one can treat nonscientific questions in a scientific way, that is to say *objectively*. And since it is my conviction that the concerns of Marx were not mainly or fundamentally *scientific*, I decided to formulate my answers in a limited number of theses.

The first publication in the 1930's of the early writings of Marx constitutes a turning point in the discussion which today has reached the international forum. Furthermore this situation is particularly paradoxical since from this time on, the thought of Marx seems to emerge *after* the triumph of the school it brought to life. It has apparently been a premature triumph since Marxism must now face, in a way, the criticism of a resurrected Marx who is making his voice heard via texts ignored by several generations of disciples.

3. Our intention is to retain, amidst the complex of disputed problems, a theme which seems fundamental to us but which appears to be left aside in the debates: the proletariat in the thought and vision of Marx. I have anticipated one of my conclusions in order to say that this negligence is in the nature of things, for to reflect on the role of the proletariat in the teaching of Marx leads to establishing a complete break between this teaching and the philosophical and political ideologies which depend upon it; moreover by carrying this reflection to its ultimate consequences, one is forced to make a clear distinction between the thought of Marx and that of Engels, in particular, if one considers the latter's attempt to systematize certain theoretical conceptions of his friend. However the role of Engels in the genesis of Marxism will not be treated in this paper.

II

1. The principal criticism made by Marx of his so-called utopian predecessors is that they failed to recognize the "historical spontaneity (*geschichtliche Selbstätigkeit*)" of the proletariat and did not bring to this group a "social science" of means and ends for its liberation. Considering the workers' struggle as an inevitable result of the working conditions imposed on the industrial proletariat by the capitalistic economy, Marx undertook—as other socialist thinkers had done before him—to bring into the open the historical meaning of these struggles. Thus while retaining the ethical implications of Utopia, Marx elaborated a theory of revolution never failing to consider himself a disciple of Saint-Simon, Fourier and Owen to whom he was linked by powerful spiritual ties. The core of this ethic based on a social theory is the postulate of the self-emancipation of the proletariat.

2. Marx conceives the political and economic organization of the

workers' struggle in the form of parties, unions and cooperatives as creations of the workers themselves and not as institutions formed from outside the ranks of the workers by elites offering themselves as guides of the ignorant masses who are incapable of grasping the meaning of their fight.

If the intellectuals have a role to play in the workers' movement, they fulfill it effectively only by bringing "elements of culture" to this movement and not a ready-made theory of philosophy, an esoteric doctrine of the course and the ends of history. (However, as "party leader," Marx no doubt had attitudes which contradict certain principles of the ethic of self-emancipation inherent in his political teachings). Nevertheless there is no connection between the sometimes ambiguous *attitude* of Marx, and, for example, the conception of the workers' party held and carried into practice by Lenin, a conception which has been erected into a *metaphysics of the party* by Georg Lukács who saw in the bolshevik party and in its leaders the embodiment of the *dialectics of history.*

3. *Marx espoused the cause of the workers before having carried out a scientific analysis of the economy based on the exploitation of man by man.* Moreover it is the ethic of alienation and not "the law of value" which is at the basis of this espousal. Historical materialism and the theory of surplus value—two "scientific discoveries" which should, according to Engels, assure the imperishable glory of Marx— were conceived by Marx after he had already formulated in two manifestoes ("Zur Judenfrage" and "Zur Kritik der Rechtsphilosophie" whose ethical inspiration is evident) the fundamental criticism of the State and of Money, on the one hand, and the liberating vocation of the proletariat, on the other.

4. Because the struggling industrial proletariat was cognizant of the defects of the economic system of which it was the principal victim, it had to find spokesmen capable of expressing and explaining the historical and ethical meaning of its refusal to accept servitude. Collective misery and the spontaneous protest of the industrial proletariat gave rise to a movement of thought, commonly called socialism in which Marx has a special place for having attempted and achieved a synthesis of doctrines that he had inherited. From then on, the importance of Marx lies in the unifying character of his teaching which aims at the *Aufhebung* (in the Hegelian sense), that is, the sublimation, of the philosophical and sociological reflection as transmitted by

generations of thinkers. This sublimation has to be realized through concrete actions and mainly through revolutionary achievements. Man has to prove the truth of his purposes by practical deeds and not by vain speculations based on nondemonstrable hypotheses.

5. Did the proletariat need Marx? From what we have just said, we might say that this question would have appeared absurd to Marx, and no doubt he would have replied in the negative. However in a sense Marx had anticipated this reply in his writings of 1843 and 1844. On the eve of becoming economist, he proclaimed:

> We do not face the world as doctrinarians armed with new principles: here is the truth, go down on your knees! We submit to the world new principles derived from the principles of the world.—We do not proclaim: desert your struggles, they are preposterous; we are going to rend the air with the true battlecry of the struggle. We show the world the reason for the struggle and that consciousness is a matter one must acquire, even against one's will.[2]

At most, Marx, in order to be able to reply affirmatively to this question, would have placed himself among this "thinking but oppressed" humanity that ought to join this suffering humanity "who thinks." It is not *his* theory but the critical theory born before his time (in the form of ideas as well as in revolutionary phenomena) and which he simply expresses in a scientific synthesis. This critical theory was "to grip the masses" by becoming a material force.

III

1. "True" or "false," every Marxism which claims to be systematized thought, or even a philosophy of Marx, represents a complete alteration of his most profound intention. The thought of Marx could not justify the birth of a political ideology, that is, the transformation of his sociological theses into norms of political action, neither as sociological theory of a determined economic system nor as an attempt to

---

[2] Marx's letter to A. Ruge of September, 1843, published in *Deutsch-Französische Jahrbücher*; cf. *MEGA*, I, 3, 574. The dash after "the principles of the world" is absent from the original text. As Professor Rubel pointed out in the discussion, he inserted it to indicate that the sentence—"We submit to the world new principles and so on"—must be taken to be said by the "doctrinarian" saying "Here is the truth" [Editor's note].

reveal the "law of the economic movement of bourgeois society." This ideology could only be born as a perversion of the ethical presuppositions which confer on Marx's teaching an extraordinary spiritual force. Marx himself apparently had the feeling of things to come when, being aware of the first attempts by his disciples of systematizing his methodological principles, he had the honesty to condemn them in saying ironically but energetically: "I am not a Marxist." To the Russian sociologist M. K. Mikhailovsky who pretended that Marx held a philosophy of history in *Das Kapital*, Marx answered that there was no reason to "metamorphose my historical sketch of a genesis of capitalism in Western Europe into a historico-philosophical theory of the general path every people is fated to tread. . . ." Marx denied then that he had given the key to a "general historico-philosophical theory, the supreme virtue of which consists in being super-historical."[3]

2. The history of Marxism up to the Russian Revolution of 1917 shows the divorce between an ideological current with revolutionary pretensions and a workers' movement marked essentially by the struggle for reforms within the existing economic system. (Germany, with a proletariat reduced to the role of electoral clientele, was the favorite setting for these phenomena.) The Russian Revolution of 1917 inaugurates the era of institutional Marxism. The sociology of Marx shows how the "historical necessity" of the accumulation of capital involves the "historical necessity" of the proletariat and, therefore, the impossibility of "building socialism" in the Russia of peasants. Marxist theoreticians, however, once they became the holders of political power, submitted the lesson of their master to a dialectical somersault. It is not the disappearance of the salaried class nor of the proletarian condition, but, on the contrary, the creation of each of these that had to be justified at the dawn of Marxism.

3. The appearance of institutional Marxism as a mystifying ideology occurred in accordance with historical determinism which Marxian sociology is quite capable of explaining. By imitating Engels, who liked to invoke the mysterious ways and the wiles of history, one could in this connection speak of the irony of fate. However that may be,

[3] This letter, written in French in 1877, was first published in 1894. For excerpts see M. Rubel, *Karl Marx, Essai de biographie intellectuelle*, Paris 1957, p. 426 ff.; for the full text, see Nicolai-On *Histoire du développement économique de la Russie, etc.*, Paris 1902, 507 ff. [Editor's note].

the answer to the question "Did Marxism help the proletariat?" can only be negative: the "historical necessity," as Marx used to say, of this perversion of ideas in no way prevents its ethical condemnation, a condemnation—and this is the irony of fate—for which Marx himself supplied the instrument. In its institutional form (in the so-called "socialist" countries) as well as in its speculative form (in the capitalistic world), Marxism today is the negation—or the betrayal—of the revolutionary ethics that animates the work of Marx: the two variants of Marxism, however, opposed they may appear in other ways, incorporate ideologies which unquestionably participate in all the economic, political, religious and moral alienations that plague contemporary societies from the East to the West. One could say that contemporary Marxism in its speculative form is, in relation to the thought of Marx, what contemporary existentialism is in relation to the thought of Kierkegaard. In their opposition to Hegel, Marx and Kierkegaard anticipated the most radical criticism that could be directed against the pseudo-socialism and existentialism of our time.

It is said and believed that since the 1917 Russian Revolution the world has entered a new epoch—that of Socialism—and that since World War II one-third of the planet has become socialist. Those who say so and think so generally choose one single criterion to justify their thesis: the abolishment of private property, called socialization of the means of production. But this thesis is confronted by another one: there is no Socialism in today's world. What is called so by sheer misuse of terms is in reality only a new and universal form of man's being exploited and oppressed by man: state monopoly or state ownership, which is as deadly as private ownership, if not more so. Instead of "Socialism," its name should be "State Capitalism" (or "Mixt Economy"). Nothing warrants the thesis that the State's control over or possession of property constitutes the means and the end toward a socialist order. If we neglect the legally established forms which seemingly regulate human relationships, we discover that man's status and thus the proletarian condition remain fundamentally and existentially the same in the so-called "Socialist" and in the so-called "Free World." Russian Marxism-Leninism had to justify the exploitation of workers and peasants and thus to build a model for the subsequent "Socialist" regimes.

4. Marx's "science" could be used to give a progressive direction to Marxist ideology whose historical function is to justify the creation

of a universal proletariat, but the scientific truth, formulated by Marx as regards capitalism, was not in contradiction with the verdict of guilt pronounced in *Das Kapital*. The revolutionary vocation he assigned to the proletariat has perhaps been betrayed by the political history of the past one-half century. However the materialistic interpretation of history teaches us that the proletarization of the world is the fundamental condition for the ultimate overthrow of things and of values. From this point of view, one could affirm that a universal proletariat "will need" Marx, that is to say, the socialism for which he fought. Judged by the catastrophic course which contemporary history is taking, this future seems to be appearing on the horizon. We are not far perhaps from the situation which Marx thought he saw in 1844 when he wrote:

> In the conditions of existence of the proletariat are condensed, in their most inhuman form, all the conditions of existence of present day society. Man has lost himself; however at the same time he has acquired not only a theoretical consciousness of his loss, but he also has been forced by an ineluctable, irremediable and imperious *distress* to revolt against this inhumanity. It is for these reasons that the proletariat can and must emancipate itself. But it can only emancipate itself by destroying its own conditions of existence. It can only destroy its own conditions of existence by destroying all the inhuman conditions of existence of present day society, conditions which are epitomized in its situation.[4]

[4] MEGA, I, 3, 206 ff.; cf. *The Holy Family*, Moscow 1956, p. 52.

4: MARX'S THEORY OF CLASS DOMINATION: AN ATTEMPT AT SYSTEMATIZATION

Wlodzimierz Wesolowski

Marx's theory of classes has been repeatedly systematized and interpreted. Although at some points these systematizations differ, for the most part they evidence many common traits, particularly if they have been written by Marxist authors.[1] Consequently a certain ensemble of assertions has become commonplace; on occasion some assertions are couched in different terms. It is not the task of this paper to restate this basic ensemble of assertions recognized by the Marxists. The purpose of this essay is different: it attempts to give a wider presentation of an element hitherto rather seldom touched upon—the concept of class domination.

Marx's theory of society like every sociological theory is an ensemble of analytical categories and assertions concerning their mutual relations, for social phenomena have many aspects and appear in extremely complex entanglements. In analytical categories some aspects or some ensembles of phenomena, as well as some of their relations, are abstractly isolated from other aspects or ensembles. They gain thereby the role of independent entities which can serve as separate "units" of analysis of a complex social reality.

However from the point of view of the degree of elaboration of such analytical categories, Marxism is not a uniform theory. The cate-

---

[1] Taking into consideration recent years alone, one can point to the following works: *Istoricheskij Materializm* ed. by F. V. Konstantinov, Moscow 1954; M. Cornforth, *Dialectical Materialism*, London 1961; J. Hochfeld, *Studia o marksowskiej teorii społeczeństwa*, Warsaw 1963; R. Bendix and S. M. Lipset, "Karl Marx's Theory of Social Classes," R. Bendix and S. M. Lipset, *Class, Status and Power; A Reader in Social Stratification*, Glencoe 1953; G. Gurvitch, *Le concept des classes sociales*, Les Cours de Sorbonne, Paris 1958; R. Dahrendorf, *Class and Class Conflict in Industrial Society*, London 1959.

gories which pertain to economic phenomena are those which have been elaborated most deeply and thoroughly in a most rigorous and systematic way. *Das Kapital* is an exposition of these. The "value" and "utility value" as the two aspects of commodity; machines, goods and money as possible forms of "capital"; the production of the "relative" and "absolute" "surplus value," the "circulation of capital"— these are only a few of those rigorously formulated categories and assertions.

The part of Marx's theory that concerns political phenomena is neither as systematic nor as precise in its presentation, and we do not have the equivalent of *Das Kapital* among Marx's political analyses. Nevertheless he has left a large number of concrete analyses of social-political phenomena, relative especially to the capitalist society contemporary to him, and from this rich variety of analyses can be derived the basis for an attempt to create a certain ensemble of categories from which it will be possible to deduct different concrete deliberations.

In this essay I shall analyze in detail phenomena which Marx and Engels described usually as *Herrschaft* and *Klassenherrschaft*. In English editions of Marx and Engels, these terms are most often translated as 'rule,' 'class rule,' sometimes only as 'domination' or 'class domination.' The use of the terms 'class rule' and 'ruling class' together with simplified interpretations of Marx's ideas has caused considerable misunderstandings in theoretical discussions of Marx's thought. One can very often find interpretations of Marx's theory of classes wherein the terms 'class rule' and 'ruling class' are understood literally. According to these interpretations, Marx allegedly states that in capitalistic society the government always does what the capitalist class wants it to do. Under this interpretation, political process is reduced to relations between the will of a class and government policy. An equation is made in an attempt to find roots of every government action in the will of the capitalist class or one of its groups.

Such an approach amounts to an undue simplification of Marx's attitude, which in reality is far more complex. Some of the concrete historical analyses by Marx and Engels do in fact point to the existence in a given country, at a given time, of precisely such a relation between the policy of the government and the will of the capitalist class. But in the more general theoretical deliberations by Marx and Engels, the term 'class rule' has a much richer and basically different content. It does not by any means signify a situation in which we deal always with a simple mechanism of realization by the government of the articulate will of the capitalist class or any part thereof.

To illustrate that the concept of *Klassenherrschaft* is much broader and refers to more basic phenomena than the current policy of a government is the goal of this paper. For denoting it, I shall be using the term 'class domination' instead of 'class rule,' because the term 'class rule' does not suggest a direct link between the will of a class and the contents of state decisions. It may very well be used for denoting a whole complex of economic, social and political phenomena. However the concept of class domination properly understood can be used as an instrument of analysis of contemporary capitalist society. Such a complex approach is markedly clear in Marx's conception of *Klassenherrschaft*.

To conclude this introduction a last remark of linguistic nature should be added. The term 'dominating class' has a rather awkward sound in the English text. Therefore I shall use the term 'ruling class' when I am writing about *a class which dominates*. Thus while speaking about the concept of "class domination," I shall also use the term 'ruling class.'

I. MARX'S THEORY OF SOCIETY

A. The Modes of Production and Types of Class Relations

Marx's theory of society has a rich history. Morcover the various interpretations, systematizations and developments often enable us to pinpoint or characterize a number of ideas as explicitly being those of Marx and Engels rather than refinements of their initial positions. Secondly the Marxism we speak of today tends to reflect the prism of amassed tradition. When this tradition aids the explication of Marx's theory of class domination, I will avail myself of it.[2]

Several authors state that the starting point of the Marxist conception of society is an acceptance of labor as the "species" feature of

---

[2] In particular, I used two systematizations of Marx's theory of society written by two Polish scholars: O. Lange, *Political Economy*, vol. I, Warsaw 1963, and J. Hochfeld, *Studia o marksowskiej teorii społeczeństwa*, Warsaw 1963.

man, distinguishing him from the rest of the natural world.[3] This labor, i.e., the purposeful, conscious activity performed with the help of artificial organs, or tools, has "created" man as a particular species of animal, has allowed him to make nature a subject of his labors and has extended his "artificial environment," which is a condition of the existence of human culture.

> This conception of the peculiarity of human existence serves as a basis of a system in which social relations of production—as the most general and, in their broadest characteristics, the absolutely repeatable relations of social human life—are being ascribed a particular role. . . . This conception in the hands of the creators of Marxism became a basis and instrument for distinguishing a number of sociological categories and outlining a certain system of relations between those categories.[4]

This system of categories and assertions concerning their relationship covers above all the category of "productive forces," pertaining to the historically determined level of the means of production and human abilities for using them, as well as the category of "relations of production" referring to the interhuman relations in the process of labor. The productive forces and the relations of production are two parts or, better still, two aspects of the process of production, representing a theoretically more complex category. Between the two aspects of the productive process there exists a certain type of regular relationship which, in more recent Marxist writings has been called "the first basic law of sociology."[5] This is the "law of the necessary conformity between the character of productive forces and the relations of production" or the law of a certain degree of mutual adaptation of the two sides of the productive process; it is this adaptation or "balancing" that enables the production to take place.

In the mutual interreaction between productive forces and relations of production, the former have been recognized by Marx as the leading factor since they are the first to undergo changes. The tools and techniques of production are constantly being perfected; the relations of production buttressed by customs or laws are more conservative and resistant to change. Within certain limits the perfected tools and new techniques of production can function within unchanged rela-

---

[3] Cf. e.g. J. Hochfeld, op. cit., p. 157.

[4] Ibid., pp. 158–159.

[5] O. Lange, op. cit., p. 23.

tions of production; however after certain decisive changes in the domain of the forces of production, their utilization demands qualitatively new relations of production. Marx exemplified this thought by citing the necessity of introducing new relations of production following the invention of the steam-machine and the weaving mill. After these relations have been established, they become in turn a factor speeding up the development of new productive forces until, after a certain time, they again become an obstacle to the development of those forces and must once more be adapted to them.

This presentation of interdependence between the productive forces and relations of production can be called a *causal-functional system of dependence* since it stresses both the causal dependence of one factor upon another and the functional role which the latter derivative factor fulfills in relation to its cause. This role can be either eufunctional (favoring existence, good action and development) or disfunctional (not favoring good action and development). This mode of presentation of interdependence of phenomena and their "dialectical interaction" is typical of Marx and can be observed in his presentation of a number of other problems.

Marx distinguished five historical modes of production: primitive community, slavery, feudalism, capitalism, socialism. These modes are characterized by their specific levels of the productive forces and of relations of production corresponding to them. Three among them: slavery, feudalism and capitalism are antagonistic while the remaining two are nonantagonistic modes of production. The antagonistic modes have a particular characteristic trait pertaining to their relations of production: these relations are based upon private ownership of the means of production. In these relations, stabilized and buttressed by a system of social norms, exists one or another principle of a determinate type of rule by determinate social groups over the very disposition of the means of production, over the process of labor and over the appropriation and distribution of the product of labor. *Every mode of production is characterized by such a principle inherent in it.*[6]

Thus in the antagonistic modes of production there is a division into those who exercise control over the means of production, the process of production, and its results and those who are deprived of

[6] Cf. J. Hochfeld, *op. cit.*, p. 161.

that control although they are direct producers of the goods. *These two groups of people form the antagonistic social classes.* In a community based upon slavery, they are represented by slaves and their masters; in a feudal society, the feudal lords and serfs; in a capitalist society, the capitalists and the workers.

The antagonistic character of relations between these classes stems from the objectively contradictory positions they occupy in production and within society. The basis of this contradiction is the private ownership of the means of production. Some people possess them, some do not. This basic difference is a source of a number of other socially important differences. In the process of production itself, it is manifest in the ruling position of some and the subordinate position of others; in the distribution of the product obtained, it is evident in the big share of the owners and the small participation of the direct producers. This latter fact causes, in turn, a number of other social consequences which can be described as the inequality of opportunities in securing education, health protection and culture.

All the above-mentioned factors determine the shaping of different types of consciousness by two antagonistic classes. To a large extent they are contradictory: among the privileged class the elements of affirmation of the existing social order are preponderant while elements of negation, or discontent prevail among the subordinated group.

Thus in the Marxist theory the characteristics of the class situation have their own particular structure conditioned by causal dependence. The basic feature (relation toward ownership of the means of production) determines a number of secondary characteristics which in the process of production are reduced to two: control over the process of production and control over the result of production. In turn, these three characteristics taken together form the basis of differences in further characteristics of social positions and psychological features. In this way a certain chain of causes and effects is formed wherein one feature conditions a number of others and they, in turn, condition still many more. But the basic definition of class relations embraces only the first three features: control over the means of production, the process of production and the product. Other features are "secondary" and certain of their ensembles can be attributed only to classes as a whole, as statistically dominant characteristics of a class, but not necessarily as pertaining to every individual member.

B. SIMPLE AND MORE COMPLEX CATEGORIES

Modes of production defined by Marx are systematized into a historic chain of development from less to more developed and efficient ones. They have been abstracted from an analysis of varied and complicated types of economies known throughout history. Therefore they constitute abstract, analytical categories in a double sense: first, because they were always manifest in concrete forms with many additional characteristics and secondly, because these concrete forms have resulted partially from an important fact of coexistence, side by side and intertwined one with another, of different modes of production, in particular, of "historically neighboring" types such as feudalism and capitalism.

The slave, feudal and capitalist modes of production are the types that very seldom, if at all, have embraced the whole of the production of a given society. Next to the latifundia of Roman aristocracy there existed petty peasant farms; next to the medieval English manors, factories and artisan workshops sprung up. Consequently we can speak only about the preponderance of a given mode of production in a historically determinate society.

An additional complication arises from the fact that besides the five basic modes of production there is, in many historical periods, a sixth specific mode of production, namely, the simple commodity production, also called small-scale commodity production. In it, the means of production remain the property of the direct producer: he employs them and the product of his labor belongs to him. It is, therefore, such a mode of production wherein we have only one class, and not two classes, antagonistic toward one another.

The existence of this subsidiary mode of production side by side with one of the dominant modes (which in addition can exist in symbiosis with one of the "historically neighboring" modes of production) constitutes another factor complicating the picture of the production system of a given society. As a result J. Hochfeld suggests establishing the following three separate theoretical categories with reference to these complicated situations: 1.) the category of the *mode of production* as a "simple model" serving to distinguish simple types of production; 2.) the category of *economic system* of the socioeconomic formation, comprising both the dominant and the coexisting modes of production, intertwined in a determinate way and thereby exerting a modifying influence one upon another; 3) the category of the *economic setup* pertaining to the actual relations of the dominant and coexisting modes of production, modified by their symbiosis and by various additional factors existing in concrete societies.[7]

These complications in the domain of economic setups influence the actual shape of a class structure. Usually it is more complicated than might be concluded from an analysis of the pure types of the modes of production. For example, in a capitalist society, besides capitalists and workers there may exist classes linked with the still lingering remnants of the feudal mode of production. In this case, the classes connected with the dominant mode of production are usually called the *basic classes* and those connected with the disappearing mode (or conversely with the one which is being born) the nonbasic ones.

One should bear in mind here that the old (e.g. feudal) mode of production sometimes is *transformed gradually* into a new (capitalist) one. In this process the feudalists are gradually assimilated by capitalists, and the serfs are transformed into petty farmers or land laborers. This process can go on for scores of years, and it produces the appearance of a whole gamut of groups belonging, to a *smaller or greater extent* (because of their characteristic features), to a certain class; they are *becoming members or ceasing to be members of a given class.*

The constant presence of the small-scale commodity economy leads to other complications in the whole picture: namely, to the appearance of "marginal groups" between the class of small-scale commodity producers and the capitalists. (Their marginal character consists in the fact that they have some characteristics of a social position of capitalists and some of small-scale commodity producers.)

The delineation of class structure is complicated by yet another factor which should be mentioned here. In the functioning of definite modes of production not only those people who can be included into one of the two basic classes are involved. This is true particularly of the capitalist mode of production. Besides the worker and the capitalist, there is the hired white-collar worker, performing a number of varied and necessary functions. He is also strongly represented in institutions belonging to the superstructure which we shall discuss later. Thus the capitalist mode of production itself causes the appearance

[7] *Ibid.*, pp. 168–169.

not only of the antagonistic classes but also of other social groups, usually called social strata.

In concluding this part of our deliberations it should be stressed that the abstract type (abstract because reduced only to a few basic characteristic features) of the mode of production and the type of class relations between basic classes linked with it constitute the basic instruments of the theoretical Marxian analysis, particularly that of the relations of power. The conception of class domination is above all a conception of relations between two basic classes, analyzed from the point of view of relationships within their basic characteristic features.

C. Basis and Superstructure

Men not only produce and enter into relations of production. They also establish legal norms, form social and political organizations and create ideologies. In Marx's view this domain of activity and social relations is not separate from and independent of production. Even as between productive forces and production relations a special, regular relationship (causal-functional) exists, so also between these two domains there is a relationship. In modern Marxist literature it is called "the second basic law of sociology."[8] This is the law of necessary conformity between the "basis" and "superstructure." The "basis" and "superstructure," in turn, are two aspects of so-called "socio-economic formations," the broadest Marxist theoretical category concerning the totality of relations in a given society.

While presenting the general outline of his theory, Marx has described the relations between the basis and superstructure:

> In the social production which men carry on they enter into definite relations that are indispensable and independent of their will; these relations of production correspond to a definite stage of development of their material forces of production. The sum total of these relations of production constitutes the economic structure of society—the real foundation, on which rises a legal and political superstructure and to which correspond definite forms of social consciousness. The mode of production in material life determines the social, political and intellectual life processes in general. It is not the consciousness of men that determines

[8] O. Lange, op. cit., p. 30.

their being, but, on the contrary, their social being that determines their consciousness.[9]

The "basis" and "superstructure" can be viewed as more or less complicated categories. According to a less complicated approach, the "basis" is represented only by relations of production typical for a given socioeconomic formation and dominant within it; the "superstructure" consists of the forms of consciousness and organization stemming from the basis and strengthening it in turn. In a more complex approach, the basis is formed of the totality of relations of production, i.e., not only the dominant relations but also other relations of production coexistent with them (because of which both the former and the latter are manifest in somewhat modified forms). Correspondingly the "superstructure" consists of consciousness and organizational forms stemming from this more complex base and strengthening that base in turn. Under the less complex approach, only the parties representing the interests of capitalists for example, would be included in the superstructure of a capitalist society that still contained in its basis the remnants of feudal economy. Under the second approach, the parties representing feudal levels would also be included.

In this context a "socioeconomic formation" can be presented both in a simplified and in a more complex way. O. Lange, while giving a simple definition (i.e., a very broad one covering the categories of Marxist sociology), describes a socioeconomic formation as the linkage of a definite type of production relations and a definite type of superstructure.[10] J. Hochfeld, also starting from the simplest and therefore most general, categories, proceeds to their greater concretization and in this connection gives this definition of a socioeconomic formation:

> A socieconomic formation is called a totality of social relations at a given time and place, distinct on account of the economic system special to it (called also the basis of economic basę) and also because of the ideological-institutional superstructure functionally subordinated to that system. In an economic system there is a dominant mode of production, characteristic for that formation; as we have already pointed out this dominant mode of production was a rule manifest heretofore in

[9] MEW, XIII, 9; cf. K. Marx, Selected Works, ed. by V. Adoratsky, New York n.d., vol. I, p. 356.
[10] Cf. O. Lange, op. cit., p. 31.

definite links with other modes of production. Because of this, both this mode itself and those other modes of production linked with it, were *sui generis* modifications of their "ideal types."

Following Marx and Engels, we call economic basis, or the base of formation, not the dominant mode of production (manifest in a real modified form of an economic setup), but the whole economic system of a given formation. A formation represents a certain entity internally balanced and harmonized because it possesses the correct links between various components of its economic system to the preponderant role which is played in this system by the dominant mode of production and the functional subordination of the ideological-institutional superstructure to the economic base. The key principle of relations between particular components of this entity is precisely this preponderant role of the dominant mode of production.[11]

I would like to point out that such an approach to "superstructure" that included only the contents of consciousness and the organizational forms, both of which stem from a given basis and serve to strengthen and perpetuate it, was introduced not so long ago by Stalin.[12] He wanted thereby to prevent inclusion into the superstructure of such forms of consciousness as mathematical sciences or certain manifestations of art that did not serve directly to strengthen a given basis (e.g., production relations). But while excluding the above contents from the superstructure, he also excluded ideological contents as well as organizational forms, which were manifest against the background of definite relations of production and which played a disfunctional role in relation to them—under capitalism, consciousness of the revolutionary proletariat and its organizational forms (political parties, educational associations and so on). Stalin proposed the inclusion of these forms only into the superstructure of a future type of society (a socialist one), and these contents are forebodings and instruments for its realization. Marx and Engels, however, included them positively into the superstructure of the contemporary (capitalist) society. A similar course was followed by many other Marxist theoreticians, i.e. Antonio Gramsci.[13]

Stalin's proposal had its advantages, but the exclusion of disfunctional elements of the superstructural type has certain drawbacks from

[11] J. Hochfeld, *op. cit.*, pp. 171–173.

[12] J. Stalin, *Marksizm i voprosy jazykoznania*, Moscow 1950.

[13] Cf. A. Gramsci, "Nowoczesny książe," *Pisma Wybrane*, vol. I, Warsaw 1961. (This is a Polish edition of "Note sul Macchiavelli," contained in the fifth volume of *Opere di Antonio Gramsci*, Torino 1949.)

the point of view of complex analyses of phenomena that are a part of a given formation, particularly of societies in which consciousness and forms of organization, disfunctional in relation to the base, are permanent. Consequently it seems more advantageous to include into the superstructure all contents of consciousness and organizational forms that originate from a given base and then to divide them into: 1) performance of a sustaining role (eufunctional) and 2) the aiming at an overthrow of a given base (disfunctional).

The theoretical categories of the modes of production, of class structure, base and superstructure which are shown here facilitate the analysis of the types of socioeconomic formation. In this analysis we distinguish three areas.

The first among them concerns a complete change in the type of "social formation," e.g., transformation of one type of social relations into another. Marx and Engels devoted much of their attention to that problem. Included in it is the theory of social revolution.

The second area is that of the "functioning" of a given formation, the daily working of its mechanisms, the definite relations among men that are typical of this formation in all different phases of life. Marx and Engels devoted much attention to these problems. In addition the mechanism of economy characteristic of capitalism in particular was thoroughly described and analyzed by them.

The third area—that of the changes in the functioning of the same formation or, in other words, the changes in some of its social relations, without changing the type of these relations—combines elements from an analysis of the first type with some from the second.

While discussing Marx's conception of class domination, I shall concentrate on the second area and attempt to show these basic features which are decisive for a certain type of social relations existing within a socioeconomic formation.

II.   THE THEORY OF CLASS DOMINATION

Marx's theory of society contains certain basic assertions relative to all known types of societies or in other words, to all socioeconomic formations. We include here the assertions on definite interaction between the productive forces and relations of production or the mutual connection between base and superstructure.

Included in this theory are assertions relative only to some formations since certain phenomena and relations are manifest only in some historical periods. Here, for example, we have assertions on the class structure which, according to this theory, is manifest only in three formations: slave, feudal and capitalist. Moreover in Marxist theory there are only assertions concerning particular formations. They refer to concrete-historical forms of certain types of phenomena and regularities of a more general character. Such, for instance, are assertions concerning the class structure of capitalist society.

In discussing the theory of class domination, we shall use as an example the rule of the bourgeoisie in the capitalist system, because Marx gave a more thorough exposition of his theory of capitalist society and because this exposition involves the theory of the class structure of that society.

Marx's theory of class domination, like his whole theory of classes, joins in certain theoretical categories the phenomena found both in the "base" and "superstructure." For the notion of class domination embraces three groups of phenomena linked with one another. Marx and Engels called them economic, political and ideological domination. Taking class domination as a certain entity, we can call those three groups "aspects" or "dimensions" of class domination.

Economic domination consists in effective control over means of production, the process of production and products. *Political domination*, the most complex of the three, is above all the state's guaranteeing of this control over means of production, its process and products. *Ideological domination* revolves around ideological consecration of this control.

The premises of the above three aspects of class domination in bourgeois society have been formed gradually within the feudal formation. We shall omit here the subject of emergence and mutual interaction of the three "initial forms" or "historical premises" of the three aspects of class domination cited above. Rather we shall demonstrate how Marx and Engels viewed these relations in a developed bourgeois society in its state of "formative" equilibrium. If we overstep those limits, it will be mainly in the "forward" direction whereby we shall point out elements that disturb this equilibrium and that establish the premises of a new type of society (a socialist one).

Moreover although under the feudal system the "initial forms" of economic and ideological domination of the bourgeoisie emerged more freely and on a larger scale than the elements of political domination, nevertheless we can only speak about the arrival of a complete class domination of the bourgeoisie at the moment that its political domination is established. Only then will the capitalist relations of ownership of the means of production, its process and product have gained their proper, fully adequate legal framework, allowing for their free and unfettered development and obtaining ascendancy over other types of the production relations. Only then could the bourgeois ideology be transformed from a subversive one into official ideology of the society.

A. The Economic Domination

In section I, B of this paper class relations were described as relations between those who exercise control over means of production, its process and product and those who are deprived of that control although they are the actual producers of goods. This control exercised over means of production, its process and product is the first aspect or "dimension" of class domination, the dimension of *economic domination*. A definition of class relations is at the same time a definition of the relations of economic domination.

As can be seen from the above definition, economic domination has three main subdivisions. They consist of: 1.) control over means of production, 2.) control over the process of production and 3.) control over the distribution of the product. These three subdivisions constitute a certain complex of phenomena linked with one another. However within this complex Marx and Engels attached the greatest importance to control over means of production. The prerogatives of that control were contained in different laws of property typical for definite socioeconomic formations. These laws represented principles according to which the specific relations of domination and subordination were shaped. The ownership of slaves, land or capital were the three basic forms of property decisive for producing a definite type of relations of subordination and domination in the process of labor and the appropriation of its products.

Even in the *Economic and Philosophical Manuscripts of 1844*, which contained the outline of Marx's theory of alienation, the basic thoughts about the relations between ownership and economic domination were present. According to Marx, the alienation of the worker in the process of production is shown by the fact that the activity identifying the species of man and representing its "natural need" (i.e., labor) is considered by the worker as a necessity imposed upon him. The alienation of the product of this labor consists in the fact that the result of the worker's activity, the product, is opposed to him "as an *alien being*, an *independent power*," although it is nothing else but his "labour which has been embodied in an object and turned into a physical thing . . . an objectification of labour."[14]

Wherein lies the source of the worker's alienation? In the property relations, Marx replies. That the product of his labor becomes alien to the worker results from its being appropriated by someone else. Moreover if the worker considers the process of labor as an alien activity imposed upon him, his attitude is caused by the fact that the labor itself does not belong to him but to someone else.

"The capitalist by means of capital exercises his power of command over labour."[15] The capital or the private ownership of the "conditions of materialization of labour"[16] represents, therefore, the *means of domination* over the process of labor and the product of the labor of others.

The mechanism of that domination was outlined in detail by Marx in his subsequent works. One could even say that the explanation of the mechanism of economic domination which was proper to the epoch of capitalism was the main motif of Marx's scientific work and its main result. According to Marx, the capitalist mode of production is characterized on the one hand by the amassing of wealth which can be used in production and on the other hand by the existence of the available manpower.

The goods themselves, be it in the form of the means of production, raw materials or money, do not as yet constitute capital. They become capital only when they can be set in motion in order to multiply their value. To achieve that, there must exist the free manpower setting in motion the means of production and multiplying in the process of production the value of the capital outlays. This labor must be free in a double sense: in the sense of having personal

---

[14] MEGA, I, 3, 83; cf. Karl Marx, *Early Writings*, trans. and ed. by T. B. Bottomore, London 1963, p. 122.

[15] MEGA, I, 3, 53; cf. *Early Writings*, p. 85.

[16] MEW, XXIII, 742; "Verwirklichungsbedingungen der Arbeit" cf. K. Marx, *Capital*, Moscow 1954, vol. I, p. 714.

freedom to dispose of itself and of freedom from the means of production. This latter condition stipulates that it must be deprived
of its own means of production, capable of providing it with
means of subsistence.

Thus under the capitalist mode of production we witness the meeting of the capitalist who has the means for effecting production and
the worker who is capable of setting those means in motion. The starting of production comes about as a result of the conclusion of a free
contract between worker and capitalist, a contract stipulating a given
pay for a given amount of work. It is a formally free contract. A
worker can accept the work or reject it. He can hire himself to X or Y.

> But the worker, whose sole source of livelihood is the sale of labour
> power, cannot leave the whole class of purchasers, i.e., the capitalist
> class, without renouncing his existence. He belongs not to this or that
> capitalist but to the capitalist class, and it is his business to dispose of
> himself, i.e., to find a purchaser within the capitalist class.[17]

Hiring oneself's to work necessitates abandonment of the right of
control over one's labor. What, how and where a worker will produce
depends on his employer. In addition because of his alienation it
usually does not matter to the worker what and how he will produce, for he treats his labor as a means of gaining a definite sum of
money and not as a creation of definite goods in which he would be
interested personally.

The focal point of Marx's economic theory is the explanation of
how the capitalist appropriates the value produced by the worker, a
mechanism that is peculiar to the capitalist mode of production. The
"secret" of capitalist production consists in the fact that the worker
receives as wage the equivalent of his labor power but not the equivalent of his work. The *value* of labor power and the value *created*
in the process of work are two different things. To put it succinctly,
one could say that during his day's work a laborer produces a greater
value than what is represented by his wage. This surplus goes into
the pocket of the capitalist and is called "the surplus value." Consequently in the process of labor, the worker not only yields his independence but also his right to the product of his labor. The essence of
capitalist production consists in producing this additional value, and

[17] *MEW*, VI, 401; cf. Marx, *Selected Works*, vol. I, p. 257.

its appropriation by the capitalist forms the essence of capitalist exploitation.[18]

The disposition of the surplus value provides the basis for making the worker dependent on the capitalist in the "next" cycles of production; the extended reproduction of capital is an extended reproduction of relations of domination and subordination. The conclusion of Marx's analysis is as follows: there is no capital without hired labor and no capitalist without wage laborers. The existence of the one is a condition for the existence of the other. The capitalist system of domination consists in uniting these two aspects of production and these two aspects of the two classes.

Under capitalist relations of labor there is an *irreconcilable conflict of interests* of the two sides, the two classes: first, because the capitalist *appropriates* for himself the surplus value produced by the worker in the production process and secondly, because the amount of this surplus value is in inverse proportion to the amount of the worker's wages. With a given amount of values earmarked for distribution between the capitalists (profits) and the workers (wages), this distribution can only be such that the augmentation of one part can take place only at the expense of the other. Discussing the possibility of improving the worker's lot as a result of the development of capitalism, Marx wrote:

> Even the most favourable situation for the working class, the most rapid possible growth of capital, however much it may improve the material existence of the worker, does not remove the antagonism between his interests and the bourgeois interests, those of the capitalist. Profit and wages remain as before in inverse proportion.[19]

The mechanism of class exploitation presented here is peculiar to capitalism. It is the mechanism of the "control over the distribution of product" as one of the selected aspects of economic domination. Other phenomena accompany this control, e.g., the fact that the capitalist has in his hands the sales of his product, thereby dominating, within certain limits, the commodity market as well. Nevertheless the mechanism of class exploitation is the main aspect of this control. It is through this form of control that the *material privileges of capitalists and the material exploitation of the workers* are realized.

---

[18] *MEW*, XXIII, 192 ff.; cf. Marx, *Capital*, p. 177 ff.
[19] *MEW*, VI, 416; cf. Marx, *Selected Works*, vol. I, p. 273.

Marx saw that this aspect of economic domination is subject to gradation. The exploitation of the working class and the privileges of capitalists can be quantitatively different. This kind of difference is influenced by two factors: the state of the labor market (supply of and demand for the labor power) and the struggle of the working class against exploitation. Marx likewise perceived that this form of economic domination, namely, "the domination over the process of labour" can also be subject to gradation. In *Das Kapital* and other writings we find remarks about English factory laws which contributed to the "humanization" of the relations of subordination of workers in the process of labor. If we realize that an interference with the relations of labor and relations of distribution is, indirectly, an interference with the rights of property, then we may state that control over the means of labor is also subject to gradation. Thus all three subdimensions or component elements of economic domination share this characteristic.

B. Political Domination

The second dimension of class domination is political domination. It consists in the legal sanctioning of determinate economic relations, or, in other words, in guaranteeing economic domination. Without appropriate state laws, a given type of domination over means of production, its process and product, although already formed within preceding economic relations, has no chance for full development or for gaining ascendancy over other types of economic relations. Only with legal guarantees by the state for the functional needs of the new economic system and like guarantees for the position and privileges of the new class can we speak about full implementation of economic domination.

Consequently Marx and Engels stated in the *Manifesto* that the class rule of bourgeoisie signifies "the imposition upon society of conditions of its existence as an over-riding law,"[20] while Engels wrote that "bourgeois legal regulations merely express the economic life-conditions of society in legal form."[21]

A state is an organ of political domination of a class. In the words of Engels: it "embodies the class rule." The state is an ensemble of

---

[20] *MEW*, IV, 473; cf. Marx, *Selected Works*, vol. I, p. 218.
[21] *MEW*, XXI, 302; cf. Marx, *Selected Works*, vol. I, p. 463.

people separated from society, acting as members or functionaries of definite institutions and enjoying on account of this special prerogatives. Their first task is the issuing of regulations binding upon all citizens of the state. The second task is the execution of those regulations. The above two tasks are as a rule carried out by separate groups of people working within the state machinery. Whereas kings or parliaments specialize in the first task, the second task is the responsibility of the administration, the police and the army.

In the writings of Marx and Engels the state is presented in two clear-cut aspects: 1) as a separate group of people and 2) as a certain set of norms guarded by those people. These norms have a longer span of life than that of particular groups of people engaged in the direct exercise of power. As a separate group of people, the state is not equivalent with society conceived as "all citizens." But as a set of norms regulating the behavior of all its citizens, the state is "an aspect of organization of society." "The state is an organization [Einrichtung] of society,"[22] Marx wrote in one of his articles. This thought was ably taken up and developed by Gramsci who argued that the differentiation between the "citizens' society" and the "political society" (adopted by Marx from Hegel) is a "methodic" differentiation and not an "organic one."[23]

In a certain sense the state is an organizer and regulator of the social life even when it leaves certain fields of life as the "private domain" of its citizens. For this domain remains such because of state laws. Consequently Gramsci wrote that "free trade" is also a sui generis "state control,"[24] since it is allowed and supported by the state while other types of economic relations are either prohibited or limited.

If, therefore, the state stands guard over definite relations (and in a class society these are relations of economic domination and economic exploitation), it is thereby an organizer, guardian and a basic instrument of economic class domination.

Depending on which type of economic relations are "organized" and "protected" by state laws, corresponding types of states were singled out by Marx and Engels. As a result Engels wrote about the

---

[22] Cf. "Kritische Randglossen zu dem Artikel eines Preussen," MEW, I, 401.
[23] Cf. Gramsci, op. cit., p. 529.
[24] Ibid., p. 530.

"slavery state," the "feudal state" and the "capitalist state."[25]

The type of state is dependent on the type of relations of economic domination which it safeguards and not on the political form of its organization and functioning (i.e., on whether it is a constitutional monarchy or a republic; whether the electoral law is universal or limited and so on). Having in mind different political systems in France from 1797 to 1850, Marx wrote:

> None of the numerous revolutions of the French bourgeoisie since 1789 was an attack on order, for they allowed the rule of the class, they allowed the slavery of the workers, they allowed the bourgeois order to endure, however often the political form of this rule and of this slavery changed.[26]

In another place in the same work, Marx distinguishes between an "overthrow of bourgeois society" and the overthrow only of its actual "form of state."[27]

Concentrating on the definition of the class contents of a state, Marx and Engels did not deny that it fulfills tasks of a public, national character. They maintained rather that the special role of the state consisted precisely in such intertwining of public and class functions that the function of the guardian of class domination could be presented as a general public function. This is manifest, for example, in the defense of property "in general," i.e., both the protection of personal property for satisfying definite individual needs as well as the defense of ownership of the means of production, the primary instrument of class domination.

The state performs its role as guardian of definite social relations (including also the relations of economic domination) by its twofold activity: establishment of laws and use of violence against those who either do not observe these laws or who act against them.

Use of violence is an important function of the state. Through its use a state becomes an organ of *political* class *oppression*. The term 'class oppression,' as used by Marx and Engels, has two principal meanings. First, it sometimes denotes the very fact of guaranteeing definite economic relations which could be called not only a relation

[25] MEW, XXI, 167; cf. K. Marx and F. Engels, *Basic Writings on Politics and Philosophy*, ed. by L. S. Feuer, New York 1959, p. 392.

[26] MEW, VII, 32; cf. Marx, *Selected Works*, vol. II, pp. 218–219.

[27] MEW, VII, 35; cf. Marx, *Selected Works*, vol. II, p. 221.

of exploitation but also relations of oppression (if only because within them a worker is but a "link" subjected to control by capitalists). This type of oppression could be called economic and does coincide with the phenomenon of economic domination.

Secondly, and this is a new element in relation to those hitherto analyzed, by the term 'oppression' Marx and Engels understand political oppression expressed in public actions of the state's law-enforcing organs (administration, police, army) against those who "do not observe laws," i.e., who act against the existing social relations. Realizing the spontaneously appearing negative attitude of the subordinated class to at least some aspects of class domination (as seen in strikes, demonstrations, uprisings and so on) Marx and Engels stressed this characteristic feature of the state. Great emphasis was also laid upon it by Lenin in his analyses concerning the situation in Tsarist Russia. Lenin, as a rule, spoke about economic and political oppression:

> According to Marx, a state is an organ of class domination, an organ for the oppression of one class by another; it creates "order" which legalizes and perpetuates this oppression by moderating the collisions between the classes.[28]

In the writings of Marx and Engels we can also find references to a third form of "oppression" or more precisely, of a special subspecies of political oppression. Here may be included various "prophylactic actions" by the government aimed at preventing political activity of those groups which are in opposition to the existing social relations. Among such actions may be included the ban on activities of workers' parties, special electoral laws, the depriving of those parties of an opportunity to gain large numbers of votes, the ban on public gatherings, obstacles for political propaganda and so on.

Thus there are different forms of political oppression. It is worth pointing out that political oppression construed as a use of violence by the state apparatus against the revolting, or disgruntled, subordinated class need not necessarily be openly displayed, although it is "potentially" always present in state activity. The fear of repression can cause the subordinated class to forego demonstrations against existing relations. However the fact that in Marx's theory of state

[28] V. I. Lenin, *State and Revolution*, in *Selected Works*, New York 1943, vol. VII, p. 9.

political oppression, a derivative phenomenon, exists relative to the state's role as guarantor of definite laws is most important. Therefore its actual appearance or nonappearance is not decisive for the existence or nonexistence of political domination. For the use of violence is but one of the instruments of maintaining class domination. Another instrument which can supplant it (and which usually exists in conjunction with it) is ideological domination.

C. Ideological Domination

Political domination does not stand alone as a factor sanctioning and strengthening economic domination. The same function—although with the application of different means—is performed by ideological domination. If the former bestows upon determinate relations of production the status of legality, the latter gives them the character of just and desirable relations. This is accomplished through the shaping of the ideological system, according to which a determinate economic setup is recognized as the best possible and most promising for all concerned. This is further achieved by propagandizing that system in such a way that the majority of society become believers in it.

In effect this ideological system is only the practice of the ruling class, translated into a general theory so as to satisfy the class' interests. In this sense it is a theoretical reflection, a superstructure over its daily activities. "Your very ideas are but the outgrowth of the conditions of your bourgeois production and bourgeois property . . ." Marx and Engels wrote in the *Communist Manifesto*.[29]

The sources of ideological domination rest not only in the peculiar monopoly of the ruling class for ideological activity (possession of education, spare time, control over media of communication and so on),[30] but they also stem from the fact that the ideology of a new ruling class is, at least in the first phase of existence of a given type of society, an expression of interests of all classes with the exception of the former ruling class; this new ruling class· is a spokesman and bearer of historical progress. In an article entitled "Status quo in Germany," written in 1847, Engels analyzed which of the then existing classes could become the spokesman and actual motive power for

---

[29] *MEW*, IV, 477; cf. Marx, *Selected Works*, vol. I, p. 223.
[30] Cf. *MEW*, III, 46 ff.; cf. K. Marx and F. Engels, *The German Ideology*, trans. by R. Pascal, New York 1960, p. 3 ff.

development in contemporary Germany. He came to the following conclusions:

> Let us sum up. The landed gentry is too impoverished, the petty bourgeoisie and peasants, as a result of their situation up to now, are too weak, and the workers, still too immature, to be able to play in Germany the role of the ruling class. . . .[31]

The bourgeoisie developing the industry, Engels continues, "is the only class in Germany which has drawn into the orbit of its interests and united under its banner at least a majority of industrial landowners, petty bourgeois, peasants, workers and even a certain part of the gentry. . . . The needs of industrialists represent, therefore, the needs of all bourgeoisie and classes which at the moment are dependent upon it."[32]

Ideological domination serves to strengthen more than economic domination does and in addition it performs the same function relative to political domination. Yet these are two separate, although related, functions. The strengthening of economic domination manifests itself in portraying the economic system as bringing benefits to all. The strengthening of political domination is demonstrated by presenting the activities of the government as an expression of interests of all classes. In this indirect way, the economic system is also strengthened.

Portraying the state as a "nonclass" or "supra-class" organ is one of the basic tasks of the ideology of the ruling class. The sharing of this conviction by people, en masse, is a genuine manifestation of ideological domination. Because of this, the state activity, which guarantees a determinate system—and consequently, determinate relations of economic domination and exploitation—gains the approval of "all."

The interdependence between political and ideological domination is by no means limited to the latter's sanctifying the former. There is also a reverse relation, i.e., political domination serves to strengthen ideological influence. The state organs are propagators of the ideology of the ruling class and play an important role in spreading that ideology. Each state organ propagates the type of society of which it forms the superstructure. In their most important normative sets, state organs invoke general ideological principles, and these acts constitute only "measures of implementation" and "practical appli-

---

[31] *MEW*, IV, 49 ff.
[32] *Ibid.*, 52 ff.

cation." Some state organs or institutions have the duty of indoctrinating citizens with a definite ideology. Such a duty, for example, is performed by state-run schools.

Gramsci probably stressed this interrelation most emphatically when he wrote:

> . . . since the state strives at producing and maintaining a certain type of culture and a certain type of citizen (and consequently a certain type of intercourse and individual relations), it must also strive towards eliminating certain habits and certain attitudes and the spreading of others; the law serves (next to schools and other educational institutions) as an instrument for achieving this goal. . . . In fact the state has to be viewed as an educator.[33]

In another place Gramsci wrote that a state represents such intertwining of different fields of practical activity "through which the ruling class not only justifies and maintains its power but also gains the active consensus of the governed."[34]

For Gramsci, class rule or "hegemony" was, in general, based upon two key elements: force and ideology, violence and leadership. Consequently in his opinion the definition of a state had to take into account not only the fact that it is an instrument of coercion but also that it is an apparatus through which the ruling class performs its "function of hegemony," i.e., the function of leadership in ideas and culture. The performing of that function allows the state to gain the active support of the "dependent classes."

It can also be said that in the situation of an "active consensus of the governed" the role of violence as means of maintaining class domination may decrease. It is not necessary to apply it to those who "support" the regime; it is reserved only for those who are dissatisfied or rebellious. Thus it may be said that *the scope of the application of force is usually in reverse proportion to the depth of ideological domination.*

III. DOMINATION AND MECHANISMS OF GOVERNMENT

Until now we were concerned with the presentation of the basic features of Marx's theory of class domination, but besides basic assertions, decisive for the unique character of Marx's theory of political

[33] Gramsci, *op. cit.*, p. 617.
[34] *Ibid.*, p. 604.

phenomena, one can find among his writings a number of very detailed analyses of political life. They cast light upon the way in which we should understand his general assertions. Consequently although the principles of those detailed analyses are not outlined in the texts as clearly as in the case of the more general assertions, they should be pondered since only then will we know Marx's theory of class domination in its entirety.

In this respect, such works by Marx as *The Class Struggles in France 1848–1850* and *The Eighteenth Brumaire of Louis Bonaparte* are very illuminating. We find in these a special Marxian approach to the analysis of political phenomena as manifest in the search for class determinations and functions of those phenomena. But at the same time we also have a clear differentation and painstaking analysis of particular "elements" of "political structure" and "political process," as we would call it today. The classes and political parties, bureaucracy and the army, the government's division into legislative and executive branches, different types of power and revolutions are merely a few of these elements.

These elements are considered in the analysis but are not expressed in rigoristic and precise analytical categories. In his deliberations on politics, in contrast to his economic writings, as I mentioned at the beginning, Marx used certain notions without worrying about their rigorous application (e.g. for denoting phenomena of the one and same kind). This concerns, among other things, the notion of political domination, which is central to our present deliberations. As a result it should be stressed at the very beginning that such notions as "political domination," "political sway," "rule" and even "governing" were used by Marx interchangeably. This does not signify, however, that Marx did not distinguish different kinds of power and in particular: 1.) *political domination*, as a legal guarantee of the existing structure of economic relations, and 2.) *governing*, as direct assumption and execution of concrete decisions by the government. In our further deliberations I shall try to explicate these differences precisely and to introduce certain typologies.

In this connection I would like to stress that the notion of "political domination," which was used by Marx quite liberally and in an unsystematic way, will here be used systematically and exclusively for denoting a phenomenon basic for Marx's doctrine: the guarantee of a definite economic system by state organs. In our present deliberations stress will be laid on analytical differentiation found in Marx's works with reference to certain human groups, certain types of power or certain mechanisms of implementing political domination.

A. The Ruling Class—Bureaucrats and Politicians

Members of a class are executors of economic domination. Industrialists exercise control over means of production, its process and product. In the third volume of *Das Kapital* Marx stated clearly that a part of that control, namely, control over the process of production, can be entrusted to paid business managers. But they are directly, in law and in fact, dependent upon capitalists.

However with political and ideological domination matters are somewhat different. Here capitalists are not executors. The existence of the state as a separate apparatus specializing in issuing and implementing laws points to the existence of groups of men distinct from the capitalist class and having special rights and duties.

With the existence of the state, Marx linked bureaucracy as a separate social stratum. He even perceived that this stratum, while directly exercising power, can strive to implement its own specific group interests (e.g., bestowing upon civil servants special privileges, material and other benefits).[35] Moreover the introduction of parliamentary democracy and the appearance of political parties was instrumental in producing yet another entity within the social division of labor. This is the type called the party politician, active in parliaments, in forming cabinets, in organizing elections and in manipulating public opinion. In his analyses of political events in France in 1848–1851, Marx clearly earmarked this group and labeled it as the "*political* and *literary representatives* of the classes." These include journalists, deputies to continuing legislative bodies and ministers of successive cabinets. Marx clearly points out that they are not simply members of particular classes which they represent. Rather in describing these political representatives of the petty bourgeoisie in France in 1849, he notes that:

> One must beware imagining that the democratic representatives are all shopkeepers or enthusiastic champions of shopkeepers. According to their education and their individual positions, they may be separated from them as widely as heaven from earth. What makes them representatives of the petty bourgeoisie is the fact that in their minds they

[35] Cf. MEGA, I, 1/1, 448–464 ff.

do not go beyond the limits which the latter do not go beyond in life, that they are consequently driven theoretically to the same tasks and solutions to which the latter are driven by material interests and social position. This is, in general, the relationship of the *political* and *literary representatives* of a class to the class that they represent.[36]

He also saw the possibility of differences in political attitudes between rank and file members of the ruling class and ideologists of that class.[37]

Generally speaking one can say that Marx distinguished: 1.) the ruling class from people professionally active in politics in the interest of that class; 2.) the ruling class from a group of people whom he described as bureaucracy, or primarily as the executive state apparatus. He also perceived the possibility of conflicts between the ruling class and its political representatives and between the ruling class and the relatively independent bureaucracy.

At the same time, however, his views were often formulated while making these distinctions or they were conceived in a way that pointed to the concurrence of two features: membership of a class and membership of a group of politicians or bureaucrats. Perhaps in his time the combination of these two features was, in relation to many persons, justified. Nevertheless it is important to see the dividing line. In general, it should be said that Marx's "models" of groups of political representatives and of bureaucrats permitted both members of the ruling class and outsiders to be represented in them.

It should also be stressed that Marx ascribed to political and ideological representatives of a class a very important social function, namely, the creation of ideology and the political program of a class. Usually a class discovers practical needs on the basis of its everyday experience. Its political and ideological spokesmen, on the other hand, give to these spontaneous discoveries the shape of a political program and the form of ready-made ideology. This problem of the roles of a class' political and ideological spokesmen was elaborated in Marxist theory both by Lenin (in relation to the leaders of the working class)[38] and by Gramsci (relative to leaders of all ruling classes or those preparing to seize power). According to Gramsci, a political party and its leaders create "the collective will" of a class.[39]

[36] *MEW*, VIII, 142; cf. Marx, *Selected Works*, vol. II, p. 347.
[37] Cf. *MEW*, III, 47; cf. Marx, *The German Ideology*, p. 40.
[38] V. I. Lenin, *What is to be done?* in *Selected Works*, vol. II, pp. 27–168.
[39] Cf. Gramsci, *op. cit.*, pp. 608–609.

B. The Mechanisms for Implementing Political Domination

In the writing of Marx and Engels we find descriptions of different ways of creating and sustaining the bourgeoisie's political domination. On the basis of these descriptions we can distinguish a few types of mechanisms for achieving class political domination. Two basic types which I should like to mention here could be called "mechanism of the class *political influence*" and "mechanism of *autocratic government*." In connection with these two, we can indicate two types of political domination that I would describe as "*direct political domination*" and "*indirect political domination*."

"Direct" political domination does not, of course, consist in the direct exercise of political power by the class as a whole. The reasons for this have been discussed earlier. The type of political domination described here as "direct" consists in a class' gaining decisive influence over the government through its political representatives who are under the influence of this class, and in turn the government is under their influence. One can also present this in the following way: a government is under the determining influence of the ruling class according to how that class applies pressure and articulates its demands; it does merely what this class expects or demand of it.

Concrete instruments of this type of domination achieved through the mechanism of class political influence are many; they may consist simply of certain limitations, giving only to the representatives of the ruling class passive and active electoral rights; they could be instruments of a total or preponderant ideological influence over the masses who possess voting rights; they could be instruments of economic pressures upon "free" voters or the government and so on.

Marx and Engels have often shown one, and sometimes several, such instruments operating simultaneously in the mechanism of class political influence and leading to "direct" political domination of bourgeoisie. In one of his early letters from England Engels wrote:

> We saw that the Crown and the Upper House had lost the position they once enjoyed; we saw how the omnipotent Lower House is elected; now a question arises: who actually rules England?—The property is the ruler. It allows the aristocracy to manipulate elections in villages and small boroughs; it allows the merchants and industrialists to influence the electoral results in big towns and often in small ones; it allows both these groups to increase their influence by means of bribery. The

rule of property was clearly recognized in the Reform Bill, through introduction of the voting privileges.[40]

In Engels' "Principles of Communism" the role of voting privileges is stressed still more emphatically, for the mechanism of class domination presented there is as follows: the only voters are those who are property owners; these bourgeois voters elect bourgeois deputies and these deputies elect the government which is, of course, an avowed representative of the interests of the bourgeoisie.

In the later works written after the introduction of universal suffrage, Marx and Engels laid stress upon another way of establishing direct domination. It consisted in the masses' electing to the parliament bourgeois representatives at a time when those masses did not as yet have their own political representatives and, above all, their own ideology. It was, one might say, political domination through ideological domination.

This way of establishing and sustaining bourgeois political domination was cited repeatedly in Marx's *The Class Struggles in France* and *The Eighteenth Brumaire of Louis Bonaparte*. Political domination of the bourgeoisie through its political parties was described there "as the outcome and result of universal suffrage, as the express act of the sovereign will of the people, that is the meaning of the bourgeois constitution."[41] At another place Engels similarly stated: ". . . the possessing class rules directly through the medium of universal suffrage. As long as the oppressed class, in our case, the proletariat, is not yet prepared to emancipate itself, it will for the most part regard the existing order of society as the only one possible and, politically, will form the tail of the capitalist class. . . ."[42]

Marx considered the kind of political domination presented here to be typical for the capitalist formation. According to this, bourgeois ideology dominated the masses, and the bourgeoisie, as a class, shaped the decisions of the government through its representatives. Consequently on several occasions he stated that a parliamentary republic is a political system characteristic of bourgeois society.

I have called all these instances "direct domination" because the government always did what the capitalist class, acting through its

---

[40] Cf. *MEW*, I, 577.

[41] *MEW*, VII, 93; cf. Marx, *Selected Works*, vol. II, p. 294.

[42] *MEW*, XXI, 168; cf. Marx and Engels, *Basic Writing on Politics and Philosophy*, pp. 393–394.

political representatives, demanded of it. But political domination can also be seen where the government listens neither to the opinions of the capitalist class nor to those of its political representatives. Rather it realizes its own ideas entirely and these are often contradictory to the political concepts of the "normal" parliamentary representatives of the capitalist class. Nevertheless the government guarantees and protects the economic domination of this class. This is an instance of "indirect domination" realized through the mechanism of autocratic government.

Such a mechanism is described in *The Eighteenth Brumaire*. Louis Bonaparte was in perpetual conflict with the Legislative Assembly which was "bourgeois" in its composition and ideology. He usually did the opposite of what the Assembly wanted in order to deprive it gradually of any real influence and, finally, to humiliate it in the eyes of the public. He eventually achieved his goals: he minimized "the political power of the bourgeoisie," i.e., its direct influence over government actions.

This, however, did not destroy the class domination of the bourgeoisie. Direct influence of the bourgeoisie was minimized so that an absolutist, caesaristic power could make use of peaceful economic domination.

> . . . the bourgeoisie, therefore, confesses that its own self-interest demands its deliverance from the danger of *governing in its own name*; that, in order to restore tranquillity to the land, its bourgeois parliament must, first of all, be muffled; that, in order to preserve its social power inviolate, its political power must be broken; that the ordinary bourgeois can continue to exploit other classes, and to enjoy his property, his family, religion and order with tranquillity, only on condition that his own class, along with all other classes be condemned to a like political nullity. . . .[43]

In the situation described above we see yet another factor that Marx considered worth stressing. It might be described as a class' passive acquiescence in the elimination of its politically active parliamentary leaders by the executive branch. Marx wrote that

> the extra-parliamentary mass of the bourgeoisie, on the other hand, by its servility towards the President, by its vilification of parliament, by the brutal maltreatment of its own press, invited Bonaparte to suppress and annihilate its press and propaganda section, its politicians and its

[43] *MEW*, VIII, 154; cf. Marx, *Selected Works*, vol. II, p. 362.

literati, its platform and its press, in order that it might then be able to pursue its private affairs with full confidence in the protection of a strong and unrestricted government. It declared unequivocally that it desired to be rid of its own political rule in order to get rid of the troubles and dangers of ruling.[44]

It can be said that in the instance described above and in similar cases we are seeing the elimination of a parliamentary political elite by an extra-parliamentary one. The former was under the direct political influence of the bourgeoisie while the latter disavowed that direct influence. However both ways achieved the political rule of the economically dominant class since both supported a determinate type of economic relations regardless of the specific ideas they were implementing. Of course, Marx did not use the term "elite." This word was introduced to the social sciences only at the end of the nineteenth century. Nevertheless from the above examples it can be seen that the phenomenon we now call "political elite" was clearly perceived by Marx.

The "direct" and "indirect" types of domination described here can be treated as "ideal" ones. In reality, however, there can be quite a number of political forms embodying mixed characteristic features. The types outlined here constitute certain analytical models which, with the help of Marx's writings, can be more fully developed and can then be used to analyze situations other than those he explicitly describes. I would like to stress at this point that the above-mentioned types appear in those analyses of Marx pertaining to bourgeois society already formed. Marx and Engels also did analyses of governments of the Caesaristic type (i.e., governments which made decisions independently of the support and articulated demands of a class or classes), but these analyses had reference to societies in a state of transition from feudal to capitalist formation. The analysis of a Caesaristic government presented here refers to the fully formed bourgeois society. It is true that Engels imagined that the reign of Louis Bonaparte marked the end of the bourgeois system and heralded a speedy transition to the socialist society as a result of a proletarian revolution. This supposition did not materialize. Therefore we can treat the Caesaristic type of government as one appearing in different periods of capitalist formation (as proved by history), and not only at its beginning

---

[44] *MEW*, VIII, 184 ff.; cf. Marx, *Selected Works*, vol. II, p. 397 ff.

or its end. Here it has been presented as just such a type, not linked with any definite stages.

As can be seen from the above analysis, in the Marxian conception of political domination the point is not so much *who is governing, but what laws govern* the behavior of the members of society. Thus the basic core of the category "political domination" is not—contrary to general intuition and even to some formulations by Marx—which particular people, employing which specific procedures, promulgate and execute laws, but rather *the contents of those laws from the standpoint of economic relations*.

It is true that those laws were often promulgated because the government (i.e., those who promulgate and execute laws) was under the predominant influence of a class to whom these laws guaranteed certain privileges. The overthrow of one class' privileged position and the transfer of these privileges to another class is the essence of social revolution. However such a revolutionary transformation of laws need not always be effected by means of direct political activity on the part of the class concerned. Sometimes it can be brought about by an autonomous Caesaristic government aiming at the formation of new relations in the country. The motives behind this decision can be several, e.g., a desire to enhance the economic or military potential of a country. History reveals many instances where the prevailing laws were not obtained as the result of a struggle by the class most interested in them but were "presented," as it were, to this class by a government free from its dominating influence. Such a situation seems to be the pattern in all those instances where capitalism was for the most part brought in from the outside rather than developed spontaneously as a result of internal processes. The elements of such a situation existed in Germany and were stressed by Marx and Engels in their works. Consequently we can say that the differentiation of these two phenomena, guaranteeing of rights and direct influence over government, although not always present in the writings of Marx and Engels (since they were not universal requisites) is clearly shown in some of their deliberations, and it is clearest in those precise instances where a need for such differentiation existed.

Certain works by Lenin concerning Russia suggest the need for an even more far-reaching differentiation. A. Jasińska in analyzing Lenin's ideas on the tasks of the proletariat in a democratic revolution came to the conclusion[45] that Lenin saw the so-called "revolutionary dictatorship of the proletariat and the peasantry" (which he called for in the Russia of 1905) as a means for introducing the capitalist order. This, in turn, would bring about the economic domination of the bourgeoisie. Thus in some transitory periods political activity and decisive influence upon the government by certain classes may lead to "economic domination" by another class.

C. Types of Interests; Interests and Will

Analytical material contained in *The Class Struggles, The Eighteenth Brumaire* and other works permits still other important differentiations to be made between various categories of interests and between interests and the politically formulated "will" of a class.

In the thinking of Marx and Engels we can distinguish at least the following kinds of interests: 1.) interests connected with a given type of economic and political domination, which we may term "general class interests"; 2.) special class interests; 3.) particular interests of the "segments" or "strata" forming part of a class.

When Marx wrote that bourgeois class domination is the imposition on society of the conditions of its own existence as a regulating norm and subordinating the whole community to its desire to enrich itself,[46] he had in mind, above all, "general class" interests, i.e., interests consisting in the possibility of making use of conditions under which the ruling class appropriates the values produced by the subordinated class.

However when Engels, in one of his works, asserted that the German bourgeois either ". . . must make its class a ruling one" or "assure for its own interests a dominant position in the legislature, administration, and jurisprudence, in fiscal and foreign policy matters,"[47] he had in mind both the general interest as well as a number of particular interests, such as appropriate tax laws, customs policy and so on. Within the framework of guaranteeing a determinate socioeconomic system, these particular policies can take different forms. They can, for example, aim only at assuring a maximum income for capitalists

---

[45] Cf. A. Jasińska, "Pojęcie i problematyka władzy politycznej w pracach Lenina," *Studia Socjologiczno-Polityczne*, no. 8, p. 92.

[46] *MEW*, IV, 473; cf. Marx, *Selected Works*, vol. I, p. 218.

[47] *MEW*, IV, 56.

or also have in mind the development needs of the country (these need not necessarily be the same), or seek the interests of other classes and strata of the population, e.g., peasants or workers.

Another possibility also exists; as one phase of its program to uphold a socioeconomic system, the government can favor the special interests of one segment of the ruling class. In *The Eighteenth Brumaire* Marx asserted that during the Restoration the interests of big landowners occupied the prime position in the government's policy; on the other hand, under the July Monarchy the interests of great bankers predominated. Big land owners and bankers were in this instance treated by Marx as two segments of the capitalist class.[48]

Another important analytical differentiation concerns the will of a class, which under normal conditions means the will of its political representatives, as well as its vested interests. Napoleon III protected the capitalist system and thus represented the interests of the bourgeoisie even though, specifically, he did not do all the things asked of him by the bourgeoisie's political representatives in the Legislative Assembly. On the contrary, he strove with all his energy to deprive them of power and to impose both upon them and the whole country *his own will*. Moreover the same Napoleon III was elected president and thereby invested with power, primarily by peasant voters. The small French farmers saw in him a spokesman for their interests and a future executor of "Napoleonic ideas." Actually Napoleon never truly represented the interests of small farmers who under his rule became enmeshed in the capitalist economy that was so ruinous to them.[49] From this analysis we can see that class interests may be one thing and the actual will of the class another thing (both in the case of the bourgoisie and the peasants). Real interests are one thing and class notions about them another. This subject matter is connected with Marx's theory of "false consciousness."

D. Class Domination and the Struggle of Subordinated Class

The antagonistic character of positions taken by the ruling and the subordinated class in the process of production, plus the exploitation of the latter, provide the foundation from which the subordinated class becomes conscious of its own interests and begins its struggle

---

[48] *MEW*, VIII, 139; cf. Marx, *Selected Works*, vol. II, p. 344.
[49] Cf. Marx, *Selected Works*, vol. II, pp. 114–426.

against exploitation and the status quo. Thinking of the proletariat, Marx called this process the transformation of a *classe en-soi* into a *classe pour-soi*.[50] Marx's ideas on the gradualness of this process and the evocation of different types of proletarian consciousness moving from a *classe en-soi* to a *classe pour-soi* was subsequently elaborated by Lenin in his theory of "trade-unionist consciousness" and "class consciousness."[51] Lenin distinguished three planes of class struggle which correspond to the three aspects of class domination presented here, i.e., the planes of economic, political and ideological struggle.

Of key importance, of course, is the political struggle which constitutes a basic weapon for overthrowing the existing economic domination. As a decisive form of such struggle, Marx and Engels envisaged revolution as the armed overthrow of the prevailing socioeconomic order, prepared and carried out through illegal means. But as shown in their works, they also attached great importance to the legal forms of the struggle, waged within the capitalist society. For this struggle is: 1.) a school for evoking the political consciousness of the proletariat and building up its political organization; 2.) an instrument for weakening the class domination of the bourgeoisie in all its three aspects; 3.) an instrument for the potential peaceful transformation of a capitalist society into a socialist one.

The conditions for waging this legal struggle within the capitalist society are of a special character. Capitalism flourished under the slogans of political equality and democracy. The democratic parliamentary republic became a political system typical of this formation. However this political system stands in contradiction to the economic regime whenever equality is lacking since, as in all class regimes, we find here the relations of subordination and dominance, the relations of exploitation.

> The most comprehensive contradiction of this constitution, however, consisted in the following: the classes whose social slavery the constitution will perpetuate—the proletariat, the peasantry, the petty bourgeois—are given political power through universal suffrage. And from the very class whose former social power it sanctions, the bourgeoisie, it withdraws the political guarantees of this power. It imposes its political rule on democratic conditions, which at every moment help the

---

[50] *MEW*, IV, 181; cf. Marx, *The Poverty of Philosophy*, Moscow, n.d., p. 173.
[51] Cf. Lenin, *What is to be done?*, in *Selected Works*, vol. II, pp. 27–168.

hostile classes to victory and jeopardize the very foundations of bourgeois society.[52]

Because of this, various means, chiefly ideological influence, are used
to sustain.

The basic weapon in the struggle of the subordinated class against
the existing class domination is composed of organizations of that
class, mainly political parties and trade unions. Depending on the circumstances, they can act legally or illegally. Their actions are not
always crowned with success, but in any case the organization of the
subordinated class is a means for *accumulating political force* which
can then subsequently be used in the struggle. Consequently alongside that political force of the dominating class that derives from economic and ideological domination, there exists a *political force of the
subordinated class based upon consciousness and organization.*

These political forces of antagonistic classes confront each other in
various battles. The outcome of the struggle, according to Marx,
depends "upon mutual relationship of forces," both as far as the goals
achievable within the capitalist system are concerned (e.g., factory
laws) and with reference to the transformation of the system itself.

I should like to stress here the *different sources* from which the
dominant and the subordinated class draw their political strength.
This difference has been pointed out by many Marxist writers. For
example, Kautsky in responding to vulgar opinions concerning the
supremacy of "economics" over "politics" (opinions which, so far as
we are concerned, amounted only to assertions that since everything
depended on the place a given class occupied in the economic system, the bourgeoisie was always stronger than the proletariat) wrote:
"historical materialism does not maintain at all that the economically
stronger and, consequently, the richer prove always to be stronger
socially."[53] Although he was guilty of overstatement when he also
categorically stated that "the capitalists are becoming stronger in economic and the proletariat in politics,"[54] Kautsky was obviously right
in his first assertion. Otherwise we would have to accept the view of
the absolute impossibility of overthrowing bourgeois domination.

In the case of an attempt to overthrow a socioeconomic system, the

[52] *MEW*, VII, 43; cf. Marx, *Selected Works*, vol. II, p. 232.
[53] K. Kautsky, *Materialistyczne pojmowanie dziejów* (Historical Materialism),
vol. II, part II, Warsaw 1963, p. 134.
[54] *Ibid.*, p. 133.

government willing to defend this system can use violence to quell the proletariat's political force. Such a development was foreseen at the very beginning by Marx and Engels, but they did not exclude a situation in which a government subjected gradually to the growing political influence of the working class is gradually and peacefully overcome by its political representatives. In this case, we would have a "peaceful revolution," the overthrow of the old economic system and the destruction of the class domination of the bourgeoisie. Of course, in such a situation various other forces defending the old order can still appear, namely, the army which may seek to strip the revolutionized parliament or government of its power. One point should be stressed, however: the analyses by Marx and Engels induce one to believe in the possibility of a variety of concrete situations.[55] In those analyses appeared, more or less distinctly, the following assertions and they are important from the theoretical point of view.

1.) A democratic political system creates the possibilities of undertaking a political struggle within the capitalist system, both for the purpose of obtaining partial gains within that system and for bringing about that system's destruction.

2.) The subordinated class is gathering together its own political force against the political force of the ruling class. While the sources of these two kinds of power are different, this in itself does not prejudge their possible size (or "weight").

3.) Revolution has two aspects, and the word, 'revolution,' has two meanings: according to one it refers to *the contents* of a social change and signifies an overthrow of a determinate socioeconomic system. Under the second meaning, it refers to *the form* of the change and denotes an illegal (from the point of view of existing laws), armed way of acquiring power.

In specific cases these two meanings can refer to two aspects of one phenomenon, of one specific revolution in which these two aspects are united. We have then a change of the socioeconomic system effected by illegal means and with the use of force. However we can also have these two aspects "separated." In such cases a change of the socioeconomic system is effected legally and without the use of violence. We are then confronted with a situation to which we can apply the term 'peaceful revolution.'

[55] Cf. H. Waldenberg, Z *historii zagadnienia form rewolucji socjalistycznej*, Kultura i Społeczeństwo, 1963, no. 4.

E. Graduality of Political and Ideological Domination

The above reasoning leads to the consideration of the problem of the graduality of political and economic domination. Besides the guarantees of definite laws that organize and protect determinate social relations (including relations of economic domination), there can appear —and usually do—various concessions guaranteed by law on behalf of the subordinated class or other classes. Their scope and extent can be varied. In the *Communist Manifesto* Marx and Engels had written that "the organization of the proletariat into a class and consequently into a political party . . . implies legislative recognition of particular interests of the workers."[56] At another place Engels wrote concerning the British Government that its principle is "to submit social reform bills only when compelled to do so and, if at all possible, to avoid carrying into effect those already existing." The "Local Government Act," he said, "is of importance only because in the hands of a government dominated by or under the pressure of the workers . . . it will be a powerful weapon for making a breach in the existing social state of things."[57] In these words Engels clearly admitted the possibility of a variety of concrete situations and of varying degrees by which the government might satisfy the workers' needs.

From the theoretical point of view, it was Engels who discussed this subject most fully in his letter to Karl Schmidt of October 27, 1890.

> In a modern state, law must not only correspond to the general economic position and be its expression, but must also be an expression which is consistent in itself, and which does not, because of inner contradictions, appear glaringly inconsistent. And in order to achieve this, the faithful reflection of economic conditions is more and more infringed upon. This is all the more true when a code of law is less and less frequently the blunt, unmitigated, unadulterated expression of the domination of a class; this by itself would already offend the "conception of justice." Even in the Code Napoleon the pure logical conception of justice held by the revolutionary bourgeoisie of 1792–96 is already adulterated in many ways, and in so far as it still exists therein must suffer each day from a gradual process of weakening because of the rising power of the proletariat.[58]

[56] *MEW*, IV, 471; cf. Marx, *Selected Works*, vol. I, p. 215.

[57] *MEW*, XVIII, 256; cf. K. Marx-F. Engels, *Selected Works*, Moscow 1955, vol. I, p. 603.

[58] Marx, *Selected Works*, vol. I, p. 385 (Letter to C. Schmidt of August 5, 1890).

Ideological domination can also be graded. In different societies and in different periods the scope of the ruling class' ideology and the extent to which it is accepted by the working masses and other strata are not equal. Marx and Engels foresaw a gradual decline of the influence of bourgeois ideology in favor of the growing influence of socialist ideology. In *The Eighteenth Brumaire* Marx wrote that "in the same measure as the actual domination of the bourgeoisie developed in fact, its moral domination over the mass of the people was lost."[59]

One can even go so far as to say that the founders of Marxism perceived two aspects concerning the domination of bourgeois ideas among the working class: 1) the quantitative aspect, as expressed in the number of adherents of a given ideology; 2) the qualitative aspect, shown by the intensity of belief in a given political creed.

F. The Problem of the "Balance of Classes"

The problem of the graduality of political domination found its specific expression in the conception of the "balance of classes." In this formulation, or rather in loose ideas jotted down here and there, the many-sided portrayal of political domination so characteristic of Marxian thought was expressed. Understanding those interpretative concepts is impossible without the analytical differentiations that I have tried to stress in this essay.

In some of their works Marx and Engels recall the existence of historical periods when there was a "balance of classes." State power was then gaining a certain "independence," i.e., it was free from demands and pressures of particular classes. Below is Engels' most general formulation which also indicates the specific periods they had in mind.

As exceptional cases, however, periods occur in which the warring classes balance each other so well that the state power, as the ostensible mediator, momentarily acquires a certain degree of independence of both. Such was the absolute monarchy of the seventeenth and eighteenth centuries, which held the balance between the nobility and the burghers; such was the Bonapartism of the first, and still more of the second French empire, which played off the proletariat against the bourgeoisie and the bourgeoisie against the proletariat. The latest performance of this kind, in which ruler and ruled appear equally ridiculous, is the new German Empire of Bismarck: here capitalists and workers are balanced against each other and are both equally cheated for the benefit of the impoverished Prussian cabbage Junkers.[60]

On the basis of this formulation it is still unknown which specific phenomena were, for Engels, accountable for the "balance" of the warring classes. However we have certain elaborations of this idea and they reveal more clearly the empirical contents which the author left hazy in his theoretical formulations. Furthermore on the basis of those empirical descriptions we arrive at the conclusion that comments about the balance of classes signify either a "balance of political forces" or a "balance of interests" and often the two taken together.

When Engels wrote that Napoleon III's coming to power resulted from the fact that "the proletariat was not yet able" and the "bourgeoisie could no longer" rule France,[61] he suggested, thereby, the existence of a balance between the political forces of the two classes. "Balance of forces" means here, so it seems, equilibrium of social-political influence. However this is not so much an equilibrium resulting from the unfettered activity of legalized parties representing particular classes (an activity which may be expressed in the number of deputies the competing parties elect to parliament) but rather stems from a still undefined, and difficult to present explicitly, readiness of the basic classes and of their allies from other classes, to defend or enforce their demands. The following opinion of Marx in The Class Struggles can serve to substantiate such an understanding of the "balance of forces."

> . . . a bourgeoisie, however, which demanded, above all, peace and security for its financial operations, faced with a proletariat that has, indeed, been vanquished but which is still a constant menace, a proletariat round which petty bourgeois and peasants grouped themselves more and more, the continual threat of a violent outbreak, which, nevertheless, offered no prospect of a final solution, such was the situation, made to order for the coup d'état of . . . Louis Bonaparte.[62]

In the following excerpt Engels seemed to be referring to a situation that was similar but which prevailed under much more peaceful conditions of the balance of political forces:

---

[60] MEW, XXI, 167; cf. Marx and Engels, Basic Writing on Politics and Philosophy, pp. 392–393.

[61] MEW, XXII, 190; cf. Marx, Selected Works, vol. II, p. 449.

[62] MEW, XXII, 515 ff.; cf. Marx, Selected Works, vol. II, p. 178.

> In Prussia . . . there exists side by side with a landowning aristocracy, which is still powerful, a comparatively young and extremely cowardly bourgeoisie. . . . Side by side with these two classes, however, there exists a rapidly increasing proletariat which is intellectually highly developed and which is becoming more and more organized every day. Therefore, alongside of the basic condition of the old absolute monarchy, i.e., an equilibrium between landed gentry and bourgeoisie, we also find the basic condition of modern Bonapartism, namely, an equilibrium between the bourgeoisie and the proletariat.[63]

These words, however, do not provide an answer to one important question: should the balance of political forces be construed as meaning the equality of those forces? Certain studies seem to suggest that the political forces of bourgeoisie and proletariat or bourgeoisie and feudal landowners were equal. Consequently one could speak about a balance in that case. However the totality of writings by Marx and Engels points out that, while not excluding the possibility of such a situation, this balance should be understood in broader terms (as it is accepted in contemporary political science): as a state in which both sides have a certain *potential of strength* and are, therefore, prepared to prevent a change in the actual balance to their disadvantage. Under this interpretation, politically *unequal* forces can be in a state of balance.

To this kind of equilibrium the words of Engels on the "compromise" between the nobility and bourgeoisie in Germany may be applied.

> Whereas in France and England the bourgeoisie proved sufficiently strong to overthrow the nobility and gain the position of the dominant class in the state, the German bourgeoisie so far has insufficient force for this. It exerts, it is true, a certain influence over the government, but every time a conflict of interests arises, it must yield to the influence of the landed gentry.[64]

The analysis of the situation in England contained in the introduction to the English edition of *Socialism: Utopian and Scientific* can serve as another example. Engels says there that in England the bourgeoisie "never had undivided sway" because "the industrial and commercial middle class had not yet succeeded in driving the landed aristocracy from political power when another competitor, the work-

[63] *MEW*, XVIII, 258; cf. Marx-Engels, *Selected Works*, vol. I, p. 604.
[64] *MEW*, IV, 43.

ing class, appeared on the stage."[65] Universal suffrage and the influence of the working class were instrumental in insuring that the English bourgeois "shared their power with the workers." In this case, too, the "sharing of power" did not mean equality of influence but rather that the working class exerted some influence with the decisive, political influence still remaining with the bourgeoisie.

All the above-mentioned examples have been referred to as "balances of political forces," although often they touched upon the question of the "balance of interests." In many statements these two aspects were joined in one. The political force of a class is mainly employed for satisfying its demands which essentially means the introduction of appropriate legislation; consequently a balance of interests could be also called a "balance of rights." Through the institution of relevant, legal norms, one can create conditions for the achievement of goals. Moreover in this case the term "balance" can theoretically signify two different states: 1) equal satisfaction of interests; 2) the satisfaction of interests of the two classes but in varying degrees.

In the analyses of Marx and Engels we usually find this second type of "balance of interests," but, it seems, this kind of balance can evolve toward balance of the first type. A relevant, concrete example is furnished by Germany's nineteenth-century history and its interpretation by Engels. In the foreword to his *The Peasant War in Germany*, he once more touched upon the role of Caesaristic governments and commented on the Bismarck era:

> The abolition of feudalism, expressed positively, means the establishment of bourgeois conditions. In the degree that nobility loses its privileges, legislation becomes more and more bourgeois.[66]

The above formulation covers the transformation of feudal laws into bourgeois ones and the evolution of the economic-legal system of Germany from one type to another. Engels goes on to say that this transformation of laws leads from the domination of feudal interests to the domination of the interests of bourgeoisie.

The conception of the balance of classes involving a balance of political forces as well as a balance of interests presents the problem of how adequate are these two aspects. Is there always an *isomorphism of these two balances*? Is the degree in which one class' political force

[65] *MEW*, XIX, 541; cf. Marx-Engels, *Selected Works*, vol. II, p. 112.
[66] *MEW*, VII, 539; cf. Marx, *Selected Works*, vol. II, p. 544.

is stronger than another's adequately reflected in the preponderance of its interests? Although Marx and Engels did not fully grasp this problem, their concrete analyses seem to point to a negative answer to that question.

The "balance of political forces" between the bourgeoisie and proletariat under Napoleon III (regardless of whether we consider it as the coexistence of equal or unequal forces) was barely equal to the "balance of interests" between these two classes. The laws of the Second Empire almost completely neglected the interests of workers. The "balance of interests" between feudalists and bourgeoisie under Bismarck by no means resulted from the earlier establishment of an appropriate balance of political forces between the two classes. Engels constantly repeated that the bourgeoisie was weak and cowardly and that its laws resulted from the government's initiative and not that of the bourgeoisie.

We now come to the question of the role that Engels assigned the Caesaristic government at moments of balance between classes. It was the role of an active organizer of political balance. The records left us often suggest that Napoleon III and Bismarck permitted certain forms of proletarian organization so that they might be used to frighten the bourgeoisie should that class ever seek to overthrow the power of the executive. Thus an absolute state power can favor the establishment and maintenance of a definite "political balance of classes."

Likewise, as is obvious from the preceding exposition, a government can become an initiator and organizer of the "balance of interests." Bismarck introduced legislation which was acceptable both to Junkers and bourgeoisie; to a certain extent it also satisfied the interests of workers.

To conclude these remarks on the "balance of classes," one other factor should be stressed. With the exception of a "full balance of classes" in the aspect of interests (laws), the existence of a "balance of classes" *does not preclude the simultaneous domination of a determinate class.* If under Napoleon III we had a political balance between bourgeoisie and proletariat, there is no doubt whatever that it existed under conditions of class domination (economic and political) by the bourgeoisie. Likewise the balance cited as example by Engels (one rather of interests than of political forces) between the nobility and the bourgeoisie under the French absolutist monarchy existed in a time, which, from the point of view of the prevailing legislation, could be described as a period of class domination by the feudalists.

Against this background it becomes possible to interpret very definitely the concept of the "independence" and "autonomy" of the state power of the Caesaristic (absolutist) type. One can also present in definite form the problem of the "independent interests" of bureaucracy, army or administration and, in general, of people who specialize in exercising power. Marx and Engels repeatedly mentioned the existence of such interests.

"Independence" or "autonomy" of the absolute power consists in independence in the state's decision-making power. But these decisions are made for society. Independently of how and by whom these decisions are made, they create new social relations and modify or affirm already existing ones. They are, therefore, always in the interests of some class since they invariably refer to a specific economic setup; they are eufunctional or disfunctional in relation to a determinate type of economic domination.

It is true that some of those decisions can be "indifferent" with respect to phenomena of economic domination. A state promulgates many laws of different social scopes and importance. A government can raise or lower the salaries of officers and civil servants and, to put the matter more broadly, it can create special privileges for the bureaucracy or professional officers. In such instances it is realizing the specific, group interests of the latter, but never is the action of the government limited to this. Even if a Caesaristic or bureaucratic government were decreeing laws aimed only at enhancing the privileges of "Caesar's clique," it could at the same time merely accept other laws relating to the functioning of the economy. The economy cannot function in a "legal vacuum." By accepting any economic legislation, such a government would fulfill not only its own bureaucratic interests but also the interests of some social class. Consequently the "rule of bureaucracy" can be instituted even while the domination of a given social class exists. In the light of Marx's deliberations these two types of power are not mutually exclusive.

The contents of Marx's theory of class domination, as presented here, deal with an important aspect of the totality of social and political relations. Obviously it does not cover all phenomena in the field of political structure and process. This subject matter has been greatly expanded in contemporary sociology and political science. Certain phenomena and processes of political life have obtained wider presentation in conceptions and studies of interest groups, power elites and bureaucracy. It seems, however, that without reference to Marx's analysis of class domination, it is impossible to present or analyze, correctly and adequately, the political life of capitalist society. Moreover it should be stressed that Marx's concrete-historical analyses presented here can provide an interesting starting point for studies on a number of problems widely discussed in theories of interest groups, power elites and bureaucracy.[67]

[67] I compared Marx's Theory of Class Domination with the "interest groups" and "power elite" theories in the articles: "Class Domination and the Power of Interest Groups," *The Polish Sociological Bulletin*, 1962, no. 1–2; "Ruling Class and Power Elite," *ibid.*, 1965, no. 1.

COMMENT
ON THE PAPERS BY M. RUBEL AND W. WESOLOWSKI
Alfred G. Meyer

I think it was Poincaré who said that natural scientists usually discuss their findings whereas social scientists usually discuss their method. However in the same way the conference participants here seem to discuss the legitimacy of their presenting papers at all, and in view of this I must determine the task of the commentator. His task would seem to be to act as a thought-promoter, as a catalyst of ideas. Consequently I have several possible choices. I could criticize the two papers. I would consider that somewhat presumptuous because I feel that the two scholars on whose papers I am commenting are much more learned in their specialties than I. Or I could attempt to tie them together; that is extremely difficult, for one paper was by a Marxist and the other by a Marxian, labels which perhaps both would prefer not to have applied to them. Therefore I have decided to present some ideas that the papers have evoked in me. In other words, I will function as an echo.

Professor Fetscher said something to the effect that the sociology of domination is one of the main themes of Marx.[1] Behind the sociology of domination lies the question: why have the achievements of capitalism (which include the machine age, the French Revolution and Hegelian philosophy) failed to liberate mankind from evil? That is the basic question Marx asks himself, and I imagine we would be able to come to an agreement that this question is still with us, perhaps more than ever. Moreover the gap between potentiality and actuality is great, possibly infinitely greater today than in the 1840's.

The question raised by Marx is still relevant to us. This leads me to another question that is before this conference in general: what is the relation of Marxian thought and of Marxism to contemporary political sociology, contemporary social science and contemporary philosophy?

Of this relationship I would advance the following ideas. I would argue first of all that we are all Marxists, whether we know it or not or whether

---

[1] Cf. p. 33 ff.

we call ourselves that or not. For we are all to some extent imbued with the ethics of Marx, we all are critics of alienation, at least in a vague sense. We need not be critics of economic exploitation or political domination but the malaise which impelled Marx to write impels all of us to some extent. Moreover I personally feel that Marxian sociology is accepted by Western political science with a certain amount of horrifying dispassionateness. By that I mean that we take alienation for granted; domination and other forms of inequality are all accepted as facts of life.

In addition I think we are all methodologically Marxists, and I would argue that contemporary social science in the Western world, particularly as I know it in the United States, is thoroughly imbued with Marxian ideas. It is thoroughly deterministic. Somehow each of us assumes that the economic system and technology have a structuring effect on society and on social and political systems. We are all to some extent convinced that we must regard the social structure as substructural and various phenomena such as ideology or politics as superstructural. I may be exaggerating, but I feel that many of us, many social scientists in the world, are functionalists. Like Marx they see society as a total system in which there is an infinite and multiple interrelationship between phenomena which must be studied in their complexity. To some extent even dialectics can be absorbed, in different terminology perhaps, by contemporary social scientists in the West. Hence when we study political systems, Marxist concepts are very much a part of our thinking. Such notions as the "ruling class" or "ideology" are familiar to and accepted by contemporary social scientists. We may use different terms: instead of using the Marxian notion of ideology, we may speak of legitimacy and legitimation or socialization. But the processes we describe are the same processes that interested Marx. Whether we study classes or interest groups or power elites, we are all interested in the strength that property in the means of production conveys, even though we express it by concepts such as access or influence.

I am interested not only in the extent to which we all are Marxists but also in the process by which we have all *become* Marxists. It is a very curious process. I would summarize it by saying that Marxist ideas have been absorbed despite Marx; that *even though* we tend to reject everything labelled "Marxist" that Marx wrote, his ideas today are very often accepted. If you trace them, and I do not know whether that has ever been done systematically, you may find that many Marxist ideas have come to us through the mediation of his antagonists, people like Max Weber, Pareto, possibly Schumpeter, and many others who sought to refute Marx and by doing so brought his ideas into contemporary social science.

I am interested also in the notion that Marxist ideas have been accepted and adopted piecemeal. We do not swallow the whole, rather we swallow it in small bites. We do not accept the structure of ideas, we accept the individual bricks of building blocks that Marx has fashioned. And that I think bears some explanation. We accept the building blocks because they are harmless or more harmless than the structure as a whole. Marx was accepted despite himself because of the relationship between the polemical nature of his writings and the revolutionary nature of his thoughts. There is a theory of resistance built into Marxism which seems to make some sense. It is difficult for any ruling class to accept the findings of any sociologist trying to prove its coming disappearance.

Moreover one reason why some of the ideas have been accepted may even be connected with the cold war. The critical, if you wish destructive, elements of Marxism provide convenient nomenclature when one wants to describe societies on the other side of the so-called Iron Curtain or on the other side of some ideological gulf. Marxist sociology has to some extent become a cold war device. We do not accept it for our own societies, but we use it for the other camp, and I am speaking of both camps.

One final reason for the piecemeal acceptance is the eclectic nature of contemporary social science in the West. Eclecticism is perhaps another word for a scientific attitude. The Western social scientist, not ideologically committed to Marxism, can discover the lacunae more easily, he can discover the internal inconsistencies, he can undoubtedly discover the misstatements and misjudgments. Eclecticism means the awareness that other kinds of analysis are possible. Wesolowski in his writings—though not in the paper he presented here—has pointed out that a class analysis is not necessarily opposed to interest-group analysis or power-elite analysis but these analyses are complementary to each other; and I think eclecticism is a realization that various approaches may be complementary to each other. The late Professor Ossowski has shown in a very interesting study under what circumstances and in what social situations one or the other method is likely to be used.

The main reason, however, why I think that the whole package of Marxism, the whole structure has not been accepted, is somewhat deeper than anything I have said so far. I have argued that we are all Marxists and I have advanced two arguments. One is that we accept some of the criticism, for example, that we are all aware of alienation. The other one is that we accept some of Marx's sociology. We accept much of the diagnosis and much of the analysis. What we do not accept in the Western world generally is the prognosis. We do not accept the belief in the self-emancipation and self-liberation of mankind. In Marxian thought this prognosis is supported by what Marx considers an analytic element. Rubel has rightly pointed out that the heart of Marxism is the theory of the proletariat, the image of a proletariat which I would describe as a theory of the chosen people. This proletariat to which Marx attributes all of the virtues of mankind liberated from alienation is the guarantor of self-liberation. Marxism is a theory of the spontaneous emergence of consciousness out of alienation. In the proletariat we have a guarantee that value and fact will merge, a coincidence of ethical goals with existential trends. The commodity becomes conscious of itself. The de-humanized liberate all humanity. Rubel may not agree with me, but I consider this a profoundly optimistic attitude and I think that in this century we no longer share this optimism. It is possible that Marx himself did not have it; it is possible that he had it before 1848 and not later. Rubel has pointed out that there are some contradictory statements in Marx; I could add some to those mentioned. I am fascinated by the fact that there is not only a theory of a proletariat in Marx but also a counter-theory which is the theory of the *Lumpenproletariat*. The theory of a proletariat asserts that misery brings out the humanity in the proletariat. The *Lumpenproletariat*, on the contrary, becomes demoralized by misery. I am not quite sure whether Marx has ever reconciled these two statements. One proletariat becomes demoralized while the other is compelled to consciousness. I would argue that no concrete study of the proletariat in the strict sense of the word will show the proletariat to have any of the attributes attributed to it by Marx, and that this is the reason why Marxism as a whole is not acceptable. Rubel has asked us to rescue Marx from the Marxists. That is a very noble task and perhaps the conference should set itself this task. It means finding a new proletariat; it means finding some force in either current or prospective society which is representative of alienation conscious of itself. I would like to be shown where this proletariat of the present or future is. Finding it or seeing it present would mean undoing the whole history of the Western world since 1848.

I might ask the conference to set itself an alternate task. Instead of finding a proletariat, we might ask ourselves whether there are any trends in history which augur the realization of the ethical, or if you wish the utopian, contents of Marxist's thought *without* a proletarian revolution. Furthermore there is one other task but I think it pales in comparison and possibly is opposed—the task of bridge-building which to some extent our Polish colleague has attempted, the task of reconciling Marxian sociology with Western sociology, of finding Marx in Western social science and of finding Western social science in Marx. This last task is opposed to the first task I have set because it is not one of utopia-building or proletariat-finding; it is simply a task of scientific analysis.

5: MARX AS A POLITICAL THEORIST

Robert C. Tucker

That Marx ranks among the major political theorists is a widely accepted opinion in our time. The histories of political thought commonly accord him a chapter or two, and the great age of political theory in the modern West is often viewed as running from Machiavelli to Marx. With the reservation that Marx's impact upon political thought may have been greater than his measurable contribution to it warranted, I see no reason to take issue with this view.

As one of the "greats" of Western political thought, Marx was in some ways a great dissenter. He radically rejected the civilization of which he was so much a part. He saw the state as coercive power wielded in the interests of property, and its legitimation was no part of his intellectual concern. Nevertheless Marx's political theory was closer to at least one main current in the classical Western tradition than might be supposed. A long line of eminent political thinkers, including Aristotle, Machiavelli, Locke and James Madison, had preceded him in offering an economic interpretation of politics, in linking the state with class interest and the property system.[1]

If justification is needed for returning to such familiar territory as Marx's political thought, it may lie in certain characteristic inadequacies of past treatments of this subject. First, exposition of the Marxist conception of history as a whole has loomed large in these accounts, and systematic analysis of the political aspect of Marxist theory has correspondingly suffered.[2] Secondly, Marx's political thought has

[1] On this point, see, for example, Charles A. Beard, *The Economic Basis of Politics and Related Writings*, New York 1957, Ch. III.

[2] The chapter on "Marx and Dialectical Materialism" in George Sabine's *A History of Political Theory*, New York 1950, is an illustration. There are, of course, exceptions, a notable one being John Plamenatz' systematic analysis of the political views of Marx and Engels in Ch. 6 of *Man and Society*, London 1963, vol. II.

mistakenly been equated with his theory of the state, which is only a part of it. And thirdly, his descriptive theory of the state has been emphasized to the neglect of his normative view, his position as a political philosopher. These comments define the tasks of the present essay. Starting with an analysis of the theory of the state in classical Marxism (by which I mean the Marxism of Marx and Engels), I will go on to present the thesis that the theory of the state, for all its importance in Marxist political theory, is not the whole of it and not even the most vital part; for Marx sees the economy as the prime historical locus of the political relationship between man and man. In conclusion I will attempt to formulate Marx's position as a political philosopher and to treat the philosophical relation between Marxism and anarchism.

I. THE STATE AS ALIENATED SOCIAL POWER

We find in the writings of Marx and Engels a twofold view of the nature of the state. On the one hand, they give the well-known functional definition of it as "an organization of the possessing class for its protection against the nonpossessing class."[3] On the other hand, the state is also defined in intrinsic terms as an embodiment in a special class of governors—politicians, bureaucracy, standing army, police, and so on—of society's power. As Marx puts it, "by the word 'state' is meant the government machine, or the state insofar as it forms a special organism separated from society through the division of labor. . . ."[4]

In so characterizing the state, Marx was expressing a view that he had developed in the formative period of his thought. Progressing toward his first formulation of the materialist conception of history in the Paris manuscripts of 1844, he had briefly applied himself to political theory. In 1843 he produced an unfinished critical commentary on Hegel's *Philosophy of Right* and some published articles summarizing the results. Applying a method of inversion of Hegelianism which he had learned from Ludwig Feuerbach, he constructed a theory of the political life as a sphere of man's alienation. Feuerbach

[3] *MEW*, XXI, 167; cf. K. Marx-F. Engels, *Selected Works*, Moscow 1962, vol. II, p. 321.
[4] *MEW*, XIX, 29; cf. *Selected Works*, vol. II, p. 34.

had extracted from Hegelianism by his method of inversion the view that religious, i.e., God-oriented man was man alienated from himself, for God was only an imaginary externalization of man's own idealized attributes.

Just so, reasoned Marx, man as citizen in the modern state, i.e., as a communal being or member of the political community, is but an idealization of real man and hence an "abstraction." Real man is not man qua citizen but man as a member of civil society (*bürgerliche Gesellschaft*), which Hegel himself, influenced by such thinkers as Adam Smith, represented as the arena of an economic war of all against all. Accordingly, the primary realm of human existence is the economy rather than the polity. Hegel's error was to treat the state as the foundation of civil society, whereas the truth is just the reverse: civil society is the foundation of the state. And the state, like Feuerbach's God, is an externalization of the powers of the species. It has a real, material existence, however, rather than a purely imaginary one in heaven. It exists as a special political organism separate from the rest of society and lording it over the latter. To overcome political alienation, therefore, man must repossess this alienated social power by revolutionary means. For "only when man recognizes and organizes his 'forces propres' as social forces and so ceases to separate social power from himself in the form of *political* power—only then will human emancipation take place."[5]

As already indicated above, Marx's early image of the state as alienated social power, a creature of society that comes to dominate its creator, persists in mature Marxism. Once historically established, writes Engels, political power is "endowed with a movement of its own" and "strives for as much independence as possible."[6] Marx, for his part, describes the "special organism" of political rule as a parasitic growth on the social body. Speaking, for example, of the executive power in nineteenth-century France, "with its artificial state machinery embracing wide strata, with a host of officials numbering half a

[5] *MEGA*, I, 1/1, 599; cf. K. Marx, *Early Writings*, ed. by T. B. Bottomore, London 1963, p. 31. For a fuller exposition of this argument, see the writer's *Philosophy and Myth in Karl Marx*, Cambridge, Mass. 1961, pp. 102–105. Marx's own recollection of his thought process in the critical commentary on Hegel is contained in his preface to *A Contribution to the Critique of Political Economy* (1859).

[6] Letter to C. Schmidt of Oct. 27, 1890, in *Selected Works*, vol. II, p. 492.

million, besides an army of another half million," he depicts this
power as an "appalling parasitic growth, which enmeshes the body of
French society like a net and chokes all the pores. . . ."⁷ In a similar
vein, Engels pictures the United States as a politician-ridden nation
where "two great gangs of political speculators" alternate in power
and at the public trough. "Nowhere do 'politicians' form a more
separate and powerful section of the nation than precisely in North
America," he elaborates. "It is precisely in America that we see best
how there takes place this process of the state power making itself
independent in relation to society, whose mere instrument it was
originally intended to be."⁸

These remarks of Engels appear in his preface to a twentieth anniversary edition of Marx's pamphlet on the Paris Commune of 1871,
The Civil War in France, and reflect one of its chief themes. Indeed,
all that the two men wrote about the Commune calls for interpretation in the light of classical Marxism's conception of the state as
alienated social power. They saw in the Commune a revolutionary
movement to destroy the state as, in Marx's words, a "parasitic excres-
cence" on the body of society, and this was a reason for their rapturous
response. The Commune, wrote Engels, signified a "shattering"
(*Sprengung*) of the former state power. By filling all posts through
elections on the basis of universal suffrage and by paying all officials,
high or low, only the wages received by other workers, the Commune
inaugurated the reversal of the historical transformation of the state
and its organs from servants of society into masters of society.⁹ This
echoed what Marx had said twenty years before. "While the merely
repressive organs of the old governmental power were to be ampu-
tated," he had written of the Commune, "its legitimate functions
were to be wrested from an authority usurping pre-eminence over
society itself, and restored to the responsible agents of society. . . .
The Communal Constitution would have restored to the social body
all the forces hitherto absorbed by the state parasite feeding upon
and clogging the free movement of society."¹⁰ For Marx, the Commune was an unsuccessful but portentous first attempt by man in

⁷ *MEW*, VIII, 150; cf. *Selected Works*, vol. I, p. 284.
⁸ *MEW*, XXII, 197 ff.; cf. *Selected Works*, vol. I, p. 483 ff.
⁹ *MEW*, XXII, 198; cf. *Selected Works*, vol. I, p. 484.
¹⁰ *MEW*, XVII, 340 ff.; cf. *Selected Works*, vol. I, p. 520 ff.

the mass to repossess his alienated "*forces propres*" and to abrogate the historic externalization of social power into the state.

There appears to exist, if not an outright contradiction, then at any rate a definite tension in the thought of Marx and Engels between their conception of the state as alienated social power and their functional definition of it as an organ of class rule. Whereas the one view propounds a dichotomy of state versus society, the other treats the state as the instrumentality of a class which in turn is a *part* of society. How, then, is it possible to conceive the state as an entity "independent" of society and lording it over the latter? The two men seem to have been somewhat uneasily aware of this problem. Engels offered a partial solution in the hypothesis that the state acquires a certain independence of society at times when no one class is clearly dominant. Citing as examples the absolute monarchies of the seventeenth and eighteenth centuries, which held the balance between nobility and bourgeoisie, and the Bonapartism of the first and second French empires, which played off the proletariat against the bourgeoisie and *vice versa*, Engels offered the generalization that there are periods when "the warring classes balance each other so nearly that the state power, as ostensible mediator, acquires, for the moment, a certain degree of independence of both."[11] This, however, would at best explain only certain instances of something that Marx and Engels elsewhere in their writings describe as a universal historical tendency; consequently the tension between their two approaches to the state went unresolved.

II. THE STATE AS ORGANIZED COERCION

Inverting Hegel's political philosophy in his critical commentary of 1843, Marx postulated that civil society was the foundation of the state and economics the foundation of civil society. He thereby arrived at the first premise of historical materialism, namely the primacy of economics in human affairs. The deeper existential significance of this familiar Marxist tenet becomes apparent only in the full context of the materialist conception of history as Marx went on to expound it in his Paris manuscripts of 1844 and then in Part I of *The German Ideology* (1845–1846). Man, in Marx's image of him, is essen-

---

[11] *MEW*, XXI, 167; cf. *Selected Works*, vol. II, p. 320 ff.

tially a producing animal who has his historical being primarily in the realm of material production. The growth process of the human species is in substance a *Produktionsgeschichte*, a process of man's production of the world of material objects that surrounds him, the "nature produced by history." Since history is chiefly a production process, human society itself is basically a society of production, i.e., a set of social relations that men enter into in their productive activity. In a well-known, later formulation of historical materialism, Marx called these social relations of production the "basis" of society. All other institutions and forms of consciousness, including political institutions and political consciousness, he relegated to the social "superstructure" arising over this foundation.[12]

Marx's theory goes on to assert that the human society of production has been deeply divided throughout recorded history. The social relations of production have represented so many different forms of a "social division of labor" between a minority class of nonproducing owners of the means of production and a majority class of nonowning producers: slave-owners and slaves in ancient society, landowning nobles and serfs in feudal society, and capitalists and wage-earning proletarians in bourgeois society. Social revolutions, the transitions from one form of society to another, have been changes in the social division of labor and mode of production arising out of advances in technology, and each such historical revolution of the social "basis" has been accompanied by a complete revolutionizing of the social "superstructure."

Every social system based on the division of labor is necessarily, in Marx's view, a conflictual system. The social division of labor is not simply a division but an antagonism, and class-divided society is society in conflict. What makes it so, according to Marx, is a postulated rebelliousness of man as producer against his life-conditions in societies of production based on division of labor. The rebelliousness is explained by the inability of man as producer to develop his productive powers freely and to the full within any given social division of labor. Thus bourgeois man could not develop the new capitalist productive powers freely within the division of labor between lords and serfs and the feudal system of landed property. Now proletarian man,

---

[12] *MEW*, XIII, 8 ff.; cf. K. Marx, *A Contribution to the Critique of Political Economy* (Chicago 1904), p. 11.

as Marx sees it, is increasingly restive because of his inability to develop freely the new productive powers of modern machine industry within the division of labor between capitalist and worker, i.e., within the confines of wage labor as the mode of production. Generalizing, we may say that for classical Marxism the rebelliousness of man as producer is a constant historical tendency which periodically rises to a peak of intensity, bursts out in a revolutionary upheaval and then subsides— but not for long—with the resulting transformation of society. The envisaged destination of the historical process is a classless society in which the social relations of production will no longer take the form of division of labor and hence will not become again a fetter upon man's powers of production.

The state, a key element in the social superstructure, is functionally defined for Marx and Engels in this theoretical context. It institutionalizes the conflict-situation in societies founded on division of labor in production, and consequently is "simply the official form of the antagonism in civil society."[13] The state according to this view is an instrumentality for waging the class struggle *from above*. The possessing class, as the beneficiary of an existing social order of production, will necessarily resist all efforts of the producer class to transform society. In doing so it will freely make use of organized coercion. To curb the ever rebellious producers and to protect the social order from the danger of overthrow, the state will use the police, prisons, the standing army, the courts and so on. Thus the state is seen by classical Marxism as fundamentally a repressive force. In Engels' words, "the state of antiquity was above all the state of the slave owners for the purpose of *holding down* the slaves, as the feudal state was the organ of the nobility for *holding down* the peasant serfs and bondsmen, and the modern representative state is an instrument of exploitation of wage labor by capital."[14]

In the work from which this passage is quoted, Engels also writes that the state historically arose as a force for keeping class conflict within certain tolerable bounds. In order that antagonistic classes might not consume themselves and society in sterile struggle, he says, "a power seemingly standing above society became necessary for the purpose of moderating the conflict, of keeping it within the bounds

[13] *MEW*, IV, 182; cf. K. Marx, *The Poverty of Philosophy* (Chicago n.d.), p. 190.
[14] *MEW*, XXI, 167; cf. *Selected Works*, vol. II, p. 320. Italics added.

of 'order'. . . ."[15] This statement must be kept in context to avoid misinterpretation. Engels does not mean that the state stands above class conflict but only that it seems to. Nor does he mean that the state is in essence a conflict-preventing or conflict-resolving force. Along with Marx, he sees the state as a *weapon* of class conflict but a weapon which, in the hands of the economically dominant class, is employed to prevent the underlying antagonism in the society from exploding into revolutionary violence. Only in this special sense does the state, in the Marxist theory of it, exist as a means of "moderating" conflict in society.

For Marx and Engels, the social history of man is a series of systemic conflicts in which the fundamental issue has been the social order itself—its preservation or its overthrow. The division of labor has bifurcated society to such an extent that the great question for every historical society has always been: how long can it hold itself together? Moreover the Marxist view of the state is governed by this underlying assumption about society. The repressive function that it assigns to state power arises logically out of the imperative needs of society as a conflictual system whose very persistence is always at stake. The state is the supreme defense mechanism of a threatened social structure; furthermore it is a mechanism that regularly must be used, often violently, because the internal threat to the system, for the reasons already explained, is continually manifesting itself in violent ways. Hence Lenin caught the spirit of classical Marxism and was merely accentuating a basic theme of its political theory when he defined the state as "organized and systematic violence."[16]

Marx's theory holds that class struggles, when they grow in intensity, become political struggles. The possessing class is ready to call out the police and the army at the slightest provocation from the producers. By the same token, the producers cannot fight their class struggles without pitting themselves against the existing state; and since the state is the social structure's defense mechanism, they cannot revolutionize the social order without overthrowing the state and taking political power, or more specifically the producers cannot transform the social foundation without tearing down the old political superstructure. Consequently Marx's political theory holds that all

---

[15] *MEW*, XXI, 165; cf. *Selected Works*, vol. II, p. 319.
[16] V. I. Lenin, *Selected Works*, Moscow 1946–1947, vol. II, p. 197.

social revolutions necessitate political revolutions. It sees the French Revolution, for example, as the political expression of the deeper bourgeois revolution in French society. However for Marx the "Thermidor" too finds its explanation in the tendency of every revolutionary new form of statehood to become very quickly a conservative force, a repressive defense mechanism for *its* social order. The state *qua* state is thus seen as in essence a conservative force for preservation of the social *status quo*. The later Leninist notion of the Communist party-state as a force for social change, an instrumentality of a long-range revolutionary transformation of society from above, is in this respect a serious modification of Marxist theory and represents one of the significant points of divergence between classical and Communist Marxism.

It follows that Marx and Engels propounded an economic interpretation of politics in both a radical and special form. Politics, in their view, is fundamentally *about* economics as defined above, i.e., about modes and relations of production and their changes. They were well aware, of course, that this conception ran counter to the general assumption of participants in political life and of those who have written about it; for this latter group had stated that political history genuinely revolves around political and moral issues, such as constitutions, forms of state, human rights, the franchise and justice. To account for the discrepancy between the real meaning of politics and what people believe about it, Marx and Engels invoked their theory of ideological thinking as false consciousness. Not only did all class conflicts tend to take the form of political struggles, but all political conflicts were also class struggles in *ideological disguise*. Such ideological disguise of economic issues as political ones was a matter of genuine obfuscation in the heads of men, including political leaders. Thus the struggles in states between government and opposition were manifestations of class conflict, but the latter was reflected in them "in inverted form, no longer directly but indirectly, not as a class struggle but as a fight for political principles, and so distorted that it has taken us thousands of years to get behind it."[17] In the same vein, Marx wrote that "all struggles within the state, the struggle between democracy, aristocracy and monarchy, the struggle for the franchise,

[17] Engels' letter of October 27, 1890, to C. Schmidt, *Selected Works*, vol. II, p. 493.

etc., etc., are merely the illusory forms in which the real struggles of the different classes are fought out among one another."[18] Elsewhere, in answering the objection that his economic interpretation of politics would not apply to ancient Greece and Rome, where political considerations really were the dominant ones, Marx declared that classical antiquity could no more live on politics than the Middle Ages could live on Catholicism, and went on: ". . . a very little knowledge of the history of the Roman republic suffices to acquaint us with the fact that the secret core of its history is formed by the history of the system of landed proprietorship."[19]

Therefore political consciousness became, for classical Marxism, a form of false consciousness, an upside-down view of reality, and common sense assumptions about political life were explained away as illusions. Marx's thinking in this regard presupposed a distinction of the Freudian type between "manifest" and "latent" meaning-content. Political consciousness was in a manifest sense about moral-political issues, but latently it was about economic ones. The underlying meaning of politics, obscure to participants and scholars alike, lay in the basic inner conflicts in the human society of production, the conflicts over modes of productive activity.

III. HISTORICAL FORMS OF THE STATE

Much of what Marx and Engels wrote about the state was expressed in sweeping generalities typified by the *Communist Manifesto's* description of the state as "merely the organized power of one class for oppressing another." To what extent were they conscious of differences between forms of government, and what importance did they attach to them? For reasons already touched on, they were much more impressed by that which all forms of government have in common than by the features distinguishing one form from another. They were not, however, oblivious to differences and did not treat them as insignificant. Though this aspect of their political theory was never systematically elaborated in detail, they did propound a kind of Marxist "comparative politics."

[18] *MEW*, III, 33; cf. K. Marx-F. Engels, *The German Ideology*, New York 1947, p. 23.

[19] *MEW*, XXIII, 96; cf. K. Marx, *Capital*, London 1933, p. 57 n.

Not surprisingly in view of the general historical structure of their thought, this was a comparative politics over time rather than across space. They tended, in other words, to assume that each successive epoch in the social history of mankind, each dominant socioeconomic formation, has its own characteristic form of statehood. On that basis there should be five different forms of government corresponding to the five forms of class society mentioned by Marx: Asiatic society, the slave-owning society of classical antiquity, feudal society, modern bourgeois society and future communist society in its lower phase during which the state would persist in the form of a "dictatorship of the proletariat." But Marx and Engels deal only very sketchily with the theme of the correlations between the types of class-divided society and the forms of government.

Influenced by the writings of British political economists, notably Richard Jones and J. S. Mill, Marx saw Asiatic society as a socioeconomic formation based on irrigated agriculture. Since the obligation of seeing to the construction and maintenance of complex and costly canals and waterworks devolved upon the state in those conditions, the centralizing power of government expanded very greatly and the state took the form of "Oriental despotism." Marx had little further to say on the social order of Oriental despotism.[20] Nor did he and Engels designate a particular form of government as characteristic of the slave-owing society of classical antiquity—an omission that may find its explanation in the diversity of forms of government in ancient Greece and Rome. They saw monarchy as the typical political form of feudal society, however, and parliamentary democracy, variously called the "representative state" or "democratic republic," as the form of government proper to a capitalist society in its mature development. It was in this "last form of state of bourgeois society" that the

---

[20] See his article on "The British Rule in India" (New York Daily Tribune, June 25, 1853) for his views on this subject. In an essay on "The Ruling Bureaucracy of Oriental Despotism: A Phenomenon That Paralyzed Marx," in The Review of Politics (July 1953), Karl A. Wittfogel hypothesizes that Marx's reticence on this theme stemmed from a reluctance to discuss the class structure of Oriental society and comments that this in turn probably stemmed from a fear of suggesting that a bureaucracy might prove the ruling and owning class in a future socialist society. This is a highly speculative explanation, particularly considering that Oriental society was not the only prebourgeois social formation concerning which Marx had very little to say. The only form of society that Marx showed any interest in analyzing in detail was, after all, bourgeois society.

class struggle was destined to be "fought out to a conclusion."[21]

The attitude of Marx and Engels toward the political institutions of liberal parliamentary democracy was ambivalent. On the one hand, they saw the democratic republic in bourgeois society as being, like all previous forms of the state, a class dictatorship. The liberal democratic state was a camouflaged "bourgeois dictatorship."[22] Its representative government and universal suffrage meant no more than the opportunity of "deciding once in three or six years which member of the ruling class was to misrepresent the people in parliament."[23] Yet Marx and Engels were not inclined to dismiss democratic political institutions as useless or unimportant. Rather they saw in them a school of political training for the working class in bourgeois society, a stimulus to the growth of revolutionary class consciousness in the proletariat. For the debate by which parliamentary democracy lived necessarily had to spread to the larger society outside: "The parliamentary regime leaves everything to the decision of majorities; how shall the great majorities outside parliament not want to decide? When you play the fiddle at the top of the state, what else is to be expected but that those down below dance?"[24]

But was it possible, as later Social Democratic Marxists came to believe, for an anticapitalist revolution and socialist transformation of bourgeois society to take place in a peaceful and orderly way through the electoral process in a parliamentary democracy? Could the workers achieve political power by democratic means and proceed by those means to change the mode of production? On one or two occasions Marx alluded to such a possibility, most notably when he allowed in a speech about the Congress at the Hague in 1872 that in England and America, and possibly in Holland as well, the workers might conceivably attain their revolutionary aim by peaceful means.[25] However it is uncertain how seriously he or Engels actually entertained such a belief, which was at variance with a fundamental tend-

[21] *MEW*, XIX, 29; cf. *Selected Works*, vol. II, pp. 33–34.
[22] *MEW*, VII, 33; cf. *Selected Works*, vol. I, p. 163.
[23] *MEW*, XVII, 340; cf. *Selected Works*, vol. I, p. 520.
[24] *MEW*, VIII, 154; cf. *Selected Works*, vol. I, p. 288.
[25] *MEW*, XVIII, 160; cf. K. Kautsky, *The Dictatorship of the Proletariat* (Ann Arbor, Mich. 1964), p. 10. See also Marx's article "The Chartists," *New York Daily Tribune* for August 25, 1852, *MEW*, VIII, 342 ff., suggesting that in England universal suffrage must inevitably result in the political supremacy of the working class.

ency of their thought over the years. Addressing himself in 1874 to believers in a nonauthoritarian revolution, Engels inquired: "Have these gentlemen ever seen a revolution?" And he went on: "A revolution is certainly the most authoritarian thing there is; it is the act whereby one part of the population imposes its will upon the other part by means of rifles, bayonets, and cannon-authoritarian means, if such there be at all. . . ."[26] It is true that later in his 1895 introduction to a new edition of Marx's *Class Struggles in France*, Engels found the Social Democratic movement to be thriving on universal suffrage and the ballot box; but even there he did not assert that the working class could actually come to power by these means. He said nothing to suggest that he had altered the view, expressed some years earlier, that universal suffrage was not, and could not be, anything more than a "gauge of the maturity of the working class." Its mission was to herald the revolutionary *dénouement*: "On the day the thermometer of universal suffrage registers boiling point among the workers, both they and the capitalists will know what to do."[27]

Marx and Engels saw in the class state not only organized coercion but also an element of deception. In each of its historical incarnations the state had been the dictatorship of a minority class of owners of the means of production, but its class character had been camouflaged. In Europe, for example, monarchy had been "the normal incumbrance and indispensable *cloak* of class-rule."[28] In addition the modern democratic republic claimed to be a state ruled by the people as a whole through their elected representatives in parliament; the control of this state by the capitalist class, and their use of it for class purposes, was concealed. This theme of the manipulation of political forms to cover up minority class rule is a minor one in Marx and Engels but merits special attention because it influenced later elitist theories of the state. In the elitist theories of Mosca, Pareto and others, the ruling class is no longer defined in Marx's manner, and the possibility of a future society without a ruling class is explicitly or implicitly denied. But notwithstanding the fact that the elitists were anti-Marxists and offered their view of the state in part as a rebuttal of Marx's, their thinking showed the impact of classical Marxist political theory. Pareto admitted as much when he praised

[26] *MEW*, XVIII, 308; cf. *Selected Works*, vol. I, p. 638.

[27] *MEW*, XXI, 168; cf. *Selected Works*, vol. II, p. 322.

[28] *MEW*, XVII, 341 ff.; cf. *Selected Works*, vol. I, p. 522. Italics added.

the "sociological part" of Marx's teaching, the idea that societies are divided into classes of rulers and ruled.[29] This basic notion, along with the tendency to see minority class rule as something concealed behind external political forms, is something for which the elitist theory is largely indebted to Marx. And it may be through this channel that Marx has had his most enduring influence upon political thought in the contemporary West.

So strong was Marx's belief in the class essence of every historical form of the state that the reality of autocracy or personal rule at certain junctures in history seems to have escaped him. Engels, as noted earlier, suggested in one passage that there were times when autocratic rulers might have become independent powers owing to a balance of contending classes in society. Marx, however, was less inclined to think in this fashion. The point is best illustrated by his interpretation of the rule of Louis Bonaparte. France seemed, Marx wrote, to have escaped the despotism of a class only to fall back beneath the despotism of an individual. But it was not so: "Bonaparte represents a class, and the most numerous class of French society at that, the *small peasants*." However the small peasants were not a unified class; and since they were incapable for this reason of cognizing and enforcing their class interest in their own name, they had to do it through a representative: "Their representative must at the same time appear as their master, as an authority over them, as an unlimited governmental power, that protects them against the other classes and sends them the rain and the sunshine from above. The political influence of the small peasants, therefore, finds its final expression in the executive power subordinating society to itself."[30]

It was an ingenious interpretation but also an arbitrary one and reflects Marx's incapacity to grasp government under any other aspect than that of rule on behalf of the economic interest of a social class. I am unable to agree with Professor Plamenatz, therefore, when he writes that Marx, in the *Eighteenth Brumaire*, showed an understanding of the phenomenon that later came to be known as fascism and, in particular, that he ". . . saw that classless adventurers could, by playing off the classes against one another, capture the State and use

---

[29] Quoted by H. Stuart Hughes, *Consciousness and Society*, New York 1961, p. 79 ff.

[30] *MEW*, VIII, 198 ff.; cf. *Selected Works*, vol. I, p. 334 ff.

it to promote interests which were not class interests."[31] It seems, on the contrary, that Marx's interpretation of Louis Bonaparte as the political representative of an inarticulate small peasantry foreshadowed the grievous mistake of Marxism in the twentieth century when it interpreted the full-grown fascisms of Hitler and Mussolini as forms of class rule by the monopoly bourgeoisie. One of the serious deficiencies of Marxist political theory is the difficulty that it inevitably encounters when it takes up the problem of personal dictatorship.

IV. THE PROLETARIAN STATE

Marx and Engels thought the state would disappear in the higher phase of the communist society, but in the transitional lower phase of communist society—society as it would exist in the aftermath of proletarian revolution—the state would survive as a dictatorship of the working class. The *Communist Manifesto* thus speaks of the proletariat constituting itself as the ruling class. In *The Class Struggles in France*, written in 1850, Marx proclaimed "the class dictatorship of the revolution, the class dictatorship of the proletariat as the inevitable transit point to the abolition of class differences generally, to the abolition of all the productive relations on which they rest, to the abolition of all the social relations that correspond to these relations of production, to the revolutionizing of all the ideas that result from these social connections."[32] Returning to the theme in a letter of 1852 to Joseph Weydemeyer, Marx declared that "the class struggle necessarily leads to the dictatorship of the proletariat" and that "this dictatorship itself constitutes only the transition to the *abolition* of all classes and to a *classless society*."[33] Finally in his unpublished notes of 1875 on the Gotha Program, Marx wrote: "Between capitalist and communist society lies the period of the revolutionary transformation of the one into the other. There corresponds to this also a political transition period in which the state can be nothing but *the revolutionary dictatorship of the proletariat*."[34]

The doctrine of proletarian dictatorship is undoubtedly an integral

---

[31] *Man and Society*, vol. II, p. 371 ff.
[32] *MEW*, VII, 88; cf. *Selected Works*, vol. I, p. 223.
[33] *Selected Works*, vol. II, p. 452.
[34] *MEW*, XIX, 28; cf. *Selected Works*, vol. II, p. 32 ff.

part of classical Marxism and its political theory. On the other hand, Marx and Engels were not inclined to go into detail on this theme and left it somewhat unclear how they concretely envisaged the future proletarian dictatorship. This paved the way for later Marxist controversy over the question. Although diverse schools of Marxist thought have recognized the doctrine of the proletarian dictatorship as an inalienable part of Marxism, they have differed, at times very deeply and bitterly, over the amount of importance to be attached to it and the proper interpretation to be placed upon it. Indeed, the theoretical and practical question of what the proletarian dictatorship would and should look like in practice, and the related question of what the founders believed on the point, directly underlay the great schism of 1917 and after between orthodox Social Democratic Marxism and the Communist Marxism of Lenin and his followers. The issue was whether or not the latter were acting as good Marxists in setting up the Soviet one-party state and calling it a Marxist "dictatorship of the proletariat." In an effort to prove in advance that this would be a valid Marxist action, Lenin in the summer of 1917 wrote *The State and Revolution*, his principal contribution to Marxist political theory. The doctrinal conflict was joined when the German Social Democratic leader Karl Kautsky published a Marxist criticism of the Bolshevik Revolution in his pamphlet of August, 1918, *The Dictatorship of the Proletariat*, to which Lenin later responded with *The Proletarian Revolution and the Renegade Kautsky*.

In attacking the Russian Bolsheviks on Marxist grounds for setting up a dictatorial regime and ruling by force and violence in the name of the proletariat, Kautsky contended that democracy and Marxist socialism were inseparable. A Marxist dictatorship of the proletariat would not be a dictatorship in the "literal sense" of suspension of democracy and rule by a single person. Rather it would be class rule by the proletariat and, as such, it would be majority rule according to the generally accepted democratic procedures and with full protection of minorities. In the proletarian context, therefore, the term "dictatorship" was to be understood in a Pickwickian sense as referring not to a form of government but rather to "a condition which must everywhere arise when the proletariat has conquered political power," namely, the condition of proletarian "sovereignty" in a society composed of the majority of proletarians. Moreover to prove that this was the Marx-Engels' viewpoint as well as his own, Kautsky cited Marx's description in *The Civil War in France* of the Paris Commune as a polity that abolished a standing army and state officialdom and operated on the basis of general suffrage and citizen rotation in elective public office. Had not Marx himself called the Commune an essentially working-class government? And had not Engels, in his preface to a twentieth-anniversary edition of Marx's famous pamphlet, expressly held up the Commune as the first example of dictatorship of the proletariat?[35]

Testimony could thus be found for a Social Democratic interpretation of the founders' views on the proletarian dictatorship. Marx did portray the Commune as a libertarian new order and hailed it as "the political form at last discovered under which to work out the economic emancipation of labor."[36] Nor was this the only evidence in support of the Kautskyan case. The *Communist Manifesto* had, after all, described the predicted future establishment of proletarian class rule as the "winning of democracy" (*Erkämpfung der Demokratie*). Much later in his criticism of the draft of the Erfurt Program of the German Social Democratic Party, Engels wrote that the working class could only come to power under the form of the democratic republic and added: "this is even the specific form for the dictatorship of the proletariat, as the great French revolution has already shown."[37]

Yet the Kautskyan interpretation of the founders' position was ultimately shaky and unconvincing, for it ignored important conflicting evidence. The very words of Engels just quoted show the untenability of Kautsky's view that Marx and Engels conceived the proletarian dictatorship not as a form of government but as a "condition" only. They saw it as the final form that the state was destined to take in history. And Engels' reference to the French revolution in this context is only one of many indications that the political *content* of the proletarian dictatorship, even within the frame of a democratic republic, was envisaged in a very different manner from Kautsky's as described above. There is adequate evidence to show that when Marx and Engels spoke of the future proletarian dictatorship, they were not using the term "dictatorship" in a merely Pickwickian sense but

---

[35] *The Dictatorship of the Proletariat*, pp. 30, 43–44, 46.

[36] *MEW*, XVII, 342; cf. *Selected Works*, vol. I, p. 522.

[37] Marx and Engels, *Selected Correspondence 1846–1895*, New York 1942, p. 486.

literally. It is true that they offered no such general definition of the term as Lenin's, according to which "Dictatorship is rule based directly upon force and unrestricted by any laws." Nor were they as explicit on the applicability of the general formula to the case of the proletarian state as Lenin was when he added: "The revolutionary dictatorship of the proletariat is rule won and maintained by the use of violence by the proletariat against the bourgeoisie, rule that is unrestricted by any laws."[38] Yet this appears to have been the direction of their thinking.

One of the indications of it is their critical reaction to the draft Gotha Program's call for a "free people's state." They objected to the idea that a "free state" should be a stated goal of the workers' party in Germany and did so on the explicit ground that a proletarian state could no more be a free one than any other form of state could. "As, therefore, the state is only a transitional institution which is used in the struggle, in the revolution, in order to hold down one's adversaries by force," declared Engels in his letter of March 18–28, 1875, to Bebel about the draft Program, so "it is pure nonsense to talk of a free people's state: so long as the proletariat still uses the state, it does not use it in the interests of freedom but in order to hold down its adversaries, and as soon as it becomes possible to speak of freedom the state as such ceases to exist."[39] Like all previous historical forms of the state, the proletarian state was looked upon by the founders of Marxism as an instrumentality of class struggle, a means of "holding down" a class in society, a repressive force. Nor did they shrink, even in their mature years, from the corollary that the revolutionary dictatorship of the proletariat would have to resort to the weapon of terror. Engels insisted on the need for a revolution to maintain itself in power by means of terror and criticized the Communards of 1871 for not having done so resolutely enough. Could the Commune have lasted a single day, he inquired, without resorting to the "authority of the armed people" against the bourgeoisie? And: "Should we not, on the contrary, reproach it for not having used it freely enough?"[40] Marx, stating in a letter of 1881 that the majority of the Commune was in no sense socialist, made clear what, in his view, a genuinely socialist government should be prepared to do on assuming power:

[38] Lenin, *Selected Works*, vol. II, p. 365.
[39] *Selected Works*, vol. II, p. 42.
[40] *MEW*, XVIII, 308; cf. *Selected Works*, vol. I, p. 638.

"One thing you can at any rate be sure of: a socialist government does not come into power in a country unless conditions are so developed that it can above all take the necessary measures for intimidating the mass of the bourgeoisie sufficiently to gain time—the first desideratum—for lasting action."[41]

All this speaks against one further argument that has been adduced in favor of the Social Democratic exegesis of classical Marxism on the proletarian dictatorship. The argument holds that the thinking of Marx and Engels underwent a democratic evolution over the years, that they moved from a youthful Blanquist tendency or Jacobinism in 1848 and its aftermath to a mature outlook that was sober, moderate and genuinely democratic. According to the Russian Menshevik leader Martov, for example, Marx and Engels originally conceived the idea of proletarian dictatorship in the late 1840's under the influence of the Jacobin tradition of 1793, with its minority political dictatorship and the Terror. But later, as Marx and Engels became convinced that conscious support of the majority of the population was required for a socialist revolution, their conception of the proletarian dictatorship lost its Jacobin content and they envisaged proletarian class rule "only in the forms of a total democracy."[42]

The weakness of this line of argument is clear from testimony already cited above. Although the mature Marx and Engels were not the flaming revolutionists that they had been in their youth, they remained faithful to the Marxian revolutionary idea and vision. It is true that they envisaged proletarian rule as a majoritarian dictatorship, but also, as we have just had occasion to observe, that democratic protection of the rights of the class minority was no part of their image of it. In their later as well as their earlier years, they saw the class rule of the proletariat as essentially a regime of revolution (a "class dictatorship of the revolution," as Marx had called it). They took it for granted that as such it would have bourgeois class enemies whom the government of the proletarian majority would have to deal with—and in their view ought to deal with—by forcible means, not

[41] Marx to Domela Nieuwenhuis, February 22, 1881, *Selected Correspondence*, p. 386.

[42] J. Martov, *The State and the Socialist Revolution*, New York 1939, pp. 57, 63. The lingering influence of this line of argument in present-day Marx scholarship in the West is to be seen in George Lichtheim, *Marxism: An Historical and Critical Survey*, New York 1961.

excluding terror. The proletarian government, like every other, would be repressive in nature.

Lenin was on strong textual ground in emphasizing this point in the controversy with Social Democratic Marxism, but that is not to say that his exegesis of the doctrine of proletarian dictatorship was correct in all details or even in all essentials. If Kautsky unduly deprecated the significance of this doctrine in classical Marxism, Lenin unquestionably exaggerated it. Not content with saying in *The State and Revolution* that to be a genuine Marxist one had to accept not only the class struggle but also the proletarian dictatorship as its outcome, he subsequently asserted that the conception of proletarian dictatorship was "the essence of Marx's doctrine" and "sums up the whole of his revolutionary teaching."[43] This was to blow up one important part of Marx's thought out of all true proportion. Furthermore if Kautsky overly "democratized" Marx's notion of the proletarian dictatorship, Lenin too construed it in a manner that Marx had not foreseen. There is nothing, for example, to indicate that Marx conceived the proletarian state as a party-state, a dictatorship of a single party ruling, or claiming to rule, *on behalf* of the proletariat. Nor did he picture it in Leninist fashion as a form of polity destined to endure through an entire historical epoch of transition to communism, for the transition itself was understood in different terms. Precisely because the proletarian state would be a regime of the immense majority in an advanced society, a majority in the process of abolishing private property and therewith the division of labor in production, it would soon lose its repressive *raison d'être* and wither away. As a "dictatorship of the revolution," it would have a short life at the close of man's prehistory. Such, at any rate, is the belief that Marx and Engels seem to have entertained.

V. THE ECONOMY AS POLITY

To our conventional way of thinking, Marx's political theory is summed up in the views treated in the foregoing pages. However the conventional view is misleading in this instance. Marx's theory of the state is an extremely important portion of his political theory and

---

[43] Lenin, *Selected Works*, vol. II, p. 362. For the passage referred to in *The State and Revolution*, see *ibid.*, p. 163.

the part that has directly influenced the subsequent course of political thought. Yet a philosophical appreciation of Marx as a political thinker cannot rest at this point. It must proceed to examine the political aspect of his economic thought.

What, parenthetically, is political theory about? One answer would be that it is about the state, since most systematic political theorizing has addressed itself to questions concerning the origin, nature, functions and limits of the state. Alternatively, one can say that the proper subject-matter of political theory is the realm of the political, which includes the state but at the same time greatly transcends it. The "realm of the political" may in turn be defined as the realm of power and authority relations among people. Such relations between man as ruler and man as subject occur not alone through the medium of the state as the sovereign political authority and public sphere of government in society. They occur in virtually every other form of society as well, starting with the family. All established human groups and institutions have their inner structure of authority, their pattern of ruler-subject relations. If they stand outside the institutional structure of the state, they are not on that account nongovernmental. Rather they belong to the sphere of private as distinguished from public government; moreover government itself, in the elementary sense of rulership of man over man, is pervasive in human society.

All this is more than ordinarily pertinent in an assessment of Marx as a political thinker. For more, perhaps, than any other important Western political theorist, either before his time or after, he was concerned with private government, particularly as expressed in the economic life of man in history. Indeed, private government in the economic life was for him the primary and decisive realm of the political, and public government—the sphere of the state—was a secondary and subordinate political field. Marx's economic interpretation of politics went along with a political interpretation of economics. If politics was "about economics," economics was political through and through.

This attribute of Marx's thought reflected the Hegelian heritage of the materialist conception of history, the influence of *The Phenomenology of Mind* in particular. His inversion of Hegel's political philosophy in the critical commentary of 1843 led him to the view that civil society underlay the state. But Marx did not for long visualize this *bürgerliche Gesellschaft* in the manner of the classical political economists, for whom it was a society of free self-interested economic men interacting as equals in the marketplace. The image of it underwent a profound transformation in his mind, as shown by his original formulation of the materialist conception of history in the Paris manuscripts of 1844. There the "economic men" in civil society reduced themselves to two archetypal figures: the worker and the capitalist. And in conceptualizing the relation between them, Marx was guided by the section of the *Phenomenology* in which Hegel had depicted the dualization of spirit into "Master and Servant" (*"Herr und Knecht"*). This was shown by the terminology he employed. He spoke of the capitalist as *"Herr,"* the worker as *"Knecht,"* and the labor itself as a condition of *"Knechtschaft"* or bondage. The fundamental socioeconomic relationship in civil society was thus politicized. The capital-labor relation became, in Marx's mind, a "politico-economic" relation of dominion and servitude, and always remained that. Indeed, this is one of the significant expressions of the underlying continuity in Marx's thought from the 1844 manuscripts to *Das Kapital*.

Not only capitalism but every previous socioeconomic order founded on division of labor came to be viewed as a realm of the political. The "social relations of production," which had formed the foundation of society in every historical epoch, were relations not simply of economic exploitation but also of domination and servitude; the pervasive form of government in history was private government in the society of production. And this followed logically from Marx's basic premises as analyzed earlier. Since each historical form of the division of labor in production had been a form of captivity for the producers, the domination of man by man was necessarily involved by the process of production. So, for Marx, man as possessor of the means of production was *ruler* over man as producer. He was so not simply as the force controlling the public government in the given society; rather his dominion over the producer was manifested first of all in the economic life itself. It was precisely as owners—of slaves in ancient society, land in feudal society and capital in bourgeois society—that men of one class tyrannized over men of another. Not surprisingly, then, Marx saw the quest for wealth and property as a kind of *Wille zur Macht*. The capitalist profit motive, in particular, was a politico-economic drive for power over man through the possession of money. "Accumulation is a conquest of the world of social wealth," wrote Marx. "It increases the mass of human material exploited by the capitalist, and thus amplifies his direct and indirect dominion (*Herrschaft*)." A footnote to this passage commented: "In his study of the usurer, the old-fashioned but perennially renewed form of the capitalist, Luther shows forcibly that the love of power is an element in the impulse to acquire wealth."[44] Thus the capitalist "economic man" was for Marx a special kind of *homo politicus*, and avarice, the ruling passion of capitalist society, was seen as a passion to conquer and dominate human beings, to rule over them in the process of exploiting their labor.

Adumbrated already in the 1844 manuscripts, Marx's political interpretation of capitalist economics received its fullest and clearest expression in *Das Kapital*. This book, which is seen as his chief treatise of political theory as well as economics, is a vast elaboration of his original picture of the relationship between capitalist and worker as *Herr* and *Knecht*. Although legally free to seek employment where he will and terminate it when he will, the worker is compelled by the necessity of earning a living for himself and his family to enter a relationship of servitude to the employer, a condition of "wage slavery." The language that Marx uses in protraying this capital-labor relation is replete with political terminology. Hence in *Das Kapital* he variously describes it as a "dictatorship of capital," "autocracy of capital" and "despotism of capital." The capitalist economic order appears here as a supremely authoritarian private realm of the political. It is a special form of command economy where the capitalist qua capitalist acts as a tyrannical ruling authority comparable to the great oriental despots of antiquity: "The power that used to be concentrated in the hands of Asiatic or Egyptian kings or of Etruscan theocrats and the like, has in modern society been transferred to the capitalists— it may be to individual capitalists; or it may be to collective capitalists, as in joint-stock companies."[45]

The despotism of capital is decentralized. The politicalized command economy is enclosed within the confines of the productive unit, which in modern society is the factory. Marx sees the capitalists ruling over men and their productive activity in the factories rather as feudal lords once ruled over serfs on their estates. He repeatedly likens the private government inside the factory to a military dictatorship,

[44] *MEW*, XXIII, 619; cf. *Capital*, p. 651.
[45] *MEW*, XXIII, 353; cf. *Capital*, p. 350.

where "The command of the capitalist in the field of production has become no less indispensable than the command of the general in the battlefield."[46] We read in the *Communist Manifesto* that "masses of laborers, crowded into the factory, are organized like soldiers. As privates of the industrial army they are placed under the command of a perfect hierarchy of officers and sergeants. Not only are they slaves of the bourgeois class, and of the bourgeois state; they are daily and hourly enslaved by the machine, by the over-looker, and, above all, by the individual bourgeois manufacturer himself." The same theme repeatedly recurs in *Das Kapital*. Here again Marx describes the workers and overseers as "the private soldiers and noncommissioned officers of an industrial army." And speaking of the factory code, he says that in it "capital formulates its autocracy over its workers—in a private legislative system, and without the partition of authority and the representative methods which in other fields are so much loved by the bourgeoisie. . . . In place of the slave driver's lash, we have the overseer's book of penalties."[47]

Because he devoted relatively very little space in his voluminous writings to general discussion of the state, it is easy to infer that Marx was only secondarily a political thinker. But such a view would be a superficial one. His major work, *Das Kapital*, was in its special way a study in rulership. Its central theme was as much political as economic. It was the theme of tyranny in modern man's life of production and of an inevitable final revolt by the worker-subjects against the "despotism of capital." Marx's economics of capitalism was quite literally a "political economy"—the phrase that he himself always used in referring to economics. To analyze it in these terms is to see Marx as the essentially political thinker that he was. His vision of the political saw the productive process itself as the prime field of power relations between man and man. And his position as a political philosopher was basically determined by this fact.

VI. THE ANARCHISM OF MARX

The central problem in the modern history of political philosophy in the West has been that of legitimizing state power, of specifying the conditions under which the sovereign ruling authority in society can

[46] *MEW*, XXIII, 350; cf. *Capital*, p. 346.
[47] *MEW*, XXIII, 447; cf. *Capital*, p. 452 ff.

be considered a rightful authority. Political theorists have addressed themselves to the basic question: What requirements must the sovereign state meet in order to be adjudged a good state? There diverse answers have generally been predicated upon the assumption that the state derives its legitimacy from fulfilling such universal needs of the citizens as the needs for security and liberty.

In these terms Marx both was and was not a political philosopher. On the one hand, he never addressed himself to the problem of legitimizing state power. But on the other hand, he did have a definite position with regard to this problem. He had a normative as well as descriptive theory of the state. Very simply and briefly, it stated that there are no conditions under which the state can be adjudged a good state. Marx believed that the sovereign political authority in society could not under any circumstances be considered a rightful authority. The state qua state was evil. Every historical example of the state, whether in the past, present or future, would inevitably partake of this evil. Accordingly Marx's normative position with regard to the state was anarchism, which may be defined as the view that state power, being evil in essence, cannot possibly be legitimized.

This formulation of Marx's political philosophy may seem contradicted by his attitude toward the proletarian dictatorship that he believed to be historically imminent. Did he not devoutly desire the coming of this dictatorship? Must he not, then, have believed it to be something good? The answer to the first of these questions is quite clearly affirmative but does not imply an affirmative answer to the second. Marx, as we have already seen, did not hold the proletarian political order to be a good or a just one; he considered it at best a necessary evil on the road of man's entry into a higher form of society which would be a good society and as such stateless. The proletarian dictatorship was only a way-station to something beyond and something different: society without a state. As a means to this end, it was desirable; as a form of state, it was not. Moreover as a state the proletarian state would doubtless be less evil than any other in history, but an evil it would be.

Marx's anarchism, like that of other political philosophers who have embraced the anarchist position, was grounded in a philosophical affirmation of freedom as the supreme human value and a belief that the existence of the state is incompatible with the realization of freedom. "Free state—what is this?" he caustically inquired in comment-

ing on the draft Gotha Program's statement that the German workers'
party aimed to create "the free state."[48] Freedom and the state, as he
saw it, were mutually exclusive concepts. Insofar as any state existed,
man would remain unfree, and liberated man would enjoy not freedom
in the state but freedom *from* it. Mankind's leap from the kingdom
of necessity to the kingdom of freedom would take place only with
the advent of the higher phase of communist society. Certain functions of public administration and direction of the processes of
production would still remain at that phase. They would not be performed, however, by a state in Marx's definition of the term ("a special organism separated from society through the division of labor").
To underline this point, Engels, in his letter to Bebel on the Gotha
Program, suggested on behalf of himself and Marx that the word
"state" be deleted from the statement of the party's goals: "We
would therefore propose to replace 'state' everywhere by 'community'
(*Gemeinwesen*), a good old German word which can very well represent the French word '*commune*.' "[49]

A final problem emerges with the recognition that classical Marxism
is committed to an anarchist position in its political philosophy. For
if we consider Anarchism not as an abstract political philosophy but
as a revolutionary movement associated with a political philosophy,
then we are confronted with the fact that Marxism was deeply at
odds with it.[50] Marxism and Anarchism were rival strains in European
left-wing radicalism in the middle and later years of the nineteenth
century. The rivalry originated at the time of Marx's break with
Proudhon in the 1840's and later witnessed the bitter feud between
Marx and Bakunin and their respective followers. The depth of the
resulting division in European socialism was mirrored in Marx's reaction to the outbreak of the Franco-Prussian War of 1870. "The French
need a thrashing," he wrote to Engels, explaining that a Prussian
victory would foster a transfer of the center of gravity of the Western European workers' movement from France to Germany, which
"would also mean the predominance of our theory over Proudhon's,
etc."[51]

[48] *MEW*, XIX, 27; cf. *Selected Works*, vol. II, p. 31.

[49] *Ibid.*, 42.

[50] To express this distinction, I here capitalize the word when referring to the
movement but not when referring to the abstract philosophy.

[51] *Selected Correspondence*, p. 292.

If we assume, as I believe we must, that the rivalry between Marxism and Anarchism was grounded in serious theoretical as well as
personal differences between their leaders, the theoretical differences
require explanation. How is it that classical Marxism, while embracing anarchism as a political philosophy, disagreed with Anarchism as
a socialist ideology? The question has generally been answered by
reference to an extremely serious difference over the strategy of transition to a stateless society. The Anarchists did not propose to create
a workers' state in the revolutionary process of leading humanity to
a stateless future. Instead they viewed the dismantling of statehood
as part and parcel of the revolutionary process. The workers' revolution itself was to be antistatist. Commenting on this position, Engels
wrote: "The Anarchists put the thing upside down. They declare
that the proletarian revolution must *begin* by doing away with the
political organization of the state. . . . But to destroy it at such a
moment would be to destroy the only organism by means of which
the victorious proletariat can assert its newly-conquered power, hold
down its capitalist adversaries and carry out that economic revolution
of society without which the whole victory must end in a new defeat
and in a mass slaughter of the workers similar to those after the Paris
Commune."[52] The two doctrines were thus at odds over the issue of
whether a state was needed for the purpose of abolishing the state. As
Lenin later put it on behalf of the Marxists, "We do not at all disagree with the Anarchists on the question of the abolition of the state
as an *aim*. We maintain that, to achieve this aim, we must temporarily make use of the instruments, resources and methods of the state
power against the exploiters. . . ."[53]

But a deeper theoretical cleavage underlay this significant strategic
difference. Anarchism did more than declare the state qua state to
be evil; it also singled out the state as the principal evil in society,
the decisive cause and expression of human unfreedom. For reasons

[52] Engels to Van Patten, April 18, 1883, *Selected Correspondence*, p. 417. The
Commune naturally caused intense controversy between the rival movements. The
Anarchists saw the Paris insurrection as an antistatist revolution, and on this
account Bakunin accused the Marxists of betraying their principles in claiming
that the program and aim of the Commune was theirs. They contended, on the
other hand, that the Commune was a proletarian dictatorship.

[53] Lenin, *Selected Works*, vol. II, p. 181. For a similar view, see Plamenatz,
Man and Society, vol. II, pp. 374, 383.

previously dealt with here, classical Marxism rejected such a view. Although it was anarchist in treating the state *qua* state as evil, it was opposed to the Anarchist doctrine on the state as the prime locus of evil. It saw man's unfreedom in the state as something secondary to, and derivative from, his unfreedom in the polity of production. The decisive cause and principal form of human bondage, and thus the supreme evil in history, was not subjection to the state but the imprisonment of man within the division of labor in production. The supreme end, therefore, was the "economic emancipation of labor" via the overthrow of the relations of domination and servitude in the economic life. The emancipation of man from the state would follow as a matter of course.

We have direct testimony from Engels showing that this was his and Marx's understanding of the opposition between Marxism and Anarchism. Bakunin's position, he said in a letter of January 24, 1872, to Theodor Cuno, was that capital existed by courtesy of the state, which was therefore the main evil to be abolished.

> As, therefore, the state is the chief evil, it is above all the state which must be done away with and then capitalism will go to hell of itself. We, on the contrary say: do away with capital, the appropriation of the whole means of production in the hands of the few, and the state will fall away of itself. The difference is an essential one. Without a previous social revolution the abolition of the state is nonsense; the abolition of capital *is* in itself the social revolution and involves a change in the whole method of production.[54]

The special anarchism of Marx and Engels must thus be seen as an anarchism directed primarily against authoritarianism in the society of production and only secondarily against authoritarianism as exemplified in the state. The tyranny from which it aimed to deliver man chiefly was that which he endured as a subject of the sovereign state of capital—the "despotism of capital."

What communism ultimately signified to Marx was man's complete and perfect freedom in the life of production. The revolutionary abolition of private property and therewith of the social division of labor between classes would lead, he thought, to the overcoming of the division of labor in all its subordinate forms. Men would no longer be bound down for life to a single form of activity; the slavery of specialization would thereby be overthrown. Even within the modern factory, the abolition of the capitalist mode of production—wage labor—would bring emancipation of the worker from bondage to a particular form of specialized work. The shortening of the working day would give him leisure, and rotation of jobs within the factory would free him from the tyranny of specialization in what remained of factory work. The economic life-process of society would be carried on by "a free association of producers,"[55] undivided into *Herr* and *Knecht*.

In his short essay of 1872 "On Authority," which was written against the Anarchists, Engels implicitly contradicted Marx's vision of the factory of the future as a realm of freedom in the life of production. "The automatic machinery of a big factory is much more despotic than the small capitalists who employ workers have ever been," he wrote. "Wanting to abolish authority in large-scale industry is tantamount to wanting to abolish industry itself, to destroy the power loom in order to return to the spinning wheel."[56] Yet a non-authoritarian existence in the factory was integral to communism itself in Marx's understanding of it, and this was a central message of his political philosophy.

[55] *MEW*, XXIII, 92; cf. *Capital*, p. 54.
[56] *MEW*, XVIII, 306; cf. *Selected Works*, vol. II, p. 637.

6: THE PHILOSOPHICAL AND SOCIOLOGICAL RELEVANCE OF MARX'S CONCEPT OF ALIENATION

Gajo Petrović

I. PRELIMINARY REMARKS

1. The title of this paper happens to be one of the longest, and this might be construed as indicative of the author's lack of modesty, but the author of this paper is not the author of its title; the latter was suggested by the organizers of the Notre Dame Conference. Moreover "The Philosophical and Sociological Relevance of Marx's Concept of Alienation" is not only a long title; it is also a broad topic and a big task. Shall we make it narrower in order to be able to consider it more carefully? Or rather shall we try to express our views as briefly as possible, to renounce long arguments and to restrict ourselves to stating only our main theses?

2. I feel certain that I would not have formulated the title of this paper in the same way, not merely because of its length, but even more because I feel that the question that it suggests starts from certain assumptions which I do not share. But are we simply to reject all questions involving assumptions that are unacceptable for us? Or is it more promising, from the viewpoint of a fruitful philosophical dialogue, to try to clarify and analyze the question suggested, to make explicit and, if necessary, to criticize some of the assumptions on which it rests but also to attempt to answer that part of the question which directs our attention to real and important philosophical problems?

3. The title may obviously be regarded as an abbreviated and neutralized form of the question: "What philosophical and sociological relevance, if any, belongs to (or is possessed by) Marx's concept of alienation?" And the question seems to suggest that there is such a thing as "Marx's concept of alienation" and that the content (or

meaning) of the concept is neither controversial nor unclear. In this way the title invites us to consider not Marx's concept of alienation "as such" but its philosophical and sociological relevance. It seems to leave open or to ignore the question whether there are some other "relevances" of the concept in addition to the philosophical and sociological ones. Are we simply to accept the alleged familiarity of Marx's concept of alienation and are we to confine ourselves to investigating its philosophical and sociological "relevance" without asking about its "relevance" for the whole of man's life?

II. MARX'S CONCEPT OF ALIENATION

1. Is there something that might be called Marx's *concept* of alienation? If by a 'concept' is meant a finished product of thought with a fixed "content" that has been made explicit by means of a definition, there is no such thing as "Marx's concept of alienation." Marx never gave an explicit definition of alienation. However if by concept is meant an essence-hitting thought of a phenomenon, regardless of whether a formal definition has been given, there is certainly a concept of alienation in Marx, because Marx really thought of the essence of alienation and he knew how to express this thought.

Again if by a 'concept' is meant a perfectly clear, complete and consistent thought of a phenomenon's essence, a thought free of all gaps, insufficiencies and difficulties, there is indeed no concept of alienation in Marx, for it is not difficult to discover a number of obscurities and incongruities in Marx's views on alienation. However if by 'concept' is meant a thought of phenomenon which despite all its defects uncovers before us the phenomenon's essence, there is such a thing as Marx's concept of alienation.

Finally if by a 'concept' is meant a thought which satisfies itself in contemplating an essence such as it is with no intention of changing it, we could not attribute a concept of alienation to Marx. He was not a "pure scientist" elaborating "neutral" theoretical concepts picturing reality passively. Rather Marx, the theoretical philosopher and practical social reformer, conceived 'alienation' to be simultaneously a criticism of alienation and an appeal for a practical fight against alienation—a call for a revolutionary transformation of self-alienated man and society.

2. Is there something like Marx's concept of alienation? If by 'Marx's concept' is meant a concept which has been created ex nihilo by Marx, a concept which was entirely unknown before Marx, it would be an exaggeration to talk of Marx's concept of alienation. Very much in Marx's concept of alienation stems from Hegel and Feuerbach; moreover much in Hegel's and Feuerbach's concept of alienation is actually not theirs. The concept of alienation is a peculiar "summary" of the whole history of Western philosophy. It was alive, under different names, from the very beginnings of philosophical thought. However if by Marx's concept one means a concept which was transformed and given a new content and life by Marx, there is certainly such a concept because Marx's view on alienation is neither a repetition nor a combination of the views of Hegel and Feuerbach. It is in many respects their most radical negation.

Marx's concept of alienation is still alive in what is best in contemporary philosophy, sociology and psychology. Would it not be more adequate to talk of the "contemporary" (instead of Marx's) concept of alienation? Although it still stimulates and inspires discussion in so many trends of contemporary thought, Marx's concept of alienation is not the only concept of alienation in our times. Some of the contemporary concepts of alienation represent a further elaboration or variation of Marx's concept, and others are very different from it. Therefore it is legitimate to talk of "Marx's concept of alienation" as something which should not be confused with those concepts which have preceded or followed it.

3. There are those who think that Marx elaborated the concept of alienation at an early stage of his theoretical development but rejected it as inadequate later. And they find it curious that many Marxists still make much use of a concept which Marx himself abandoned. However is it really of decisive importance for others whether a thinker permanently retained or at one time repudiated some of his views? Even if Marx had renounced his own concept of alienation, it would not simply annihilate what he had previously written on it and even if Marx had come to regard his own concept of alienation as worthless, we may regard it as precious; furthermore we may be right.

On the other hand, is it really true that Marx in his later writings renounced "alienation"? It is well known that Marx and Engels in their German Ideology and in the Communist Manifesto criticized philosophers for representing the historical process as a process of self-alienation of man and for speaking about the "alienation of man's essence." But is it not "curious" that the allegedly "discarded" concept of alienation reappeared in the later writings of Marx, that it was explicitly used not only in that unfinished manuscript which is now known as *Grundrisse der Kritik der politischen Ökonomie,* but also in his undisputed masterwork *Das Kapital?* And is it not so that even in those works where Marx seemingly rejects the concept of alienation, its compounds serve as leading ideas and tacit presuppositions?

4. How are we to get at what is authentically Marx's view of alienation? Shall we try an "objective reconstruction" of his views on the basis of his texts? It would be possible to collect all of Marx's texts dealing with alienation, to compare them mutually and to analyze them carefully. It would also be possible to study all the works of Marx with the intention of making explicit what they implicitly say about alienation. This would require much space, time and patience, but it is theoretically possible. There is only one objection to such a procedure: it would probably contribute more to the distortion than to the elucidation of the essence of Marx's thought, for Marx's "concept" of alienation is a live thought that includes open questions and unsolved difficulties. Therefore to bring to life the essence of Marx's "theory" of alienation is not merely to repeat what Marx has already said, but to think in the spirit of Marx about the problems which he thought of, to contribute to solving difficulties which he fought with, and to open horizons which he only vaguely anticipated.

Will we not add something extraneous to the essence of Marx's thought in this way? Perhaps. But nevertheless the essence of a thought is not only what it in fact contains. Therefore the essence of Marx's thought is also what it includes merely as a possibility of further development. It is impossible to say what Marx really thought of alienation without saying many things which he actually never thought. To excavate the inner riches of a theory is certainly a risky undertaking, but there cannot be any life or theory if we are not ready to take some risks.

5. Marx's concept of alienation has in it something of that broadest and seemingly most natural meaning that is suggested by the etymology and morphology of the word—the meaning that alienation is the process or the state in which something becomes or has become alien to something else. But Marx's concept of alienation cannot be identi-

fied with such a general common sense idea. From the standpoint of common sense, self-alienation can be only a special case of alienation; for Hegel and Marx every alienation is a special case of self-alienation, because there is no alienation where there is no self.

If every alienation is self-alienation, things cannot be alienated either from themselves or from each other; it is also impossible to talk of the self-alienation of nature. There is no self-alienation where there is no self. This does not mean that the concept of alienation is entirely inapplicable to "dead" things and nature. Both single things and nature as a whole can be alienated from man, but these cases of alienation are only special forms of man's self-alienation, forms of the alienation of man from his own essence.

6. Every alienation is self-alienation both for Hegel and Marx, but while for Hegel the self which alienates himself from himself is the Absolute, for Marx it is man. Everything which happens is for Hegel a part of the circular process of alienation and de-alienation of the Absolute Mind, and man is the Absolute in the process of de-alienation. For Marx there is no Absolute Mind and nature is not an alienated form of any mind. The whole of human history is a process of alienation and de-alienation and conversely there is no alienation or de-alienation without and outside human history.

However there is only one step from Hegel to Marx, not only because in addition to the self-alienation of the Absolute Mind Hegel admits the self-alienation of the Finite Mind or man but also, and in the first order, because only owing to and through the Finite Mind does the Absolute Mind become self-aware, "returns" to himself from his self-alienation in nature. This means that without the finite mind the Absolute Mind cannot be de-alienated, but that which cannot de-alienate itself cannot alienate itself from itself either. In this way the Absolute Mind is basically dependent on the Finite Mind. It is not the Absolute Mind but the Finite Mind which is the subject of self-alienation and de-alienation.

7. Both Feuerbach and Marx reject Hegel's view that nature is a self-alienated form of the Absolute Mind and that man is the Absolute Mind in the process of de-alienation. For them man is not a self-alienated God, but God is a self-alienated man—he is merely man's essence abstracted, absolutized and estranged from man. Whereas Feuerbach thought that the de-alienation of man can be reduced to the abolition of that estranged picture of man which is God, Marx

stressed that religious alienation of man is only one among the many forms of man's self-alienation. Man not only alienates a part of himself in the form of God, he also alienates other products of his spiritual activity in the form of philosophy, common sense, art, morals; he alienates products of his economic activity in the form of commodity, money, capital; he alienates products of his social activity in the form of state, law, social institutions.

There are many forms in which man alienates the products of his own activity from himself and makes of them a separate, independent and powerful world of objects toward which he is related as a slave—powerless and dependent. However he not only alienates his own products from himself, he also alienates himself from the very activity through which these products are produced, from the nature in which he lives and from other men. All these kinds of alienation are in the last analysis one; they are only different forms or aspects of man's self-alienation, different forms of the alienation of man from his human "essence" or "nature," from his humanity. The self-alienated man is a man who really is not a man, a man who does not realize his historically created human possibilities. A nonalienated man on the contrary would be a man who really is a man, a man who fulfills himself as a free, creative being of *praxis*.

III. THE PHILOSOPHICAL "RELEVANCE" OF MARX'S CONCEPT OF ALIENATION

1. Contrary to what might be expected, I am ready to "confess" that Marx's concept of alienation has no "philosophical relevance." This is not to maintain that it is "philosophically irrelevant." The concept can be neither philosophically relevant nor philosophically irrelevant simply because it is primarily a philosophical concept.

If by "relevance" we mean "the state or quality of being relevant," and by being relevant, "bearing upon" something other than that which is relevant, a philosophical concept cannot be "philosophically relevant." One can ask about the philosophical relevance of a sociological, economic, legal, religious, literary or any other nonphilosophical concept; but it would be curious to ask about the philosophical relevance of a philosophical concept.

The question of the philosophical relevance of Marx's concept of alienation taken literally is based on the assumption that this is a nonphilosophical concept. Therefore the only adequate answer to it can be the criticism of this assumption. However the question might really be a not quite precise formulation of the question about the philosophic scope and value of the concept, and this question can be answered only by asking ourselves what place, if any, the concept has within the scope of philosophy.

2. Some philosophical adversaries of Marx's concept of alienation think that the concept has no place in philosophy because it is too special or too narrow. Only the most general concepts—they say— deserve a place inside philosophy, as the most general "theoretical" inquiry into the nature of the world. The concept of alienation does not possess such a generality. Those who want to exclude Marx's concept of alienation from philosophy by means of such an argument obviously have either a peculiar idea of Marx's concept of alienation or a dubious idea of what kind of generality is a prerequisite for philosophy. They either think that Marx limited alienation to one special aspect or field of man's being, for example to economics, politics or psychology or they believe that all concepts which aim at characterizing man are too special for philosophy.

However both assumptions are untenable. In speaking of "alienation," Marx did not have in mind only economic, political or psychological phenomena, he had in mind also the self-alienation of man as a whole being—a "phenomenon" which is so general that it cannot be studied by any special science. And on the other hand, those who think that even the most general problems of man are not philosophical, because man is merely one special being in the universe, overlook that regarded from the standpoint of quality man contains in himself everything that is in the world.

3. Some philosophers would be ready to concede that the concept of self-alienation belongs to philosophy, if anywhere, but they insist that the concept should be excluded from every theory because it is self-contradictory. Furthermore it might seem that alienation is by definition a polyadic relation which presupposes at least two terms, two entities which are alien to each other so that it would be self-contradictory to say of one single entity that it is alien to itself, i.e. self-alienated. Where there is only one self, there can be no alienation. Alienation requires two.

However such a simple argument starting from one and two would be valid only if man were absolutely simple, if being one he could not consist of (or be divided into) two or more parts; and it is obviously invalid if we assume that a man is self-alienated when he is internally divided in such a way that his two parts are alien to each other.

If one objects that in such a case one should not speak of the self-alienation of the self but about the mutual alienation of the parts of the self, one could answer that talking of self-alienation instead of simply the "internal division" or "split" of man into two alien parts has the function of suggesting the following points: a) the division into two mutually alien parts was not carried out from the outside, it is the result of an action of the self itself; b) the division into alien parts does not annihilate the unity of the self; despite the split, the self-alienated self is nevertheless a self; and c) it is not simply the split into two parts that are equally related to the self as a whole: the implication is that one part of the self has more right to represent the self as a whole so that by becoming alien to it the other part becomes alien to the self as a whole.

4. One way to clarify and specify the inequality of the two parts into which a self-alienated self is split is to describe the self-alienation as a split between man's real "nature," or "essence," and his factual "properties," or "existence." The self-alienated man in such a case is a man whose actual existence does not correspond to his human essence. A self-alienated, human society would be a society whose factual existence does not correspond to the real essence of human society.

Some philosophers would be ready to grant that by defining self-alienation in such a way an appearance of avoiding contradiction has been produced, but they would insist that contradiction has really remained. Alienation of man's existence from his essence is a contradiction in terms, because man cannot be man without his human essence. A thing's essence is something owing to which a thing is what it is, and if a thing has alienated itself from its own essence, it is no longer the same thing. In other words, either the being in question is not alienated from man's essence, and then it is a man; or it is alienated from man's essence, and then it can be anything whatsoever, but it cannot be man.

There is something in such an argument. If a man were a thing and if one should conceive of man's essence as something shared by all men, then somebody alienated from man's essence could not be a man in fact either. But are we entitled to assume that man has essence in the same sense in which nonhuman things have it? Or is there a difference in principle between all other beings and man so that man's essence is not what all men have in common, but what man as man can and ought to be? The question might seem difficult; however if we answer it in the affirmative, there need be no contradiction in the concept of self-alienation.

5. Some critics of alienation would agree that the concept of self-alienation is not self-contradictory, but they would insist that it is untenable because its use is inconsistent with certain indisputable "philosophical truths" that have been not only accepted but even discovered (or at least elaborated) and given a special prominence by Marxism. As the most important among such truths, the view of man as a historical being is cited. The concept of the self-alienation of man—they say—presupposes, and has no sense without, the concept of a permanent, unchangeable essence or nature of man; and it is certain knowledge of our time that man has no eternal, unchangeable properties but rather that he changes and develops historically.

However it is not difficult to see that the historical view of man excludes not every kind of man's essence but only an everlasting, unchangeable nature or essence of man whereas "essence" implied in the concept of alienation need not be of this kind. Moreover the essence of man as conceived by Marx is neither an unchangeable part of man's factuality, nor an eternal or nontemporal idea toward which man ought to strive; it is the totality of historically created human possibilities which at each stage of man's historical development can be, and really is, different. To say that man alienates himself from his human essence would then mean that a man alienates himself from the realization of his historically created human possibilities. To say that a man is not alienated from himself would, on the contrary, mean that a man stands on the level of his possibilities, that in realizing his possibilities, he permanently creates new and higher ones.

6. Some would be ready to grant that the concept of alienation does not exclude history in the sense of a series of changes, but they would insist that it is incompatible with the view of history as an open process leading to the emergence of ever new qualities. The concepts of self-alienation and de-alienation—they would maintain—can be useful within the framework of a view of history as a closed, circular process having its beginning in an original nonalienated society where man's existence corresponded to his essence, and an end in a

final de-alienated society representing a return to (or an ameliorated form of) the original harmony between existence and essence.

However Marx's concept of alienation, as it was sketched above, does not necessarily imply a nonalienated original or future society where there is no split between man's essence and existence. If an animal becomes man at the very moment when its existence ceases to be determined by its essence, when he becomes free either to realize his human essence or to alienate himself from it, it means that even in the beginning of his development man can be self-alienated. And if man's essence is a set of historically created human possibilities, then at any given stage of his evolution (even at the most advanced one) man can be alienated from it, i.e., below the level of his possibilities.

The requirement of de-alienation that is naturally suggested by the very concept of self-alienation does not imply a circular character of the historical process nor does it demand an end of history. The requirement is not a call for a return to something that has already existed because to be de-alienated means to be able to fulfil one's own human possibilities and to create new and higher ones. In other words, not the return to the past but the projecting of a new future is the core of de-alienation.

It would also be wrong to interpret de-alienation as a terminal of history. Some Marxists, it is true, have really thought that absolute de-alienation is possible, that all alienation, social and individual, can be once and for all abolished; the most radical among the representatives of such an optimistic view have even maintained that all alienation has already been eliminated in principle in socialist countries, that it exists there only as a case of individual insanity or as an insignificant "remnant of capitalism"; but such a view cannot be attributed to Marx. Rather from his basic views it would follow that only relative de-alienation is possible. It is not possible to wipe out alienation once and for all, because human "essence" or "nature" is not something given and finished which can be fulfilled to the end. However it is possible to create a basically nonalienated society that would stimulate the development of nonalienated, really human individuals, but it is not possible to create a society that would produce only nonalienated, free, creative individuals and that would exclude every possibility of anybody's being self-alienated.

7. Some philosophers would be ready to grant that Marx's concept

of alienation is neither self-contradictory nor inconsistent with any indisputable philosophical truth. They would concede that it may be used in discussion about man in general and contemporary man in particular, but they would insist that everything which can be said by the help of this concept can be said not worse—and perhaps even better—without it. Although not definitely "bad," the concept is unnecessary or, more mildly, not indispensable.

There is some truth in such a view. Much of what can be thought by the help of the concept of alienation can also be thought without it, and the word "alienation" is certainly not indispensable. However is it so that all that can be thought by the help of alienation can be equally well thought without it?

Some people think that "alienation" is merely a pseudophilosophical term for such concrete phenomena as, for example, private property, the existence of classes or class exploitation. According to such a view, instead of talking about the "self-alienated" and "nonself-alienated society" one could talk simply about the "class-society" and "classless society."

The most obvious objection to such a view would be that it assumes that the concept of self-alienation can be applied only to societies, whereas Marx applied it both to societies and to individual men. An attempt to save the reduction of alienation to class oppression from this objection by saying that it is possible to define the self-alienated man in terms of self-alienated society (by defining "self-alienated man" as "the man of self-alienated, i.e., class society") would not help, because according to Marx even in a self-alienated society some men can be basically nonself-alienated and in a basically nonself-alienated society some men can be self-alienated.

However this is not all. There are at least two more serious objections to the identification of self-alienation with class rule. First, if every class society is a self-alienated society, this does not mean that only class society can be self-alienated and that every self-alienated society must be divided into social classes. Self-alienation can exist even in a classless society. Second, even if only class society were a self-alienated society, this would not mean that "class society" and "self-alienated society" are only different names for the same concept. The two concepts have different contents and can be defined independently of each other.

Therefore it would be possible to make the distinction between class and classless society and still dispute the division of societies into "self-alienated" and "nonself-alienated." There would be nothing "contradictory" or "illogical" in such a proceeding. However this would mean to remain in the limits of a scientistic, empirico-positivistic approach to society—appropriate for describing external facts and properties but unsuitable for uncovering their inner connection and essential meaning from the viewpoint of man as a whole—and that would also mean to be unable to find a theoretical foundation for the requirement for a revolutionary change of the existing class society. We may be able to describe in all details the class structure and class struggles of our society, but we are not entitled to say either that we know it or that we have good reasons for fighting against it unless we have succeeded in grasping it as an inhuman, self-alienated form of human society.

8. Many of those who regard the concept of self-alienation as not indispensable would agree that the concept cannot be reduced to the concept of class rule or class exploitation. In contrast to such concepts as "class rule," "class struggle" and so on, which are descriptive, the concepts of self-alienation and nonself-alienation are evaluative. When we characterize a society or an individual as self-alienated, we do not add any new information to its description, we simply express the opinion that it is not as it should be. Why then should we use such complicated terms as "self-alienation" and "nonself-alienation"? Why should we not simply use old, well-known terms such as "good" and "bad" (or "moral" and "immoral")?

The suggestion might seem acceptable. However the concepts of alienation and de-alienation as conceived by Marx are neither descriptive and factual nor prescriptive and evaluative. To characterize an individual or a society as self-alienated or nonself-alienated is neither to mention some of its empirically ascertainable properties nor just to express one's moral indignation about it. It is a characterization of the ontologico-anthropological nature of the man or society in question, a characterization which moves neither on the level of pure factual "is" nor on the level of pure moral "ought." It belongs to a "third" realm which is really "first."

Man is not only what he is, but also what he can and ought to be. Yet man is not a sum of "is" and "ought." Before we analyze him into "is" and "ought," he is already someone in essence and it is for this realm of "essence" (which precedes the split into the realm of facts and the realm of values) that the concepts of alienation and non-self-alienation are used. They are only two among the concepts aiding in analyzing man philosophically, as a free creative being of *praxis*. In addition they have a function for this realm, and they cannot be replaced by any concept serving either to describe the factual existence of man or to prescribe for him ideal moral rules.

9. One might be ready to admit that in addition to scientific concepts necessary to describe objectively the factuality of man and value concepts serving to judge morally what is good and what is bad in him, one also needs "ontological," or "ontologico-anthropological" concepts in order to analyze the essence or essential structure of man. However one might insist that the family of such concepts need not include the Marxian concept of "alienation," that what is said by the help of this concept can also be said by the help of some non-Marxist philosophical concept. Instead of speaking about self-alienated and nonself-alienated man and society, should we not speak, for example, about "human" and "inhuman" society and man (or about more and less human society and man)?

The suggestion might seem plausible. However the attributes 'human' and 'inhuman' cannot be identified with the attributes 'non-self-alienated' and 'self-alienated.' I think that no really human society (or man) can be self-alienated and that every inhuman society (or man) is self-alienated, but I do not think that the concepts "inhumanity" and "humanity" must necessarily be defined in terms of self-alienation and de-alienation. It is logically possible, for example, to divide man and societies into human and inhuman according to whether they correspond to an outside ideal or standard of humanity. To be inhuman in such a case would not mean to be alienated from one's own historically created human possibilities but to be unable to achieve a high goal prescribed from outside.

In this way, far from being eliminable from philosophy by the help of the concepts "human" and "inhuman," the concepts of "self-alienation" and "de-alienation" are indispensable for clarifying one special interpretation of those concepts, that interpretation in which to be human or inhuman means to be "faithful" or "unfaithful," "equal" or "unequal" to his own creative possibilities.

10. One might admit that the concept of alienation cannot be fully replaced by any of the traditional non-Marxist philosophical concepts, but insist that among specifically Hegelian and Marxist concepts

there are some which make the concept of alienation necessary. Moreover some Marxists and Marxologists have been inclined to identify "alienation" with "objectification," the process of projecting human potentialities through man's productive activity into external objects. However Marx clearly distinguished between objectification and alienation and sharply criticized Hegel for having identified objectification with alienation and the suppression of alienation with the abolition of objectivity.

To be sure, there have been Marxists who thought that there is no essential link or connection between objectification and alienation, that alienation is something arising quite incidentally out of objectification. Marx on the contrary thought that in every objectification lies a possibility of alienation so that as long as there is objectification, there will be a "danger" of alienation. However this is not a sufficient reason for simply identifying objectification and alienation.

Some Marxists and Marxologists have been ready to draw the distinction between objectification and alienation, but they were inclined to think that all alienation can be reduced to alienation arising out of objectification, to the alienation of man from the results of his objectifying activity, so that consequently the whole problem of alienation could be reduced to the problem of enumerating and describing in detail the forms of man's objectification.

However according to Marx the alienation of man from the products of his activity is only one form or aspect of alienation. Man alienates himself not only from the products of his own activity, he alienates himself also from his fellow men who produce together with him and from the nature in which he lives and which always lives in him. Moreover he alienates himself from his own productive activity through which he creates objects, transforms and humanizes nature and collaborates and communicates with other men. In other words man alienates himself from his essence, from his own human "nature," from what he as man can and ought to be.

IV. THE SOCIOLOGICAL RELEVANCE OF MARX'S CONCEPT OF ALIENATION

1. If the question about the "philosophical relevance" of Marx's concept of alienation strictly taken has no sense, the same need not hold for the question about its sociological relevance. And indeed, if we

agree that the concept of alienation is basically philosophical (and not sociological), the question about its sociological relevance naturally arises. What, then, if any, is the "sociological relevance" of Marx's concept of alienation?

According to one view, the mere fact that alienation is a philosophical concept indicates that the concept is sociologically irrelevant. All philosophical concepts—it is said—are irrelevant for sociology. It would be possible to argue against such a view; however I shall content myself with the remark that those who regard all philosophical concepts as irrelevant for sociology demonstrate in this way that a certain pseudophilosophy (the positivistic one) is very relevant for their own sociology.

2. Some sociologists have been ready to grant that philosophical concepts may be useful in sociology, but they would insist that all concepts belonging to such a branch of philosophy as axiology (or at least to its sub-branch, ethics) should be kept apart from sociology as well as from every other empirical science inquiring into the nature of what is (not what merely ought to be). According to their view, alienation is an axiological, and also more precisely, an ethical concept. Therefore although the term might be useful in the context of moral discourse, it ought to be abandoned within the sociological context.

There are at least two defective assumptions in such a view. One is the assumption, which we have criticized above, that the concept of alienation as conceived by Marx is a value concept. Another is the idea that "pure sciences" without any "axiological" or "ethical" presuppositions or ingredients are desirable and possible. Without undertaking a criticism of this second assumption here, we shall merely observe that a value-free science is an illusion of dubious value.

3. There are sociologists who do not deny that philosophical concepts, including axiological ones, may be relevant for sociology, but they maintain that Marx's concept of alienation is one of those philosophical concepts which have no sociological relevance.

The concept of alienation—they argue—cannot be of any use for sociology because the phenomenon of alienation exists in different guises, in practically all societies, in small, egalitarian, cooperative and agricultural societies no less than in big, non-egalitarian, competitive and industrial ones. But if the phenomenon of alienation is so universal, why should it mean that the concept of alienation is not useful?

Would it not follow rather that it has an extremely wide use in sociological analysis, that it is indispensable for analysis of every society
that has existed so far?

4. An opposite objection to the sociological relevance of Marx's
concept of alienation (sometimes found in the same authors) is that
the concept is too narrow or too eccentric to be suitable for sociology.
Some sociologists have maintained, for example, that for Marx and
Engels "alienation" was a romantic concept with a preponderantly
sexual connotation, a concept for depicting a man whose way of
thinking is determined by his repression of sexuality.

Even if it were so, the concept could have a sociological significance. Sexuality is not utterly unimportant. However it is far from
true that the concept had such a meaning for Marx. Those who
interpret him in this way show only that they are themselves more
interested in sexology than in sociology.

5. Some have argued that the concept of alienation in Marx,
although it might be sufficiently clear for philosophical purposes, is
not sufficiently clear for the purposes of sociology, while others have
added that the impression of the "unclearness" of the concept is the
result of the fact that there are here several different concepts hidden
behind one single word.

We have also maintained above that there are differences and inconsistencies in Marx's view of alienation. However there is still a definite
basic view of alienation in Marx: the view according to which to be
self-alienated is to be alienated from one's own essence so that a self-
alienated man is a man alienated from his human essence, and a
self-alienated society, one that is alienated from the essence of human
society. And the question is whether such a concept of alienation has
some sociological relevance or not. Is it the sole task of sociology to
describe and classify social phenomena according to some external
characteristics, or is it also to study them as *human* phenomena characterizing social man and human society?

6. A number of sociologists have maintained that the concept of
alienation is essentially "critical." Regarding it as a defect, some of
them have tried to "save" the concept by removing the "critical" or
"polemic" components from it. Others have insisted that this is an
undertaking doomed to fail because the critical or polemic components of "alienation" belong to its essence. Both of them were in a
sense right: those who wanted to "save" the concept were right in

their basic intention; those who wanted to reject it, for in their view the concept is basically critical.

However they were wrong in the common fundamental assumption that a sociological concept must be devoid of critical content. Man is not man insofar as he is not critical toward other men and toward himself, and science is not science unless it has a critical attitude toward the "object" and "results" of its investigation. The idea of an "uncritical" science using "neutral" concepts is a contradiction in terms. And the idea of an "uncritical" sociology is, in addition to that, a direct support for an apologetic social theory justifying the existing social order.

7. Some have insisted that the concept of alienation is inapplicable in sociology because no reliable objective criteria for measuring the alleged phenomenon of alienation can be found. In order to justify the use of "alienation" in sociology, others have tried to find criteria and standards for measuring it. The application of these standards has sometimes led to unexpected and curious results (such as, for example, that physicians in a hospital for the mentally ill are more alienated than most of their patients and that average "normal" people are more alienated than either the mentally ill or the doctors who treat them).

Is this to be interpreted as a sign of the defectiveness of the standards applied or as a sign of their fruitfulness? Shall we try to find better criteria and standards for measuring alienation or should we come to see that it is senseless to look for a numerical expression of man's self-alienation and nonself-alienation (or de-alienation)? The tacit assumption of the requirement for measuring alienation is the opinion that man's essence, humanity and inhumanity are measurable quantities.

Instead of trying to find criteria for measuring alienation, should we not question the assumption common to those who want to exclude alienation from sociology because it is not strictly measurable, and to those who try to find criteria for measuring it, the assumption that all sociological phenomena must be measurable? Should we really confine sociology to the investigation of measurable phenomena? Or should we conceive of it in a broader way?

8. Some would be ready to admit that sociology can investigate phenomena which are not measurable, but they would insist that sociology has to do only with phenomena which are empirically ascer-

tainable. The phenomena of alienation can be studied by sociologists only if we can define it in terms of empirically observable qualities.

We do not deny that phenomena of alienation can be observed empirically, but we think that there can be no universal empirical criteria for distinguishing between alienation and nonalienation. This would be possible if, and only if, self-alienation were a decline from an eternal, fixed, permanent, unchangeable human nature and if that unchangeable human nature were definable in terms of empirically observable characteristics. However neither is alienation a decline from such an eternal essence of man, nor is man's essence something directly observable.

Does this mean that the phenomenon of alienation should not be studied by sociology? Or does it mean that sociology should not be reduced to an inquiry into empirically observable phenomena?

9. The question whether Marx's concept of alienation could and should be used in sociology comes down to the question whether sociology has to acquiesce in the allegedly "objective" description, measuring and classification of empirically ascertainable facts, or whether it has also to say something about the human meaning and value of those facts. The controversial problem here is not "alienation" but the nature, meaning and scope of sociological inquiry.

If the concept of alienation is of basic importance for sociology, this does not mean that it should be used without discrimination always and everywhere and that its uncritical use can serve as a substitute for critical sociological inquiry.

V. THE HUMAN "RELEVANCE" OF MARX'S CONCEPT OF ALIENATION

1. Our task has been to say something on the philosophical and sociological relevance of Marx's concept of alienation. In trying to fulfill this obligation, we have attempted to show that the concept is not merely philosophical; it is a concept of great importance for sociology. Yet it is no less relevant for other social sciences and for psychology, as well as for art and literary criticism. In all spheres of theory it is a critical concept that directs the investigation toward the seeing of problems in their essence and integrity. The concept is relevant not only for theory; it is also of great importance for man's real

life and for the practical struggle for a really human man and social community.

2. Marx's thesis that contemporary man and contemporary society are self-alienated is not only a pure "thesis," it is at the same time an invitation to change existing man and society. Moreover it is not an invitation to any kind of change. If existing man and society are basically self-alienated, this means that the fulfillment of man and the realization of a really human society are impossible without their revolutionary transformation.

If we were to characterize existing man and society simply as insufficiently human, then the way out could be found in the gradual, further development of humanity, but if it is a basically inhuman, self-alienated society, no such gradual change will do. What is needed is a radical revolutionary change of existing man and society. Thus the "concept" of alienation is also a call for the revolutionary transformation of the world.

3. Some think that de-alienation could be carried out on an individual plane without any change of the social structure or "external conditions," through an internal moral revolution or by application of certain medicopsychiatric therapies. Others think that de-alienation can be carried out only on a social plane through a transformation of the social structure, primarily through changes in the sphere of economy that will be automatically followed by corresponding changes in all other spheres of life.

However alienation is a phenomenon found both in individual men and in human society and it dominates not just this or that side of man's life but the whole man. Therefore the road to de-alienation leads neither only through transformation of the external conditions of man's existence, nor only through the change of his individual "inner" self. The de-alienation of social relations is a precondition for a full development of nonalienated, free human personalities, and free human personalities are a necessary precondition for the de-alienation of social relations. From this theoretical circle there is no theoretical way out. Rather the only way out is the revolutionary social *praxis* by means of which men, changing their social relations, change also their own nature.

4. The question about the decisive or essential sphere of man's de-alienation is justified only if we do not forget that the difference between the essential and unessential is very relative. Perhaps the

most fundamental form of man's self-alienation is the split of his activity into different "spheres" in an external, mutual relationship. In accordance with this, we may say that the essential sphere of de-alienation is not a special sphere but the "sphere" of the relations between the spheres, the "sphere" of the struggle for overcoming the split of man into mutually opposed spheres.

This does not mean that the existing difference between the spheres should be ignored or disputed. In the whole of history up to now, in the interaction among the different spheres, the determining role in the last analysis has belonged to the economic sphere. Therefore the fight for de-alienation of this sphere has a special significance. Only we should not think that the struggle for de-alienation in other spheres is without significance. We should also beware of the illusion that it is possible to carry out the de-alienation of the economic sphere while remaining within the limits of that sphere.

5. The problem of de-alienation of economic life cannot be solved by the abolition of private property. The transformation of private property into state property (be it a "capitalist" or a "socialist" state property) does not introduce an essential change in the situation of the working man, the producer. The de-alienation of economic life requires also the abolition of state property, its transformation into real social property, and this can be achieved only by organizing the whole of social life on the basis of the self-management of the immediate producers.

However if the self-management of producers is a necessary condition for the de-alienation of the economic "sphere" of man's life, it is not also a sufficient condition. The self-management of producers does not lead automatically to the de-alienation of distribution and consumption; it is not sufficient even for the de-alienation of production. Some forms of alienation in production have their root in the nature of contemporary means of production and in the organization of the process of production so that they cannot be eliminated by a mere change in the form of managing production. Some ways of struggling for de-alienation have already been found and verified; others have to be invented and tested.

6. From the requirement of abolishing the independence of "spheres" of man's existence, the sphere of philosophy cannot be exempted. And consequently the de-alienation of man should mean, among other things, the overcoming of philosophy in the sense it has

had up to now. Philosophy should cease to be a narrow special branch of knowledge. It should develop as a critical reflection of man about himself and about the world in which he lives, an auto-reflection which penetrates the whole of his life and serves as a coordinating force of all his activity. As a concept which implies the negation of philosophy, the concept of de-alienation is not merely philosophical, it is metaphilosophical.

COMMENT
Marx W. Wartofsky

Petrović set himself a difficult task in this paper. He proposes first to give an analysis of the concept of alienation that primarily deals with a number of hypothetical criticisms or interpretations (or rather misinterpretations). Secondly, he seeks to define not only its relevance to sociology but also its human relevance with regard to the distinction between economic alienation and personal alienation. Finally Petrović proposes a metaphilosophical thesis concerning the disalienation of philosophy itself. I cannot say that Petrović succeeds in this complex and difficult assignment which he sets for himself, but he raises questions of great importance as well as practical, not narrowly theoretical, relevance. I think that this is all to the good. In his own analysis at this Symposium and in a number of his other papers, Petrović has succeeded in exhibiting the relevance of the concept of alienation to contemporary philosophical discussion.

My comment will evolve around three central points. First, I would like to make a few remarks about the concept of alienation itself in order to clarify for myself and with respect to Professor Petrović's formulation of it what I think it means. Secondly, I will consider what I think is a paradoxical question in Petrović's formulation of the concept. And finally I will treat the very interesting remarks Petrović makes on alienation in a classless society.

From everything Professor Petrović has said, I think it is clear that alienation is not a simple concept, but, like other major philosophical notions, it is a complex one whose boundaries are not simply given by a specific application to one or another phenomenon of alienation or by paradigm cases. Petrović is right in holding that one cannot simply identify the concept with its particular form in one or another application, in one

or another field or phenomenal exemplification. One cannot simply identify it, for example, with Hegel's notion of the self-alienation of Absolute
Spirit; or with Feuerbach's critique of religious consciousness as the
alienation and objectification of human essence in some "other" superhuman form; or with Marx and Engel's notion of man's alienation of his
essence in labor, that is, in the objectification or the externalization
(*Entäusserung*) of his practice in the objects of production and in production relations (that is, in Marx's notion of the fetishism of commodities).
These are different ways in which the concept of alienation has classically
been formulated. However one could add to these phenomena of alienation all those manifest instances of psychological, personal and esthetic
alienation in which the concept is elaborated, appropriated by others and
transformed and in which it finds its application in various ways. Let me
cite a few examples of how diffuse the concept has become: the underlying mechanisms of projection and transference in Freudian psychology,
however metaphysically abstract or methodologically isolated they become,
are in their conceptual derivation the heirs of the Hegelian-Feuerbachian
phenomenology; the influential family of esthetic theories which developed
around the concept of *Einfühlung*, the so-called empathy theories of
Worringer, Lipps, Vernon Lee, Santayana and others inherit this same
general concept of alienation. Moreover it has of course become the commonplace of contemporary American sociology, so that "alienation" is on
every schoolboy's lips and is used to characterize everything from American
voting behavior to American sexual behavior, to the revolt on campus, to
the fragmentation and dehumanization of modern art. Thus the concept
practically reeks with relevance. But this relevance is largely uncritical, and
"alienation" becomes, in effect, both a vulgarized and a glib concept—a
"dead metaphor."

Petrović is, and rightly so, concerned with it in another way. Somewhere
in this indifferent and diluted spread of the concept, he seeks some formulation of alienation which is philosophically and critically fundamental and
is in such a way that not every phenomenon of alienation nor even all
of them together reveal the essence of the concept. The notion of essence
here is such that one does not discover what the essence of a thing is by
grouping together all things of a certain kind and finding out what they
have in common. The circularity of that procedure is enough to destroy
the definition of essence, because one could not know what to group
unless one already had a notion of what it was that these things had in
common. Consequently Petrović seeks his answer in some notion of
human essence which enables alienation to become fundamentally the
self-alienation of human essence or of human being. One should note that
the English translation of the German 'Wesen' is terribly awkward here
and consequently leads one to commit numerous Platonistic errors.

'Human Essence,' or 'Human Being' with a capital 'B' has all the overtones of a Platonistic or Hegelian idealist essentialism; generally the German 'menschliches Wesen' is better translated as simply "the property of being human." Even though the term 'property' is no better than the term 'essence,' it seems less imposing.

It is precisely here that the problem lies and it is here that I think Petrović ultimately fails to reach a satisfactory or a clear resolution of it. The difficulties, one should admit, are notorious. Plato wrestled with the dialectical problem of the relation of essence to its embodiment in many of the dialogues and especially in the *Parmenides*. It lies at the core of Hegel's dialectic, involving as it does the knotty problem of so-called Concrete Universals. I would urge all to read Feuerbach's doctoral dissertation as a prelude to reading his *Essence of Christianity* to see how complex a problem the notion of "species-concept" (*Gattungsbegriff*) presents for Feuerbach (since it is after all fundamental to his definition of man's species-consciousness, his awareness of himself as a member of a species.)

What then is the problem in Marx's own terms? Man creates his own humanity. Therefore man is self-created essence by means of his *praxis*, that is, by means of his characteristic activity. And for Marx this does not mean any activity whatever, nor simply a phenomenal account or descriptive survey of what men do from day to day. Therefore it is not a sociological field-work problem to discover what *praxis* is. One does not go out and watch people, take notes, and then discover what their *praxis* is. Rather there exists previously a notion of what men do that is distinctive of their humanity. In counterdistinction to the idealist tradition, which was the first to formulate or identify man's being, or his being human, with his activity, Marx chooses not the activity of consciousness but what he called "sensuous concrete human practice" from which consciousness itself is said to be derived. Certainly the notion that man's being is identical with his characteristic activity is quite clear in the whole idealist tradition. Descartes' *Cogito* is probably the sharpest and clearest formulation of it: Man is a thinking being, he is what he is insofar as he thinks. His being is his thinking. In *The German Ideology*, in criticizing the German idealists and the idealist tradition in general, Marx characterizes basic human activity by describing it as the production of the means of existence and the production of men, that is, human reproduction. If anything is systematically essential to the materialist's concept of alienation, it is this. According to the thesis of historical materialism, from production there evolve the modes of organization of production—the production relations—and closely related to these are the modes of organization of the production of men, i.e., the family and everything that this entails, e.g. the division of labor. In Marx's view these are the biological and social foundations of human society. One should say then that the self which is required, as Petrović suggests, if alienation is to exist in the first place is itself the product of this dialectic, of man's relation to the production and reproduction of his own existence.

This is still abstractly conceived, but at least the materialism is quite clear as opposed to the classical idealist formulation of this alienation, e.g. in Hegel. Only with the development of Marx's political and politico-economic works does the fuller, and more specific, analysis begin to fill out the philosophical, materialist-humanist program of the earlier works.

Petrović assumes all this as background and proceeds then to raise the question as to how the self-alienation of man from his essence is to be overcome. But here we run into either a conceptual tangle or an outright paradox which I hinted at earlier in talking about the difficulties of the concept of essence and of human essence. Man has no eternal, Platonic, essence from which he is alienated. The concept of *such* an essence is rather itself the fantastic or symbolic form of alienation theory, exhibited in the theories of the fall from grace, the doctrine of original sin and the Platonic theory of forms. Instead, man creates his own essence, becomes human or humanized by the very evolution of his *praxis*. That is, his being human is nothing apart from the *humanizing* practice in which he engages. Marx insisted in fact that the historical evolution of class society by its unfolding of the possibilities of the universal system of production and exchange was the precondition for this humanization; that is, the precondition for rising beyond the hypothetically "unalienated" but brute life of some primitive economy, the myth of the unalienated state of nature which Hobbes and Rousseau, and Plato before them, already knew and said was a philosophical fiction. (Sometimes, unfortunately, it appears even in Marx's interpretations as if there were some such primordial unalienated state, and I think that Petrović is right in de-emphasizing this. Recent anthropological study reveals what a misleading myth this notion of the state of nature is, how untrue this is even about so-called primitive or preliterate societies.) Thus man comes to be humanized in the very process of recognizing his humanity, that is, in his evolving awareness of himself as a species being. Not only is this Feuerbach's argument, but it is also retained by Marx. One becomes human in recognizing that one is a member of the human species, in beginning to discover one's *self* in the *other* where the *other* is an exemplification of one's own essence, either as God or as Christ or as an Ideal Being of some sort. But Marx made the condition of this species-awareness itself the practical condition of the production of man's existence and not simply the reflective awareness which Feuerbach dealt with and which, Marx claimed, derived from the facts of social production and grew with the development of local, national and international economy. Consequently this *selbst-Entäusserung*, the *self-externalization* or *self-projection*, of human essence as an object of awareness is never the abstract *praxis* of mental life, but rather it takes place in the process of social and economic and political activity itself. Obviously then this *Selbst-Entäusserung* is going to develop and change with the development and change of social, political and economic life. Therefore it cannot be a static or eternal essence but one which changes or evolves along with human historical development. So long as history remains history, so long as its essence is a transformation of the present, that is, as long as history essentially involves change (excluding the question of whether this change is inevitably progress), so long does human essence undergo change and transformation. On these grounds, the notion that there is no static essence follows from the fact that man produces his essence in his practice and his practice is in itself constantly being transformed and is transforming his environment. Strictly speaking, then, man can come to know his essence only by *praxis*. This activity changes historically; and what is more, if Marx is right, the historical change is lawful, can be described scientifically; consequently the charting of the transformation of human essence is in effect no more than the charting of the transformation of that *praxis* in which man makes history, for in making history he makes himself. In this process of constant change his essence is continuously undergoing transformation.

To this point, the analysis is effective; however one then encounters the concept not of *selbst-Entäusserung* but rather *selbst-Entfremdung*, i.e. *self-alienation*, that is the pejorative notion of the separation from one's essence, implying the failure to realize the possibilities of one's essence or one's humanity. This is no longer the characterization of history or the historical evolution of *praxis* but of a normative, valuative characterization of an aspect of history. Petrović argues that this normative connotation adds nothing to the descriptive content of alienation but rather undertakes a valuative approach to the question. In production as in social life, man's essence is alienated, estranged from him insofar as he becomes himself the abstracted essence of production relations. That is, he becomes characterized simply by the phenomena of his *praxis*. His human essence is replaced by the forms in which his *praxis* itself becomes alienated from him in commodities or in his relation to other men in class society or in his relation to the means of production, or to his own labor in its externalized form as a commodity, that is, labor power. This is a characteristic of alienated production and its concomitants in alienated exchange and alienated distribution; and this alienation is to be overcome, according to the thesis, in a socialist society (using "socialist" now in the usual way). Professor Petrović has a special view about how one ought to use the term "socialist" and "communist": the "communist" is an earlier stage, "socialism" is an advanced stage. I refer you to a paper of his on this subject in the journal *Praxis*. This alienation is to be overcome when the production becomes socialized.

Petrović raises a question, as to whether in fact human alienation can be overcome simply by the overcoming of the economic alienation of man in capitalist production. Furthermore he says that it cannot, that alienation is not simply to be identified with one of its phenomenal manifestations in production but rather that the concept of alienation, if it has any force at all, applies to what he calls the "whole man." And here this economic activity is only one aspect of man, his activity as a producer is only one aspect of his existence. Consequently alienation may continue because in social production or in socialized production, even under socialism, the technology of production itself may still produce alienation, e.g. the alienation that the technology of the large automated industry would produce. (It is interesting that Professor Tucker in his paper pointed to this same feature in Engels' article on authority and claimed here that Engels was taking issue with Marx's former idealized view of the factory.) Thus there remains a residue of alienation even when the material foundation out of which the alienation supposedly derives, the production relations in which man's essence is alienated from him in all of these ways, are overcome. There remains the alienation of man from himself in perhaps personal terms.

My problems with this formulation are essentially two. On the one hand, if in Petrović's view we regard human essence as the capacity for creating new possibilities, then the problem becomes one of asking whether alienation can ever be overcome or whether it is built into human essence itself. I should like to distinguish here between formal essence and concrete, applied or historical essence. If it is man's formal essence that he is always free to create new possibilities, then his essence is precisely his creation of new possibilities, that is, man can never overcome the alienation of any given stage of his development because he is always producing possibilities beyond those which he could possibly have met or achieved at a given time. As with his shadow, he can never catch up with his ideal self because he keeps creating and recreating it in the course of his activity. On the other hand, if the formal essence of man is that he is a being who is capable of alienating himself (to put it in this perverse form), then it would seem to be built into his frame that what makes him human is his capacity for self-alienation. Human beings can alienate themselves, animals cannot. That seems to be the direction in which this argument heads. If this is the case, then I think it tends partially away from what I think the materialist conception of alienation would have demanded, because this formal concept—namely, that man is a being such that he is capable of alienating himself, that is, producing possibilities which he may not realize, which he may choose not to realize —seems to me to move away from what I think Marx's materialist conception of alienation was, his transformation of Hegel's and Feuerbach's notion. Moreover it moves from this in the direction of the existentialist characterization of man as essentially alienated, or divided being, and hence proceeds to the ontological characterization of man as a somehow intrinsically *divided being*. This, I think, leads in the direction of a sort of Platonistic (I hesitate to say Heideggerian) Marxism in which, at the bottom of all of this real activity, there is something even more fundamental, some formal essence that is something which makes man man, namely his freedom not to be able to fulfill himself. This is a negative and perverse version, admittedly, of which the positive form is Petrović's view of man's freedom to be able to create new possibilities.

This problem appears to be a dialectical one. I do not think it is resolved in Marx. I do not think it is resolved in Marxism. I am very happy that Petrović raises it, but I think it needs some more tough thinking. The other side of this is that if all possibilities were realized there would be no alienation, and if there were no alienation, man's creative freedom would be at an end. This is the "end of history" argument which Petrović correctly criticizes. The essence would then become static and if it became static it would not be what we formally defined it as, namely, that kind of thing which constantly is capable of transforming itself in *praxis* and of creating new possibilities. We would have in effect Kant's *kingdom of ends* in which *is* and *ought* are identical and in which we have the kind of being that some theology speaks of, i.e. God's being in which essence and existence are one. I think the kind of theology which would be most akin to this notion of essence would be Augustinian in which the essence is created by the very fact of the absolutely free act of God's willing this or that. God does not have an essence to conform to, He creates His own essence by His own action. I think there are in fact strong voluntarist and Augustinean elements in Marx and in Marxism, but I think they have to be carefully construed.

The other problem I see with this is: How does one come to *know* one's essence? I think Petrović is keenly aware of this problem too, especially when he talks about it with respect to the relevance of the concept of alienation to sociology. How does one know one's essence and how does one know that one is falling short of it? If it is a question simply of describing what men *do*, then in fact there is no description of the essence but only of their existence. The distinction is an important one methodologically in many fields. Recently it has become a rather fundamental though trivial distinction in linguistics—trivial in the sense that everyone knows it and knows what it means as a distinction between *competence* and *performance*. A speaker may be competent if he knows the grammar of the language. A description of the grammar is therefore a description of his competence. He may stumble, he may speak incomplete sentences, he may have a headache, he may go to sleep; that is his performance which has nothing to do with his competence. I think this distinction makes sense in many fields, including sociology. But then one does not come to know one's essence by doing sociological field work. Rather here is the need for sociological theory which Petrović says is at the same time not simply descriptive theory but normative, valuative theory. However the question still remains, how does one come to know, in a sociological theory, what human essence is? If one poses it as a formal question for science, then I think one loses the sense that Marx had of it and which I think Petrović retains, namely, that one comes to know one's essence in *praxis* itself, and not outside of it, not standing outside and describing it externally. But this is not novel. In addition I feel that Petrović lapses into vague and sometimes pious phrases that do not go beyond a characterization of this "essence" in such terms as "free creative being of *praxis*" or "historically created human possibilities." These are all good initial programmatic distinctions. But how does one characterize "free creative being of *praxis*"? How does one make it the object of a concrete analysis, of what the "free creative being of *praxis*" *is at this time, in this place?* Consequently I think the problem begins where Petrović ends, or at least he alludes to a broader spectrum at the very end when he begins to talk about the problems of alienation in socialist society. We have here a different problem but it is also a concrete one. And in this sense I would like to distinguish what I called before a Platonist element. (I should not call it Platonist, for it runs through Aristotle as well.) Let me rather call it *formalist* element, in the sense of what Marx rejected in formalism, namely, its abstractness and its lack of concrete, historical application. The formalist definition, just as Aristotle's "happiness is activity in accordance with virtue" does not tell one what the concrete conditions of happiness are. It tells one formally that whatever they are they are in accordance with one's nature. Another instance is Kant's categorical imperative. It does not tell one what to do concretely; it only says that whatever one does, the formal conditions it would have to meet are such that man could rationally will it to be a universal maxim. Since these conditions are definitional, they are empty formulations. Similarly, to talk about human essence is empty until what it means to talk about "free Creation of human possibilities" or the "overcoming of alienation" becomes concrete talk about what human essence is *now* under *these* circumstances such that it needs to be fulfilled in a different way than it is being fulfilled at present. And this of course is the "criticism of the here below" that Marx thought philosophy ought to accomplish and which Petrović says it ought to undertake. In this sense Petrović's very interesting discussion on alienation in classless society, I think, requires a still deeper and fuller analysis.

7: MARX'S THEORY OF ETHICS

Svetozar Stojanović

I

In the history of Marxism and Marxology two kinds of interpretation of Marx can be easily distinguished. One might be called nonethical and the other ethical. I shall argue in the spirit of the latter, namely that Marx's writings have considerable ethical content that could be used as a starting point to work out a Marxist normative ethics. However at present there exists no such ethics, at least none satisfactory and worthy of Marx's name. Why?

Several reasons are usually cited and from them I can accept a political one, namely Stalinism which prevented work on the development of the true Marxist ethics. However the root, in my opinion, goes much deeper and can be found within Marx's own writings. I shall try to show that unless some theoretical obstacles contained in these writings are removed, the efforts to create a Marxist evaluative ethics will not succeed.

II

In attempting to develop this thesis it is necessary to consider two questions: what has served as a basis for a completely nonethical interpretation of Marx and what are the reasons usually given by those who claim that Marx's writings have no ethical content, indeed that they *could not* have such content?

First of all it is a fact that Marx himself wrote that he had transcended the domain of philosophy and entered the field of a "real, positive science." Consequently he thought that he was the founder of scientific socialism in contrast to a utopian one. Secondly there are several of Marx's would-be antiethical and antimoral statements. For instance:

a. Communism is for us not a state which is to be established, an
ideal to which reality will have to adjust itself. We call communism the
real movement which abolishes the present state of things.[1]

b. The communists in general preach no *morality*, which Stirner does
extensively. They do not make moral demands upon men—to love
another, not to be egoists, etc. On the contrary, they know very well
that egoism as well as self-sacrifice is, in certain circumstances, a necessary form of the self-assertion of individuals.[2]

c. Law, morality and religion have become to him [the proletariat]
so many bourgeois prejudices, behind which just as many bourgeois
interests lurk in ambush.[3]

d. *Moral* is *"impotence in action."* Every time it fights a vice it is
defeated. And Rudolph does not even rise to the standpoint of an
independent moral, based at least on the consciousness of *human dignity*. On the contrary, his moral is based on the consciousness of human
weakness. He is a *theological* moral.[4]

The group of interpreters, both Marxists and non-Marxists, who
usually cite the above quotations in support of their contention that
Marx's writings are nonethical, include Werner Sombart, Benedeto
Croce, Karl Kautsky, Max Adler, Rudolph Hilferding, some neo-Kantians, Lenin, Lucien Goldman and so on.

The consequence of this interpretation is that either there has been
no work done among the supporters of a Marxist ethics, or an ethical complement to Marx has been unsuccessfully sought in Darwin
(Kautsky), Darwin and Kant (Ludwig Woltmann), in Kant alone
(some neo-Kantians) and so on.

III

The group who believes that Marx's writings lend themselves to an
ethical interpretation includes among others Eduard Bernstein, Maxi-
millian Rubel, Karl Popper, John Lewis and Eugene Kamenka. However within the group some members consider the doctrine of Marx to
be purely ethical and nonscientific while others contend that it is

[1] MEGA, I, 5, 25; cf. *The German Ideology*, transl. by R. Pascal, New York
1960, p. 26.

[2] MEGA, I, 5, 227.

[3] MEW, IV, 472; cf. K. Marx-F. Engels, *Selected Works*, Moscow 1955, vol.
I, p. 44.

[4] MEGA, I, 3, 379; cf. K. Marx-F. Engels, *The Holy Family*, Moscow 1956,
p. 265.

partly ethical and partly scientific. I myself would join the latter division. Again one should note that these members are both Marxists and non-Marxists. The following texts of Marx are some on which this group could base its assertion:

a. The social principles of Christianity preach cowardice, self-contempt, debasement, subjugation, humility, in short, all the properties of the *canaille*, and the proletariat, which does not want to be treated as *canaille*, needs its courage, its consciousness of self, its pride and its independence, far more than its bread.[5]
b. [In his Address to the First International Marx spoke of] the simple laws of morals and justice which ought to govern the relations of individuals.[6]
c. The standpoint of the old materialism is civil society, the standpoint of the new materialism is human society or socialized humanity.[7]
d. [Marx pleaded for] an association in which the free development of each will lead to the free development of all.[8]

Furthermore the writings of Marx are full of ethical language. For example, in his *Manifesto of the Communist Party* Marx very often uses such words and phrases as the following: "crude self-interest and unfeeling 'cash-payment,'" "oppression," "degradation of personal dignity," "unashamed, direct and brutal exploitation," "ruthlessness," "modern enslavement by capital," "subjugation," "masses of workers are slaves" and so on. If anyone remarks that these are mainly Marx's political and not scientific writings, I could easily reply by quoting *Das Kapital*.[9]

Marx was from his early to his last writings, i.e. both in his, as he put it, philosophical and scientific phase, one of the greatest and most radical humanist thinkers in history. Morever he was an heir of the great European humanistic-ethical tradition. Having taken seriously the ideals of the great Western democratic revolutions, he, on the basis of them, strongly and rightly criticized the capitalist society. Of course, he did not dwell on these ideals but tried to develop, deepen and further concretize them. All of this has been recognized and praised by many important non-Marxist thinkers. A Marxist could hardly pay a greater tribute to the humanistic and ethical ideals

---

[5] *MEW*, IV, 200.
[6] *MEW*, XVI, 13; cf. Marx-Engels, *Selected Works*, vol. I, p. 385.
[7] *MEGA*, I, 5, 535; cf. Marx-Engels, *Selected Works*, vol. II, p. 404.
[8] *MEW*, IV, 482; cf. Marx-Engels, *Selected Works*, vol. I, p. 54.
[9] See, for instance, vol. I, chapters 4, 7, and 13.

of Marx than, for instance, Karl Popper did in his *The Open Society and Its Enemies.*[10]

Marx's most fundamental ideal was that of a free, socialized, creative, many-sided, integral, autonomous and dignified personality. The more specific content is given to it by his ideas of dealienation, the abolition of social, especially class, inequalities, withering away of the state and so on. In brief, Marx's opus is, in my opinion, rich in the humanistic-ethical content that could and should be used to develop a normative ethics.

IV

However despite all these possible textual references, some interpreters have asserted that the doctrine of Marx is ethically empty and necessarily so. Before attempting to comment on this assertion, we must address ourselves to another: namely, that Marx claimed to be only a scientist and made some (allegedly) antiethical statements, despite the ethical content of his writings. For this I can see only two possible explanations.

1. Either he did not notice the ethical content of his own thought, or

2. He meant by 'science' something rather different than the "value-free" science that his nonethical interpreters have had in mind. In line with this, his allegedly antiethical and antimoral statements were in fact directed only against moralism and a certain kind of ethical language usage.

The first alternative seems to me very improbable in regard to a man of Marx's calibre, particularly if we bear in mind the extent of the ethical contents of his writings. However in my mind there are several reasons for the second alternative. First, *all along* Marx used evaluative language including that of an ethical nature. If he had thought this to have been irreconcilable with the realm of "real, positive science," he would have tried to stop using it the moment he wanted to enter this realm. Secondly, Marx never made, explicitly or implicitly, such a distinction between evaluative and cognitive statements as has been assumed by his nonethical interpreters. Thirdly, we must never forget that he was Hegel's follower and that Hegel,

[10] 4th ed., London 1962, vol. II, ch. 22.

rejecting Kant's dualism, claimed the unity of *Sein* and *Sollen*.

It seems to me that when entering the scientific stage, Marx changed his mind only as to the legitimacy of independent uses (from cognitive statements) of evaluative statements. In other words, he did not then try to avoid using them if and only if he thought they could be logically supported by cognitive statements. To add another point, he thought that in science cognitive statements play a primary role and evaluative statements only a subordinate one.

I believe that Marx's *implicit* meta-axiological and meta-ethical views were cognitivistic. Consequently he could continue to use evaluative and ethical language and at the same time believe that he was still only in the field of science. Many Marxists correctly write that the works of Marx contain considerable material for a normative ethics, but they wrongly assume that despite this he was merely a scientist. Together with Marx they make a cognitivist fallacy. However we should not overlook the fact that in Marx's time the cognitivist idea was by far the prevailing one in the theoretical self-consciousness of philosophers and scientists, for it was almost half a century before the first modern and systematic meta-axiological and meta-ethical studies began. Only in our century have philosophers rather clearly distinguished between evaluative and cognitive statements and found out the nature of their interrelations.

All the texts of Marx quoted in division II except one, can easily be interpreted in accordance with what I have said as being antimoralistic and not antimoral. The whole context of the exempted text—"Law, morality and religion have become for him [the proletariat] so many bourgeois prejudices, behind which bourgeois interests lurk in ambush"—shows, however, that it is directed only against bourgeois morality and not morality as such. I also believe that the other texts of Marx which are or might be quoted by his nonethical interpreters could be explicated in support of my thesis. Moreover if any counterexamples exist, they would not destroy my claim but rather point out that on some occasions Marx hesitated.

There are two principal characteristics of the moralism that Marx opposed:

1. the use of moral language which is independent from cognitive language and which achieves primary importance in comparison with cognitive language to criticize the existing morality and simultaneously to preach the new "true" morality;

2. the belief that significant moral change and reform can be effected in this way.

The counterpart of moralism in practice is ethicism in theory. Utopian socialism was essentially moralistic and ethicist. As is well known Marx was in the beginning primarily a humanist-moralizing thinker. His ideological commitment was liberal and only after that socialist. Very quickly he wanted to become a scientific, in contrast to a utopian, socialist.

Marx's aversion toward moralism cannot be explained, or at least to any extent, by his personal moral characteristics, as for example Karl Popper attempted: "Marx avoided an explicit moral theory, because he hated preaching. He was deeply distrustful of moralists who usually preach one thing and do the other."[11] For Marx did have the respect for at least some utopian socialists' personal morality although he opposed their moralism, simply because he wanted to replace moralistic socialism by a scientific one. In contrast to the utopian, moralistic socialism Marx tried to follow two principles:

1. he used ethical language only if he thought it could be logically supported by cognitive language and to attach exclusively a secondary importance to the former;

2. instead of putting his hopes into moral preaching, he insisted on the need of changing social conditions resulting in immorality; to acquire the knowledge for these conditions he plunged into the scientific investigation of the existing social reality, its supporting forces, its tendencies and laws, possibilities for and carriers of its eventual change and so forth. That was the only way of breaking into the causes of the existing immoral order. Utopian socialism tried to deal primarily with the effects instead of the causes. That is why it was powerless, inefficient and naive.

Against this background it is not difficult to understand why cognative language became of primary importance to Marx. In the forefront was his effort to show the necessity and lawfulness of replacing capitalism with socialism. The ethical criticism of capitalist reality was only of secondary importance for him. And the *explicit* ethical justification of socialism as his cause was the least important for him. These have misled some of his interpreters who have come to the wrong conclusion that there necessarily was no place for ethical ideas in Marx's theory.

[11] *Ibid.*, vol. II, 385.

Marx's only implicit meta-ethical cognitivism has been doubly misleading. Some interpreters, not having noticed it and having taken into account Marx's statement about the pure scientific nature of his doctrine, have been misled and have concluded that it did not have and could not have any ethical content. From such people, even if they are Marxists, it is, of course, unreasonable to expect any effort to develop a normative ethics based on Marx.

The others, however, have been misled to think that there is a basis in Marx for a *scientific normative* ethics. Much time and energy have been spent in trying to create a "scientific Marxist normative ethics." Since normative ethics, including a Marxist one, cannot be a science, all these efforts have been doomed to failure. But still it is possible, in my opinion, to work out a Marxist normative ethics *using*, among other things, all relevant scientific knowledge as cognitive premises or reasons for ethical statements.

V

The primary characteristic of Marx's thought is activism. Its core consits of these categories: practice, freedom and self-realization of man as man. The underlying principle of this activism is some sort of *moderate* historical determinism expressed in the following way: "Men make their own history. But they do not make it just as they please; they do not make it under circumstances chosen by themselves, but under circumstances directly encountered, given, and transmitted from the past."[12]

Marxists should start seriously considering, developing and justifying this middle of the ground position between extreme historical determinism and extreme indeterminism. While in post-Marxian Marxism this (possibly convenient) scheme has been mainly repeated, in some other philosophical orientations serious and detailed works on historical determinism and freedom have been written. Of course, one cannot say that they resolved the problem, but only came a little closer to it. The final solution is expected only by a naive person who does not know that this is one of the eternal philosophical problems.

Unfortunately Marx did not consistently hold a *moderate* historical deterministic view. Some of his texts reveal an internal conflict and

[12] *MEW*, VIII, 115; cf. Marx-Engels, *Selected Works*, vol. I, p. 247.

tension between moderate and extreme deterministic inclinations. One has to bear in mind that Marx belonged to the nineteenth century science in which rigid determinism of natural science still was a theoretical and methodological ideal.

VI

Marx correctly stressed the influence of the economic, especially of the class-economic, position of man upon his morality. One's moral views often really are ideological rationalizations of his economic-class interests. If today we try to penetrate formally identical abstract moral ideas of various people in order to identify different contents expressing and rationalizing different social interests, it is at least partially due to the impact of Marx. His idea of the ruling morality as the ruling class morality may also be fruitful. All these ideas are, in my opinion, important for ethics and particularly for the sociology of morals. It may be that they are commonplace now. If they are, it is to Marx's credit.

However, some of Marx's formulations of the moral "superstructure" being determined by the economic "foundation" are so much overdone that Engels found it necessary in his last letters to warn that they should not be understood literally.

Some Marxists seem to think that they can at the same time do both things—on the one hand, to hold such *extreme* formulations of economic determinism and, on the other hand, to insist upon the work on Marxist normative ethics, assuming that there is a possibility of its significant influence. It is, however, impossible to have one's cake and eat it too. If morals were *fully* dependent upon and determined by economic conditions, there would be no chance whatsoever for the formative and reformative function of moral and ethical statements. The *only* way of exerting influence upon people's moral life would consist in changing their economic position.

VII

Some of Marx's statements on the necessity of socialism are so rigid that they verge on fatalism, for example the following ones:

"But capitalist production begets, with the inexorability of a law of Nature its own negation."[13]

Marx approvingly cites one of the reviewers of his Das Kapital:

Consequently, Marx only troubles himself about one thing; to show, by rigid scientific investigation, the necessity of successive determinate orders of social conditions, and to establish, as impartially as possible, the facts that serve him for fundamental starting points. For this it is quite enough, if he proves, at the same time, both necessity of the present order of things, and necessity of another order into which the first must inevitably pass over; and this all the same, whether men believe or do not believe it, whether they are conscious or unconscious of it. Marx treats the social movement as a process of natural history, governed by laws not only independent of human will, consciousness and intelligence, but rather, on the contrary, determining that will, consciousness and intelligence. . . .[14]

In the following passage Marx holds a moderate deterministic conception treating social "laws" as "tendencies," and at the same time holds an extreme deterministic view according to which social laws function with "iron necessity": "Intrinsically, it is not a question of the higher degree of development of the social antagonisms that result from the natural laws of capitalist production. It is a question of these laws themselves, of these tendencies working with iron necessity."[15]

"And even when a society has got upon the right track for the discovery of the natural laws of its movement—and it is the ultimate aim of this work, to lay bare the economic law of motion of modern society—it can neither clear by bold leaps, nor remove by legal enactments, the obstacles offered by the successive phases of its normal development. But it can shorten and lessen the birth-pangs."[16]

Engels' definition of freedom, taken over from Hegel, as "awareness of necessity" is consistent only with the extreme deterministic passages in Marx. It easily can be shown that this definition of freedom is untenable. Real freedom is possible only within Marx's moderate determinism. Let me state quite briefly what I argued at length

---

[13] Cf. Wright C. Mills, The Marxist, New York 1962, p. 67 (Manifesto).

[14] MEW, XXIII, 26; cf. Capital, Moscow 1955, vol. I, p. 18 (Afterword to the 2nd German edition). Italics are mine—S.S.

[15] Ibid., 12; cf. Capital, p. 8 ff. (Preface to the first German edition). Italics are mine—S.S.

[16] Ibid., 15; cf. Capital, p. 10. Italics are mine—S.S.

elsewhere. Moderate determinism believes that there is more than one historical possibility but that the number of historical possibilities is limited. Freedom, then, is the ability to choose between them and to realize the chosen possibility.

Let us suppose for a moment that the rigid deterministic theses of Marx are true. In other words, we shall assume that socialism is inevitable in the sense that people are able, as it were, only slightly to assist or render more difficult this necessity. What then would be the consequences for a corresponding normative ethics?

I shall take for granted that the function of such an ethics should be: a) morally to justify a socialism which is inevitable, and b) morally to oblige people to bring it about. The first part (a) of the job should and could be done even if Marx were right in saying that there was no possibility whatsoever, so to say, to add something to or to take away anything from the necessity of socialism. Even that which is absolutely necessary still could be good or bad. But the second part (b) of the job has sense only if human activity can make any difference to what happens. Morally to oblige someone to do something is rational only to the extent in which it is in one's power to do it. However according to the above quotations of Marx, people can do very little about the historical course. Therefore they can have very little moral responsibility for it.

It follows, I hope, that Marx's doctrine, by being (in some of its parts) strictly deterministic, frustrates ethically its own cause. There is not much sense for a rigid determinist to urge people to be morally concerened about making socialism emerge. However Marxist normative ethics, by its very Marxist nature, has to do this and in addition must be primarily a social ethics.

Just because he sometimes thought that socialism, no matter what people do, was inevitable, Marx did not feel the need of trying to give an *explicit* ethical justification of socialism. Even less did he want to present to the people the moral obligation of trying to realize it. This has misled some of his interpreters to think that his works are, and necessarily so, without any ethical content. Karl Popper,[17] Isaiah Berlin,[18] H. B. Mayo[19] and some others also were misled to conclude

---

[17] *Op. cit.*, chapter 22.
[18] *Karl Marx*, London 1948, p. 140.
[19] *Democracy and Marxism*, New York 1955, p. 231.

that Marx identified historical necessity with the moral criterion.

Let us pause for a moment to deal with Popper's interpretation which is the most worked out of these three. The only text he quotes to support it is the following one of Engels:

> Certainly, that morality which contains the greatest number of elements that are going to last is the one which, within the present time, represents the overthrow of the present time; it is the one which represents the future; it is the proletarian morality. . . .

First of all, it is not at all clear that Engels here regards historical necessity as the moral criterion. But even if he did, from that it would not follow that Marx did the same. More important, Popper did not quote Marx and I believe could not simply because there is, in my opinion, no text in Marx that explicitly or implicitly is of that nature. Tucker[20] rightly rejects Popper's interpretation, reminding us that Marx first arrived at the idea of a good society and only later became persuaded of its inevitability. Of course, this counterargument is not by itself conclusive. Popper could still insist that in his second phase Marx was an ethical historicist. I believe, however, that Popper cannot prove this either. I should like to add that *psychologically* the idea of an ethical justifiability of socialism led Marx to believe in its inevitability, and not vice versa. Marx was an extremely optimistic and progressivistic thinker. *Logically*, however, the moral criterion and historical necessity are for Marx independent from each other.

But let us return to the main line of this paper. Marxist normative ethics should invite and morally obligate people to use all their efforts in effecting socialism. However to be able to do this, it must renounce Marx's extreme deterministic formulations. Moreover instead of speaking about the inevitability of socialism, it is, in my opinion, more acceptable to consider socialism as a *real historical possibility tending strongly to realize itself*. Today not even the survival of humanity, let alone socialism, can be thought of as inevitable. Whether socialism will come about or not *completely* depends on people and their actions. Only such a Marxist doctrine may conceive of people as *fully* morally obligated to actualize socialism.

---

[20] R. Tucker, *Philosophy and Myth in Karl Marx*, Cambridge, Mass., 1961, p. 21.

COMMENT

A. James Gregor

I undertake comment on Professor Stojanović's paper with mixed sentiment. First of all, I heartily applaud what I understand to be his intention,
that is to say, his desire to satisfy the demand for a viable normative ethics.
But, on the other hand, I am not at all convinced that he has succeeded
in justifying his use of the adjectival qualifier "Marxist" with which he
characterizes his attempt. Moreover I think his analysis is, in several critical
respects, mistaken and confused. I should like to treat these considerations
in reverse order.

With regard to the last consideration, Professor Stojanović attempts to
support his claim that Marx was, in some significant sense, concerned with
issuing imperatives which were distinguishably ethical. Professor Stojanović
is admirably candid in recognizing that contemporary ethics clearly distinguishes between evaluative and cognitive propositions. Professor Stojanović, nonetheless, seems convinced that Marx issued or wished to issue,
in some sense or another, specifically ethical imperatives. As evidence for
his claim we are offered four quotations from the thousands of pages of
Marx's correspondence and publications—quotations that have an unmis-
takeable normative resonance. Two of these (from the *Economic and
Philosophic Manuscripts of 1844* and the *Holy Family* written in the
same year, the year before Marx's efforts at what he himself called "self-
clarification")¹ originate in the period when, by Professor Stojanović's own
admission, Marx was still a "liberal." In other words, two of the quotations
date from the period of Marx's development generally recognized as
"immature" and could be mustered to support any interpretative thesis
only with considerable reservation, for Marx had not yet developed his
mature views. The third quotation originates in the *Communist Manifesto*
which Professor Stojanović recognizes was a "political tract" serving an
admittedly exhortatory purpose. The sole remaining quotation is indeed
from Marx's maturity, found in an Address written in 1864. Unfortunately,
Marx left us his own opinion concerning its merit in the present context.
On November 4, 1864, he wrote Engels that the "sentiment" of the members of the International Workingmen's Association had forced him to
include references to "morality" and "justice" in his Address but, he added
quickly, that he had framed those references "in such as way that they
[could] do no harm."²

¹ *MEW*, XIII, 10; cf. K. Marx-F. Engels, *Selected Works*, Moscow 1955, vol.
I, p. 364.
² *MEW*, XXXI, 15.

Professor Stojanović, in other words, could have selected a more substantial sample of quotations to support his point. The four cited do not support the thesis that Marx was interested in issuing serious moral imperatives. At best Professor Stojanović's references indicate that in Marx's youth, before he had developed a specifically Marxist position, he entertained such locutions and that when he sought to impel men to action, Marx used language calculated to that end whether he felt such language had any independent significance or not. Still less do such quotations suggest anything about what Marx understood to be the relationship between such language and a serious normative ethics.

Professor Stojanović goes on to indicate that Marx frequently used the language of moral indignation. This is perfectly true. Marx's writings abound with language that indicates moral approbation and disapprobation. Certainly Marx thought such language appropriate. The real question, it would seem, is how Marx analyzed such language. And here Marx was painfully specific. In all his mature statements Marx entertained an essentially monofactorial thesis. The "material life conditions" determine definite forms of "social consciousness" which include "legal, political, religious, esthetic or philosophic" expression.[3] In *Das Kapital* this is expressed: "the mode of production determines the character of the social, political and intellectual life in general. . . ."[4] Twenty years before, in the first full statement of the materialist conception of history, Marx maintained, "Our conception of history depends on our ability to expound the real process of production, starting out from the simple material production of life . . . [and to] explain the whole mass of different theoretical products and forms of consciousness, religion, philosophy, ethics, and so on."[5]

How Professor Stojanović is prepared to handle this issue is difficult to say. On the one hand he admits that Marx was guilty of a "cognitivist fallacy." This seems to mean that Marx made grievous errors in the analysis of ethical language, that he somehow thought that ethical imperatives could be unpacked without remainder into descriptive propositions. Marx certainly seems to have been guilty of this (no more guilty, Professor Stojanović would add, than most of the thinkers of the nineteenth century the majority of whom were guilty of the same simplism). The long and short of it seems to be that Marx's analysis was simply wrong.

But Professor Stojanović goes on to add that while Marx was "antimoralist" he was not "antimoral." What this means is hard to determine.

---

[3] MEW, XIII, 9; cf. *Selected Works*, vol. I, p. 363.

[4] MEW, XXIII, 96; cf. *Capital*, Moscow 1954, vol. I, p. 82 n.

[5] MEGA, I, 5, 27; cf. K. Marx and F. Engels, *The German Ideology*, New York 1947, p. 28.

Certainly Marx was not antimoral. He was convinced that morals, like all intellectual products, was a derivative by-product of the material conditions of life. He certainly would not legislate against the use of injunctions, prescriptions, proscriptions, exhortations, approbation and disapprobation. What he consistently maintained was that such uses could only be explained by reference to descriptive propositions about the material conditions of life, to "derive," as one contemporary Marxist put it, "moral concepts from the material conditions of life. . . ."[6]

Most ethicists, not to speak of meta-ethical theorists, are opposed or completely indifferent to moral preachments as such. They are concerned with the status of ethical propositions and they are certainly not antimoral in whatever sense Professor Stojanović is employing the term. What they are concerned with, just as Marx was, is with determining the status and character of ethical propositions vis-à-vis cognitive and noncognitive components.

Marx seemed to believe, as Professor Stojanović appears ready to grant, that ethical propositions are derivative or secondary products, generated, in some obscure way, by material conditions of life. Most people concerned with ethics recognize that facts have some *relevance* for ethical judgments. Marx, on the other hand, seems to have been convinced that facts *explain* ethical judgments. This seems to be the real issue and Professor Stojanović, with admirable intellectual independence, appears to have taken up his position with the non-Marxists.

Professor Stojanović seems to artfully dodge the central issue by maintaining that Marx used ethical language "only if he thought it could be logically supported by cognitive language and to attach exclusively a secondary importance to the former." This, of course, can mean almost anything. Most contemporary ethicists recognize that arguments about moral questions, which are not trivial, logically involve our beliefs and assumptions about psychological, sociological, economic, as well as any number of other relevant, facts. Furthermore the facts we muster tend to support our moral conclusions in an argument form not unlike that analyzed by Aristotle over two thousand years ago. Facts are logically relevant as minor premises in any argument in support of a normative judgment. What this has to do with a specifically *Marxist* ethics is obscure. That we are now much more sophisticated in marshalling our facts, that we now consider, among a host of other things, class and economic interest,

---

[6] W. Ash, *Marxism and Moral Concepts*, New York 1964, p. xi. Engels, in his *Anti-Duehring*, *MEW*, XX, 87 ff; English, Moscow 1962, p. 131, maintains precisely the same thesis: "We maintain . . . that all moral theories have been hitherto the product, in the last analysis, of the economic conditions of society obtaining at the time."

in the appraisal of our own and our opponent's ethical arguments is of sociological interest but hardly of profound ethical moment. Marx may have made us better sociologists, but I doubt whether it can be said that he significantly influenced our analysis of ethical language.

All this seems somewhat confused in Professor Stojanović's account. No one suggests that there is "no place for ethical ideas in Marx's theory." Marx specifically seeks to explain the origin, nature and status of ethical conceptions. What critics maintain is that Marx's explanation is mistaken. And Professor Stojanović seems to grant as much. For it is Marx's "strict determinist position" that is the source of his faulty analysis of ethical language. And Professor Stojanović rejects Marx's determinism.

What we are left with is Professor Stojanović's programmatic suggestion that we work out a normative ethics "using, among other things, all relevant scientific knowledge as cognitive premises or reasons for ethical statements." But this has been part of the ethical enterprise at least since the time of Aristotle. And Aristotle was not a Marxist. The only effort Professor Stojanović makes to justify the characterization of his proposed ethics as Marxist is to identify its core conceptions: "practice, freedom and self-realization," concepts which are not now, nor have they ever been, specifically Marxist. Such concepts, as a consequence, are neither Marxist nor informative. Practice, freedom and self-realization can, and have in the past, meant almost anything. Unless their meaning is specified with some precision such invocations are completely vacuous. But even with such specification I fail to see that we have moved one step closer to resolving serious ethical issues or succeeded to an analysis of the language of ethics capable of compelling general assent.

Since Professor Stojanović is prepared to abandon all the major tenets of classical Marxism that have provoked the objections of philosophers in the past, and what remains is a real sentiment to pursue the substance of discussion, I recommend that we abandon the adjectival use of "Marxist" when we undertake to discuss ethics. Its use generates confusion and breeds animus. What we are all concerned with is ethics and its analysis, pure and simple. I heartily recommend Professor Stojanović's paper as evidence of how far contemporary Marxists are prepared to go to join in our common enterprise.

8: THE INDIVIDUAL AND HISTORY

Karel Kosík

I

In contrast to the usual practice which never takes titles literally and pays little attention to them, I should like to draw the reader's attention to the conjunction 'and' standing between the words 'history' and 'the individual' and to consider its special function. An individual remains an individual, but if he gets into the proximity of history, he becomes either the great individual making history or the helpless person being crushed by history. The historical individual views history differently than the average individual. Does this mean that there are two kinds of history—one for the historical individual and one for the average individual? Is the real individual only the one who makes history and real history only that which results from the activities of the historical individual; or is this an extreme view and the correct position is held by those who stress what the great individual and the average individual have in common and consider history as a chain of events in which all have their share and in which everyone may show his abilities? *Which* individual and *which* history have we in mind when we speak about the relationship between history and the individual?

Their mutual relationship seems self-evident and, what is more, seems to suggest the proper approach to the problem, "The Individual and History." If we know what is history and what is the individual, we should also be able to recognize their relationship. However this way of thinking assumes that the individual and history are two units which are independent of each other and which can be recognized in isolation and that later their mutual relationship can be sought.

The relationship between history and the individual is expressed in mutually exclusive theories; one maintains that history is made by great individuals while the other states that history is made by superindividual forces (Hegel's "World Spirit," the "forces of production" of simplifying Marxists, the "Masses" in the view of the Romantics). On first sight these views seem to exclude one another. However by penetrating further, we find that they have very much in common, that one conditions the other and that they percolate. What they have in common is that they consider the making of history a privilege granted to some selected factors: either to great individuals or to hypostatized abstractions. In order that Man may interfere with history, he must, according to one view, differ from other individuals seeking the same goal, that is, who also want to make history; his historical greatness depends on the degree of his difference from the others. In the perspective of the great individual, people may be divided into two groups: the majority is merely the material of historical events and is subject to history, whereas the second group is made up of individuals wanting to play a historical role; they must, therefore, become each other's enemies. Historical individuals create for themselves a world in which they stand up to those who oppose or may oppose them.

The individual becomes a historical being to the extent to which his particular actions have universal *Geltung*, that is, bear general results. As history exists only as continuous, the theory of the great individual must state whether history ceases to exist, or is interrupted, in those periods which lack any great individual and in which "there is a rule of mediocrity." If the actions of great individuals do not fall within a certain continuity of events and have no share in creating it, history breaks up and is replaced by the chaos of isolated and discontinuous events. If the continuity of history—created, according to this theory, by the actions of great individuals—is admitted, the particular activity of each great individual clashes with the existing universality of history. The great individual either denies this universality in his words (and by this he does not destroy its existence or his dependence on it), or he recognizes it and becomes the conscious representative of the universality. At this moment the individual proclaims his particular activity to be the immediate expression of universality and History itself is manifest in his actions, Being itself resounds in his words. Thus the great individual that first appeared as the maker of history turns out to be an instrument of History.

The results that follow from this approach are, in fact, the starting point for those who hold the opposite view. In the universalist theory the individual becomes a historical factor if through his actions he expresses rightly the tendencies and trends and/or the laws of the superindividual formations or forces. History is a transcendental force, the processes of which may be accelerated by the great individual or may be given a particular historical tinge by him, but he cannot destroy or fundamentally change this force. Whatever the importance of the great individual's role in these conceptions, his mission is not at all enviable for two reasons. Such an individual is a historical automaton founded on the proper calculation of knowledge (information) and will (action); these are adequate elements of his function, and all the other human qualities are redundant or subjective from the point of view of his historical role. The great historical individual of this theory is not identical with the universally developed individual, i.e., with the personality. As the great individual has the function of an accelerator and modifier in history, a second question arises: will not his existence become superfluous or outdated as soon as both functions may be performed by "someone" or "something" more perfectly and not accidentally (as the individual's existence is considered to be accidental)? The view that considers great individuals as particular beings realizing general laws leads ultimately to the conclusion that their functions may be performed more reliably and with greater efficiency by those automatic institutions that can be managed by average individuals; this is in line with the prophetic views expressed by Schiller, Hölderlin and Schelling:

> In such institutions everything is of some value only if it can be expected and accounted for with certainty. . . . Consequently those who are least distinguished by their individuality, the average talents and the mechanically educated souls, get to power and manage affairs in such institutions.

The logical outcome of this theory of the great individual is the defense of average individuals.

The individual may be great, that is influential and powerful, even while he is not a personality. The greatness in question does not spring from the individual's personality, his spirit or his character but from the power which he exercises as the result of certain circumstances and by which he makes history. The individual with the greatest power may simultaneously be the individual with the least individuality.

Hegel and Goethe were correct in defending the hero, i.e., the great or historical individual, against the views of the butler. But the but-

ler's idea of the great individual is not a view from below, i.e., a ple-
beian criticism, because the butler is not the hero's opponent but his
complement. The hero needs the butler as witness to his human weak-
nesses (he represents a means of making them public); this is the way
society learns that the hero remains *human* even in his responsible
and exhausting historical function. The great individual is not only a
hero who, through his actions, is different from others, but he is also
a human being (he loves flowers, plays cards, cares for his family, and
so on) and in this respect he does not differ from other people but is
like them. What, however, is indicated by the butler's view and what
the uncritical public accepts as the great individual's human nature
is, in fact, the degradation of human nature to an anecdotal and secondary level: the human side appears in the form of insignificant
details or in the sphere of private life.

The butler belongs to the great individual's world and his view does
not bespeak any criticism but only a direct or indirect vindication
expressed in stories, in the betrayal of background secrets or in slander
and minor intrigues. This is the explanation of why we encounter the
ridiculous, the comic, the humorous, the satirical only in marginal
anecdotes that have no historical value in this conception of history
and the individual. Such history means gravity, self-denial, seriousness;
moreover, according to Hegel, a period of happiness is something of
an exception in it. The butlers may tell anecdotes about their masters,
but the ridiculousness of a certain historical individual and the comic
side of his doings can be revealed only through another view which is
inaccessible to butlers and servants.

Both theories, however contradictory they seem to be in details, fail
because of their common inability to solve the relationship between
the particular and the general in a satisfactory manner. Either generality is absorbed by particularity, and history becomes an irrational
and senseless process in which every particular event appears with a
general meaning and in which there is only arbitrariness and chance;
or the particular event is absorbed by generality, which means that
individuals are mere instruments, that history is predestined and that
people only seemingly make history. In the latter view we may discover a remainder of the theological doctrine that considers history to
be a scaffolding with whose help a building is erected; the scaffolding,
as the sphere of temporality, is of an ontological nature that differs in
principle and is, therefore, separable from the building that bears the

signs of eternity. In the view of St. Augustine, the *machinamenta temporalia* and the *machinae transiturae* are qualitatively different from what they help to build: *illud quod manet in aeternum*. If the metaphysical assumptions of this theory are repudiated but the view of the qualitative, ontological difference between "scaffolding" (the temporary thing) and the "building" (the thing outside of time) is accepted in a transformed and therefore implicit and unclear likeness, we are faced with a bastard-like idea that has catastrophic consequences. Hegel's "cunning of history" is outwitted. By using and wearing out particular passions and interests, pure generality, undefiled by particularity, does not originate but leads to a generality in which particularity is embedded. In order not to be discredited, generality seeks to turn particularity into an instrument, but this cunning is outwitted. "The scaffolding" with the help of which the building of history is constructed cannot be removed from "the building itself." Particularity and generality are interlinked and the attained goal bears some likeness to the sum of the means employed.

II

The principle of universality and the principle of particularity, through which the relationship between history and the individual is expressed in the form of rigid antinomies, are not only abstractions which fail to express the concreteness of history but also only appear to be principles: these principles are not the *beginning* and the *foundations* (*principium*) from which the movement springs and in which reality is manifest; they are rather deduced and petrified degrees or stages of this movement. In disclosing the shortcomings and contradictions of the two theories, we may discover certain dialectics in which the relationship between history and the individual is no longer expressed by means of antinomies but rather as a movement in which the inner unity of the two members is constituted. This new principle is the *play*.

Terms referring to plays and games may be found in every meditation about history, e.g., 'part,' 'masque,' 'peril,' 'victory,' 'defeat' and so on; the idea of history as a play or a game is quite common in German classical philosophy. Schelling illustrates this in *System of Transcendental Idealism*:

If we think of history as a play in which everybody who shares in it may play his part freely and use his own discretion, we can imagine a reasonable denouement to this confused play only in the sense that there exists "One Spirit" which makes everyone compose his part, and that the poet, whose mere pieces (*disjecti membra poetae*) the individual actors are, has previously harmonized the objective success of the whole play with the freedom of the individual actors, so that in the end the outcome should be quite reasonable. If, however, the poet were independent of his play, we would only be actors who performed what he had composed. If he is not independent of us but manifests and reveals himself only successively through the play of our liberty, so that without this liberty he himself would not exist, we become fellow poets in composing the whole, and independent inventors of the particular parts that we play.[1]

In *The Poverty of Philosophy* Marx characterized the materialistic idea of history as a method "which investigates the real profane history of the people in each century" and which "describes these people both as authors and actors of their own drama. As soon as you describe these people as the actors and authors of their own history, you have come back . . . to the true beginning."[2]

For the time being, I leave aside the differences in the views of Schelling and Marx since I am primarily concerned with the meaning of the idea that identifies history with a play. In the idea of the play as the principle of the individual's unity with history we no longer confront linear abstractions but rather find that the various heterogeneous elements are united through some inner link. The individual and history are no longer entities independent of each other but are

---

[1] "Wenn wir uns die Geschichte als ein Schauspiel denken, in welchem jeder, der daran Theil hat, ganz frei und nach Gutdünken seine Rolle spielt, so lässt sich eine vernünftige Entwicklung dieses verworrenen Spiels nur dadurch denken, dass es Ein Geist ist, der in allen dichtet, und dass der Dichter, dessen blosse Bruchstücke (*disjecta membra poetae*) die einzelnen Schauspieler sind, den objektiven Erfolg des Ganzen mit dem freien Spiel aller einzelnen schon zum voraus so in Harmonie gesetzt hat, dass am Ende etwas Vernünftiges herauskommen muss. Wäre nun aber der Dichter unabhängig von seinem Drama, so wären wir nur die Schauspieler, die ausführen, was er gedichtet hat. Ist er nicht unabhängig von uns, sondern offenbart und enthüllt er sich nur successiv durch das Spiel unserer Freiheit selbst, so dass ohne diese Freiheit auch er selbst nicht wäre, so sind wir Mitdichter des Ganzen, und Selbsterfinder der besonderen Rolle, die wir spielen" *Werke*, München 1927, vol. II, p. 602.
[2] *MEW*, IV, 135; cf. *The Poverty of Philosophy*, Moscow.

interlinked by a common base. The theories mentioned earlier considered participation in history to be a privilege; either they did not explain a number of features or else distorted them by means of forcible constructions which disagreed with experience. History as a play, however, is open to everyone and to all; history is a play in which the masses and individuals, classes and nations, great personalities and average beings, all partake. It is a play as long as all people have a part in it and as long as *all* parts are included and no one is excluded. All genres are fully developed in historical tragedies, comedies and grotesque plays. We cannot agree with those who transform the tragic in history into the tragedy of history or the comic in history into the comedy of history, because here one aspect of history becomes absolute and is raised above history itself; this view also disregards the inner relationship between the various aspects and history as a play.

As every play requires actors and audiences, the first of the basic assumptions of the interpretation of history as a play is the relationship of Man to Man, of Man to other people; the basic *forms* of this relationship are indicated in grammar (I-You, I-We, They-We and so on) and its *concrete content* is determined by its position in the totality of social and historical conditions and circumstances (slave, capitalist, pope, revolutionary and so on).

The relationship of Man to Man and of Man to other people may become a play, if a second assumption is fulfilled: each actor or player, on the basis of the encounter of his actions with those of others, learns to know, or may learn to know, who the other individual is and who he is himself, but he may also disguise his intentions, hide his face, or be deceived by others. The relationship of people in the play becomes concrete through the dialectics of acting and knowing. The individual performs a certain historical role within the framework of what he has learned and what he knows. Does this mean that knowledge and action are variables, that the individual performs his historical role more perfectly the more he knows? The real actions of the individual are not based only on the *quantity* and *quality* of information (correct or incorrect knowledge, probable and uncertain information) but especially on the way it is interpreted. Consequently efficiency of actions is not and need not be adequate to the quantity and quality of knowledge since rational activities may be interwoven with irrational actions. The relationship between action and knowledge is realized by way of calculation and forethought, by way of premature, timely or belated information and actions, by way of conflict between what is expected and what is unexpected. The third assumption is the relationship between past, present and future. In the metaphysical conception of history the future is determined on the general and basic level and is open and uncertain in details: these secondary factors, which cannot disturb or interrupt the basic predestined trend, open up the field of activity to significant and insignificant individuals. The principle of play undermines this metaphysical determinism inasmuch as it neither conceives the future as ready-made on the basic level nor as complete in details but rather considers the future a wager or risk, and uncertainty and ambiguity, a *possibility* penetrating into the basic tendencies and details of history. Only the interplay of all three assumptions or elements comprise the play of history.

The differences between the theories of Marx and Schelling, as we have cited them are as follows: in Schelling's view, history is both the appearance of a play and the play of appearance, whereas Marx considers history to be a real play and a play of reality; to Schelling history has been written before people perform it and the play of history is prescribed, for only thus may the

> entire arbitrary play of freedom which each individual plays for himself (*aus dem völlig gesetzlosen Spiel der Freiheit, das jedes freie Wesen . . . für sich treibt*) become something that is reasonable and harmonious (*etwas Vernünftiges und Zusammenstimmendes*).

This predestination of history turns the historical play into a sham drama and degrades people to mere actors and finally to puppets. With Marx, on the other hand, the play of history must be performed before it is written, in fact, be first played in order to be written, because its course and outcome is in the play itself, that is, it is part of the play, springs from the historical activities of individuals. Schelling had to place the creator (Providence, Spirit), the one guaranteeing the rationality of history outside history or more specifically outside the play, whereas for Marx the rationality of history was simply the rationality *in* history which is realized through the struggle with the irrational. History is a real drama: its outcome, the victory of reason or nonreason, of freedom or slavery, of progress or obscuratism, is never decided beforehand outside history but only within history and its events. Consequently the elements of uncertainty, incalculability, openness and inconclusiveness that *appear* to active individuals as ten-

sions and things that cannot be foreseen are the constituent components of real history. The victory of reason is never decided definitely
at any point: to claim this would mean to annul history. Every epoch
fights the battle for *its* reason with *its* nonreason and every epoch
realizes an attainable degree of reason through its own means.

This infiniteness of history assigns to the present its real meaning as
the moment of decision and returns to each individual his share of
responsibility for history. To leave the definite solution of anything
to the future means a surrender to illusions and mystification.

In history there are not only actors but also spectators; one and the
same individual may at one point take an active part in events and
at another time only look at things. There will be various types of
spectators: he may be a person who has already played and lost his
game or he may not yet have entered the play and may view it with
the intention of some day taking part in it; moreover there are persons
who are actors *and* spectators simultaneously, who as participants in
the play contemplate its meaning. There is a difference between views
about the *meaning* of the play and contemplation on how to acquire
the technique and rules, so that the play will have meaning for those
who consider it as an opportunity to assert themselves.

Can the individual grasp the meaning of the play that is performed
in history? Is it necessary to step out of history to learn what history
is, i.e., is it first necessary to lose in history to discover its truth? Or
is it necessary to perform the play to the very end, inasmuch as its
meaning is revealed to the individual at the moment of death and
death is the privileged moment in which truth reveals itself? Twelve
years after the French revolution, Hegel wrote in his notes about the
reasons for the fall of Robespierre:

> The necessary happens but each part of necessity is usually assigned to
> individuals. One is the prosecutor and advocate, the second is the judge,
> the third the hangman; but all are necessary.

Hegel's necessity, however, is an illusion because he evokes the
appearance of unity where there is contention, he obscures the sense
of the individual roles and identifies the play with a play which has
been *agreed upon* beforehand. History is not a necessity which happens but a happening in which necessity and chance are interwoven
and where lords and serfs, hangmen and victims, are not components
of necessity but exponents in a struggle which is never previously

decided and in which mystification and demystification play their parts. Either the victims discover the play of the hangman, the accused that of the judges and the heretics, that the play of the inquisitor is a false one: they refuse to play the parts assigned to them and thus spoil the play. Or else they do not discern it and submit to the play, which deprives them of their freedom and independence: they evaluate their actions and look at themselves through the eyes of their fellowplayers and express this surrender and loss of their own personality in the prescribed formulae: *Ich, Stinkjude* (I, bloody Jew . . . and so on). Since they act and speak as captives of their counterplayers, they do not escape their confines, and therefore it seems to future observers that they played a *prearranged* play.

III

The conception of history as a play solves a number of antagonisms that could not be overcome by antinomic principles; it introduces dynamics and dialectics in the relationship between history and the individual; it breaks out of the limitations of the one-dimensional view and shows history as an event of several dimensions. Still this solution is not satisfactory either. On the one hand, history as a play cannot be identified with a play as such because the play of history differs in a number of essential points from a real play. On the other hand, the principle of the play may be used not only to explain history, but human life in general and, in this sense, a consistent solution must have the capacity to explain the relationship between history and human existence. Apart from this, we must explain why a play may become a principle disclosing and showing the dialectics of history, i.e., ask whether this principle discloses the dialectics of history fully and adequately and whether the play is history's true principle, in the sense of source, beginning and foundations.

Does an individual turn into a historical individual only if he enters history or is drawn into it, and does history originate only in consequence of an individual's activity? In this view, as history originates from the chaos of individual actions and is the law of relations that are independent of every individual, the acting individual is *originally* unhistorical and history is constituted only subsequently. The individual is historical only as the object of history, that is, as far as he is *determined* by his position in the line of time, in the historical context and in the social and cultural pattern.[3] Further history appears as an object, i.e., as a product of individual actions in which the objective process governed by recognizable laws which we call history, originates.[4]

If we reduce history to an object, i.e., to the objective process governed by recognizable laws and either resulting from the chaos of individual actions or predestined by a superindividual factor to which the great individual is related as an instrument and the ordinary individuals as a component part, we include in the foundations of history the notion of reified time. This notion of reified time in the theory of history manifests itself as the supremacy of the past over the present, of recorded history over real history, as the absorption of the individual by history. History as a science of past events investigates completed history, that is, is interested in history as it has passed. If history is the object of science and represents the past in the outlook of the historian, it does not follow that real history has only one time-dimension or that the one time-dimension marks history's concrete time. The historical event, which is examined by the historian as a past event and about which he knows how it passed and what its results were, in reality passed in such a way that its outcome was not known to its participants and the future was present in their actions as a plan, as a surprise, as an expectation, as a hope, i.e., as an incomplete happening. The laws of the objective processes of history are the laws of completed past events that have already lost the historicity which was based on the unity of three dimensions of time which are now reduced to one dimension, to past time. These laws have only a general character and in this sense are laws of "abstract history" in which the most essential factor has disappeared, namely, historicity.

The principle of the play might disturb the metaphysical antinomic conception and discover dialectics in history because, in the foundation of history, it anticipated the three dimensions of time. But it cannot explain its discovery and therefore recognize that the play itself has a time structure and is based on the three dimensions of concrete time.

The relationship between history and the individual is not only a

[3] In this sense, the historical position of the individual is interpreted among others by Dilthey, Ges. Schriften, vol. VII, p. 135.

[4] "Processus objectif, régi par des lois connaissables que nous appellons l'Histoire," G. Lukács, Existentialisme ou Marxisme, Paris 1948, p. 150.

question of what the individual can do in history but also what history can do with the individual. Does history tend to support the growth of the individual or does it tend to support the growth of anonymity and impersonality? Has the individual a voice in history or are the possibilities of his activities and initiative limited in favor of institutions? Marx and Lukács refused the romantic illusion that there exist certain privileged spheres that are protected from the expanding process of reification. Romanticism petrified disconnected realities in the authentic spheres of poetry, idealized nature, love, childhood, imagination, dreaming, which are powerless historically, and in reified reality in which the socially important events take place; it also creates the impression that the privileged spheres first mentioned are largely immune to reification and may become automatic sources of authentic life. As in the criticism referred to here, historicity was not consistently linked with the individual, and Marx's most important philosophical discovery, the notion of *praxis*, was interpreted more or less as a social substance *outside* the individual and not as a structure of the individual himself and of all individuals. The analysis of the reified modern industrial society's relationship to the individual led to practical consequences opposed to those that were intended.

The discovery which revealed modern society's depersonalization and disintegration of the individual, as well as his tragic position within the given possibilities and realities, that discovery which rightly stressed that only the revolution, as a collective action could stop the individual's fixation, failed to answer the question of what the individual should do so *long* as this reification continues. The criticism asserted that objective reality appears to the individual as a complex of ready-made and unchangeable things toward which the individual may have a positive or negative attitude, accept them or refuse them; in addition it also admitted that only the social class is capable of effecting practical changes of reality. There is no doubt that the individual cannot change reified reality, but this does not entail that the individual should *primarily* be defined in the light of reified reality or that he exists only as an object of reified processes. By reducing the individual to a mere object of reification, history is deprived of human content and becomes an empty abstract scheme. The existential moments of human *praxis* like laughter, joy and fear, and all forms of concrete, everyday, common human life, such as friendship, honor, love and poetry, are separated from historical actions and events as if they were "private," "individual" or "subjective" affairs. Or else they are seen in the light of a one-sided, functional dependence and become subjects of manipulations (manipulations of honor, courage and so on).

Man cannot exist except as an individual, but this does not mean that every individual is a personality or that the individual, claiming for himself the right to individualism, cannot live the life of the "masses." Similarly the social character of the individual does not entail a denial of his individuality, and human sociability does not conflict with personal anonymity. If we understand individualism as a priority of the individual before the collective, and collectivism as subjecting the individual to the interests of the whole, according to the slogan "Gemeinnutz geht vor Eigennutz" (public interest comes before self-interest), the two forms are identical in that they deprive the individual of responsibility. Individualism means the loss of responsibility in that Man as an individual is a social being; collectivism means loss of responsibility insofar as Man remains an individual even in the collective.

There is a difference in principle, whether Man as an individual disintegrates in social relations, whether he is overwhelmed by them and deprived of his own appearance so that hypostatized social relations employ uniform and anonymous individuals as their instruments (in which case the transposition seems to represent the supremacy of the all-powerful society over the powerless individual), or whether the individual is the subject of social relations and freely moves within them as in human and humanly respectable surroundings of people retaining their own appearances, i.e., of individualities. Individuality is neither an addition nor an unexplainable irrational remainder to which the individual is reduced after subtracting the social relations, historical situations and contexts and so on. If the individual is deprived of his social mask and underneath there is no hint of an individual appearance, this privation bears witness only to the worthlessness of his individuality, not to his nonexistence.

The individual may enter history, i.e., the objective processes and its laws, because he is already historical in two senses: he is always the actual product of history and simultaneously the potential maker of history. Historicity does not come to the individual after his entry into history or after his being dragged into it; rather, historicity itself is the prerequisite of this history, i.e., of history as an object and law. Historicity pertains to every individual; it is not a privilege but the constituent element of the structure of human existence that we call *praxis*. History as an objective structure, and historical events, could not be introduced into the life of the individual in any way if the individual were not marked by historicity before such introduction. Historicity does not protect the individual from becoming a victim of events or toy in the play of circumstances and accidents: historicity does not exclude chance but includes it. Historicity does not mean that all people might be Napoleons and did not become Napoleons merely "as a result of certain circumstances," or that in the future after the removal of reification, all people would become Napoleons.

The historicity of the individual is not only his ability to evoke the *past*, but also his ability to integrate in his individual life what is *generally* human. Man, just like his *praxis*, is always *imbued* with the presence of others (his contemporaries, his predecessors, his successors) and he takes over the present and transforms it either by acquiring autonomy or not acquiring it. Autonomy means: first, to stand, not to be on one's knees (the natural posture of the human individual is to hold up his head, not to be on his knees); second, to show one's own face and not to hide behind a borrowed mask; third, to portray courage, not cowardice; and fourthly, to remain *aloof* from oneself and from the world in which he lives and to include the present in the totality of history, so that in the present may be distinguished the particular and the general, the accidental and the real, the barbaric and the human, the authentic and the nonauthentic.

The well-known dispute about whether the imprisoned revolutionary can be free and whether he is more free than his jailer is based on a fallacy: the dispute is based upon a confusion about the difference between freedom and autonomy. In jail the revolutionary is deprived of his freedom, but he need not lose his autonomy.

Autonomy does not mean to do what others do or to do something different than others, but neither does it mean to do something regardless of others. Autonomy is an independence of or isolation from others. It means establishing contacts with others in which freedom can exist or can be realized. Autonomy is historicity, the center of the activity in which the instantaneous and the "metatemporal," the past and future, unite; it is the totalization in which universally human qualities are reproduced and revived in the particular (the individual).

The individual can change the world only in cooperation and conjunction with others. But even in reified reality and change of reality and in the interest of a really revolutionary change of reality, every individual as an individual has *occasion* to express his humanness and preserve his autonomy.

In this connection, we can understand why the *goal* of effecting structural changes in society and achieving the sense of revolutionary *praxis* is, for Marx, embodied neither in the great individual nor in a powerful state nor in a potent empire nor in a prosperous mass society, but is rather

> the development of that rich individuality which is universal in its production and its consumption, and whose labour no longer appears as work but as the full development of the activity itself, in which natural necessity has disappeared in its immediate form, . . . the universality of necessities, abilities, enjoyments, forces of production, etc., of individuals produced in the universal exchange . . . free development of the individuality . . . and the cutting of society's necessary labour to a minimum, to which reduction the individual's artistic and scientific education corresponds, because of the time which is now free and the means which have now been created for all.[5]

COMMENT

A. James Gregor

Commenting on papers delivered by colleagues is, at best, an onerous responsibility. Such a responsibility requires that the enterprise be undertaken with conscious and scrupulous good will, a will to devote oneself

---

[5] "die Entwicklung der reichen Individualität, die ebenso allseitig in ihrer Produktion als Konsumtion ist und deren Arbeit daher auch nicht mehr als Arbeit, sonder als volle Entwicklung der Tätigkeit selbst erscheint, in der die Naturnotwendigkeit in ihrer unmittelbaren Form verschwunden ist . . . die im universellen Austausch erzeugte Universalität der Bedürfnisse, Fähigkeiten, Genüsse, Produktivkräfte etc. der Individuen . . . die freie Entwicklung der Individualitäten . . . und die Reduktion der notwendigen Arbeit der Gesellschaft zu einem Minimum, der dann die künstlerische, wissenschaftliche etc. Ausbildung der Individuen durch die für sie alle freigewordne Zeit und geschaffnen Mittel entspricht. *Grundrisse der Kritik der politischen Ökonomie*, Berlin 1953, pp. 231, 387, 593.

wholly to the unbiased search for meaning and truth. But more than that, such a responsibility presumes the capacity on the part of the commentator to understand what is being said. I can, without hesitation, certify to my own good will. What I cannot certify is my ability to understand what Professor Kosík has said. The reason I entertain such misgivings will become apparent in the course of my comments.

I am not concerned with the introduction to Professor Kosík's paper—his account of various "metaphysical" interpretations of history. I have not understood much of that, but I do not think this constitutes a serious disability since I do not think understanding it would substantively assist me in understanding the remainder. My difficulties become serious only when Professor Kosík begins the exposition of his own views.

In Part II of his paper Professor Kosík seems to maintain that he is searching for a "principle" which is the "beginning" of history, the "foundation from which . . . movement springs, in which reality is manifest. . . ." He evidently respects "universality" and "particularity" as such principles. I find myself in *prima facie* agreement with him—because I am not sure that any *principle* can be conceived as the beginning of history, the foundation from which movement springs and in which reality is manifest. I cannot seem to fathom what it means to say that a principle is the beginning of history much less the foundation from which movement springs. Is the principle a part of history or only the foundation from which it springs? Metaphors employing "beginning," "foundation" and "springing" suggest, it seems to me, that the principle under consideration *precedes* and is *extrinsic* to history, while the insistence that the principle is that in which "reality is manifest" suggests that the principle is *immanent* in history. All of which leaves me somewhat confused.

Now Professor Kosík has attempted to assist me by identifying his principle. Once the principle with which he is concerned is identified one would expect that my puzzlement would abate. Unfortunately it seems that I have failed Professor Kosík again, for he informs me that the principle of history is the *play*. The principle of history, the principle which constitutes its beginning, the foundation from which movement springs and in which reality is manifest, is the *play*, the *drama*. I remain puzzled.

I must confess that I have never thought of the drama, the play, as the principle from which all movement in history springs or in which reality is manifest. Needless to say, I have frequently heard historians refer to the "role" people "played" in history. But I always thought that this exemplified picturesque speech and patter. Never once did I imagine that the principle of history was being revealed. And I must further confess that even after having submitted myself to Professor Kosík's paper several times

I still do not know what it means to say that the principle of history is the play . . . or the drama . . . or the game. Certainly people will talk of the "drama" of history, or even the "game" of history. But surely such locutions are metaphorical. Their authors do not usually pretend to be advancing a knowledge claim. In speaking of the drama of history, one does not seriously maintain that he has discovered that history really *is* a drama, still less that the *principle* of history *is* the play.

Conscious, apparently, of the reader's bewilderment, Professor Kosík goes on to indicate that he will really concern himself with the idea that "identifies history with a play." Then I find myself thrice confounded. Either the play is the *principle* from which all movement springs, in which reality manifests itself or it is *history.* One cannot seem to have it both ways, for if history is the play and the play is the beginning or the foundation of history, then it would seem that history is the beginning or the foundation of history—which is not very informative.

But then I am not at all sure what to make of the identification of history as a play. By the middle of his paper Professor Kosík informs us that "history as a play cannot be identified with a play as such because the play of history differs in a number of essential points from a real play." Such an analytic distinction seems to be promising. History is not a play at all. It is something *like* a play. Significant disanalogies obtain between history and a play. It is only necessary to specify them. In this regard we are told, first of all, that "history as a play . . . is open to everyone and to all. . . ." Now certainly this is a significant difference between any play we might be familiar with and history as a play. Then we are informed that not only does everyone, as such—but whole "classes" and "nations" as well—take part in history as a play. Not only does history as a play have a staggering cast of characters, but the cast includes hypostatic entities as well. More peculiar still is the fact that history is a play in which we are sometimes actors and sometimes spectators, apparently in something like an audience participation program. Certainly a most uncommon sort of play. But more than all that, history is a play, Professor Kosík tells us, that is written only after it is performed. A most extraordinary play. One begins to wonder in just what sense *is* history a play? As far as I can determine history is a play in so far as history has a *meaning.* Certainly plays are expected to have meanings, if not a meaning. History, according to Professor Kosík, has, in fact, a meaning. He talks about *the* meaning of the play that is performed in history. It seems that the meaning of the play is freedom and independence and living the authentic life, because Professor Kosík talks about plays within plays some of which are "false" plays and "false" plays deprive men of their freedom and independence and authenticity. One should refuse to play an "assigned" part in such a "false" play. This seems to be what Professor Kosík is saying.

My reasons for hazarding such an interpretation rests on what Professor Kosík seems to say concerning history, historicity, *praxis* and autonomy. He tells us, first of all, that *historicity* is the most essential factor in or the "prerequisite" of history. Then he proceeds to tell us that "historicity . . . [is that which] we call *praxis*." This seems to establish an equivalence. Then he tells us that "autonomy is historicity." This seems to establish their equivalence. Thus by simple substitution we have *historicity* equivalent to *praxis* and since *historicity* is also equivalent to *autonomy*, all three are substitution instances of each other and we can say that historicity, or *praxis*, or autonomy is the most essential factor in or the prerequisite of history. All that seems necessary at this point is to discern what any of the three terms, historicity, *praxis* or autonomy, mean. And Professor Kosík is quick to provide just such a definition:

> Autonomy means first, to stand, not to be on one's knees . . . ; second, to show one's own face and not to hide behind a borrowed mask; third, to portray courage, not cowardice; and fourthly, to remain aloof from oneself and from the world in which he lives and to include the present in the totality of history so that in the present may be distinguished the particular and the general, the accidental and the real, the barbaric and the human, the authentic and the nonauthentic.

All of which suggests that Professor Kosík thinks that history is a peculiar kind of play, which is not really a play at all but which has a meaning. The meaning of the play is autonomy which is the essential or prerequisite of history, which is really a play which is not a play. Autonomy, which is *praxis*, which is historicity, means that one should not be on one's knees, should not wear a mask, should be courageous and should not confuse the particular with the general, the accidental with the real, the barbaric with the human and the authentic with the inauthentic. Such an account is, of course, preposterous and I am sure that Professor Kosík intends nothing of the sort. It seems to indicate that I have not understood anything Professor Kosík has labored so hard to convey, a fact which grieves me, for he approves of many things dear to all of us. I know that Professor Kosík advocates a personality for each individual and that he objects to depriving men of their freedom, independence and appearance. I am sure that we are all convinced that men should have freedom and independence—and that each should certainly have an appearance.

There are, I am sure, many other convictions we share with Professor Kosík and I look forward to the time when he chooses to give us a Marxist account of them.

A REJOINDER

K. Kosík

From the many conceivable kinds of philosophical polemics, Professor Gregor has chosen the one which is most considerate and gentlemanlike to the opponent: his basic objection amounts to saying that he does not understand what I am saying. This objection is of course a quite current flattery among philosophers. Indeed, whenever did a philosopher understand another philosopher; in particular, whenever did living philosophers understand each other?

Accordingly, I should like to thank Professor Gregor for having given me the opportunity to articulate my conception in a clearer and more intelligible way.

First, I wish to stress that it was not my intention to promulgate a new and further principle of history or to claim that history is a play. The critical and polemical part of my paper I may summarize as follows:

a) the deterministic conception of history does not leave a place open for the activity of individuals and it cannot explain concrete history;

b) the relationship between history and the individual cannot be solved by proceeding from a conception of history uncritically accepted or by confusing the historical individual with the great individual;

c) the conception of history as a play represents a progress as opposed to the deterministic conception but still it is not satisfactory.

My own conception which is contained in the third part of my paper may be summarized as follows:

a) there is an intrinsic connection between history and time; real historical time is three-dimensional and therefore cannot be reduced to one dimension, for example, the past;

b) once one has realized that time is the foundation of history, it becomes possible to grasp the connection between history and the individual; for then history and the individual are not two independent magnitudes but rather have a common foundation, namely, three-dimensional time;

c) accordingly, I do not look for a principle of history which is above and outside history; rather, I try to show that time is history's foundation. From this point of view I am trying to indicate the connection between, but not identity of, *historicity*, *praxis* and *autonomy*.

To my commentator's friendly invitation to give a Marxist interpretation of these concepts, I may say,

first, that my whole paper precisely is an attempt to treat this question—an attempt which may of course be considered problematic and questionable, and,

secondly, that as difficult as it may be for all philosophers, including Marxists, to advance a satisfactory treatment of the problem of freedom, the individual and history, it ought to be clear that Marxism does *not* entail either a negation of the individual in terms of a history consisting of suprapersonal forces or an interpretation of the individual as a means.

Part II:

The Impact of Marx and Marxism on the Non-Communist World

9: MARX'S IMPACT ON EUROPEAN SOCIALISM

Gerhart Niemeyer

Upon closer scrutiny, "Marx's impact on European socialism" turns into a number of equations with many variables. It presupposes an entity called "socialism" which on its historical path encounters one Karl Marx. Supposedly Marx then changed or reconstituted this entity. On the other hand, one can hardly imagine Karl Marx as a phenomenon without this socialism which he became cognizant of and which helped to constitute him and his ideas. Marx was a living person, an identifiable substance. Socialism, by contrast, received its identity at least partially through Marx's awareness and classification of what he and Engels called by that name. This awareness, an aspect of Marx's process of self-realization, in its turn became a phenomenal factor changing socialism in the public consciousness. It would take more than a brief paper to untangle these complex relationships. At any rate, an inventory of "socialism" at the time of Marx's arrival in Paris seems to be a useful starting point.

I

The term 'socialism' is a name meant to establish a collective identity of a number of public phenomena. Lorenz von Stein acted as the namegiver in 1842 when he listed a number of common characteristics in the movements and ideas which he gathered under the designation "socialism and communism in France." First and most prominently, he linked these phenomena with the then new distinction between state and society from which resulted theses about supposed "contradictions" between political forms and social structures. Next he focused on the notions of freedom and equality stemming from the French Revolution and the shift of these aspirations from the political to the economic realm. The problem of freedom and equality viewed in the economic perspective was called "the social question," a question frequently linked with the institution of private property. Then again von Stein pointed to the aspirations of a new subdivision of society, now called "class," the industrial workers. They were often referred to as the "most miserable and most numerous class," which designation conferred upon them an ideological significance. "State and society," "freedom and equality," "the social question," "the working class," "private property"—all of these were the main elements in Lorenz von Stein's composite picture of "socialism."

However other features did not easily fit into this descriptive definition. The air was full of charges of "inherent contradictions" in the present social order and of speculations about a future society that would be free from all such contradictions. Among these speculations were quite a few that centered neither in the working class nor in the property question but rather in other alleged causes of present disharmony and other hopes of future harmony. If such speculations are included in the definition, there are "socialisms" that envisage no solution of the "social question" and no role for the proletariat. Extending the horizon still further, one notes that the fall of the *ancien régime* in France had caused much guessing about the age that would ensue, most of which centered in the characteristics of an industrial, technocratic and utilitarian society rather than in socialism.

Lorenz von Stein's depiction of socialism should be further enlarged to comprise the eighteenth century. Long before the "working class," the "industrial age," the alleged "contradictions between state and society," we have socialisms rooted in a rejection of religion or morality or both. One has in mind such names as Meslier, Morelly, Mably, Deschamps and many others. They rejected the social order and, indeed, civilization as such as false and inhuman and appealed from it to an alleged order of nature which they postulated as free from oppression and vice, particularly the supposed root-vice of avarice, since common labor, common property and common consumption were said to bar all shortcomings of human existence. Here was a kind of antitheistic religion, or antimoral ethics in terms of which many intellectuals formulated a message of world-immanent salvation and coupled a worship of "nature" with a total rejection of history as embodied in the past and present social orders.

Another school of thought accepted historical societies and civilizations but saw them as products of an automatically propelled forward and upward movement of the "total mass of mankind" (Turgot) in which impersonal forces would weave patterns of inevitable progress out of self-seeking human activities. In lieu of an appeal to nature, we have here an appeal to alleged "laws of history" construed as an evolutional necessity and yet crowned with a vision of millennium that was ultimately borrowed from Christianity.[1]

What is remarkable is that both those who believed in the perfection of the "order of nature" and those who put faith in the beneficence of historical causal laws met in their hopes for a new and transfigured world, a "world that will change its nature without ceasing to be the world in which we live concretely."[2] It seems that this kind of "metastatic" hope, the vision of a radically different human existence in this world, is the real common denominator of socialism. Von Stein would have done better to call socialism a gospel of world-immanent redemption from common human evils and social shortcomings. Its characteristic note is the pulling of transcendental hopes into politics and economics, the mutation of charity into social engineering and the replacement of the love of God by the love of "humanity." This characterization would have permitted a significant distinction between socialism and what one might loosely call the "labor movement."

Like all ideological movements, socialism had its incubation period, which ended just as Marx appeared in Paris. At the time of Robespierre, socialism was not yet fully articulated, even though one notes a few steps in the socialist direction. But already in Babeuf's conspiracy, which was meant to carry through Robespierre's ultimate intent, a considerable articulation of communism was attained. After a dormant period, socialism and communism finally crystallized in a number of variations during the period from 1830 to 1848. Bazard definitively formulated Saint-Simonism in 1829. Buonarroti published his account of Babeuf's conspiracy and message in the thirties, and around these concepts Blanqui organized his cadres. Lammennais

---

[1] The merging of the concepts of evolution and the millennium appeared first in Thomas Burnet's semiscientific, semiprophetic speculations about evolution culminating in a terminal world conflagration from which a perfectly harmonious world society would be born. Cf. E. L. Tuveson, *Millennium and Utopia*, Berkeley 1949.

[2] E. Voegelin, *Israel and Revelation*, Louisiana 1956, p. 452. Voegelin proposes the term 'metastasis' for this kind of hope.

brought out his first important work in 1832, Proudhon his in 1840, Louis Blanc in 1841. In 1838 Considérant summed up Fourierism, and in 1840 Cabet wrote his Voyage en Icarie. These, plus a number of quickly founded and quickly disappearing revolutionary societies and periodicals, were the crests rising above the ground swell of a drive for a world, new in harmony yet the same in substance and energy. From 1789 on, seekers for this new world hopefully looked on every revolution as the magic wand that would effect a basic change and, when the morning after revealed that nothing basic had changed, immediately resolved to try again, more radically. Thus 1789 was followed by 1792 and 1796; the July Revolution of 1830 by uprisings in 1832, 1834 and 1839; the February Revolution of 1848 by the June revolt of the same year; and the dreamed-for democracy and universal suffrage by the call for "social dictatorship."

In the Paris of 1843 Marx encountered: a great multitude of revolutionary societies, revolutionary journals and books, new versions of the millennarian gospel every few years and in all of this the turbulent convergence of three currents—the destructive rationalistic fury of the Enlightenment, the gestation of an immanentist Gnostic[3] religion and the real or supposed pressure of newly emerging social elements. Socialisms in France oscillated back and forth between these three, now stressing one over others, then seeking to combine all of them into a single formula. How did this activity appear to Marx, and how did Marx appear in the perspective of French socialism and communism?

II

Marx, too, looked for a total metamorphosis of the world, which he called "this dehumanized world," "this political animal world," out of the negation of which he expected to obtain the "true reality," the "social truth." If the common denominator of socialism is the commitment to the vision of a never experienced harmony in the setting of this empirical world, socialists would differ from each

---

[3] The term 'gnostic' has been applied to modern ideological movements by G. Quispel, Gnosis als Weltreligion, Zürich 1951; H. Jonas, Gnosis und spätantiker Geist, Göttingen 1964; The Gnostic Religion, Boston 1958; and, most prominently, by Eric Voegelin, The New Science of Politics, Chicago 1952, and "Religionsersatz," in Wort und Wahrheit XV (Jan. 1960), pp. 5–18.

other in the choice of some single factor of experience to which they would reduce the problem of present evil and future perfection. Marx, confronted with these various constructions, had to make his place among them. It is instructive to see which ones he rejected. First, in repudiating traditional religion he also repudiated the endeavors of Saint-Simon, Fourier, Comte and Feuerbach to replace Christianity with a new immanentist cult, a civil religion designed for the utility of the new society. Secondly, he scorned Proudhon's insistence on justice, i.e. normative reason, and Lassalle's kindred emphasis on the state. Thirdly, he found no attraction in Morelly's and Fourier's (and, to some extent, Helvétius') reduction of social order to the passions and their confidence that the passions, once released from false constraints, would prove to be unfailing sources of harmony. In other words, Marx discarded the spiritual, rational and appetitive elements of human nature as experiential assumptions from which a metastatic world could be constructed. At the same time he insisted that "the new world must be positively elaborated." Thus Marx proclaimed his fundamental distrust in the elements known to compose human experience, and consequently one looks in vain for the materials from which he could take the stuff of such positive construction.

Marx's total critique of man and his faculties is first cousin to that of St. Augustine who also saw human loves, reasoning powers and appetites bent and perverted by man's inclination to prefer himself or some created good to the Creator himself. Like Marx, Augustine was persuaded that man in this fallen condition could not be counted upon to produce a genuinely harmonious social order, real peace or true justice. Unlike Marx, though, Augustine never lost sight of Creation's original goodness even in man's most perverted strivings and what is more, he perceived the action of divine Grace in its healing of human corruption and never attributed to evil a positive reality. The love of God is thus man's true orientation to being, the beacon of order in the midst of corruption.

Curiously enough, we find a similar idea in Marx. In September, 1843, he wrote to Ruge: "Reason has always existed, but not always in reasonable form." In other words, present disorder contains the hidden essence of real order. From this premise Marx drew the programmatic conclusion that "the critic can begin with any form of theoretical or practical consciousness and, from the forms characteristic of present reality, develop the *true reality as its norm and its final destiny*" (italics mine). Critique here becomes the tool to establish not-yet existing truth through the negation of the given, unreasonable forms of theoretical and practical consciousness. Such a Hegelian program could make sense on an assumption that consciousness evolves through successive dialectic stages of unreason with each stage more closely approaching the ultimate from which point alone the entire movement could be recognized as that of reason. But without the assumption of a *logos, physis,* or even Absolute Mind, how can one expect to find a hidden "norm" or "final destiny" in present unreason? Marx postulated that consciousness derives from modes of production. On this evidence, the critique of present forms of theoretical and practical consciousness could at least lead to the underlying forces of production rather than to anything like a *telos.* Thus Marx's program as stated to Ruge could not be implemented. It was based on a Hegelian faith in the *eidos* of history but had jettisoned the indispensable Hegelian metaphysics.

It is the contention of this paper that the key to Marx is his insistence on a Hegelian program of critique in spite of his rejection of Hegelian metaphysics. In his letter to Ruge he speaks of the "ruthless critique of everything that exists." The term 'ruthless' already indicates the form which "critique" would have to take in Marx's view; moreover critique must become practical action, or, more precisely, armed force. This requires power, and power adequate to a total critique could be found only in "the masses." Consequently the masses would have to become the armed force of critique. This would come about, however, only as the result of "radical needs." At this point Marx proceeded to that definition which set him off from all the other socialists who thought of the proletariat as "the most miserable and most numerous class," the "suffering class" or, at most, the "industrial class." Marx's program called for a negative power, a mass element with "radical needs," and he defined it as an "estate that is the total loss of humanity," the "actual dissolution of order," a class that "is nothing." Obviously he specified what was needed for his program of total practical critique rather than describing what could actually be observed. The meaning of this definition is that Marx, desiring to draw the truth from the false forms of present reality and unable to accomplish this by intellectual procedures, shifted his task to the revolutionary armed force of nihilistic masses. Man's "true reality" would be liberated through the proletariat's "nothingness." This *productio ex nihilo* would take the shape of a massive insurrection, not a mere seizure of power but rather a total subversion that would not even "leave the pillars of the house standing."[4] Hegel's futurism, minus the "Absolute Mind," thus was turned into a blind faith in the salutariness of total destruction.

Marx's formula for this faith is "negation of the negation." Again Marx embraced Hegel's logic while rejecting Hegel's metaphysic. Provided that consciousness, representing the becoming of the Absolute Mind, is the reality of political order, a dialectical upward motion of consciousness would indeed proceed by way of negation of any given stage of order to a new and higher one. In the Hegelian perspective, no society or stage of consciousness would be wholly devoid of all reason, although every one of them would have a flaw until the final stage of "absolute knowledge" was attained. Had Marx applied the concept "negation of negation" in Hegel's sense, even with his materialistic modification of Hegel, the "bourgeois society" would have been described as the "negation of the feudal society" that, in turn, was the negation of a previous type and so on—each phase drawing its elements of rationality from the negation of the predecessor's flaws and all of them participating in the rationality of the entire process of becoming. Now Marx's "negation of the negation" does connote the uprising of the proletariat against its bourgeois masters, but what is negated by this negation is not merely the bourgeois society, i.e., one of the phases of history. Rather the proletarian revolution negates the "negation of humanity," and that negation has another name in Marx's vocabulary: alienation. Not only the bourgeois society but *all* types of society known to the historian fall under the category of "alienation," a general condition in which man is estranged from his life process, himself and his species. What is more, "alienation" appears not as a late fruit of decadent civilization but rather, similar to Freud,[5] as an organic flaw in the whole of humanity's known existence, since it stems from the division of labor which is connected with

---

[4] The quotations in this paragraph are from *Zur Kritik der Hegelschen Rechtsphilosophie* (1844).

[5] Cf. *Civilization and Its Discontents*, where Freud traces civilizational neuroses (his symptom of human alienation) to the late primates who began to walk upright, thus lost their limitation of sexual activities to the periodical olfactory stimuli and established the family with all its subsequent repressions.

such elementary facts as the sexual act and takes its first acute form in the separation of manual and intellectual work. 'Alienation' is Marx's term not for one phase of history but for mankind's entire recorded existence. Nowhere in that experience can Marx find anything that speaks of man's "true reality." All human history has been a continuous negation of humanity. While Hegel's "negation of the negation" is a passage of consciousness from a phase of more to one of less imperfection, a motion conceived in accordance with the known processes of the human mind (whatever one may think about its projection into the historical future), Marx's "negation of the negation" is a leap from a totally false human existence embodied in all historical societies into the harmony of a dreamworld, or, in ideological words, from the nonlife of the past and present into the "true reality" of the transfigured future.

That leap could be made only once and only by one negating force: the proletariat. For only the proletariat's revolution could "change the world." It is true that Marx had chided philosophers for merely "interpreting the world" and had added: "The point, however, is to change it." In this way Marx appeared to reserve the responsibility for change to philosophers of his persuasion. But Marx, the philosopher, no more accepted this charge than his predecessors. He had passed it on to a rebellious mass of people and concluded that their rebellion could not be ordered at will. A proletarian revolution would not come unless and until the proletariat became *conscious* of itself and its task as well as emotionally *indignant* about the "insufferable power" under which it chafed. This puts Marx back on the track of Hegel's dialectic of consciousness from which he supposedly had departed when he shifted from total intellectual critique to practical radical revolution. The consciousness of the proletariat could not be willed into existence. The philosopher, after all, could not change the world. He could do nothing more than to reflect on the requirements of change and then wait for these requirements to become realities.

There are in Marx two historical dialectics, rather than one. The first consists of the alleged laws of change from one type of society to the other, through economic developments conducive to legal and political upheavals. The other is the dialectic of alienation. The first, an explanation of how societies rise and fall, can be called a first cousin to the cycles of Polybius and the corso and ricorso of Vico. The reduction of power to property, the upward push of a formerly ruled class, the periodic breaking up of legal and political structures followed by the creation of new ones—all this is not an implausible picture by any means. If corroborated by concrete evidence which Marx failed to supply, this dialectic might serve as a useful tool in the prediction and assessment of historical developments, and it is in this capacity that Toynbee tried to make use of it in his *Study of History*. If this were indeed something one could rightly call a "law" of historical change, the change would go on and on. However nothing in this dialectic indicates a climactic end or even a necessary upward direction of the movement. All it says is that human institutions carry in them the germ of social decay and mortality.

The other dialectic is not concerned with periods of decline and reconstruction. It is a dialectic of redemption, or, to use Marx's own term, "the emancipation of mankind." Reversely one might call it a message of redemption through dialectic, the dialectic of consciousness. Instead of a series of changes, this dialectic envisages only one change: from alienation to the realm of freedom. History is divided not into a series of successive phases but rather into Before and After, or "animal existence" and the full human life. Passage from the old to the new occurs by force of man's awakening consciousness of his condition and the awareness of the whole of history. Marx himself points up this dialectic by declaring in the *Communist Manifesto* that the proletarian revolution differs from all other revolutions, and thereby he places it in a class of one. Simultaneously denying this attribute to other classes that have been instrumental in effecting the laws of historical change he calls the proletariat the "only really revolutionary class." Nor does the proletarian revolution belong to the series that is characterized by the cycle ownership-power-economic innovation (new property—revolution—new power). It is not new property but "consciousness of its historical mission" which constitutes the proletariat's subversive power. Georg Lukács[6] has argued that proletarian consciousness has nothing to do with the actual thoughts and feelings of workers but rather consists in the "identity of subject and object, theory and practice, freedom and necessity." It is a consciousness that already transcends the dualities from which man suffers in this vale of alienation. Another term of Lukács by which he designates the revolutionary energy is "troubled consciousness" that recognizes and thereby

[6] *Geschichte und Klassenbewusstsein*, Berlin 1923.

overcomes man's present condition. While the first dialectic of Marx, that of periodic social change, belongs to the realm of socioeconomic necessity, the dialectic of redemption is a dialectic of man's self-awareness and thus occurs in the area of human freedom.

The two dialectics can be distinctly traced in Marx's works. In the *Communist Manifesto*, for instance, the rise of the bourgeoisie is described in terms of the discoveries, new trade routes, the development of manufacture and later of large-scale industry, the opening of a world market and the enormous increase of capital. In connection with each of the economic developments Marx reports some corresponding political "progress." Subsequently he outlines the supposedly parallel rise of the proletariat in utterly different terms. No economic developments, no achievements of political "progress" mark the path of the proletariat, only a series of battles and engagements in the course of which the proletariat is said to become a class. This is the dialectic of struggle, of consciousness, of conscious unity. Not only the *Manifesto* but also *Das Kapital* presents a drama of consciousness rather than a process of material necessity. *Das Kapital* is structured like Dante's *Inferno* in that it takes the reader through increasingly hellish circles of alienation, starting with commodities and commodity production through the "fetishism" of money, the subservience of commodities to the desire for capital and finally concentration, centralization, and the annihilating pauperism and industrial reserve armies. At that lowest point, when the movement cannot descend any further, comes the dialectic redemption, the "expropriation of the expropriators."

It is almost customary to identify Marx through his historical materialism. Actually Marx himself made relatively little use of the materialistic dialectic of social change, so little in fact that Kamenka could remark of historical materialism that it is a "theory formulated loosely, ambiguously, without proper care, never demonstrated in a single case, frequently ignored and virtually subverted in the discussion of concrete social developments."[7] Marx presented only a rough sketch of this dialectic in the *German Ideology*, restated it in most sweeping terms in the *Communist Manifesto* and summed it up in one neat, all too neat, page in his Preface to *A Critique of the Political Economy*. The brief chapter on "Primitive Accumulation" in

[7] *The Ethical Foundations of Marxism*, New York 1962, p. 140.

Das Kapital is limited to one single country. Nowhere does Marx make an attempt to test his theory in a general morphology of history. Engels did when he encompassed mankind's history and prehistory in his slender volume *Origin of the Family, Private Property, and the State*, but that work at decisive points does not even corroborate Marx's ideas. Regardless of what Marx said and what the literature about him asserts, one must conclude that the materialistic dialectic of periodic change occupied a back seat in his mind and that his love was for the dialectic of alienation, the passage from false existence to true reality. This we must regard as the core of Marx.

Why, then, would Marx have two dialectics? The answer is contained in a phrase of the *Communist Manifesto* where Marx, having first described the rise of the bourgeoisie according to the necessity of economic development and accretion of social power, passes on to the treatment of the proletariat with the words: "A similar movement is going on before our eyes." What he then describes is actually not at all similar to the rise of the bourgeoisie as noted above. The remark, however, serves a purpose. The proletarian revolution represents the emancipation of mankind. By passing it off as a movement "similar" to one of the periodic changes of social order, Marx creates the impression that the redeeming event must come with inexorable necessity. Or, to put it differently, Marx seeks an ultimate goal of "true reality," a "final destiny" of man. The comparison of the proletariat's mission with the economically determined rise of the bourgeoisie de-emphasizes the final cause but stresses an efficient causality, suggesting that such causality is fully knowable and reliable. An important side-effect results from this. The vision of redemption by a class that "is nothing," a full future life issuing from present total dehumanization is too absurd to be rationally accepted. That a merely negative consciousness would have that kind of power would have to be taken on faith and blind faith at that. Now when Marx asserted that the proletarian revolution was a movement "similar" to one of these changes that occur with regular necessity, he removed the requirement of faith and substituted for it what looked like a scientific prediction. For this kind of reassurance, a loosely knit theory of superficial plausibility supported by a smattering of evidence would do, in fact it would be preferable to a carefully elaborated theory with a full battery of tests that would merely challenge opposition. For when one's glance is kept steadfast on the ultimate result of future freedom, it is only out of the corner of one's eye that one notes the alleged causal necessity which supposedly guarantees the eventual realization of this future. The millennium could now be possessed as if it were a fact, and faith never entered into the picture.

III

The above assessment provides us with a key to the difference between Marx and the socialism and communism of the mid-nineteenth century. Marx believed in the redeeming power of the negative consciousness; all other socialists put their trust in some kind of positive consciousness. Babeuf, who was the father-in-revolutionary-spirit of Blanqui, had pursued the realization of the rights of man as originally proclaimed by the Jacobins. Everyone concerned with the "social question" envisaged some sort of positive solution. Those whose attention centered in the proletariat deserving a place in the sun had a variety of plans about the distribution of political power, civil rights, cultural benefits and wealth. Most socialists announcing the message of a wholly new world proclaimed positive principles that were to govern it, principles drawn from this or that assumption about human nature and society. Such purposes engaged the will in constructive tasks in legislation, power arrangements, economic organization and cultural initiative. They also implied reliance on the power of normative reason to engineer positive goodness in the world.

Marx had stepped out of this circle when he decided that man was impotent to will justice and that radical negation alone contained any hope of real life. He had hit on the concept of a "class with radical chains" as the power substratum, whose "radical revolution," i.e., movement of total destruction, would accomplish what no philosopher could plan and no statesman directly will. This introduces into Marxism a typical waiting attitude, a deliberate renunciation of the intent to create beneficial results. Marx, of course, demanded that the philosopher, instead of contemplating the world, engage actively in the task of changing it. But this was not a positive activism directly creating a redeemed humanity. Revolutionary negation alone had that creative power. The will of the philosopher, i.e., the revolutionary leader, must focus on the struggle of the "class in radical chains," i.e., on the means and methods of tearing down the house of the present society, including its pillars, all the while trusting that from total negation would emerge eventually the harmony of the total man. Marx prohibits the revolutionary will to commit itself to an ideal blueprint. Pending the advent of the future world, goodness is wholly negative. It is the duty of the revolutionary will to concentrate on the task of destruction.

Even though the problem of the state never loomed very large in Marx's attention, it is here that the difference between him and other socialists comes to its practical point. Socialists of the constructive variety, who envisaged some kind of social engineering, looked on the state as their foremost potential instrument of positive change. They thought in terms of constitutional arrangements, new laws and different administrative practices. Marx from the outset tended to brush the state aside; in his *Critique of Hegel's Philosophy of State* he had called the state a "mere illusion," mainly because he assumed that all social and political power ultimately roots in the ownership of the means of production. On this evidence, Marx would have to conclude logically that the proletariat which by definition had no property could not wield political power and could have no state of its own. Engels, somewhat naively, did indeed draw that conclusion, but Marx again abandoned the materialistic dialectic and based his position on the dialectic of alienation. For him the proletariat was not so much the "most miserable" and the "suffering" class as the incarnate power of negation which required a machinery of political might as a tool of a negatively oriented struggle. Marx assigned to the proletarian political regime the task "to make despotic inroads on the rights of property" and to "sweep away by force the old conditions of production"—wave upon wave of destructive measures "outstripping themselves" and then "necessitating further inroads."[8] In other words Marx differed from other socialists in looking upon the state as a necessary but primarily destructive instrument. In keeping with this view, he spoke of the revolution, in so far as he defined it in his writings in the early fifties, not as a program of new constitutions, laws, rights and institutions but rather as a dialectic growth of the negating force, a movement from original weakness, through defeat, to greater strength, further defeat and further increase, accompanied by a simultaneous process of dissolution in the fabric of extant social power. In

[8] *Communist Manifesto.*

his 1875 *Critique of the Gotha Programme*, Marx indicated that this dialectic of power and struggle would continue even after the proletarian overthrow of the bourgeoisie through a period of transition whose length could not be predicted. It is the "accentuation of the negative," the exclusive attention to the dialectic of negating power, that is practically the chief meaning of the term 'scientific socialism.'

IV

European socialism began its period of major organizational growth about fifteen years after the 1848 disaster. At that time it was everywhere oriented along non-Marxist lines. In England first the Chartists and later the Fabians maintained a positive attitude toward the state. French socialism was predominantly Proudhonist and thus imbued with ideas of justice, mutualism and other positive principles of social order. Lassalle created German socialism and gave it a strong appreciation of the state that he hoped to control through universal suffrage. Bebel, who was no Lassallean, later confessed that he "like almost all who then became socialists got to Marx by way of Lassalle." Trade unions formed everywhere without any help of Marxist ideas. Apart from unions, other workingmen associations arose for educational purposes, consumers' cooperation and a sharing of cultural goods. Much of this had already taken fairly concrete shape before Marx's influence made itself felt on the second rebound, as it were. In Germany, Marx was accepted as an absentee leader after Lassalle's death which coincided with the founding of the First International. In France, and elsewhere, Marx's stock rose steeply after the Paris Commune and Marx's successful mythification of that event. The most important factor in Marx's upsurge during the seventies was, of course, the publication of *Das Kapital*. In Russia, where *Das Kapital* appeared translated in 1872, Marx's ideas became the center of a newly formed socialist movement under the leadership of Plekhanov. But in that country, by contrast, the alternative to rising Marxism was not a socialism of positive constructive intent but rather a tradition of revolutionary nihilism complete with its own literature, organization and terroristic practice. The influence of this tradition, in the person of Bakunin, could also be felt in Italy. Apart from that, though, European socialism in general aimed at economic improvements, legislative protection of workers, universal suffrage, civil rights of association and free opinion, cooperative institutions and cultural opportunities for the poor. State ownership or management figured as a means to obtain some of these objectives. To use the language of Lorenz von Stein, European socialism was a movement to assert workingmen's interests through the intervention of the state in the processes of society.

What, then, was Marx's impact on this movement? First, it occurred mainly in the realm of theory. The time for Marx's practical direction of European socialism had come and gone. In the First International, Marx and Engels never held undisputed sway, and when they finally triumphed over Bakunin, the hour of victory also marked the beginning of the International's end. Marx never returned to a position of practical political power. His influence, then, was that of his and Engels' books, mainly *Das Kapital*, to which should be added the *Anti-Dühring*, particularly in its abbreviated form: *Socialism, Utopian and Scientific*. This influence was great and sustained. In the nineteenth century, Marx was the last of the great socialist system builders (forgetting Dühring, for the moment), who made his entrance when the Fouriers, Owens and Saint-Simons were already nearly forgotten, and the Proudhons and Lassalles had shot their bolts. Marx's was the only system of socialist thought that made its bid *after* the socialist movement had become organized, conscious and active in many countries and the need for an ideological foundation had come to be acutely felt. The delay in completing *Das Kapital*, which Engels so often deplored, actually redounded to Marx's greatest advantage in that people who already were engaged in practical activities now turned to Marx as a source of rationalization of their programs. On the other hand, Marx's belated entry also resulted in certain limitations on his influence. English socialism never came even close to Marxism until after 1945. In France, only one among many competing groups was Marxist. Only in Germany and Austria Marx attained something like a dominating influence over a country's entire socialist movement, even though Lassalle's influence never wholly disappeared and eventually reasserted itself powerfully.

All over Europe, socialists sought to participate in, or gain influence over, the state. In France, a socialist became a cabinet minister before the end of the century. German Social Democrats eagerly sought not only a parliamentary majority but also power positions in local government. In Belgium, Holland and Sweden, socialist parties pursued the objective of universal suffrage which is essentially an alternative to seizure of power by direct action. In England and Germany, socialists moved the governments to pass legislation in the workers' interests. Many of these advances were small, to be sure. All the same, the trend pointed in the dirction of legislative solutions of the "social question" and the problem of working class political participation.

Marx's influence, injected into this stream of activities, may be defined through the three "proofs" in which he himself summed up the gist of his message in his letter to Weydemeyer of March 5, 1852: "proof" that classes appear as a result of certain developments in economic production; "proof" that the struggle between classes must eventually culminate in the dictatorship of the proletariat; "proof" that the dictatorship of the proletariat will give rise to a classless society, i.e., a realm of harmony and freedom. The conviction that Marx had indeed proved these three points found wide acceptance among people of socialist persuasion. As a result, socialists began to believe that a future millennium could be expected on the basis of "scientific prediction." Otherwise sober men and women who hitherto had worked for the improvement of their conditions and were committed to the idea of social reforms, now abandoned themselves to moods of radical negation and the cultivation of a permanently revolutionary force, which in turn forbade them to tolerate reforms except as stratagems for the purpose of increasing revolutionary strength. Two generations of European socialists entertained the illusion that their reformist practices and their revolutionary theories were compatible with one another.

Thus Marx's influence can be traced in attitudes that had been alien to the socialist movements and could at most be found among Bakunin's adherents. Socialists began to look on history as if it were a causality of purposeful motion superordinated to human wills and to assent to some vague obligation according to which one ought to conform to history's alleged necessity; they substituted a knowledge of history for ethics. They began to think of the proletarian revolution in terms of the end of "all that exists," and at the same time to take it for granted as if it were an indisputable historical fact. They swallowed all this as if it did not require faith, or at least as requiring faith only in Marx and his alleged "proofs" which faith came easy to people who, while admitting not to have understood Marx's Das Kapital, were convinced that his economic language certified the method of strictest science. Thus Marx supplied a quasi-religious vision to people who were under the impression that in giving themselves to it they never had to compromise their inviolate rationality.

As a result, European socialism, insofar as it came under Marx's influence, acquired two faces. On the one hand, it worked within the state and aimed to gain influence in, and possibly to hold control over it. On the other hand, it moved in an ideological dreamworld without a state and envisaged radical destruction as a supposedly certain road to a free and harmonious society. Neither its opponents nor its adherents could tell which of the two faces was the real one. Much unnecessary fear issued from this split personality of European socialism, and much harshness on both sides was the unhappy result.

Had the two faces of European socialism been able to dispute with each other, their argument would have concerned mainly the evaluation of the state: a structure of order in the eyes of one and a power for destruction in the other's eyes. As long as socialism was nothing more than a group of minor sects, that argument would have been purely academic. But by the end of the century, socialist parties were powerful enough in many countries to wield real influence, so that the support of, or opposition to, this or that piece of legislation or cabinet became a weighty responsibility. It was then, when socialist parties had to decide no longer on abstract concepts but on practical policies, that the split in socialism's personality grew into a fissure between two factions. The fissure manifested itself in the first decade of the twentieth century. Finally it was a supreme test of one's attitude toward the state, the outbreak of the war in 1914, that caused it to widen into a rupture between two camps. In 1914 one could clearly see that the face of European socialism which had been turned toward the *second reality*[9] of a millennium had not been the real one. Out of the test of 1914 grew the split into Social Democracy and Communism. But one can also say that it was 1914 that marked the beginning of a gradual separation of European socialism from Marxism, a separation that is now more or less complete in all major socialist (as distinct from Communist) parties.

Marxism's union with European socialism had turned out to be a passing affair: it lasted no more than one-half of a century. After the

[9] The concept of a "second reality," i.e. a fictitious world built up in man's mind and then confused with and substituted for the real world, stems from Robert Musil's novel *Der Mann ohne Eigenschaften*.

bond had weakened and in some places approached dissolution, Marxism found new homes: one in the various branches of Russian revolutionary nihilism, another with the disaffected Western intelligentsia where it became a kind of academic *ersatz*-religion of metaphysical discontent. As for European socialism, it outlasted its dalliance with Marx. All the same, the forty some years of Marxist gnosticism have left their indelible mark. European socialism once had been confident in its supposed possession of an infallible "science" of historical destiny. When that "science" turned out to be mere fiction, European socialists felt the void of a profound disappointment and found it hard to regain their former self-assuredness. While under Marx's spell, they had pushed aside other possibilities of justifying and rationalizing their cause, for instance, Christian socialism, so that it is now extremely difficult for a socialist to find his place among the current views of man and society. European socialism has grown into a movement characterized by practices and organizations rather than consistency of ideas.

As for Marx, he belonged structurally to a lineage of millennarian ideologies which first arose as Christian heresies in the late Middle Ages, later merged with scientific ideas of evolution in the seventeenth century, and appeared entirely without any reference to their biblical sources in the eighteenth century. Their common characteristic is a future society on earth, free from authority, government and law, and immune to vice, poverty and war. Marx had combined this ex-Christian heresy with the notion of "laws of history," meaning the causally inescapable succession of certain "phases" or types of society. This idea was the eighteenth century's substitute for Augustine's theology of history which had been publicly disestablished by Voltaire. In both regards, Marx was of an ideological lineage that had just about spent itself by the middle of the nineteenth century and of which he was the last prominent representative. De-Christianization lent some strength to Marx's message so that it could appear as if it were a real alternative, but on the other hand the socialist movement with which it merged had already adopted strong reformist views which always resisted the radical nihilism of Marx. While socialism, after the Marxist interlude, continues as a movement of welfare policies, Marx now occupies a position befitting his ideological genealogy: the prophet of history proclaiming a world-immanent salvation to men who have ceased to believe in God.

10: MARX AND AMERICAN DEMOCRACY[1]

Maximilien Rubel

I

In proportion as our means of information and communication have become more powerful, we find ourselves less prepared to resist the terrorism of words and myths. At the same time, there is an increasing contrast between our scientific knowledge and technical skills and our incapacity to establish harmonious relations which would allow mankind to live without fear of war, starvation and disease.

Among the words which are charged with all our hopes and fears, there is one which seems to express the common faith of all peoples and political regimes: democracy. It has a magical effect on our minds and has thus become the stakes for which the rival hemispheres of our world seem ready to accept total war.

In dealing with the nineteenth-century problems of a historical scope, we must take great care to separate the concepts we are using from the connotations they may have acquired in our century. This is particularly necessary when dealing with a subject like "Marx and American Democracy." In using the word 'democracy,' we are tempted to associate it with the experience we have acquired in our time which is often considered as the fulfillment of the democratic ideals of the past century. This is all the more true when the word 'democracy' is related to the body of doctrines of a thinker like Marx, doctrines assumed to have been wholly or largely realized under the name of Marxism in, at least, one-third of the world.

It is my intention in this paper to distinguish as clearly as possible Marx's own ideas from those of Marxism of any kind. Whatever we may believe of the intellectual and practical consequences of the

[1] This paper originally was delivered at Wesleyan Ohio University on April 22, 1966.

teachings of Marx, we must always keep in mind that they were formulated in a certain historical context. Consequently the question of whether the so-called Marxist achievements of our time correspond to Marx's ideas cannot be passed by without a critical confrontation of Marx's expectations and the present day reality, whatever label it may wear.

Thus speaking of Marx's "communism," I am excluding systematically every connection between the notion held by Marx and modern so-called socialist or communist regimes.

II

Marx started his intellectual career by participating in the political struggle conducted by the German liberals and democrats in the 1840's against Prussian absolutism and the feudal remnant of the Prussian state. He was a practical liberal and a democrat before he held a theoretical conception of democracy. His articles in the *Rheinische Zeitung* reflect his philosophical culture rather than a historical and sociological insight into the problems of his time. Although spellbound by Hegel's system during his university years, Marx succeeded in escaping from the seduction of Hegel's political philosophy through the study of Spinoza. Feuerbach's and Spinoza's doctrines on democracy and human liberty conceive of human perfection in the realm of nature and society while they provide the individual with a chance of freedom through wisdom and love. Marx held an ethical notion of democracy before he started his historical and sociological studies. Moreover he formulated this notion in opposition to Hegel's idealization of the monarchical state and its bureaucratic institutions.

In an unpublished manuscript intended to be an exhaustive criticism of Hegel's political philosophy, Marx describes democracy as "the solved riddle of all constitutions," as "the essence of all political constitutions," and "man socialized as a particular constitution" in the same way as Christianity is the essence of religion—"man deified in the system of a particular religion."[2]

Commenting on this early opposition of Marx to Hegel, Professor Easton correctly states: "Here is Marx's first conception of socialism

---

[2] *Kritik des Hegelschen Staatsrechts*, MEGA, I, 1/1, 434 ff.

in outline."[3] I would add that the subsequent critique by Marx of the *Bill of Rights*, while including the rejection of the bourgeois form of democracy, does not involve an absolute rejection of democracy. On the contrary, *true democracy* has to be realized in a communist society. But democracy, in Marx's eyes, is not only an aim in itself, it is also a means which, if it is respected by the bourgeois regimes, must finally turn against the dominant class. It is evident that the conquest of political power is guaranteed to the proletariat through the normal functioning of democracy; while concealing a dictatorial relationship between exploiting and exploited classes, a real divorce between fundamental rights and material oppression, the exploitation of the majority by the ruling minority, bourgeois democracy, through the instrumentality of the universal suffrage, will necessarily lead to the triumph of the working class. But, in order to achieve this aim, universal suffrage has to be changed—as Marx will declare shortly before he died—from an instrument of dupery into a means of emancipation. Thus bourgeois democracy grants to the working class political emancipation and ultimately social or total emancipation.

III

Marx's idealistic vision of democracy, as opposed to Hegel's metaphysics of the state (defined by Hegel as the embodiment of the moral Idea) was difficult to relate to any existing state at that time, whether in Europe or in America. However what Marx had in mind was a humanist vision of a social order conceived as an ethical postulate or aim and as the leading norm of political action.

In order to confer on his postulate or aim a maximum of historical and sociological evidence, Marx left the public scene (after the suppression of *Rheinische Zeitung* where he fought as a liberal against Prussian censorship of the press). He buried himself deeply in the study of the revolutionary history of France, England and America, and it was through these historical studies that Marx obtained the empirical evidence that *political* democracy must—under certain material and moral conditions—result in *social* democracy, that is to

---

[3] Address for a symposium on "Alienation," organized by the Society for the Philosophical Study of Dialectical Materialism, Chicago, Apr. 29, 1956.

say in *communism*. We must always keep in mind that Marx then conceived communism as *humanism*.

The following definition is quoted from the Paris manuscripts of 1844 (known as the *Economic and Philosophical Manuscripts*):

> Communism is . . . , for the next stage of historical development, a *real* and necessary factor in the emancipation and rehabilitation of man. Communism is the necessary form and the active principle of the immediate future, but communism is not itself the aim of the final form of human society.[4]

In other words, the aim of communism is *humanism* which Marx defines in the same *Manuscripts* as the

> . . . final resolution of the antagonism between man and nature, and between man and man. It is the true solution of the conflict between existence and essence, between objectification and self-affirmation, between freedom and necessity, between the individual and the species. It is the solution of the riddle of history and knows itself to be this solution.[5]

I must insist greatly on the fact that Marx arrived at this position (as a communist and a humanist) not by studying political economy but by his historical studies after the suppression of the *Rheinische Zeitung*. His extant notebooks of this period show that for the most part he was interested in European history, and especially in the history of the bourgeois revolutions of England, France and the United States. Among the historical literature from which he took large excerpts, we find extensive notes from Thomas Hamilton, a Scottish writer who described the United States at the beginning of the 1830's. Hamilton's *Man and Manners in America* was published in 1833 and appeared in German in 1834.[6] Marx read this work and made his extracts during his Kreuznach period, that is to say, on the eve of his taking up the cause of the workers' emancipation. Although there is no mention of other sources on America excerpted in the notebooks available at present, we know of two other documents read by Marx probably at the same time: Alexis de Tocqueville's *On Democracy in America* published in 1835 and 1840, and Gustave de Beaumont's

---

[4] MEGA, I, 3, 126; cf. Karl Marx, *Economic and Philosophic Manuscripts of 1844*, trans. by M. Milligan, Moscow 1961, p. 114.

[5] MEGA, I, 3, 114; cf. *Economic and Philosophic Manuscripts*, p. 102.

[6] Thomas Hamilton, *Die Menschen und die Sitten in den Vereinigten Staaten von Nordamerika*, Nach der 3. engl. Aufl. übersetzt von L. Hout. Zwei Teile. Mannheim 1834.

Mary or Slavery in the United States published in 1835. In his Paris exile, Marx interrupted his historical studies, and after the failure of the Deutsch-Französische Jahrbücher (which incidentally contained his first communist profession of faith) he began his economic studies.

IV

It is my conviction that Marx's vision of American democracy and of its revolutionary potentialities—a vision which he derived from the readings mentioned—was decisive for his adopting, as early as 1843, the workers' cause, even before he started his critical analysis of the capitalist system.

In fact, these readings differ from the classical studies on European revolutions in that they are remarkable by their foreboding tone. They do not only give descriptions; they express hopes and fears, admiration and criticism, enthusiasm and indignation. Moreover they instructed Marx on what one may call the discernible collective mentality of the different classes of American society. What strikes one when reading these documents is, above all, an impression of violent contrasts but also latent antagonisms which announce social conflicts of unimaginable vehemence.

Two of these authors, Alexis de Tocqueville and Thomas Hamilton, are interested not only in American reality but also in the problematic content of this reality. It is not American democracy as it really functioned which was the main concern of the French and Scottish visitors but its concealed potentialities of upheaval. What Tocqueville saw in America was, as he wrote, more than America; what he sought there was the image of democracy itself. Tocqueville's book begins and ends with the same magic invocation which is moreover what I would call the leitmotif of the whole work: equality. The more Tocqueville advanced in the study of American society, the more he perceived the "equality of conditions" as the fundamental fact from which all others seem to derive. He saw in the gradual development of this equality a "providential fact" and a "Divine decree," and he wrote: "is it conceivable that the democracy which has annihilated the feudal system and vanquished kings will respect the citizen and the capitalist?"[7]

[7] Alexis de Tocqueville, Democracy in America, trans. by H. Reeve, London 1838, vol. I, p. XVI.

What Tocqueville considers as a divine decree will become with Marx a "historical necessity," namely, the inevitable evolution from capitalism to socialism, or—to put it in Hegelian terms—the unavoidable "negation of negation" as expressed by the abolition of the capitalist mode of production through the instrumentality of the modern working class. Tocqueville may have transmitted to Marx his religious emotion as laid down in the following honest confession of the French aristocrat.

> What appears to me to be man's decline is advancement to the eye of the Creator and Preserver of men; what afflicts me is acceptable to him. A state of equality is perhaps less elevated but is more just; and its justice constitutes its greatness and its beauty. I would strive, then, to raise myself to this point of the divine contemplation, and thence to view and to judge the concerns of men.[8]

Hamilton, like Tocqueville, a visitor to the United States although an earlier one, evidenced in his account of America the same historical instincts as Tocqueville. Marx could not remain indifferent to certain striking facts as reported by Hamilton. We have seen that in spite of this fear that democracy may lead to the tyranny of the majority, Tocqueville was essentially optimistic about the social and economic prospects of democratic regimes. As for Hamilton, his insight upon certain economic features of American society allowed him to recognize a tendency which, in Marx's conception, could become a decisive factor in America's future, namely, the class struggle.[9]

Commenting on what he calls the progress and tendency of opinion among the people of New York, Hamilton describes the "separation" which rapidly takes place between the different orders of society. He speaks of the "operative class," which has formed a society under the name of "the WORKIES" and is "in direct opposition to those who, more favored by nature and fortune, enjoy the luxuries of life without the necessity of manual labor." The first demand of these workers is "equal and universal education." The existence of an aristocracy of knowledge, education and refinement, they argue, is "inconsistent with the true democratic principle of absolute equality." These are the moderates of the party. But there are others who go still further. They constitute the *Extreme Gauche* and boldly advocate the

---

[8] A. de Tocqueville, *De La démocratie en Amérique*, ed. by A. Gain, Paris 1951, vol. II, p. 453 ff. The second volume, published five years after the first, that is, in 1840, has not been translated by Reeve. [Editor's note]

[9] Cf. Marx's excerpts in *MEGA*, I, 1/2, 135 ff.

introduction of an agrarian law and a periodical division of property.

Hamilton predicts that America is destined to become "a great manufacturing nation" with a laboring population congregated in masses and exposed to the perpetual fluctuations of the market, menaced by commercial crises. And then he enounces a prophecy in the purest "Marxian" style and speaks of the "suffering class" in which will be "deposited the whole political power of the state." Thus democracy must lead, according to Hamilton, to "anarchy and spoliation"; it is only a question of time and it will depend on peculiar circumstances of every country. In England, the process will be faster. In the United States with the great advantages they possess, it may last longer, but, says Hamilton, "the termination is the same. The doubt regards time, not destination."

Marx had only to substitute for the words "anarchy and spoliation," used by the aristocratic Scotchman, the word 'communism,' as he did with Tocqueville's concept of equality; he had only to give to Hamilton's premonitory warnings the theorical coating; and American democracy as seen by Thomas Hamilton and Alexis de Tocqueville would constitute one of the inspiring elements of the theory of social revolution which Marx elaborated during the two or three years preceding the edition of the Communist Manifesto.

From that time, Marx showed keen interest in American economic and political development, particularly after the conquest of the Pacific coast, the discovery of the gold mines in California and the phenomenal growth of railroad networks of the country. One can find in Marx's and Engels' writings of this period a real glorification of the civilizing task the United States would have to assume in "dragging the recalcitrant barbarian peoples into civilization" and thus playing on an international scale, in modern times, the role which Italy played in the Middle Ages and England afterwards.

It is not possible to analyze here Marx's attitude toward the United States as compared to tsarist Russia with respect to the political history of the European powers particularly during the Oriental crisis and the Crimean War. Let me only remind you that Marx's phobia for Russia led him to pronounce the most definite warnings against the tsarist messianic strivings toward world domination; this can be explained by his profound hatred of the absolute state as represented by the tsarist regime; in Marx's eyes, the economic alienation of man is embodied in money and capital, in the same way as man's political alienation is symbolized by the state, be it democratic or absolute.

However democratic institutions, be they "bourgeois," are among the main prerequisites for the political action of the working class.

Despite the fact that Marx's main work, *Das Kapital*, is primarily the result of a study of British capitalism, American economy did not cease to preoccupy him, as is illustrated by the numerous references to American capitalism in his studies and writings.

But it was the outbreak of the American Civil War which furnished Marx with an opportunity to turn his attention not only as an economist and a sociologist but also as a democrat and revolutionary to the unrolling of the struggle.

All that Marx wrote about the Civil War reflects remarkable understanding of the political evolution of the United States since the War of Independence as well as a profound comprehension of the development of the Southern cause which led up to that outburst.

> . . . the true people of England, of France, of Germany, of Europe, consider the cause of the United States as their own cause, as the cause of liberty, and despite all paid sophistry, they consider the soil of the United States as the free soil of the landless millions of Europe, as their land of promise, now to be defended sword in hand, from the sordid grasp of the slaveholder. . . . The people of Europe know that a fight for the continuance of the slavocracy—that in this contest the highest form of popular selfgovernment till now realized is giving battle to the meanest and most shameless form of man's enslaving recorded in the annals of history.[10]

From the outset Marx understood the conflict between the North and the South as a struggle of two diametrically opposed social systems, the one being based upon slavery and aristocratic law and the other on free labor and popular rights. Let me quote a few excerpts from Marx's articles written for *Die Presse* of Vienna in 1861–1862:

> The whole movement was and is based, as one sees, on the *slave question:* not in the sense of whether the slaves within the existing slave states should be emancipated or not, but whether the twenty million free men of the North should subordinate themselves any longer to an oligarchy of three hundred thousand slave-holders; whether the vast territories of the republic should be planting-places for free states or for slavery; finally, whether the national policy of the Union should take armed propaganda of slavery in Mexico, Central and South America as its device.[11]

The present struggle between the South and the North is, therefore,

---

[10] *New York Daily Tribune*, Nov. 7, 1861; cf. MEW, XV, 326 ff.
[11] *Die Presse*, Oct. 25, 1961; cf. MEW, XV, 338.

nothing but a struggle between two social systems, between the system of slavery and the system of free labor. The struggle has broken out because the two systems can no longer live peacefully side by side on the North American continent. It can only be ended by the victory of one system or the other.[12]

Marx's state of mind with respect to the significance of the struggle and the revolutionary prospects of American democracy has found passionate expression in the address to Abraham Lincoln, which he wrote at the occasion of Lincoln's re-election in the name of the General Council of the International Working Men Association.

In drafting the address, Marx had to take into account the feelings and convictions of the various members of the Council composed by different political tendencies; but on the other hand, it must be recalled that the main characteristic of Marx's position as a social theorist was precisely to start from human reality and human aspirations and not from some sweeping generalizations and indisputable dogmas.

Let me then quote a few passages from Marx's congratulating address to Lincoln after the latter's election.

> From the very beginning of the titanic American strife the workers of Europe instinctively felt that the star-spangled banner carried the destiny of their class. . . . When for the first time in the annals of the world an oligarchy of 300,000 slaveholders dared to inscribe "slavery" on the banner of armed revolt; when on the very spot where hardly a century ago the idea of a democratic republic had first sprung up, whence the first Declaration of the Rights of Man was issued, and the first impulse given to the European revolution of the eighteenth century . . . then the working classes of Europe understood at once . . . that the slaveholders' rebellion was to sound the tocsin for a universal holy crusade of property against labor, and that for the men of labor not only their hopes for the future but even their past conquests were at stake in that tremendous conflict on the other side of the Atlantic. . . . The workers of Europe feel sure that as the American War of Independence initiated a new era of ascendency for the middle class, so the American War against slavery will do it for the working classes. They consider it an earnest of the epoch to come, that it fell to the lot of Abraham Lincoln, the single-minded son of the working class, to lead his country through the unprecedented struggle for the rescue of an enchained race and the reconstruction of a social world.[13]

[12] *Ibid.*, Nov. 7, 1861; cf. *MEW*, XV, 346.

[13] *Der Social-Demokrat*, Dec. 30, 1864; for the English version, cf. *Daily News*, Dec. 23, 1864, and *Reynold's Newspaper*, Dec. 25, 1864 (both London). Cf. *MEW*, XVI, 18 ff.

I have restricted my inquiry to some views of the main aspects of what I would call Marx's *explicit* position on the political problems connected with American democracy. Lack of space prevents me from going into more details on Marx's idea with respect to the workers' movement in the United States particularly after the Civil War and the establishment of the General Council of the International Working Men Association in New York in 1872. Yet this is a problem which cannot be separated from Marx's general theory of the relationship between the economic structure of capitalism and the political struggle of the working class. At the same time, the question cannot be avoided as to whether the history of American capitalism and the workers' movement in the United States can, or cannot, be considered as a validation of Marx's social theory. These problems are permanently debated by scholarly Marxists and anti-Marxists. I would like to recall only that neither Marx, nor Engels after Marx's death, was doubtful about the final outcome of the evolution of American capitalism. In this respect let me quote a statement made by Marx in 1879 to an American journalist whether "the European socialists look upon America's movement as a serious one?" Yes, was Marx's answer, "it is the natural outcome of the country's development." And after having refuted the opinion that the movement "was imported by foreigners," then having emphasized that "socialism was not merely a local, but an international problem, to be solved by the international action of workmen," Marx declared:

> We see everywhere a division of society. The antagonism of the two classes goes hand in hand with the development of the industrial resources of modern countries. From a socialist standpoint the means already exist to revolutionize the present historical phase. Upon Trade-Unions, in many countries, have been built political organizations. In America the need of an independent workmen party has been made manifest. They can no longer trust politicians. Rings and cliques have seized upon the Legislature, and politics has been made a trade. But America is not alone in this, only its people are more decisive than Europeans. Things come to the surface quicker. There is less cant and hypocrisy than there is on this side of the ocean.[14]

If I may express my personal feelings about the validity or the invalidity of Marx's judgments, I would refer less to his explicit formulations than to the nonformulated implications which can be derived

[14] *Chicago Tribune*, Jan. 5, 1879.

from his social theory. The particular history of the birth and evolution of American society offers the key to the understanding of the particular features of the workers movement in this country. Remember that Vernon L. Parrington in beginning his monumental work on the *Main Currents in American Thought* could write this phrase: "The American Revolution remains after a hundred and fifty years somewhat of a puzzle to historians." Remember also that the true historiography of your country started (I hope I am not wrong) with Frederick Turner's theses as exposed in his remarkable book on *The Frontier in American History* in 1893 which can be considered as the best "Marxist"—I apologize for using this absurd epithet—interpretation of American history, an interpretation you can find in elementary form, it is true, in various writings of Marx dealing with the extraordinary historical adventure which is constituted by the territorial growth of the United States.

If you would ask me what Marx would think today of American democracy, I would not hesitate in answering that if he saw the actual and the virtual contrasts of contemporary American society, on the one hand, and the material and moral potentials of this country, on the other hand, he would consider that the United States possess, dialectically speaking, the best chances to give the world model of a humanist society. As a matter of fact, there is no country in the world today which implements to the same degree the human and technical conditions of a society in which, to quote Marx's definition of communism, "the free development of each individual is the condition of the free development of all." But these *potentialities* are contrasted absolutely, with the *actual* moral and political conditions of the same American society of our time: the concentration of wealth and power deprives the so-called "affluent society" of the advantages of highly mechanized industry, as measured by standards which Marx considered as corresponding to human dignity. As an American author put it recently: "Perhaps the ideal of a social and economic democracy—the hope of society erroneously said to exist in the United States today—will at least serve as the stimulus for its ultimate creation."[15]

[15] G. Kolko, *Wealth and Power in America*, New York 1962, p. 133.

11: MARXISM AND LATIN AMERICAN DEVELOPMENT*

Helio Jaguaribe

I. EARLY SOCIALISM

A. APPEARANCE OF SOCIALISM

Socialism appeared in Latin America in the 1840's primarily because of European immigrants and secondarily because of the indigent thinking of some intellectuals. The socialism brought by the European immigrants, mostly Italian, Spanish and German workers and some French émigrés of the revolution of June, 1848, and of the Paris Commune, was as varied and heterogeneous as the composition of the newcomers.

The French émigrés of 1848 were mostly Fourierists while the later "communards" were chiefly Proudhonists. Among the German workers, Marxism was predominant and they were responsible, particularly in Argentina, for the final preponderance of Marxism in the socialist movement. However it was the anarchist and anarcho-syndicalist tendency, brought principally by the Italian and Spanish immigrants, which prevailed in the late nineteenth century and which has been particularly important, even in a later period, in Mexico (around the Casa del Obrero Mundial and the Confederación Regional Obrera Mexicana) and in Argentina (group of La Protesta). These two groups have offered the strongest opposition to Marxism in the labor movements. Until the early 1920's, the anarcho-syndicalists kept their movements separated from the socialists. After the Second International and the split of the socialists, the anarcho-syndicalists, in

* Due to the great length of the paper originally delivered by Professor Jaguaribe at the Notre Dame Symposium, we are publishing only the second part of the author's contribution. Professor Jaguaribe will publish the paper in its entirety elsewhere. [Editor]

Latin America as elsewhere, joined the former and maintained their opposition to the Communist parties.[1]

Among the early Latin American intellectuals who engaged in the formulation of social ideas two groups were formed: first, those who developed really socialist ideas, mostly under the influence of the French Utopians, the Chileans—Francisco Bilbao (1825-1863), San Tiago Arcos (1822-1874), Martin Palma (1821-1884)—and in Peru, Manuel Gonzalez Prada (1848-1911); secondly those who became libertarian thinkers as Argentina's Esteban Echeverria (1805-1851), the author of Dogma Socialista (1839), and Chile's José Victoriano Lastarria (1817-1888).

B. THE PRE-MARXISTS

Pre-Marxist socialism has been relevant in Mexico, Peru, Brazil, Argentina and Chile. These countries were also the ones where the influence of Marxist ideas was significant before the organization of the Third International and the spreading, under its orientation, of Communist parties throughout Latin America.

In 1861 a Fourierist Greek tailor, Polonio C. Rhodakanaty, started the socialist propaganda in Mexico and with his disciples founded the Gran Circulo de Obreros de Mexico in 1870. They were responsible for publishing, in that same year, the first translation in Latin America of the Communist Manifesto. The Mexican labor and social movement, however, as in the other Latin American countries, followed the anarchist line. With some scattered groups throughout the country in the last third of the nineteenth century, the anarchists reached a major influence only with the Mexican Revolution. Ricardo Flores Magón (1873-1922) and his brothers have been the principal animators of this later anarcho-syndicalist movement that culminated with the foundation in 1906 of the Casa del Obrero Mundial and later in 1917 of the Confederación Regional Obrera Mexicana, better known by its initials CROM.[2]

Casa del Obrero Mundial was one of the most active groups dur-

[1] Victor Alba, Históriá del Movimineto Obrero en America Latina, Mexico 1964, p. 85 ff.
[2] Victor Alba, Las Ideas Sociales Contemporaneas en Mexico, Mexico 1960, p. 119 ff.; Marjorie Ruth Clark, Organized Labor in Mexico, Chapel Hill, N. C. 1934, ch. 2.

ing the Mexican revolution. Mobilizing the workers in favor of Carranza and Obregón, they contributed with "red battalions" entirely formed by workers and organized by the unions to the victory of the revolution.

Social thought in Peru came later. There were a few anarchist groups at the end of the nineteenth century. In that country, however, practically without immigrants and industries, the development of socialism and social ideas resulted only from the work of the intellectuals. An interesting fact is the circumstance that Peru, which remained a very traditional and patrician structure until after World War II, produced the three greatest social thinkers of Latin America: Manuel Gonzalez Prada (1848–1918), José Carlos Mariátegue (1895–1930) and Victor Raul Haya de la Torre (1895–   ).

Prada was the only one who was a pre-Marxist. Moreover his personality and work, relatively unknown outside Peru, deserve much wider interest. A well-educated member of the Peruvian aristocracy, he was the first to understand that the political troubles of his country were not due, ultimately, to the faults of the contending factions and their leaders but to the existing socioeconomic structure that kept the masses, particularly the Indians, alien from any participation in the national affairs while a small group of patrician families controlled all the sources of wealth and power and used the state to protect and perpetuate their privileges.[3]

Early socialism in Brazil was associated with the ideas and spirit of the June Revolution of 1848 and found its local representatives among the radical liberals of the province of Pernambuco. The movement of which Antonio Pedro de Figueiredo (1814–1859) was the intellectual leader because of his journal O Progresso (1846–1848), spawned a revolution in that province in 1848–1849. Until the formation of the Communist Party in 1922, other social movements have predominantly evidenced anarchist tendencies and for the most part have occurred among the Italian immigrants in São Paulo.[4]

The Argentina Italian immigrants have made the most important center of anarchism in Latin America. Although earlier the French socialists exerted some influence through the émigrés of the Paris

[3] Federico de Onis et al., González Prada, New York 1938; William Rex Crawford, A Century of Latin American Thought, Cambridge 1944.

[4] Vamireh Chacon, História das Idéias Socialistas no Brasil, Rio de Janeiro 1965.

Commune, the Italian anarchists asserted their predominance with Erico Malatesta (1854–1932) and particularly Pietro Gori (1869–1911) who in 1892 established the periodical *La Protesta,* which remained active for more than thirty years and which made him the most influential leader of anarcho-syndicalism in Argentina. For a long period the anarcho-syndicalists have exerted throught the Federación Obrera Regional Argentina (FORA) a dominating influence on her labor movement. That influence declined after the Third International and practically disappeared with the Peronista movement which acquired and maintained the control of Argentina's labor.[5]

In Chile, as in Peru, although at an earlier time, social movements were also started by the intellectuals. Francisco Bilbao, previously mentioned, published in 1844 his *Sociabilidad Chilena* and founded in 1850 along with San Tiago Arcos the Sociedad Igualdad. This first attempt of a popular and democratic movement whose three basic principles were 1.) the sovereignty of reason as the authority of authorities, 2.) the people's sovereignty as the basis of all political life and 3.) universal love and fraternity as the moral rule was immediately considered a subversive danger and dissolved by the government some months later; in addition their leaders were sent into exile. However the efforts of Bilbao and San Tiago Arcos were continued by some radical liberals in the course of the next three decades and later by Malaquias Concha (1859–1921) who in 1855 founded a periodical, *La Igualdad,* and in 1886 after separation from the radicals created a new Sociedad de la Igualdad. In 1887 that society became the Democratic Party which was for a certain time the political vanguard of social and popular movements in the country. Yet in the next generation that Socialist tradition acquired a Marxist line.[6]

II. THE SECOND INTERNATIONAL PERIOD

A. THE MARXIST PARTIES

Generally it can be said that the Latin American labor and social movements started under the influence of the French socialists (mostly Fourier), became predominantly anarchist and anarcho-syndi-

[5] Alba, *História,* 89 ff. and ch. 9.
[6] Julio Cesar Jobet, *Les Procursores del Pensamiento Social de Chile,* Santiago 1955, vol. I, ch. 1.

calist in the late nineteenth century and finally at the end of the last and in the first three decades of this century culminated in Marxism. However the influence of Marxism, besides being posthumous to Marx's life, evidenced more of an intellectual climate than effective organization and systematic doctrine. Only Argentina has had, and then in the period of the Second International, a Marxist party sufficiently close to the European models; this resulted precisely because Argentina in that period had so many features of a transplanted European society. The Argentinean Socialist Party, even before its transformation into an alienated instrument of the conservative forces —since the "década infame"—never became a mass party and always represented the immigrant more than the native worker.[7]

The Argentinean Socialist Party of Partido Obrero International was created in 1894. The party was founded by one of the small pre-existing socialist groups, the Agrupación Socialista, organized two years earlier and composed principally of Italian and French immigrants. After changing its name to Centro Socialista Obrero, the Agrupación called other socialist groups, notably the German workers of the Vorwärts, to join them in the foundation of the Partido Obrero. The Germans, then engaged in a campaign for the extension of political rights to the immigrants, did not want to affiliate themselves with a party until they achieved their former goal. In 1895, however, the Vorwärts group, and the recently created Centro Socialista Universitário together decided to join the Partido Obrero, which changed its name to Partido Socialista Obrero Argentino. José Ingenieros of the Centro Universitário was appointed the first secretary of the Central Committee. In the same year the name of the party was once again changed to Partido Socialista, and Juan B. Justo (1865–1928), who became the great leader and personal embodiment of the party, was selected its secretary.

The party had, as it can be seen, a rather appropriate origin from a Marxist standpoint: it resulted from an association of manual workers with intellectuals, by the initiative of the former and with an international spirit not only stated in its bylaws but effectively represented by the multinational composition of its membership. The fact that the Argentinean native workers were not attracted by the party

---

[7] Jorge Aberlardo Ramos, *Revolución y Contrarrevolución en la Argentina*, Buenos Aires 1957, p. 343 ff.

did not seem, at the time, to have any significance. The working class, then, was mostly composed of immigrants, and the nationals were either members of the higher classes or *peones* living in the countryside or still keeping their rural outlook in the city. This composition of the working class proved to be much more important than was originally foreseen. For the party was never able to overcome its foreign perspective and posture, a limitation which was, for the socialists of that time, particularly difficult to detect and to evaluate precisely because of their internationalist credo and their Marxist prejudices against any form of nationalism and any approach that would not pretend to be valuable from an international point of view. Founded to be the party of the working class and the great masses, the party was not able to extend its appeal beyond the restricted circle of specialist workers, mostly immigrants, and still less to mobilize the great masses. Eventually it gained academic and political respectability and became representative of a certain sector of the middle class, mostly composed of intellectuals and bureaucrats, who at the theoretical level adopted the most radical view but in a purely abstract form—a view which was essentially unconnected with their sociohistorical conditions and their concrete lives.[8]

Chile was the other Latin American country where Marxist socialism, although less systematic and with less continuity than the Argentinean Socialist Party, asserted itself in the beginning of the century. In spite of its looser organization that led to many futile attempts to constitute a socialist movement and to many ups and downs in its career, Chilean socialism ultimately reached a national importance which was never attained by the Argentinean socialism, and its meaning as a mass movement, usually in coalition with other parties of the Left, has been increasingly confirmed and reinforced by effective popular support.

Chilean Marxist socialism, after a long pre-Marxist past and after some unsuccessful attempts at organization principally in 1887 by Malachias Concha and members of his Democratic Party, was finally launched in a continuous form by Luis Emilio Recabarren (1876–1924), a former member of Concha's party and a typographer who became the great labor and socialist leader of his country. Recabarren's party was founded in 1912 under the name of Partido Socialista

8 Alba, *História*, p. 123 ff.; Ramos, *op. cit.*, p. 286 ff.

Obrero, and the story of Recabarren was an unending effort of the labor and socialist organization to receive from the conservative forces recognition and acceptance of his legitimate elections and hence his right to represent the working class in Parliament. After the Russian revolution the group followed the Leninist line and affiliated with the Third International. His never explained suicide in 1924, after returning from a voyage to the Soviet Union, has been interpreted by some as a final disenchantment with the Russian revolution.[9]

The coming years were crucial for Chilean political life: adoption in 1925 of a new Constitution (putting an end to the parliamentary stalemate existing since 1891), dictatorship of Ibañez in the late 1920's and the short-lived Socialist Republic in 1932. This latter event, proclaimed by a coup led by Col. Marmaduque Grove (1878–1961) on June 4, 1932, if unable to achieve the revolutionary purposes of its radical members, made a lasting impact on Chile and created the conditions that facilitated a succession of left coalitions from the "Bloque de Izquierdas" (1934–1935) to the Popular Front (1936–1941) and later the "Frente Popular" (FRAP) since 1957.[10]

B. Marxism and the Intellectuals

The influence of Marx on Latin American intellectuals has been almost completely posthumous. This fact could be explained by the socioeconomic backwardness of the region, which had not yet started its industrial revolution and which was lagging farther behind in cultural and education areas. Similar socioeconomic conditions—although with a net cultural advantage in their favor—did not, however, prevent the penetration of Marxism among the Russian intellectuals in Marx's own lifetime. It seems more pertinent, therefore, to attribute the Latin American intellectuals' late reaction to the French cultural imperialism, which was in its heights in the region until the 1920's and which tended to submerge Marxism beneath a wave of French positivism and eclecticism.

In that light it was not surprising that the only Latin American intellectual who was contemporaneously well aware of Marx's works

[9] Julio Cesar Jobet, *Recabarren*, Santiago 1955.
[10] Alberto Edwards Vives and Eduardo Frei Montalva, *História de los Partidos Politicos Chilenos*, Santiago 1949, p. 200 ff.

was the germanophile Tobias Barreto of Brazil. That extremely curious character, living in the Brazilian Northeast between the provin-
cial capital of Recife and his small native town of Escada—where he
published a paper in German of which he probably was the only local
reader—was quoting Marx among his cherished German philosophers.
His real understanding of the substantial aspects of Marx's writings
was more questionable than his information about them. While he
followed Marx's criticism of the utopian socialists (in part, certainly,
because they were French) and he acknowledged at the same time the
conditioning of man by the economic process and, what is more, the
historical nature of the latter and its changeability by man, he was led
to contradictory apologies for Bismarck and his role—placed by him
above social conflicts—and condemned the opposition to Bismarck.
Tobias Barreto's famous "Discurso em mangas de camisa" (jacket-
less speech) in the inaugural address of the Popular Club of Escada
(1877), founded by him, was as close to Marxism as it was possible
for one with his kind of intellectual confusion.[11]

After the interval of one generation, or more specifically in the
beginning of the twentieth century, Latin American intellectuals
started reacting to Marx. In Mexico, Antonio Caso made the first
explanation and critical discussion of dialectical materialism. In 1908
he founded the Ateneo de la Juventud, an agency for updating Mexican culture, spreading it to the people, promoting greater understanding of Mexican reality and encouraging the modernization of the
country. In 1912 the Ateneo created the Universidad Popular, which
was so influential in the course of the Mexican Revolution in developing and spreading a social-minded conception of democracy and
in attempting a synthesis between Western ideas and the national
requirements and character.[12] A generation later, Vicente Lombardo
Toledano, as an independent Marxist, played a relevant role in the
1930's and 1940's between the legacy of the Mexican revolution and
Marxism-Leninism, between the Mexican government and the labor
force and between the official party and the working class.[13]

In Brazil, Marx's writings, after their isolated earlier discussion by
Barreto, exerted a continued but moderate influence on the next two

[11] Chacon, op. cit., p. 265 ff.
[12] Alba, Las Ideas, p. 139 ff.; Crawford, op. cit., p. 276 ff.
[13] Vicente Lombardo Toleoano, Escritos Filosóficos, Mexico 1937; La Per-
spectiva de Mexico-Una Democracia del Pueblo, Ed. del Partido Popular 1956.

generations. Euclides da Cunha (1866–1909), author of the classic *Ōs Sertoes* (The Backlands), understood and supported the central theses of Marx. In 1901 he founded in Saō José do Rio Pardo the International Club, Sons of the Work, for the divulgation of Marxism, which he called "rationalism." Silverio Fontes (1858–1928), a physician converted from positivism to Marxism and a propagandist of the Republic, was the first Brazilian Marxist militant and attempted through his periodical *Ā Questao Social* to impregnate the republican movement (so conservative and middle-class minded) with a social content. Manuel Bonfim (1868–1932), only ten years younger than Fontes but historically belonging to the second republican generation, reflected in his works a Marxist view of Brazilian and Latin American society within a nationalist and regionalist framework.[14]

In Argentina, José Ingenieros (1877–1925) introduced the ideas and the *praxis* of Marxism before the end of the last century and was one of the founders of the Socialist Party. His theoretical work, however, was less influenced by Marx than his social ideas and remained, as a whole, within the frontiers of positivism. Juan B. Justo (1865–1928) was the most important political theoretician of Marxism at the end of the last and the beginning of this century while Anibal Ponce was the chief philosophical interpreter of dialectical materialism. Justo's Marxism was typical of the Second International period: democratic, reformist and implicity revisionist with a strong influence of Spencer's evolutionism. In Paris in 1895 he revised the first translation into Spanish of *Das Kapital*. In the same year he joined the Socialist Party and in the next founded the Centro Socialista de Estudios. The Biblioteca Obrera (1897) and the Universidad Popular (1904) expressed his constant concern with the education of the masses. Unlike Justo, Ponce was a pure scholar of strict Marxist orthodoxy. His work principally involved the dissemination of Marxism, either for the instruction of the workers (*El Vento en el Mundo*) or on a scholarly level (*El Momento Actual de la Filosofia, Educación y Lucha de Clases*). Under the harassment of the reactionary climate of the 1930's, he was obliged to emigrate to Mexico where he spent his last years.[15]

[14] Chacon, *op. cit.*, pp. 282–293 and 356–362.
[15] Luis Farré, *Cincuenta Años de Filosofia en Argentina*, Ed. Penser 1958, ch. 4 and 6; Crawford, *op. cit.*, p. 116 ff.

In Peru, however, the influence of Marx in Latin America had its most important intellectual repercussion evidenced in the works of José Carlos Mariátegui (1895–1930) and in the ideas and activities of the young Haya de la Torre. Mariátegui was in his short life the most original Latin American Marxist. His activities were divided between studying and travelling in Europe, undertaking a theoretical work of interpretation of Peruvian and contemporary realities (combined with an intense aesthetic interest) and engaging himself in a militant effort of organization of a popular movement along the lines of independent Marxism. La Escena Contemporanea (1925), Siete Ensayos de Interpretación de la Realidad Peruana (his most famous book, 1928) and three posthumous books, Defensa del Marxismo (1934), El Alma Matinal y outras Estaciones de Hombre de-Hoy (1950) and La Novela y la Vida (1955) have been his most important writings. To these should be added numerous articles published in the review founded by him in 1925, Amauta. He affiliated his Socialist Party, founded in 1926, to the Third International but always maintained an independent position.[16]

Haya de la Torre, also born in 1895, was much less an intellectual and much more a politician than Mariátegui. His great originality corresponded with his youth and the initial phase of his career. However in the 1930's he understood that in the conditions of Latin America —particularly of Indo-America, which corresponded to his Peruvian, Mexican and Centro-American experience—the Marxist thesis could not be adopted in its entirety and without an organic adjustment to the new reality. Indo-America was a preindustrial and predemocratic region, confronted with the problem of promoting her own development and getting rid of the imperialist domination closely associated with the local oligarchy. In such conditions, the struggle for Latin American development and emancipation could not have been molded in the conventional class-struggle model of the industrialized countries of the West, but rather it had to lead to an alliance of all the progressive forces of Indo-America under the leadership of the intellectuals and working class against the Anglo-American imperialism and their oligarchical associates. This conception led Haya de la Torre, while in exile in Mexico and Paris in 1924–1925, to create the Alianza Popular

[16] José Carlos Mariátegui, Obras Completas, Lima 1959, 10 vols.; Crawford, op. cit., p. 182 ff.

Revolucionaria Americana (APRA), conceived as a supranational Latin American movement and represented, in each country, by a national branch. Accepting those tenets of Marxism compatible with "aprismo" and maintaining the closest relationship with Marxism-Leninism short of subordination to the Comintern, Haya de la Torre engaged in a desperate and heroic struggle for organizing the Peruvian masses in a Peruvian aprista party. Although winning over the largest sectors of public opinion and obtaining repeated majorities in the popular vote, Haya de la Torre was never allowed by the Peruvian military, then completely identified with the traditional oligarchical establishment, to take office or even to freely propagate his ideas. That long and systematic rebuke by the army ultimately affected the validity of Haya de la Torre's views and of APRA's socio-political doctrine. The leader and the movement became increasingly conservative partly from the necessity of constant compromise and partly by the weight of age until finally they were driven to the reactionary camp. New forces, such as Belaunde's Acción Popular on the moderate Left and the Izquierda Revolutionaria on the radical Left, have superseded APRA's appeal to the urban masses and the new generation of politicized campezinos. In his creative and original period, Haya de la Torre was very influential not only in Peru but in the Caribbean and Central American areas as well as in Mexico. Moreover such men as Romulo Betancourt, founder of the Venezuelan Acción Democraticá, Pepe Figueres of Costa Rica and the Cuban Autenticos, were apristas.[17]

III. THE THIRD INTERNATIONAL PERIOD

A. FORMATION OF THE COMMUNIST PARTIES

The Russian revolution and the organization of the Third International had a diverse effect on Latin American popular and labor movements. Wherever the Socialist Party was well organized and adjusted to the role of trying to increase its influence by liberal-democratic forms, the Leninist line was repealed. In its 1919 Congress convoked to discuss the issue, the majority of the Argentina party in accordance with Justo and against Enrique del Valle Iberlucea (who

---

[17] Luiz Alberto Sanchez, *Haya de la Torre y el APRA*, Santiago 1955.

stressed his conviction of the impossibility of implanting socialism in Argentina by electoral means) decided to remain outside the Third International. While some of those who favored the acceptance of Lenin's twenty-one points joined the faction that had split in 1917 to form the Partido Socialista International and organized together the Communist Party, del Valle remained in the Socialist Party.[18]

The opposite case was the one of the Peruvian and Chilean socialists whose respective leaders, Mariátegui and Recabarren, highly respected and esteemed in their parties, took the initiative of joining the Comintern, the latter in 1921 and the former in 1926. The tradition of independence of these leaders, however, was at variance with the total discipline and conformity exacted by the Third International from the member parties. When both leaders died a few years after the affiliation with the Comintern, the new leadership stressed the difference between the pre-Communist and the really Communist phases of the parties.[19]

A different situation occurred in most of the other Latin American countries where the popular and labor movements were neither conservative nor radical, either because they simply were inarticulate and unorganized or because they were not molded in a predominantly Marxist form.

The Mexican revolution had amalgamated the anarcho-syndicalist tendencies of the Casa del Obrero Mundial and of CROM with the petty-bourgeois radicalism and anticlericalism of Calles, together with what remained of the agrarianism of Zapata. All these tendencies had been and were much more intuitively felt than rationally articulated and consequently were expressed in terms of practical politics rather than in any theoretical form. Therefore from that point of view nothing should formally oppose the possibility of imparting a more consistent formulation through the categories of Marxism-Leninism to the ideas and the practice of the Mexican revolution. The fact that the revolution was already an old process which had definitely divided Mexican society between groups favoring it and groups resisting it did not allow for a transplanted ideology, committed to purposes which were then alien to Mexican national urgencies. Consequently the foundation of the Communist Party in 1919

[18] Cf. Alba, História, p. 137 ff.
[19] Cf. Jobet, Recabarren, p. 55 ff.; Robert J. Alexander, Communism in Latin America, New Brunswick, N. J. 1957, pp. 177 ff. and 222 ff.

by two competing groups, (where the group of M. N. Roy, a Hindu, prevailed) acting only in response to Comintern directives was without any effect on Mexican society for a long time.[20]

The establishing of the Brazilian Communist Party in 1921 by Astrogildo Pereira, Otavio Brandão and a tiny group of militants, most of whom defected from anarcho-syndicalism and Communism because of Lenin and the Russian Revolution, was for some years an insignificant event. The Party did not rise to political importance or penetrate the labor movement—which was kept under the control of the anarcho-syndicalists—until Luis Carlos Prestes joined it in 1934. Prestes, the most prestigious of the "tenentes" of the revolution of 1924, marched his famous column through Brazilian western wilderness for four years, resisted the loyal troops until, forced to give up, he fled with the survivors into Bolivian territory where they took asylum. From that time reading and meditating in exile, Prestes gradually became more radical and revolutionary. In 1930 he refused to join most of his former comrades in a new attempt at revolution, which was at that time successful. He no longer believed in radical-liberal ideas and became a convinced Marxist, formally joining the Brazilian Communist Party in 1934 after returning from a trip to the Soviet Union.[21]

With the co-leadership of Prestes, the Communists, following the popular front strategy then adopted by the Comintern and with some military support, successfully organized a large left coalition, the National Liberation Alliance. Overrating their means and miscalculating the reaction of the rest of the army, they tried in October, 1935, to seize the control of some garrisons in Rio de Janeiro, Recife and a few minor places. Completely reduced after a brief but wild fight, the Communists suffered a setback from which they have never fully recovered and were reduced to political impotence until the last years of Vargas' New State, 1943–1945.

B. Deterioration of the Anti-Communists

The division and conflict between socialists and Communists have been harmful for both in Latin America as elsewhere. The Commu-

---

[20] Cf. Alba, *Las Ideas*, p. 215 ff.; Alexander, *op. cit.*, p. 319 ff.

[21] Cf. Everardo Dias, *História das Idéias Sociais no Brasil*, p. 10 ff.; Alexander, *op. cit.*, p. 93 ff.

nists, where they have been strongly opposed by well-organized socialists, as in Argentina, neither reached any political importance nor succeeded in controlling the labor movement. However the Socialists, on the other hand, displaced to the right by the Communists, have tended to join the reactionary camp (at least objectively) and as a result have left the masses deprived of political orientation, a typical occurrence in Argentina. Since 1940 the populist movements have achieved the mass mobilization that Socialists and Communists had failed to promote.

Conversely where a working compromise could be achieved between socialists and Communists, as in Chile ("Bloque de Izquierdas," 1934–1935; "Frente Popular," 1936–1941; FRAP, 1957 onward), the alliance was able to prevent the formation before World War II of local fascist governments and after the war have succeeded in improving the situation of the masses and in establishing conditions for the consensual adoption of important socioeconomic changes.

Systematic anti-Communism has also proved to be fatal for nonsocialist organizations, as APRA. In contrast a cautious coexistence with the Communists, as Cardenas in Mexico and post-New State Vargas in Brazil, has reinforced the popular and progressive meaning of such regimes, and consequently this has largely guaranteed their mass support and their margin of success in promoting economic development and social change.

C. The Failure of Communism

In the long period that has elapsed since the foundation of the Third International, the Communist activity in Latin America measured by its ability to inspire successful local revolutions, has resulted in complete failure. The only country which became Communist, namely Cuba, has done so for reasons and by ways entirely alien to both international and Cuban Communism.[22] Moreover their lack of success at instigating revolution or in coming to power in any Latin American country (the Arbenz regime not being a real exception to that rule), the Communists have not even been able to become a large mass party, except in the special case of Chile and there only as

[22] Cf. Wyat MacGaffey and Clifford R. Barnett, *Twentieth-Century Cuba*, New York 1965, p. 275 ff.; René Dumont, *Cuba, Socialisme et Dévelopement*, Paris 1964, p. 28 ff.

partners of a left coalition which has always been led by the socialists.

The Communists' efforts in the trade union movement have brought them much better results, for they have succeeded in controlling, chiefly in the period of World War II, some key unions and confederations of the region; this relative success did not bear any proportion to their endeavors, and it was not given excessive signification. Their influence in the labor movement has consistently proved insufficient in achieving any major and durable political gain; consequently they functioned only as representatives of labor, professional and economic interests.[23]

The reasons for the failure of the Communists have been many and complex and only a very brief survey can be given here. They will be considered in historical terms and a distinction will be drawn between the central purposes of international Communism for Latin America and the empirical process of the relationship of each Communist party with the society in which it was operating.

Conceived by Lenin and maintained by his successors, until the recent polarization and decentralization of the Soviet bloc, as a highly centralized system of parties under the severe discipline and control of the Soviet Union, they have always been commanded by the national interest of the "fatherland of socialism." In the initial phase (1919–1924) when the world revolution was considered to be imminent and was actively pressed forward by the Soviets, it was clearly not in their interest to divert from the strategic centers of Europe energies and means desperately needed there in a probably vain attempt to win the backward countries of Latin America to socialism. In the succeeding years until World War II, the Soviet Union, no longer convinced of the short-term possibility of world revolution, concentrated on her own development and used the Communist parties for her external protection, not for effectively trying to seize power in other countries. The antifascist league absorbed the period of the war. Only after the war with the conception of the national liberation wars and the conversion of socialism, to a large extent, from a system of redistribution of wealth to a model for socioeconomic development, was Communism geared to objectives immediately and directly connected with the local conditions and interests of Latin America and other underdeveloped countries. At that time, however,

[23] Cf. Robert J. Alexander, *Organized Labor in Latin America*, New York 1965, p. 18 ff.

the Communist bloc had lost its monolithic cohesion. Communism, as a theory, had become with Stalinism doctrinaire and sectarian and had lost most of its moral appeal and cultural validity. The international situation, on the other hand, with the nuclear stalemate preventing, if precariously, the outburst of a major war, had implicitly consolidated for each of the superpowers their respective areas of hegemony, and Latin America was thus placed under the unchecked control of the United States.

From the point of view of the empirical relationship of the local Communist parties to their respective society, the most relevant observation to be made, until the recent shift of emphasis (due to the Chinese and Vietnamese experiences) from city workingmen to countryside peasants was that the Communist movement in Latin America was suffering from a double limitation. The first was the poor position of the proletariat in rural or insufficiently industrialized backward countries too weak to play the role of the transforming force of society. The second, and perhaps even more serious, was the fact that in the Latin American conditions of unlimited labor supply, large unemployment and a very low cultural level of the masses, the urban workers were hardly convertible into a class of revolutionaries or even of radical political fighters. In their routine daily life there was and is so much to lose in risking a job and so little to gain in short-run, perceivable terms from the eventual seizure of power that, in practice, the working class tended to be passive and docile. Moreover the unemployment of the masses and the fact that the intellectuals have been easily absorbed by the middle class establishment hardly allowed the formation of cadres of really professional revolutionaries.[24]

In spite of their failure, however, the Communists have played in the recent decades a most relevant role in Latin America, as in all backward areas, in general. The first positive aspect of their contribution was to maintain pressure on conventional Latin American governments and their imperialist supporters, and hence to force on the more advanced sectors of the international and local establishments the dilemma of either accepting some sort of fascist rule in order to maintain the status quo or embarking on reformist programs for the social emancipation and economic development of the area and their masses.

[24] Cf. Espartaco (Anibal Pinto) "Critica del Modelo Político-Economico do la Izguierda Oficial" Trimestre Economico 1964 (31) pp. 67–92.

The second positive aspect has been the preservation of the liberating meaning of Marxism, despite all the deformations brought about by the practice of Stalinism. Adhering to their position of spokesmen for the masses and the exploited classes, the Communists—whatever their real title for such role—have fostered in the masses the hope for a possible final conciliation between practical politics and the emancipation of man.

The third relevant contribution of the Communists, although not planned by them in that way and for that purpose, has been the practical demonstration that economic development can be achieved, in predictable time, by countries starting from the most backward levels. Conceived as a humanist theory of the de-alienation of man and the redistribution of material and spiritual goods, Marxism, in its Leninist and Stalinist versions, has become a model for socioeconomic development.[25] In the Latin American countries, whatever the efforts of anti-Communist propaganda, on the one hand, and the awareness, on the other hand, of the tremendous prices to be paid for the achievement of development by the Communist model more and more sectors of the population are being led to conclude that this model at least affords reliable prospects of success, if and when all the other alternatives prove to be ineffective. Furthermore they have come to understand that the highest price for development is cheaper than the price for no development at all.

IV. THE LATIN AMERICAN REVOLUTION

A. ECLA and the Marxian Legacy

It was not only by the dialectic of positive-effects-through-failure, the theme of the preceding section, that Marxism has given a significant contribution to recent Latin American occurrences. More important was the influence of the Marxian legacy in the creation, by ECLA and the new Latin American intelligentsia, of the new theory of Latin American development and revolution.

These theoretical developments were begun in a systematic form after World War II with the creation, as one of the specialized agen-

---

[25] John H. Kautsky, *Political Change in Underdeveloped Countries*, New York 1962, p. 57 ff.

cies of the United Nations, of the Economic Commission for Latin America (ECLA) and better known by its Spanish-Portuguese initials CEPAL. Staffed by Latin American economists and other social scientists, ECLA, under the creative and inspiring leadership of the Argentinean economist Raul Prebish, has made in the late forties and early fifties an impressive theoretical effort at analyses of Latin American socioeconomic problems and at preparation of concrete policy schemes and programs for the promotion of the development of each of the Latin American countries and of the region as an integrated whole.[26]

B. The Central Thesis

The central thesis of CEPAL can be described as a highly sophisticated combination and adjustment to Latin American conditions of post-Keynesian economics with Mannheimean and post-Mannheimean sociology, including in addition some other ingredients of the Marxian legacy.

The general conception of CEPAL can be understood as a theory of asymmetry in the relations between the center—the industrialized countries in general and the United States in particular—and the periphery—the underdeveloped countries in general and Latin Amer-

[26] Among ECLA's main publications the following deserve special attention: a.) Early Phase, Basic Themes: *The Economic Development of Latin America and its Principal Problems*, U.N. 1950; *Economic Survey of Latin America*, 1949; *Theoretical and Practical Problems of Economic Growth* (E/CN 12/222, 1951); *International Cooperation in a Latin American Development Policy* (E/CN 12/359); b.) On Planning: *Economic Development, Planning and International Cooperation* (E/CN 12/582/ Rev. 1); *Progress in the Planning Field in Latin America* (E/CN 12/627); *Agriculture in Latin America: Problems and Prospects* (E/CN 12/686); *Problemas y Perspectivas de la Industrializacion Latinoamericana* (E/CN 12/664); c.) On the terms of trade: *Stabilizing the Terms of Trade of Underdeveloped Countries*, Economic Bulletin for Latin America, VIII, no. 1, March 1963; d.) On the Common Market: *The Influence of the Common Market in the Economic Development of Latin America* (April 1959, E/CN 12/01/13); e.) On monetary questions: *Economic Development and Monetary Stability: The False Dilemma*, Economic Bulletin for Latin America, VI, no. 1, March 1961; *Inflation and Growth-Summary of Experience in Latin America*, Economic Bulletin, VII, no. 1, 1962; f.) On structural questions: *Development in Latin America: Sociological Considerations* (E/CN 12/646); ACLA (Raul Prebisch) *Towards a Dynamic Development Policy for Latin America* (E/CN 12/680, 1963).

ica in particular.[27] This asymmetry presents three main aspects. First is the uneven division of the gains of trade between the center and the periphery in favor of the former and to the detriment of the latter, due to deteriorating terms of trade. Based on evidence gathered by a 1949 United Nations study on the British terms of trade from 1876 to 1946, CEPAL explained how the comparative increase of the prices of its imports (mostly capital goods) and decrease of the prices of its exports (mostly primary products) continuously drains from Latin America to the developed countries part of her regional product.

Secondly, CEPAL stressed the difference between the income elasticity of demands for imports of the center compared to that of the periphery. Due to Engels' law (the percentage expenditure on food is, on the average, a decreasing function of income), the income increase in the two poles affects in a different form their reciprocal demand for the other's supplies, and this is detrimental to Latin American trade.

The third point emphasized by CEPAL is that protectionism plays a different role in developed and underdeveloped countries. In the former it interferes with the optimal allocation of resources; in the periphery, because of disguised unemployment in agriculture and a natural increase of population that cannot be absorbed there, protection of industy is required from the point of view of resource allocation.

The main conclusions drawn by CEPAL are:

1.) the indispensability of the programming technique; 2.) the necessity for the state to be at the same time central planner, active promoter and close controller of the process of development; 3.) the imperative of Latin American economic integration in order to give the area the benefits of scale saving, diversification of production and increased intraregional trade as well as a strengthened international position of bargaining and competition; 4.) the urgency of structural reforms in order to effect a substantial reduction of class privileges, sectional and regional imbalances and to adjust Latin American institutions and socio-political practices to the requirements of modernization.

[27] Cf. Albert O. Hirschman, *Ideologies of Economic Development in Latin America* in *Latin American Issues,* Ed. by A. O. Hirschman, New York 1961, p. 12 ff.

After placing its emphasis until the early fifties on the necessity of economic planning and state action, CEPAL, during the late fifties, stressed the need for Latin American economic integration only to transfer its main attention in the 1960's to the problem of structural reforms, aimed at increasing the productivity of agriculture, incorporating the marginal masses into the modern and productive sector and redistributing the income among regions and classes in order to augment the capacity of investment and the purchasing power of the market. As has been said by ECLA in a recent document (*Towards a Dynamic Development Policy for Latin America, 1963*), 5% of the Latin Americans have 30% of the region's income while 50% have a chance of getting only 20% of the income. The income relationship between the higher and lower strata is of a ratio of 15 to 1. To increase the regional per capita growth from 1% per year to 3% per year (largely acknowledged to be the minimum "sound" rate of growth) that relationship should be reduced to 11 to 1 while a 9 to 1 ratio would allow a real annual per capita growth of 4%.[28]

C. The New Intelligentsia

The process of intellectual renewal that has made CEPAL possible and that has been reactivated by CEPAL work corresponds to the appearance of a new Latin American intelligentsia earnestly engaged in the task of thinking Latin American problems in the perspective of the culture of our time and in looking at our time in the perspective of Latin America. The central concern of this intelligentsia is to achieve a scientifically reliable understanding of the Latin American reality and, at the same time, to search for a new *praxis* which could consistently and realistically lead to the socioeconomic development of the region and the personal development of Latin American man.

In this sense, the kind of problem confronting the new Latin American intelligentsia is similar to the one with which Marx was confronted in his own time: how to understand the world in order to transform the world in accordance with its rational understanding. As Marx, and with the help of the Marxian legacy, the new intelligentsia looks for an answer to that question in terms which might provide the reciprocal foundation of theory and *praxis*. There is not

[28] Cf. ECLA (Raul Prebisch), *op. cit.*

an integrated and complete solution for such questions, but there is a common approach to it and there are some basic common features among the works and activities of the new generation of Latin American intellectuals dealing with it.

At the risk of conveying too much of my own ideas in what is purported to be a broad, objective picture of a general trend of thought, it seems possible to me to summarize this approach and these common features around four main points.[29] The first is the emphasis on the regional approach. Latin American countries have no meaning in isolation—even in the special case of semicontinental Brazil—because of the insufficient availability for each of the necessary natural and human resources for their development and because of the technological requirements of our time and the socio-political conditions internal and external to the Latin American countries. Moreover since the spontaneous factors of unity are already fairly considerable and the obstacles for the regional economic integration, particularly in South America and between South America and Mexico, are far from insuperable, it would be inconceivable not to make use of this advantage. A relevant aspect of this question is the parallelism and even large margin of coincidence between the problems of regional and national integration. If the latter should logically precede the former, the fact that the obstacles to be overcome in both cases are practically the same and the social forces favoring or opposing national integration in both cases are basically the same make the two problems a common one.[30]

The second point is the functional approach to the problem of socioeconomic development. The new Latin American social scientists consider it a gross simplification of reality to pretend that either "capitalism" or "socialism," albeit in their contemporary and much more comprehensive and eclectic versions, should be the appropriate models, nor do they believe in a synthesis or combination of both. There is no single right model for development because the requirements vary according to the structure of each society and its relative stage of development. What should be said, therefore, is that the multiple variations of situations and of stages of underdeveloped

[29] Cf. Claudio Véliz, ed., *Obstacles to Change in Latin America*, London 1965.
[30] Banco Interamericano de Desarrollo (Ed. by Felipe Herrera), *Factores para la Integración Latinoamericana*, Mexico 1966.

societies are ideally reducible to a limited number of typical cases to which corresponds a limited number of typical models for development. Moreover failure to adopt some fundamental measures at critical junctures in a society's life tends to lead to structural deterioration in any society, perhaps so severe as to produce a new structural type that would need a different kind of developmental model.[31]

The third aspect of this trend is the conception of the role of the nation—and of nationalism as a collective commitment to the nation —in the process of development. It has been already pointed out how in the Latin American case nationalism and regionalism tend to coincide in their essential features. The aspect to be emphasized here is the fundamental role of the nation in the promotion of development. This is an aspect that has been entirely misunderstood by Marx whose thinking in that respect was biased by the internationalization of liberal capitalism and by his own excessive economicism as well as by the fact that his experience and reflection were made in and from the ambit of developed societies and not dependent and underdeveloped ones. The nation is understood by the new Latin American intelligentsia—although within the strict limits of an historicist view of society—as being, in the first place, a built-in mechanism for increasing the functionality of the mass-elite relationship. In the second place, the nation is seen as a protective shield against other countries' nationalism. In so far as the nationalism of one country tends to be detrimental to another country which is unprepared to counter with its own nationalism, it follows that the overcoming of nationalism should be started with appropriate guarantees by the most powerful and influential countries. Empirical observation, however, indicates how the super-powers have retained and developed their own nationalism in the course of the last decades to the extent that the United States had to readjust some of her deepest traditions (e.g., nonaggression) to meet the demands (as they are being officially formulated) of her present foreign policy; the USSR was also obligated, against the formal text of Marx, to use Great Russian nationalism as a powerful aid in the promotion of her internal development and national defense.[32]

[31] Cf. Helio Jaguaribe, *Desenvolvimento Economico e Desenvolvimento Politico*, Rio de Janeiro 1962, ch. 3–7.

[32] Cf. Helio Jaguaribe, *O Nacionalismo na Atualidade Brasileira*, Rio de Janeiro 1958, ch. 1, 4, 5 and 18–22.

The fourth point to be noted, directly connected with the first three, refers to the limits and conditions of viability of the Latin American nations. Some of them—the Central American ones and the Caribbean Islands—due to their inadequate size, among other reasons, no longer can exist as individual states and can only develop in the broader context of an integrated Latin America. However even the largest Latin American countries, such as Brazil, Mexico and Argentina, cannot remain underdeveloped forever and still maintain their national integrity. In a world which is being rapidly organized around some few powerful poles of development and stratification, there is a historical deadline for achieving socioeconomic development within a given national configuration. Societies failing to do this will be submitted in the course of time to disruptive pressures. This problem is now being faced by Latin America. Although it does not seem possible to determine when Latin America's deadline for national and regional viability will arrive, it can be assumed, in view of recent events and existing circumstances, that such a deadline is not too remote and is likely to be reached in the next two or three decades. If this hypothesis is valid, either the Latin American countries—particularly key nations like Brazil, Argentina and Mexico—will achieve a minimum level of socioeconomic development in that lapse of time, or their national configuration will be disarticulated by disruptive processes that will affect the whole of Latin America. In that case, however, the resulting conflict, which would tend to pit the rural-central backward sectors against the modern coastal cities, would also reach uncontrollable proportions. Even if the United States interfered in order to prevent such an explosion by helping the forces of the local establishments to contain their own masses, the unsolved contradictions between the huge backward central regions and the tiny strip of the advanced coastal cities would likely be more powerful than any military system of containment.[33]

Timely and appropriate development, within the framework of the national states in the ambit of a regional Latin American Community, is both a realistic goal and an indispensable necessity. The failure to achieve such goals would probably precipitate Latin America into a continental revolution for which the Chinese revolution may possibly be an archetype and the Vietnam war, amplified to an

[33] Cf. Banco Interamericano, *op. cit.*, ch. V.

incomparably larger dimension, might be a term of reference for understanding the consequence of foreign intervention.

The cautious conditional optimism and the alternative sense of tragedy implied in this brief sketch of the conceptions of the new intelligentsia seem to be the most characteristic features of an outlook that recognizes itself as the last formulation of rational reformism or the first warning of inscrutable revolution.

12: MARXISM AND THE MOSLEM WORLD: THE MIDDLE EAST

Helène Carrère d'Encausse

Marxism, an ideology conceived by its founding fathers within the perspective of the industrial societies of the West, tried to solve the problems peculiar to these societies. Until recently it generally paid very little attention to the underdeveloped societies of the East. In its temporal undertakings Marxism, developed and often reinterpreted by the successors of Marx and Engels, has triumphed largely in non-Western agrarian societies.

It is in this connection that the Islamic world raises a very curious problem. Except in the Islamic territories of the old Russian Empire where a revolution occurred, in the wake and by the force of the Russian Revolution, the revolutionary efforts of the Communist have so far failed in Moslem territory. (Note the succession of dramatic failures in the Middle East—Iran: 1919, 1945–1946, 1953; Iraq: 1947–1948, 1952, 1958 and so on.)[1] Moreover each of these failures contributed more and more to the weakening and disorienting of the revolutionary organizations which in fact had appeared ready to take over the destinies of their countries. This prompts us to ask three questions:

1.) Is there, first of all, a problematic peculiar to the study of the relations of Communism and Islam?

2.) Are there, on the other hand, in Islamic society elements which favor resistance to or the penetration of Communism?

---

[1] For a rapid survey of events in this region, cf. W. Z. Laquer, *Nationalism and Communism in the Middle East*, 2nd ed., New York 1957; and M. Halpern, "Middle East and North Africa," *Communism and Revolution: The Strategic Uses of Political Violence*, ed. by Cyril E. Black and Thomas P. Thornton, Princeton 1964, pp. 303–331.

3.) Is the revolutionary history of the Middle East during this past half century explained by a peculiarity linked to the Islamic character of this society? Does it tend to evolve in new directions, or does it continue to follow the course of traditional ideological perspectives?

I.   THE FACTS ABOUT THE CONFRONTATION OF MARXISM AND OF ISLAM

The first problem we face in our analysis is that of discovering the precise categories in terms of which one may compare Communism and Islam. For many specialists have emphasized that no comparison is possible because it involves two heterogeneous phenomena, a religion and an anti-religious ideology. Others—without being too precise about what categories they were referring to or by merely arguing that Communism might also be seen as a religious phenomenon— have attempted to establish at all levels rigorous comparisons between the "ideological principles" of Islam, Communism and Capitalism.[2]

It is clear that we cannot classify Islam and Marxism in the category of religious phenomena. For Islam is, above all, a religion while Marxism certainly does not correspond to the usual definition of a religion.[3] Does this imply that in their temporal activity these two movements never confront each other and never converge? At least in the Soviet Union, history has demonstrated the opposite. Bernard Lewis has noted that the problem of heterogeneity and doctrinal incompatibility is characteristic of most religions.

> The same thing can be said with equal truth of Orthodox, Catholic or Protestant Christianity, or of Judaism or of any other religion worthy of the name. However, this doctrinal incompatibility has not prevented many followers of these religions from becoming Communists.[4]

Unable to place ourselves in a satisfactory way within the purely religious framework, it seems possible to us, following other scholars of Islam whose works have opened up extremely fruitful perspectives on Islamic research,[5] to have recourse to the sociology of knowledge

[2] J. P. Roux, *L'Islam en Asie*, Paris 1958.

[3] According to G. Gurvitch it must be of a "mystico-ecstatic" type.

[4] B. Lewis, "Communism and Islam," ed. by W. Z. Laqueur, *The Middle East in Transition. Studies in Contemporary History*, London 1958, p. 311.

[5] W. Montgomery Watt, *Islam and the Integration of Society*, London 1961.

and to place the phenomena analyzed within the framework of ideologies as described by Mannheim.[6]

Considering the two entities Islam and Marxism as ideologies, can we detect in their history and doctrine elements of comparison, favoring a confrontation? I think we can answer in the affirmative both in regard to certain basic data and to other more accidental data.

The first fundamental element of comparison is, I think, the weight of history and society in Islam and Marxism. Islam differs from other religions, be they revealed or not, in that it gives an extraordinary place to these two elements and thereby reveals itself nearer to Marxism than to other religions. The integration of history in the Moslem *Weltanschauungen* is a very important phenomenon which has been well explained by W. C. Smith,[7] for he states that contrary to Christianity for whom history, if it is of any importance, is neither final nor decisive; Islam is first of all a rehabilitation of history. Indeed Islam considers that, until the seventh century, the history of men was marked by a permanent deviation. All the prophets sent by God to earth failed to make their message heard:[8] either because their followers limited or distorted its meaning or because they adored the messenger and substituted him for Him who sent him. It was only in the seventh century with Mohammed that divine revelation was properly understood and that truth was finally incarnate in history through the foundation of a society which had as its starting point and purpose to bring God's truth into the world. This rehabilitation of history, this commitment in history, fundamental in the Islamic conception, has as a corollary the place ascribed to society in Islam. One fact is evidence of it, the date chosen as the starting point for the life of Islam in the world: the year 1 of the Hegira is the year 622 A.D. This choice aptly illustrates the difference between the Moslem and Christian conceptions. By linking the date of its beginning with the year of the birth of Christ, Christianity shows clearly its link with Jesus. The history of Islam is linked not to the Prophet as such but rather to the historico-socio-political phenomenon of the birth of the *community*, for 622 was the year in which Mohammed

[6] K. Mannheim, *Ideology and Utopia: An Introduction to the Sociology of Knowledge*, London 1936, p. 173ff.

[7] W. C. Smith, *Islam in Modern History*, Princeton 1957.

[8] The Moslems give a privileged place here to Abraham who succeeds in establishing in an enduring way the doctrine of monotheism.

and his companions left Mecca for Medina in order to form a separate society with its own laws, the *Umma*, which would conquer political power, and then carry this power across the world. Thus the fundamental basis in the Moslem perspective is neither the life of the Prophet nor the moment when his message was revealed but the creation of a community which explicitly announces its plan of installing the kingdom of God on earth.

This decisive place given to history, the will to realize a social ideal in this world, is also found in Marxism. Essentially there is a fundamental difference between these two ideologies: Marxism is exclusively temporal in outlook while Islam sees everything in the twofold context of the temporal and the eternal. However our purpose is not to deny these differences nor to minimize them but rather to note that alongside these differences there are analogies from which other elements of comparison derive. In an attempt to define Islam and Communism in the perspective of a comparison, Maxime Rodinson writes:

> Islam, like Communism, seems to us to relate to a type of grouping attested, moreover, by more or less pure forms. We would prefer incidentally to call them *movements* rather than groupings to do justice to their dynamic character. One might call them militant ideological movements with a socio-political program and totalitarian aims.[9]

Totalitarianism is another analogy between Marxism and Islam, linked to their conception of history and of society. If Marxism in its beginnings, in the organizations inspired by Marx and Engels was not very totalitarian, it tended to become so when it became incarnate in States, when the ideology acquired an earthly aim. Islam was in its beginnings and for a long time totalitarian to the extreme. For centuries it dominated and directed all the areas of social and private life, integrated in its ideological system all the external environment and sacralized the whole life of man and of society. For centuries nothing in Islamic society, nothing in the most ordinary acts of daily life from the most trivial to the historic expansion of the community, was foreign to Islam. The Koran and the Sunna constitute a corpus of reference works whose authority is absolute, an almost closed corpus, and thereby more intangible and sacred than the corpus of Marxist texts to which the successive ideological leaders have brought many

[9] M. Rodinson, "Problematique de l'étude des rapports entre Islam et Communisme," *Correspondance d'Orient*, Brussels 1961, no. 5, p. 8.

refinements. Initially this totalitarian aspect of Moslem ideology was re-enforced in a certain number of countries where Islam developed through an authoritarian political tradition. Indeed in certain countries of the Middle East, Egypt, Iraq and in central-Asiatic khanates, economic life depended on irrigation which entails a strong, centralized power in order to initiate and realize activities whose importance extends beyond the capacities of individuals. In a word one finds there then, "hydrolic" societies[10] where from pre-Islamic periods, religion unified society and nature in the person of the sovereign god and priest;[11] Islam, with its force of integration, which W. Montgomery Watt[12] has emphasized, would build upon these tendencies and would develop them. The totalitarian character of Islam appears even more clearly in the brutal rupture it created between *Dar ul Islam* and *Dar ul Harb* (the domain of Islam and the domain of war), which required of the faithful a merciless struggle, the *Djihan* (or Holy War) and which closely linked spiritual progress to the earthly and historic mission of Islam.[13] There again the analogy with Marxism, at least in its contemporary forms, appears.

In the temporal development of Islam there are other aspects which permit a comparison with Marxist ideology. The adventure of Mohammed and of his companions was based on the effort of a subjugated man whom injustice and oppression had aroused. The Koran is, in many ways, a revolutionary text which has a great quantity of invectives against the powerful, a defiance and appeal to the justice and to the equality of men. Moslem faith, born of a social and national protest and expressed by the freest and most lucid spirits of Moslem society of the seventh century, became a mobilizing and conquering ideology, which rallied vanquished peoples without effort and often against their will,[14] gave birth to an earthly empire based on an ideal

---

[10] K. Witfogel, *Oriental Despotism*, New Haven 1964.

[11] P. Vidal-Nacquet, Introduction to the French edition of K. Witfogel, *op. cit.*, p. 11.

[12] Watt, *op. cit.*

[13] The Moslem martyr gives his life while fighting for the extension of *Dar ul Islam*, that is for the extension of the area under Moslem domination; this does not follow the Christian idea of the martyr whose martyrdom is not linked to an historical victory.

[14] The conversion of the conquered peoples was often due to the wishes of the conquered. In fact, conversion permitted them to acquire the same status as their conquerors, especially in fiscal matters. In this way they escaped the *Djizziah*, a tax imposed on the infidels.

of justice and was probably the first temporal realization of an explicit ideology in history. In triumphant Moslem society one could find both the privileged role given the poor, concern for individual humility and the constant preoccupation with the temporal success of the community.

Thus by a certain conception of the destiny of man on earth, of his place in the community, of the role of the ideology in his life, but also in history, the Moslem *Weltanschauung* is not totally foreign to Marxism.

Surely the analogies noted have two implications. On the one hand, we are dealing with two entities which are comparable in certain ways. But, on the other hand, we could argue that the fundamentally totalitarian character of Islam, as well as the totalitarian character of Marxism, at least in its earthly undertaking, prevents in the end any confrontation between these two ideologies and above all implies an absolute impossiblity of their coexisting at any level.

In fact we must view this alleged incompatibility based on the totalitarianism of ideologies with the same precautions used to examine the argument of their heterogeneity. If we wish to understand the present reactions of Moslems towards Communism, we cannot limit ourselves to the vision of Islam as it emerged in the seventh century and maintained itself in its triumphant period. For ideologies are variable phenomena subject to mutations; Mannheim has rightly insisted on this point.

It is clear that Islam was profoundly transformed by its withdrawal from temporal undertakings.[15] The triumphant ideological movement became progressively an ideology in a pure state, thus tending to lose its totalitarian aspect, and gradually gave way to ideas, princi-

---

[15] This retreat begins with the fall of Bagdad in 1258. Although Moslems, Turkish and Persian, would continue to assure the temporal greatness of Islam in the world, very significant changes appear as early as this time in the Moslem *Weltanschauung*. The spread of Moslem mysticism (*sufism*) during the medieval period involved a certain re-evaluation of history and of temporal values. The individual is more important than society, the eternal than the temporal. However *sufi* vision remains limited and Sunnite orthodoxy prevails for the majority of Moslems who remain attached to the historical process. However in the *institutions of Islam*, this detachment from the temporal also has a few repercussions, notably in the substitution of the authority of the *sultan* for that of the *caliph* which gives to the temporal head of the community an explicit independence from the spiritual power.

ples and aspirations foreign to the Islam of the seventh century.[16] Many factors favored this evolution. The first was the reversal of the political situation which Islam had known in its period of triumph. From the eighteenth century on, the decline of Islam was aggravated by the development and penetration into the East of a West whose exuberance and pressure were going to take away from Moslem society the grip it had previously held on the world. Moslem society had no ideals by which it could compete with this exuberence, except the disarray of the political and spiritual transformations it knew since the fifteenth century and its inability to explain the changes which had occurred in the world. Certainly sovereigns like Mahmud II or Mehmet Ali, conscious of this failure of Moslem society to adapt to the world of the nineteenth century, tried to solve the problem by reform measures, but their efforts were too fragmentary and ended by liquidating the order which had existed up to that time without succeeding in endowing Moslem society with new structures. The uneasiness of Moslem society in encountering these changes, which the faith and order of Islam no longer explained, in recognizing the growing divorce between the history of the world and the history peculiar to the Moslem community (which up to then had coincided) would be expressed a little bit everywhere in Moslem lands. This disquiet and disarray yielded to a powerful intellectual movement of renewal which, whatever the directions it took to find solutions for the problem of Islam, would modify profoundly Moslem ideology by tearing it away from its isolation and totalitarianism and by forcing it to open itself to new perspectives that were often totally alien to it.

This is not the place to study the history of the reform movement which overtook the Moslem conscience in the nineteenth and early twentieth centuries from Arabia to the Indies. We evoke it because, under certain of its forms, it opened the door to new ideological dimensions, and principally to the national one. As early as the eighteenth century Moslem reformers of India,[17] specifically the successors of Shah Walyullah of Delhi, reflected upon the decadence of Moslem society and introduced, along with the idea of spiritual reform, the idea of a political reform based on national liberation. Closer in time

[16] "Enrichments" of this kind have existed since the seventh century, but for a long time Islam integrated and Islamized them. For example, Plato was considered a disciple of Moses, the precursor of Mohammed.

[17] W. C. Smith, *Modern Islam in India, A Social Analysis*, 2nd ed. Lahore 1947.

to us, Djamal ad din al Afghani[18] truly integrated the West into the Moslem view by realizing that the West threatened Islam in its totality and not just with respect to a limited time and place. The concepts *Islam* and *West* became present as historical phenomena at once in conflict and yet linked together. If now this idea seems trite, we need to remember, in order to understand the profoundly original aspect of the thought of Djamal ad din al Afghani, that until then the Moslem conscience had succeeded in considering all foreign ideas and values by integrating them into the Moslem frame of reference. It was primarily in the Moslem possessions of the Russian Empire that this effort of reflection took on the most original direction and went the furthest. In the nineteenth century at Bukhara, the most backward of the Central Asiatic emirates, but also one of the most famous of the former Moslem cultural centers, Ahmad Donish, whose thought is comparatively unknown, opened up many new avenues for the intellectual evolution of Islam. A contemporary of Djamal ad din al Afghani, Ahmad Donish analyzed the problems of the Moslem community not only in the light of the glorious past but also by taking into consideration the liberal ideas which were troubling the Russian Empire.[19] His work clearly reveals the influence of the nationalist and democratic thought which he saw developing in Russia. For him, the salvation of the Moslem community lay in an understanding, a knowledge of Western thought and techniques, not their Islamization. For him too—and here the influence of utopian Russian socialism is clear—salvation implies a fundamental re-examination of the structures of society. A few decades later the thought of Donish would be developed and brought to the level of action by another Moslem from Bukhara, Abdur Rauf Fitrat.[20] In a work written with passion between 1910 and 1914, Fitrat took up the earlier reformers' questioning about the decline of the Moslem community; in addition he took into consideration two historical facts which profoundly disturbed the

[18] Nikkie R. Kiddie, professor at the University of Los Angeles, is preparing a work on Djamal Ed-din which will certainly shed very important light on him. In France, the journal *Orient* has published important extracts of the work of Djamal Ed-din.

[19] The work of Ahamad Donish remains in part unpublished; cf. I Muminov, *Uzbekiston Ijtimoi falsafii tafakurning tarihidan*, Tashkent, 1960, pp. 116–143 (in Uzbek) and H. Carrère d'Encausse, *Réforme et révolution chez les Musulmans de l'Empire russe, Bukhara 1867–1924*, Paris 1966, pp. 109–115.

[20] Carrère d'Encausse, *op. cit.*, pp. 172–182.

consciences of Russian Moslems in the twentieth century: the Revolution of 1905 and the defeat of the Russian Empire by Japan.

In a world filled with a revolutionary spirit, in which at least the military superiority of the West began to be questioned, the need for the Moslem world to adapt quickly to the new realities was evident. Abdur Rauf Fitrat substituted for the nostalgia of a glorious but already distant past a program of action which aimed to restore Moslem society to its temporal grandeur and to see the relations between Western society and the non-European world dominated by it in new terms. As regards internal affairs, this program implies a re-evaluation of structures, social relations and ideas prevalent in Moslem society. Fitrat challenged everything that religion had sacralized by invoking against an outworn social order, based on religion, the revolutionary religion of the Prophet. He denounced the past use of religion by privileged classes to hide the exploitation of man by man and the struggle for power. In short, the society he advocated, while claiming links to Islam, integrated values which owed more to Western liberalism than to Islam. Likewise in the defense of the community against the West, Fitrat, while insisting like Afghani on the link between Islam and the national concept, defends the idea of a national struggle as an end in itself. Even more he enlarged the Pan-Islamism of his predecessors which reduced all national demands to the fundamental conflict of Islam against the infidel to a revolutionary Pan-Asianism, a general uprising of all peoples oppressed by the West against the oppressor. This tendency, new to Islam, is also found at the same period in the Afghan Mahmud Tarzi whose paper, *Siraj-ul Akhbar*, carries on the masthead the motto: "Asia for the Asiatics." The position of Fitrat, like that of Mahmud Tarzi, takes into consideration the evolution of Moslem ideology, at least in its most advanced form as expressed by the reformers on the eve of World War I.

Of course, this was the thought of only a small fraction of Moslem opinion. The masses, living in Moslem lands, remained attached to their traditional ways of thought and occasionally took the side of the traditionalists against every effort of the innovators when a conflict arose. But the spirit of the innovators gained ground and the events that overturned the Russian Empire in the early twentieth century had considerable echoes in the nearby Middle East, both influencing the political structures and profoundly disturbing the conscience of the people. The defeat of Russia by Japan opened minds to the idea of a revenge of non-European peoples on the West,[21] and hence to the idea of a solidarity of the oppressed which extended beyond the boundaries of Moslem society. Thus in Iran and in Turkey, the revolution of 1905 had, in good part, brought about the political reforms of the years 1906–1911.

It is clear that on the eve of the war and of the Russian Revolution, Moslem ideology had been profoundly reinterpreted, and the new currents of thought which had sought to describe in theory the new situation of the community opened up the formerly totalitarian ideology in two essential directions. One seeks the renewal of tradition, cleansed of the accretions and all the dross accumulated over the centuries; this effort, promoted by the Wahhabis, led to what, following the Egyptian philosopher Abdel Malek, we shall call *Moslem Fundamentalism*.[22] The other is the liberalism borrowed from Western ideology of the nineteenth century which also evokes the first manifestations of a nationalism which had its own ends.

In the half century which has passed since the Russian Revolution, new elements have appeared and modified Moslem ideology. In this regard two problems have been decisive. The national problem achieved significant prominence during World War I when the diverse adversaries tried to manipulate the aspirations to independence by playing off opposing peoples one against the other. In fact, this weapon—which the European allies brandished against the Austrian-Hungarian Empire and Germany against the Russian Empire[23]—was used particulary to awaken the national conscience in non-European countries. The Russian Revolution of 1917 stressed the right of peoples to determine their own fate, and the Comintern, from 1920 on, was going to assert the necessity of applying this principle to the countries of the East.[24] The triumph of the Russian Revolution in

[21] Cf. for example B. Vernier, *Qedar, carnets d'un mehariste syrien*, Paris 1938, p. 102, which recalls the repercussions of the event in the Arab Orient.

[22] Anouar Abdel-Malek, *Anthologie de la littérature arabe contemporaine*, vol. II, *Les Essais*, Paris 1965, pp. 9–33.

[23] At the Lausanne Conference of 1916, organized by the *Office of Nationalities*, which had in principle as its purpose the breaking up of the Austria-Hungarian Empire, the Moslems of Russia accused the Russian Empire, while the Algerians, Tunisians, and so on, demanded the condemnation of the French and English colonial empires.

[24] D. Boersner, *The Bolsheviks and the National and Colonial Question*, Paris 1957.

Moslem lands implied not only the liberation of nations but also the rapid transformation of underdeveloped societies. And this latter point provokes the second problem of the Middle East. As early as 1919, at the time of the formal independence, states as important as Egypt and Iraq had to face the problem of social development. Neither of these two problems—national independence and development—found a lasting solution[25] before the Second World War. However after 1945, political developments would change radically and quickly. Unions and political parties developed from 1920 on in Arab countries. The beginning of industrialization brought to the towns and the oil fields new social groups which, cut off from their rural roots, were to integrate in an environment in which the weight of Moslem tradition yielded to new social needs. At the same time, the collapse of colonial systems, the extension of the socialist world not only to Europe but also to Asia, have upset fundamentally the international context and made it more radical. The problem is, henceforth, to organize the newly independent states, that is, to opt for new forms of social and political organization. The men who preside over the destinies of the new states, all those who reflect on these options became aware—when referring to the experience of the years 1920–1940—that neither traditional Islam nor the innovating currents, fundamentalism and liberalism, could solve their problems. The Moslems of the two reformist currents, who were supported at least by the urban masses, sought new solutions by turning quite naturally to Marxism which had succeeded as a triumphant ideological movement, and which seemed able to solve the problems of underdeveloped societies.

II. THE COMMUNIST-MOSLEM CONFRONTATION
IN SOVIET RUSSIA

The first Communist experience in Moslem lands, that is, the Soviet experience, is extremely important because it gives us a concrete example of the encounter of the two ideologies, Islam and Communism, and raises various problems. Under what conditions does such a confrontation take place? Is there coexistence? Who decides? And at what price?

[25] H. Carrère d'Encausse and S. Schram, Le Marxisme et l'Asie, 1853–1964. Paris 1964.

The most enlightening example in the Soviet Union is that of the Central-Asiatic States both because of their preservation of a very ancient national tradition—contrary to the Tatars of Kazan, for example, who were subjected to Russian rule and to Christianization from the sixteenth century on—and because of their proximity to the Middle East. In Central Asia the triumph of the Revolution evidenced itself in two ways: it was either purely Russian, that is, colonial, clashing with the natives in Russian populated zones;[26] or else it was (and here we come to the heart of our subject) the result of Moslem reform movements which had struggled for years for the renewal of Moslem societies. This was the case notably in the protected States of Bukhara and Khiva where between February and October, 1917, the leaders of the national reform movement deliberately began cooperating with the Bolsheviks because the liberals in power in Russia, after February, 1917, did not seem to them capable of supplying answers to the national problem. Having come to power in the summer of 1920 after a very hard struggle against traditionalist forces, the Moslem innovators who had joined the Bolshevik party en masse had to safeguard their independence while attempting to overhaul the structures of society. Their experience resulted in failure for an external reason (after 1920, with the subsiding of the European revolution, the Soviet state had to proceed with the reconstruction of the old Empire) but especially for an internal reason, the inability of the Moslem masses to accept quickly an order which broke radically with its mode of thought and earlier convictions.[27] Does this mean that Moslem ideology set up an insuperable barrier to Communist penetration? The initial shock was certainly very hard. When in Central Asia, formerly the Central Government of Turkestan—the zone of Russian colonization—the Soviet government attacked Islam within the framework of its global antireligious struggle, when it closed the places of worship, confiscated the wealth of pious foundations, and forbade Moslem teaching, the shock to the popular mind was enormous. It was so enormous that when Soviet power adopted the N.E.P., it tried to reconcile the Moslem masses by cancelling these drastic measures. Later the anti-Moslem struggle was resumed along with the whole antireligious struggle in Soviet Russia. It was extremely violent

---

[26] G. Safarov, *Kolonial'naia revoljucià—opyt Turkestana*, Moscow 1921.

[27] Ryad Hassan, *L'Egypte nassérienne*, Paris 1963.

from 1930 to 1941, moderate between 1941 and 1946; since then it has been cunning, permanent, and it seems not very coercive.

Consequently if one tries to see what has come of it after a half century's experience of the ideological encounter of Islam and Communism in Soviet Russia, what can we say? On the one hand, there has been a remarkable power of resistance in Islam, but it has been a resistance stemming not from faith but from national interest. Islam lives in Soviet Russia, less because a relatively small number of mosques, attended incidentally by the aged, remain open for worship than because a certain number of rites and practices (a great number of which do not belong, in fact, to Moslem society, but have been Islamized over the centuries) explicitly affirm the existence of a Moslem community distinct from the Russian community. Thus one notes in Islamic parts of the Soviet Union that the practice of circumcision has been preserved as symbolizing the entry into the Moslem community, especially in towns and there even by Communists who emphasize their atheism. Thus the Islam seems to be connected with national self-affirmation. In the realm of religion the Islam has been compromised in the Soviet Union; the empty mosque and lack of interest in faith go hand in hand with the progress of education and the development of society. However as a national symbol it has increased in importance. On its part, Communism in Soviet Russia has also very clearly adjusted to Islam. Even though fifty years ago it was possible to believe that a bitter antireligious struggle in an area where the 1917 level of education was very low would be ineffective, that the destruction of the infrastructure on which religion was based, namely, society of classes, would cause the superstructure to collapse by itself, it has become rather difficult today to consider as "survivals" a phenomenon which thrives in so obvious a way. However Soviet power has, especially since 1946, for reasons of internal order and external propaganda, granted a place to Islam. Of course officially Islam like every other religion remains a false ideology which mystifies the popular consciousness. However when delegations from non-European countries, especially Moslem delegations, visit the Soviet Union, the program always includes a visit to the *spiritual leaders of the Moslems of Central Asia*, which leaders are alleged to symbolize the coexistence of Communism and of Islam. This is true from the point of view of external propaganda, but from the domestic point of view conciliation is no less evident. Thus one can read in the republican press of the Soviet Union these past twenty years the same indignant articles on "Islamic survivals" evidenced by great celebrations of religious ceremonies (marriages, circumcisions, and so on) in the presence of local dignitaries of the State and of the Party, or again, by pilgrimages to holy places. It becomes rather difficult at the present time to look at these articles as much more than a display of Platonic disapproval, for they demonstrate that one can with complete impunity participate in Moslem ceremonies, and at most they give handy explanations (itineraries, schedules, and so on) on the means a Moslem has to participate in them. However one can speculate whether, in certain cases at least, Soviet power does not consider Islam as a possible outlet for the national sentiment of the non-Russian peoples?

Thus the concrete, administrative, and no longer only ideological, encounter of Islam and of Communism has, on the ideological level, resulted in a certain compromise in which the two ideologies confronting each other have been reinterpreted somewhat in the direction of a rapprochement. Soviet Moslems try to show that Marxism corresponds to a purely Islamic revolutionary tradition,[28] that nothing in Islam before it deviated—that is, was used for class interests—was against the ideas advanced by Marxism. Thus there is a "recovery" of the Moslem past, of the Koranic tradition as well as of the great figures of Islam like Ali Shir Navai,[29] or again, of heroes of the reformist thought like Aini, who rejoined the ranks of the Communist Party, or of Mullah Behbudi.

But what has been the price of this conciliation for the Moslem of the Soviet Union? Instead of the colonial environment left by the Tsarist empire to Soviet power in which illiteracy reigned and instead of an economic and social backwardness analagous to what the Middle East then knew, there is at present a society much more advanced than the other Moslem societies. Of course this society, as do all others in Soviet Russia, still experience real economic difficulties; moreover the progress of the Central Asiatic republics is not compara-

[28] This attempted conciliation does not exist just in Soviet Russia. One of the most remarkable examples of it is the poem of Mohammed Iqbal, "Lenin, the choir of angels and the injunction of God" where he attributes to Allah a thought that Communism would never disavow that "the day of the sovereignty of the masses is approaching."

[29] Cf. the novel of Aibek, Navai, Moscow 1946 (translated from Uzbek by P. Sletov) in which Mir Ali Shir Navai is portrayed as a precursor of Communism.

ble to the evolution of the advanced societies of the West; they do not belong in the same perspective as the Soviet Russian-American race but in the perspective of the modernization of societies in the course of development. When Egyptians or Pakistanis visit Uzbekistan, they are not thinking of the American way of life but of themselves; and there the prodigious effort at education, the quality and the quantity of teaching at all levels, the development of a purely native research, the progressive substitution of native economic and industrial staffs for the Russian staffs (within the limits of the demands of the political system), the modernization of society, and the standard of living— all show that the Soviet Union has found solutions to the problems of the development of its Moslem peoples. I am interested here in giving neither an overall judgment nor a moral judgment of the Soviet effort but to observe that when representatives of Moslem peoples visit Moslem regions of Russia, the judgment they take back is dominated by a twofold impression. The work of development and of modernization is real; the Moslem peoples have learned how to reconcile their national and Islamic identity with Communism.

III. THE EVOLUTION OF COMMUNISM IN THE MIDDLE EAST

Moslem ideology progressed from a traditional body of doctrine to an implicit ideology that realized the needs and aspirations of contemporary Moslem society. This was partially effected by the continual "radicalization" of the Middle Eastern political environment, the international evolution and the Moslem Soviet example.

Until 1950, the history of the Communist movement in the Middle East remained essentially the history of groups of isolated intellectuals cut off from the masses whose audience was extremely limited. In the 1920's such groups developed in three countries—Egypt, Palestine and Turkey. In Egypt at this time the weakness of Communism resulted for several reasons. First of all Egyptian Communists were divided into several rival groups whose factional quarrels totally blinded them to the real problems of their country. Communism did not find in the 1920's a national social basis in a country where a powerful movement of national vindication, the Wafd, led by native bourgeois, defended a coherent program for satisfying Egyptian aspi-

rations for independence.[30] The position of groups which claimed to
be Marxist, when confronting the Wafd, is not easy to define. On
the national plane they could add nothing to the exigencies of the
Wafd. On the social level they preached an agrarian reform which the
native peasantry could not, in its state of misery and backwardness,
comprehend. In addition they tried to promote a workers' movement
of revolt which the Wafd in power with Sa'ad Zaghlul easily broke
up in 1924. In short, the followers of these groups, and this probably
was their principal weakness, were particularly important among the
minorities of Egypt-Jews, Armenians and Greeks. This also became
one of the principal causes of internal weakness of the Turkish Communist groups, most of whom were led by minority groups,[31] and of
the Palestinian Communist party[32] which from 1925 on, despite
orders to become Arab, remained in the eyes of the Arabs an offshoot
of the Zionist movement. In these three countries the Communist
parties or groups ran into the same internal and external obstacles.
The masses, still deeply attached to Islam and to their traditional
structures and open only to nationalistic revindications, found in
national movements which all more or less stemmed from or were
linked to the Moslem currents of renewal in the nineteenth century,
representations of their aspirations. Communism, which in the 1920–
1930 years presented itself to the Middle East in all its antireligious
intransigence which emphasized the social problem[33] and challenged
the dynamic role of the native bourgeoisie, clashed profoundly with
the national conscience. Moreover the Comintern did not facilitate

[30] Anouar Abdel-Malek, Egypte, société militaire, Paris 1962; and M. Colombe,
L'évolution de l'Egypte, 1924–1950, Paris 1951.

[31] Cf. Laqueur, op. cit., chapter VI.

[32] The Communists of Palestine were at first regrouped in the Mifleget poalim
socialistim (socialist workers party) which broke up in 1921. A Communist Party
of Palestine was formed which admitted for a long time that it was unable to
regulate, on the one hand, its attitude toward Zionism, and on the other, to win
a following among the Arab masses.

[33] At the Congress of Baku in September, 1920, the Moslem Communist representatives of Russia, basically Turkestanians, opposed the leadership of the Comintern. They tried for the first time to theorize the problems of the revolution
in an essentially Moslem colonial environment. They emphasized that the class
solidarity between the Western proletariat and the Oriental colonial proletariat
was infinitely weaker than the actual solidarity between all the classes of oppressed nations and those in exploiting nations. Hence there exists the need to
adapt revolutionary ideology, that is, socialism, to the special conditions of the

the task of the national Communist parties and on occasion (as happened in Turkey[34]) supported explicitly anti-Communist national governments. Hence after a short period of activity, the Communist groups established in the Middle East broke up (Turkey) or vegetated (Egypt). It was only in the years before the Second World War that the theoretical revisions of the Comintern gave these groups new perspectives for action. Indeed the rise to power of Fascist regimes in Europe, the necessity of cementing the union of "democratic" powers led the Comintern to redefine the direction of the action of the Communist Party.

This was evidenced by Middle Eastern reaction in the years 1936–1940 to the increasing prestige of National-Socialist Germany. The power of this country which had been defeated by the Anglo-French colonizers less than twenty years before and the retreats of France and of Great Britain which the national movements of the East effected contributed to the German myth in this area.[35] Consequently Soviet Russia as well as the mandate powers felt the need to use all the national forces against German ideological penetration. Until then suspect, partly or completely illegal, the existing Communist Parties which had national importance and which were not merely representatives of minorities, were engaged in anti-Fascist national fronts. This explains why these discredited groups, like the Egyptian Communist Parties, did not play a role at this time while the mandatory powers and Soviet Russia saw with satisfaction the development of Syro-Lebanese and Iraquian Communist Parties created around the 1930's. Contrary to the parties created elsewhere in 1920, the Syro-

Orient; first of all, ideological conditions (to find an understanding between socialism, the ways of thinking and the structures of Moslem society); then, the political conditions (to grant a priority to the national struggle over the social struggle, to let at this stage, in the absence of a proletariat, the national bourgeoisie assume the leadership of the movement). These positions were condemned by the leadership of the Comintern which in its final theses recognized only the possibility of finding a place for the national movement at the side of the social struggle and substituted for the leadership of the national bourgeoisie as advocated by the Moslems, that of the poor peasantry of the Orient, cf. *Pervyj s'ezd narodov vostoka,* Baku, 1–8 Sentjabr' 1920 g, Stenograficheskia Otchet, Petrograd 1920.

[34] Cf. Laquer, *op. cit.*

[35] Local "National-Socialist Parties" appear in most of the Middle Eastern countries. In Iraq in 1941 this tendency led to the Fascist coup d'état of Rachid Ali al Ghilani which the population viewed favorably.

Lebanese and Iraquian Communist Parties were Arab Parties,[36] especially the first whose leaders, clearly aware of the internal realities of their countries, had been appointed in the Soviet Union. Their position was not made easier. To make a common front with the national groups of the country, they necessarily stressed the national struggle and not the social problems. However in the mind of the masses the national struggle was first of all the struggle against France and Great Britain, and consequently it was not very easy to reorient it in the direction of an alliance of all the democratic powers against Fascism. The existence of the popular front in France facilitated such an about-face for the Syro-Lebanese Communist Party, yet the soft pedalling of the orders for national liberation, if it permitted the Communist Party to have a legal activity and hence to develop and improve its organization, did not favor its acquiring a hold on the masses. Until the defeat at Stalingrad the Fascist-like parties had infinitely higher prestige in the Middle East.

Thus from 1920 until the end of the Second World War, the masses of the Middle East remained, on the whole, attached to their traditional values, that is, to Islam and to the national fight led by the native bourgeoisie. The local Communist Parties, already weak and hampered by the directives of the Comintern, could only develop at the level of an action confined to a few social levels—workers (who were not numerous), minorities, intelligentsia. The policy of Soviet Russia at the end of the war did not contribute to improving their positions. On the one hand, the Soviet claims—quickly withdrawn moreover—on Tripolitania or Eritrea and on the Straits[37] and, on the other hand, the support granted at one time to the revolutions that gave birth to the republics of Azerbaidzhan and of Mahabad[38] in Northern Iran profoundly troubled the popular conscience of the Orient. Behind these republics of Iran there lurked the threat of a

[36] Although one of the leaders of the Syrian Communist Party, Khalid Begdash, was a Kurd, nonetheless he always identified himself with the Arab cause and remains at the present time still the most prestigious figure of Middle Eastern Communism.

[37] On this last point cf. Department of State, La verité sur les rapports germano-soviétiques de 1939 à 1941, Paris 1948, notably p. 196; and Peter Kleist, Entre Hitler et Staline, 1939–1945, Paris 1953, pp. 208, 225, 246ff., 259, 261.

[38] Cf. G. Lenczowski, Russia and the West in Iran, 1918–1948: A Study in Big Power Rivalry, Ithaca, N. Y. 1949; and by the same author, The Middle East in World Affairs, Ithaca, N. Y. 1952.

rapid disintegration of States having minorities (multinational Iraq was particularly prone to this problem). If this particularly "hard" attitude of Soviet Russia, so little in conformity with the expressed national aspirations, lasted only a very short time (in 1947 order was restored to Iran, and Soviet Russia made no more territorial demands), the party line assigned by Soviet Russia to the Communist movement continued to impose a very heavy burden on the evolution of local Communism.

The last years of Stalinism were dominated by a Manichean conception of the world and of international relations. The division of the world into two irreconcilable blocs left no place for intermediary political solutions. However the postwar years were marked by so many countries gaining their independence that the political choices of these countries were limited; either one had to open up the national struggle to a fight for social liberation, or according to Soviet analysis, the newly acquired independence remained purely formal, "juridical," for the national bourgeoisie in power would lead the country back into the orbit of imperialism. The local Communist Parties, constrained to secrecy, found themselves necessarily thrown into the opposition and were led to renounce all the work of the national movement which the governments in power had inherited. In the 1950's the local Communist Parties seemed, after the plush period of collaboration with the national movements of the years 1936–1945, to have returned to the situation of 1920, that is, of minority parties without a hold on the masses because separated from the national needs. The material conditions of the local Communist Parties (numbers, press and so on) seemed to express this state of things.[39] In actual fact, however, things were going quite otherwise, for the very problem of Communism was no longer seen in the Middle East in the same terms as in 1920. First of all, ideological conditions, as we have pointed out, had been considerably modified. The implicit ideology of the Moslem masses had integrated new situations and needs; the existence of a growing industrial proletariat, especially in Egypt and in Iraq, modified the very character of society. Moreover the national movement which had dominated the whole life and political action of the Middle East since 1920 changed its content during the

[39] "The Background of Soviet Policy" in The Middle East in Transition, pp. 388–398.

1950's. The evacuation of the national territory was everywhere achieved or in the course of being so. The objective was no longer to chase the foreign oppressor but to assure the sovereignty of the national state not only in reconquering national identity, but also within the reconquered state to assure the diverse classes and social categories access to material and cultural resources.

Social problems were seen in relatively clearer terms than in the past in proportion as the nationalization of Iranian oil, or of the Suez Canal, and the constantly increasing concessions of representatives of foreign capital prevented the native bourgeois in power at this time (the one that had led the national movement in the past, and having won, sought quite naturally to safeguard its privileged position) to withdraw in order to justify the economic and social problems behind the "imperialism which pillaged national resources." After a long period of maturation, the masses had from the 1950's on a keen awareness of their desire for radical changes. Here, once again, the Communist problem would be seen in very ambiguous terms. On the one hand, there was the problem of local Communist Parties. The theoretical re-evaluations of the Twentieth Congress[40] opened up to them new possibilities for action. While affirming an intermediate course between the two extreme camps, while affirming that with the continued strengthening of the socialist camp the independence gained could be guaranteed, Soviet theoreticians rehabilitated the national bourgeois governments of the underdeveloped world.[41] Everywhere Communist Parties have been obliged to go along with this revision which implied for them—to the extent they were not mass parties capable of directing national States—the necessity of supporting the governments in power. Their program has been completely centered on the national theme and discarded into the background the needs of social transformation and, first of all, of agrarian reform. Thus the Communist Parties of the Middle East gradually came to adopt a moderate line which advocated national interests rather than socialism. This attitude reverts to the one they had between 1936 and 1945, but it takes place on another level of development of the new nations, and because of this, the problem of socialism is raised in the Middle East, *outside the local Communist Parties*. As a result of the series of revolutions in most Middle Eastern countries between 1954

[40] *Ibid.*
[41] *Ibid.*

and 1965, army-dominated administrations[42] replaced bourgeois-led national administrations. These new regimes seized power in the name of social justice and proclaimed their determination to work quickly for economic progress.

The defeat of the Iraquian Communist Party in 1958–1960 offers an excellent illustration of the difficulties which beset the Communist Parties of the Middle East. The revolution of July 14, 1958, had been interpreted throughout the world as a Communist *coup d'état*, and the United States had sent troops at the time to Lebanon to meet the eventuality of a pro-Soviet democratic government. In reality, the success of the revolution was due to the conjuncture of diverse forces. In 1957 the democratic parties of Iraq (Communist Party, National Democratic Party, Istiklal, Baas) had secretly—for all parties had been outlawed since 1954—regrouped into a *Unified National Front*. This Front, and especially the Iraquian Communist Party, were solidly founded in the cities among the workers and the intelligentsia and were awaiting the opportunity to take action. The Iraquian revolution of July 14 was the work of the army led by General Kassem. Popular elements supported by the Iraquian Communist Party joined it.[43] During the first months of its existence the young Iraquian republic showed the circumstances of its birth by constantly leaning to the left.[44] Although the parties had not been legalized, they reorganized the *Unified National Front* in November, 1959.[45] On the second day

[42] Soviet theoreticians are at present trying to analyze the true meaning—sociologically—of this layer of militarists who have seized power in almost all the Middle Eastern countries. There is in this an extremely important new effort at understanding. Cf. G. Mirskij and T. Pokataeva, "Klassy i klassovaia bor'ba v razvyvaiushchikhsia stanakh," *Mirovaia Ekonomika: Mezhdunarodnye Otnoshenia*, 1966, pp. 57–70.

[43] In its program of 1960, the Iraquian Communist Party stressed this aspect by recalling "the support brought to our heroic national army by our great people," *Orient*, 1960 (13) p. 189.

[44] General Kassem rehabilitated the memory of the Communist "martyrs" of 1949, amnestied the Kurd leader Barzani and authorized him to return to Iraq, abolished the tribal law, re-established trade unions, promulgated a law for agrarian reform; a legal purge was organized. Above all the new government found places for members of all Communist tendencies as individuals and not as members of an outlawed party, including Kurds.

[45] Despite its illegal character, this regrouping obtained publication of its charter in the official press and permission to hold a series of meetings with the help of the *organization of partisans for peace* (notably December 30, to protest against the visit to Iraq of the American General Roundtree).

of the revolution the Iraquian Communist Party began publishing a newspaper, Ittihad al Chaab, which cultivated in the country a constant climate of revolutionary tension, one favored by attempts of rightist elements to recover power. This was the case at the time of the riots of Mosul in March, 1959. The republican regime did not collapse at Mosul because of the resistance of democratic organizations,[46] above all those of the Communists and the Kurds. The Communist Party of Iraq thought that the time had come to draw the consequences from the role it had played since July 14 in the establishment and defense of the republic and of the hesitations of General Kassem to commit himself completely to the Left.[47] As early as September the Central Committee of the Iraquian Communist Party had tried to evaluate the importance of the Iraquian revolution and the direction it would take. It had emphasized that the only revolutionary experience the Communists of the Middle East had known up to that time was the Iranian experience of 1953. What to them was fundamental and new in the Iraquian revolution of 1958 was the "mobilization of large masses of people" which gave it a profoundly progressivist character and caused a reverberation which could not fail to be felt throughout the whole Middle East. After the riots of Mosul, the Iraquian Communist Party decided that the time had come to orient the regime in an irreversible way to the Left and to demand the return of freedom for the parties, hence the recognition of its legal existence and its participation in the government.[48] General Kassem tried to avoid the problem of admitting the Communists into the government by hiding behind the "need for a period of transition" in order to come peacefully to the use of democratic insti-

[46] The putsch of Mosul took place at the very moment that the first congress of partisans for peace was meeting in the city. The conspirators, led by Colonel Aldal Wahab Chaouaf, arrested the leaders of the partisans for peace, then proclaimed an insurrection followed by the local garrison. The forces of the people which put down the insurrection, became mixed with the partisans of Peace.

[47] General Kassem tried to appease both the Left and Right at the same time. He offered the Left: withdrawal of the Bagdad Pact (March 24), ratification of the Soviet-Iraquian agreement (March 25), permission to publish a new Communist newspaper al Insanya (Humanity) (April 1), the constitution of a trade union liaison committee, the return and regrouping of Kurdish refugees in the Soviet Union around their leader Barzani and so on. . . . Kassem granted the Right of return to the Shammar tribe of Syria which reassured the conservative forces.

[48] Ittihad-al-Chaab, April 29, 1959, published by Orient, Oct. 1959, p. 195.

tutions. He seems to have been haunted during the following months by the twofold worry of not shocking Middle Eastern and international opinion by opening the way to power for the Iraquian Communist Party and, on the other hand, of not throwing this party into the opposition by bluntly opposing its demands. In this way, while delaying the "democratic period," he multiplied concessions to the Left in order to appease it. The Iraquian Communist Party took advantage of this period to arouse popular protest.[49] On July 14, 1959, the first anniversary of the Revolution, a veritable riot took place at Kirkuk as well as in other Iraquian towns between the traditionally quarrelsome Kurds and Turkomens in these regions. The riots were dramatic, accompanied as they were by very important massacres, and they were deliberately provoked by the Iraquian Communist Party. General Kassem reacted brutally and with the help of the army re-established order and launched a big campaign to clean out the Communists. However the collapse of the Iraquian Communist Party seems to have been caused more by its own retreat than by the firm attitude of General Kassem, for it seems clear that the Iraquian Communist Party could have thrown Iraq in July, 1959, into a new revolution. Why did it not do so? At the very moment of the rebellion, the Central Committee of the Iraquian Communist Party met in the presence of Khalid Begdash, the old leader of the Syro-Lebanese Communist Party who came from Moscow in order to preside. Khalid Begdash was the most respected personage of Middle Eastern Communism and in a sense its historic leader; moreover he had never entered into open conflict with the Communist Party of the Soviet Union. His presence in the dramatic days of 1959 as President of the Iraquian Central Committee took on a special significance; he spoke as a representative of the Communist Party of the Soviet Union. We know from the press of the Iraquian Communist Party, which published the report of this session, that the Central Committee criticized itself and condemned the line that had led to the riots. In addition it emphasized "the lack of education of the masses and a bad misunderstanding of the real condition of the country," the "underestimation of the other political forces of Iraq," and "the

---

[49] It was very great during this period. For example, the peasants in many places seized by force hundreds of hectars of land which were to be distributed to them as a result of the agrarian reform which became very difficult to apply.

sectarian and negative attitude of the Iraquian Communist Party toward other parties."[50]

The line which the Party would have to follow henceforth,[51] declared the Central Committee of the Iraquian Communist Party, was one of "cooperation with the government" and of "collaboration with all classes hostile to imperialism and feudalism, that is, with the lower and middle class national bourgeoisie, besides the workers and the peasants." At the beginning of 1960 political parties were again allowed to organize (Law of Jan. 1, 1960). The Iraquian Communist Party[52] presented its charter which indicated its options: a *National Front* appealing to all classes and national forces as well as to the collaboration of workers, management and private capital; modernization of the economy by respecting private property and without endangering the capitalistic system; freedom to exercise political rights; freedom of association and of organization and so on. Thus the Iraquian Communist Party returned to the line advocated by all the Communist Parties of the Middle East. The advice or pressure exercised on it through the intermediary of Khalid Begdash is easy to understand. When the threat of a government with Communist participation in Iraq came up, the disquiet of various governments, and first of all, of the Egyptian government, was very great. They extensively exploited the massacres of Kirkuk against the Communists through an appeal to national Arab opinion as well as to Moslem opinion. Soviet Russia could not approve of an operation which would gravely compromise its whole policy of cooperation with national governments that in turn were very sensitive about their independence as regards the West and that were neutralist. Moreover these national governments had until then been fully reassured by the moderate attitude of the local Communist Parties. At the same time, the Soviet Union was justified in asking if the success of the

[50] *Ittihad-al-Chaab*, Aug. 3, 1959; *Ibid.*, Aug. 23, 1959.

[51] *Pravda*, Aug. 17, 1959.

[52] In reality, this was a question of a fragment of the Iraquian Communist Party which split up at this time into two groups, one led by Abdel Kader Ismail Bustani, publisher of the *Ittihad-al-Chaab*; and the other by Daoud Sayigh, founder in 1941 of the Iraquian Communist league (*Rabitat Chouyouyin al Iraqiyin*) who would oppose the Iraquian Communist Party (*Hizb al Chouyouyin al Irakin*) founded by Youssouf Salman Youssouf. Restored to good standing in the party, Daoud Sayigh founded at the time of the second split of 1959 a rival paper, *Maabda*. His group would receive permission to exist legally in January, 1960.

Communist movement in Iraq, which probably would have provoked a stiffening of the national governments of Nasser's type, would not have compromised the fortunes of socialism in the Middle East.

For the basic ambiguity of the evolution of the Middle East at present, namely, the fact that the local Communist Parties are almost everywhere obliged to secrecy, does not imply that socialism does not have any chances. It simply indicates that its cause is not represented by Communist Parties but by governments that in other ways can give proof of solid anti-Communism. The problem which the groups in power in the Middle East face, as elsewhere in the underdeveloped world, is that of material progress, and the choices are limited if this is to be obtained in a short time. Industrialization, the key to the evolution of the underdeveloped world, can be realized either by private capitalists or by the state. Many variations can exist in the relations established between capital and the state, but the essential question is to know who holds the power to opt and to decide. However the extent of the effort needed in the underdeveloped world is such, the sacrifices leading to it are so important, that an ideology clearly is necessary to mobilize and to exalt both the efforts and the end pursued and to promise a radical reform of the structures of society. In Iraq before 1958 and in Iran, the leaders chose a development that required passing through liberal capitalism. The State intervened moderately in order to regulate the evolution, and the United States granted substantial material aid to this project. However the failures suffered in these two countries evidenced how little the ideology of capitalist society meant for underdeveloped societies and how few people were affected by it. Quite naturally, the Socialist option was accepted as much by certain leading groups as a means of mobilizing the whole nation around radical reforms as by the masses for whom this choice seemed the one which most directly concerned the oppressed. This was the direction, for example, which Nasser's Egypt took. It is interesting to note in this regard that the Egyptian revolution of 1952 was the work of the army alone, without any popular participation.[53] As soon as it came to power, the government of Nasser, while putting the Communists in prison and while avoiding mention of the word "socialism" in its first theoretical text,[54] mani-

---

[53] P. Y. Vatikiotis, *The Egyptian Army in Politics*, Bloomington, Ind. 1961.
[54] Gamal Abdel Nasser, *Philosophie de la révolution*, Cairo 1957.

fested a constant concern to overturn completely the economic and social structures of Egypt. This is evidenced by the presence at Nasser's side of a man as steeped in Marxist culture as Khalid Mohhiedine and by Nasser's frequent use of opinions formulated by Communist theoreticians.[55] On the practical level, the law of 1952 on agricultural reform involved the process of destroying feudalism which had dominated Egyptian society up to that time. However since 1961, Nasser has made clear his options with the adoption of some twenty "socialist" laws aiming at three objectives: the re-enforcement and enlargement of the public sector, the continuation of agrarian reform and the redistribution of the national revenue. These measures may seem limited but considering the state of Egyptian society prior to 1952, they have a revolutionary character about them. These were completed by the charter of 1962, by the new nationalizations at the beginning of 1964, by the pure and simple expropriation of the big landowners, by the preparation of a second Five Year Plan on more scientific bases than the preceding one and with outside financing coming primarily from socialist countries, and finally in March, 1964, by the liberation of Communists who were still interned. Surely President Nasser wanted to distinguish between *Arab socialism* and Marxism.

> Some people call us Marxists. This is absolutely false. However, we do know what Marxism is. It involves a philosophy which has its importance. One third of the world's population is Marxist. But Marxism denies religion. This is the basic difference which makes us oppose it. Our socialism is one thing, Communism is another.

And again:

> Our Socialism is the socialism explained in the charter. It is neither merely materialistic nor merely spiritual and it is not Marxist. It has its source in the very conditions of our country, where the problem was to prevent exploitation, to permit people to have the means of production in their hands, to substitute the alliance of the working forces for the preceding coalition of reactionaries with feudalism.

[55] "At the moment of accepting important American loans, the leaders of the military movement had a non-militant Marxist theoretician, who also translated Marx and Lenin into Arabic, come. He gave them a course on Imperialism, the final stage of capitalism. They turned down the loan." M. Rodinson, "Le problème des partis communistes en Syrie et en Egypte," *Cahiers internationaux*, Feb. 1958, p. 83.

One can see the road taken by Nasser's team in pursuing the social-ist choice by noting that, if during the first years of the regime they insisted on the essentially pragmatic character of the Egyptian revo-lution "not founded on a specific theory elaborated in the silence of the study of a philosopher or theorist," the charter of 1962 specifies that a "true socialism, a sane socialism ought to be established in a scientific way."

That President Nasser insists on keeping his distance from Marxism by insisting on the peculiar character of Arab socialism is natural. He thereby follows the same aspirations as those of Middle Eastern soci-ety which, on becoming nations, seeks to achieve a synthesis between two ends, the recovery of identity and modernization. It tends, thus, to integrate Marxism in the national movement, to raise the internal problems of the national body, instead of making a local transposition of revolutionary schemas resulting from other experiences. To the extent it joins this profound aspiration, Nasser's experience receives the approval of Egyptian Marxists even if some think that Nasserism has reached its limits and that, at the present stage, it blocks a revolu-tion accelerated toward social revolution.[56]

However the Egyptian example is not an isolated one; on the con-trary, other governments tend to follow it under various forms and to show that the reference to socialism seems important to them. It is so for the Baath in Syria which defends poor peasants still very attached to Islam against the ulimas. However here it is a question of a lay ideology whose principal ideologist, Michel 'Aflak, is moreover Christian.[57] Likewise in Iran the sovereign seems to be trying at pres-ent, in order to save his throne, to follow the path of a "white revo-

[56] It is interesting to see in this regard the respective positions of the two brilliant representatives of Arab Marxist thought at the present time. On the one hand, Anouar Abdel Malek, Egypte, société militaire, Paris, 1962; and Anthologie de la littérature arabe contemporaine, vol. II: Les Essais, Paris 1965. On the other hand, Hassan Ryad, L'Egypte nassérienne, Paris 1963, who contrary to Abdel Malek, who is favorably prejudiced in favor of Nasser's experience, analyzes in a very detailed way the chances of an Egyptian evolution beyond Nasserism.

[57] The judgment made in this connection on the reforms of the Baath in Syria is extremely affirmative as formulated by Soviet theoreticians. Cf. Ju. Ostro-vityanov, "Proshloe i nastoyashchie nacional'nogo socializma partii Baas," Miro-vayja Ekonomika i Mezhdunarodnye Otnoshenija, 1966 (1), pp. 44–51; and even Khalid Begdash, "La Syrie sur une voie nouvelle," Orient, Feb. 1965, pp. 109–133.

lution" which claims to be both socialist and Moslem but which shows primarily the repercussion of the socialist ideology, even under the modified forms in the popular mind of the Middle East.

Thus we see clearly in what direction these revolutions of recent years in the Middle East have taken. On the one hand, the Communist Parties, prisoners of the line ordered by Soviet Russia, confine themselves to supporting governments that are national, neutralist or favorable to Soviet Russia and demanding only that freedom of expression and of organization be granted them. On the other hand, the national governments take the path of reforming their fundamental structures by claiming to be socialist while raising the national or Islamic flag. Does this mean that this evolution is irreversible? It is quite clear that those who have been eliminated from power, those who have been dispossessed by the current reforms, as well as the Moslem religious authorities whose ideological monopoly is strongly contested, can be tempted to resist this current by brandishing against the groups in power the green flag of Islam. Already in the Middle East there is a reaction in this direction with the Pact of Islam.[58] In North Africa the weight of religious tradition hangs so heavily that it slows down all efforts to develop or to socialize.[59] However, and we have insisted on this point, the implicit Moslem ideology of the contemporary Middle East has largely integrated the aspirations toward a rapid and radical evolution toward modernization and social justice.[60] Under these conditions we may well wonder whether a monopolization of Islam by forces hostile to socialism would not end in the masses' losing their faith as they emerge from their moral and material misery.

---

[58] A recent work which is very enlightening in this regard: Maarouf Dawalibi, Nazarat Islamia fi ilishtirakiya al-Saourya—the author deplores the spiritual emptiness of the Arab world and the "snares" due to the importation of ideologies which are foreign to it, especially Marxism. To remedy this he preaches the formation of a Moslem Alliance.

[59] Samir Amin, L' Economie du Maghreb, Paris 1966, vol. II, Les perspectives d'avenir, p. 221.

[60] M. Rodinson, Islam et Capitalisme, Paris 1966, p. 237 ff.

13: MARXIAN SOCIALISM IN THE FAR EAST

Masamichi Inoki

I. TWO ELEMENTS OF MARXISM

In order to understand the relationship between Karl Marx's theory of revolution and Marxian Socialism in the Far East, we must first note that Marxism as originally formulated during the 1840's consisted of two major elements—a theory of human alienation and communist revolution and a theory of German revolution.

A. THEORY OF HUMAN ALIENATION AND COMMUNIST REVOLUTION

The first illustrates Marx's attempt to extend Ludwig Feuerbach's critique of religion to a criticism of political and economic conditions, to locate the roots of self-alienation in capitalism and to achieve the full emancipation of man under Communism through the liquidation of private ownership of means of production. Stimulated by Engel's "Umrisse zur Kritik der National-Oekonomie" (1843), Marx began to conceive this theory in "Zur Judenfrage" (1843), further developed in the Ökonomisch-philosophische Manuskripte (1844), and roughly completed in Die deutsche Ideologie (1845–1846).

It was succinctly summed up in the Communist Manifesto and was substantiated with great detail in the first volume of Das Kapital. Marx claimed in "Zur Judenfrage" that the economic life of civil society constituted the most extreme form of human alienation, and in Das Kapital he demonstrated with numerous examples drawn from the history of British capitalistic development how human alienation was intensified in a capitalistic society. Marx concluded Das Kapital not only by describing the emergence of the proletarian class—the embodiment of human self-alienation—as the gravedigger for capitalist society but also by recognizing its awakening to class consciousness and its rising to class struggle. The higher the capitalistic development is, the maturer the objective conditions for the coming of Communist revolution are. In other words the more advanced a capitalist country becomes, the nearer it draws to a proletarian revolution.

What came to occupy a central place in Marxism after the 1850's was historical materialism, formulated in Zur Kritik der politischen Ökonomie (1859). According to this concept, "the old social form will never disappear until all the productive forces that can operate within it have unfolded themselves to the last, and new higher production relations cannot develop until material conditions for them mature in the womb of the old society." In other words in the theory of human alienation and Communist revolution, the emphasis fell on objective conditions for a proletarian revolution, and in addition the proletarian guidance of the revolution tended to be relegated to the background. Thus the Marxian theory which the German Social Democratic Party embraced under the leadership of its theorist Karl Kautsky was a vulgarization of the theory of capitalistic development set forth in the first volume of Das Kapital and was characterized by a highly deterministic and fatalistic tone. The Erfurt platform did touch on revolution, but its emphasis lay in the belief that the objective conditions for a proletarian revolution would ripen as capitalism advanced and as it neglected the organizers and the driving force of the revolution, the proletariat.

If the German Social Democratic Party in the age of anti-Socialist laws appeared revolutionary, it stemmed from the need to resist Prussian militarism. An entirely different situation arose when the anti-Socialist laws were repealed in 1890 and as the laboring classes came to share in the benefits of prosperity in a maturing capitalist economy. Kautsky did not cease to use a revolutionary language, but the practical activities of the German Social Democrats evidenced reformist tendencies. Edward Bernstein's revisionism arose out of his efforts to harmonize the theory with the practice of the German Social Democratic Party by facing up to the reality of the practical reformism and by theorizing on it.

Although Bernstein's revisionism was rejected at the party convention, the German Social Democratic Party and other parties belonging to the Second International discarded the theory of Communist revolution and turned to a theory of socialistic reformism. Engels' declaration, immediately before his death, that a peaceful revolution had now become possible through parliamentary channels by the simple exercise of universal suffrage demonstrated that one of the co-founders of Marxism who survived until the 1890's had, for all practical purposes, become a revisionist himself.

B. Theory of Revolution in Backward Germany

The second element of Marxism, a theory of German revolution, Marx made his immediate and practical concern during the 1840's. In his "Zur Kritik der Hegelschen Rechtsphilosophie. Einleitung," written in 1843–1844, Marx compared England and France, the two advanced nations of Europe, with Germany, then a relatively "backward" country and pointed out that in Germany where the bourgeoisie had gone prematurely reactionary, a bourgeois democratic revolution on the British or French model would be impossible. Therefore, he asserted, the only type of revolution that could be achieved in backward Germany would be a Communist revolution led by the newly rising class of the proletariat, the very embodiment of human alienation. In the *Communist Manifesto* Marx and Engels further illustrated this thesis by their observation that the Communists were paying their chief attention to Germany by their forecast that in Germany a bourgeois revolution would immediately turn into a proletarian revolution, and by their frequent reference to the permanent revolution at the time of the revolutions of 1848.

The theory of human alienation and Communist revolution was, of course, inseparably linked with the theory of German revolution; the former theory dealt in a general way with the proletarian Communist revolution while the latter theorized about the coming of such a revolution specifically in Germany. However an essential difference existed between the general and the particular theory of Communist revolution; in the former, the emphasis fell on explaining how self-alienation was intensified under capitalism and on analyzing objective conditions for the coming of a proletarian Communist revolution, whereas in the particular theory the accent was on the *proletarian* evidence of the revolution since it was impossible to effect a bourgeois revolution in Germany.

To further corroborate his position, Marx employed Hegel's philosophy as a medium for arriving at this conclusion, for he felt that unless one argued from German classical philosophy, specifically that found in Hegel, one's thesis would inevitably lead to an anachronism. Marx explained the highly abstract character of Hegel's theory of the state by saying that it simply reflected the abstract nature of human rights guaranteed by the modern state to which the French Revolution had given rise. In other words Marx attempted to show through his critique of Hegel's philosophy that political liberation, or bourgeois revolution, in England and France was a half-way measure and a deceptive one at that.

What kind of revolution, then, ought German revolution to be? Marx maintained that political liberation, or bourgeois revolution, raising Germany to the level of England and France would not be enough, and consequently the task for the German revolution must be to attain the next state—the liberating of man. Moreover because the German bourgeoisie had become reactionary, he concluded that a political revolution could not be anticipated in backward Germany but that there was a better prospect for universal human liberation.

As the agency to achieve this universal liberation of man, Marx pointed to the proletariat—"a class which does not really fall into any existing class in civil society, but rather represents the liquidation of all classes . . ., in a word, a class which embodies the total loss of humanity and which for this reason can hope to recover itself only through the fullest recovery of man." As such a special class, the proletariat "incarnates the dissolution of society."

I have indicated that Marx did not advocate German revolution for the purpose of emancipating the modern laboring class, the bourgeoisie, which was just beginning to emerge in Germany at that time; rather Marx, in his search for the driving force to achieve universal human liberation, hit upon the proletariat. "Just as philosophy finds its material weapon in the proletariat, so does the proletariat find its spiritual weapon in philosophy." These words of Marx show that the idea of the proletariat was to him not an experiential concept but rather a philosophical category.

This theory of revolution in backward countries disappeared after the February and March Revolutions. However in the twentieth century it has been revived by Lenin in Russia, a backward country of Europe at that time. Lenin's concept of "revolutionary democratic dictatorship of the proletariat and the peasants," reinforced by the theory of uneven development, led to the idea that czarist Russia, as the weakest link in the chain of imperialism, might become the first country to plunge into a proletarian revolution.

In this sense, therefore, Lenin's theory of Russian Revolution in the opening years of the twentieth century was a revival and extension of Marx's theory of German revolution formulated in the 1840's. One important difference between them was that to Lenin the proletariat was not a philosophical category as it was to Marx but rather the living reality in Russian society—the working class closely allied with peasants who constituted five-sixths of her total population. While the Russian proletariat supplied destructive and radical revolutionary energies commonly shared by the working class everywhere during the early state of industrialization, the peasants in turn provided forces pushing toward land reform.

The theory of revolution in backward countries, formulated by Marx and adapted by Lenin, asserted that in backward countries lacking a vital objective condition for socialism—productivity—the proletariat instead of bourgeoisie would be the agent for achieving a democratic revolution which in turn would change into and lead to a socialist revolution. In short, the emphasis was not on the substance of the *Communist* revolution, but rather on the driving force, the proletarian guidance of the revolution.

II. MARXIAN SOCIALISM IN JAPAN

A.

There are in Japan today two political parties professing Marxian Socialism—the Communist Party and the Socialist Party. The former unconditionally supported Peking's policy until recently while the latter, a member of the Socialist International, is under the strong influence of the Communist Parties in Moscow and Peking. Although the Japanese Communist Party holds only five seats in the House of Representatives of the National Diet and although the Socialist Party holds 144 seats, the membership of the Communist Party, numbering nearly 150,000, is estimated as roughly three times that of the Socialist Party.

Initially Marxian Socialism was spawned in Japan by the radicalist movement which arose in defiance of the new Meiji government during the last quarter of the nineteenth century, and the ideology of this phase was influenced by the thought of Jean J. Rousseau and Herbert Spencer as well as by the Russian idea of the *Narodniki*, heroically standing against suppression by the czarist regime.

The second phase of Marxian socialism was characterized by protestant leadership and by an active interest in social reform. Among the top six leaders of the Social Democratic Party founded on May 30, 1901, all but Denjirô Kôtoku were Christians.

Immediately after being formed, the party was ordered by the police to disband. From this it became obvious that there was in Japan at that time little chance of achieving social reform by gradual and constitutional process through the National Diet. Consequently the leadership of the Socialist movement slowly shifted from Christian moderates to radical materialists.

Thus in the third phase of the party, following World War I, the labor movement grew in Japan under the powerful impact of Wilsonian democracy and the Bolshevik Revolution. Yet since the government followed a policy of ruthless suppression, to attain universal suffrage seemed impossible, and this in turn effected a division within the Party: anarcho-syndicalism, advocated by Sakae Osugi, and Bolshevism, recently imported from Soviet Russia, vied with each other for leadership of the proletarian movement. At first a romantic anarcho-syndicalism prevailed over the abstruse Marxian theory, but gradually Bolshevism oriented toward Soviet Russia became dominant. Hitoshi Yamakawa, Kanson Arakawa, Tetsu Nosaka, Eizô Kondô and Seidô Takatsu in rapid succession were converted to Bolshevism, and these men together with the original Marxist, Toshihiko Sakai, founded in July, 1922, the Japan Communist Party which won recognition at the Fourth Congress of the Comintern in November of that year.

In addition to the Communist Party which continued to exist as an illegal party, three proletarian parties were founded in 1926: the Worker-Peasant Party, a lawful left-wing group led by Ikuo Oyama; the Social Democratic Party, based on social democracy and with Professor Isoo Abe as chairman; and the Japan Worker-Peasant Party, led by Hisashi Azô and Jusô Miwa and professing a middle course. The Social Democratic Party, the right wing of the proletarian movement, was led by Christian social reformists; however the left-wing and the middle-course parties were both heavily oriented toward Marxism. Moreover the Worker-Peasant Party often serves as a lawful instrument of the Communist Party. The present Japan Socialist Party is derived from both the Worker-Peasant Party and the Japan Worker-Peasant Party while the present Democratic Socialist Party can be traced back to Isoo Abe's party.

B.

The Marxism of the Japan Communist Party was conditioned by three factors. First we may mention the rigor of governmental suppression. From its founding in 1922 to the crushing blow dealt immediately prior to World War II, the Communist Party, being an illegal party, was constantly subjected to ruthless suppression. Unlike the Communist Parties in Western Europe, it never had an opportunity to make a broad and open appeal to the people by holding forth the popular front policy adopted by the Seventh Congress of the Comintern in 1935. Instead the Japanese Communist Party virtually gave up its lawful activities and concentrated its desperate efforts in effecting a violent revolution. It is important to note, however, that it was not through a systematic analysis of Japanese society that the party reached the conclusion that a violent revolution was inevitable but rather it started out with the premise that a violent revolution was a necessity and from this viewpoint surveyed Japanese society. Moreover the possibility of a violent revolution was never questioned; it was assumed at the outset.

For less than five years—from Japan's surrender in August, 1945, to the purge of the Central Committee members by General Mac-Arthur in early June, 1950—the Japanese Communist Party could carry on its activities with relative freedom. Since 1952 when Japan recovered her independence, the Party has existed lawfully, yet because it considers its immediate enemy to be the United States linked with Japan through the United States-Japan Security Pact, it must by necessity live in constant fear of government suppression. Many leaders of the Communist Party of the pre-war days had been forced to renounce the Party and have since the end of the war been "reconverted" to Communism; consequently their previous prison experiences explain a strong persecution complex noted among Japanese Communists.

The second factor that conditioned the Japanese Communist movement was its lack of a broad base among the masses except for a brief period after World War II. A vanguard party without the support of the masses, the party has been shot through with sectarianism, and its intraparty relations are governed by a patriarchal oyabun-kobun hierarchy. As of June, 1965, the Party's central organ, *The Red Flag*, reportedly sold 200,000 copies and its Sunday edition more than

700,000 copies, yet the Communist Party controls none of the major labor unions. Even today the Party cannot be said to have set its roots broadly among the masses. Therefore we may conclude that Japanese Communism has its base among the outsiders alienated from society, that it exhibits strong signs of sectarianism and elitism, and that it tends to be dogmatic and deductive rather than empirical.

Thirdly, the Japanese Communist Party, ever since its founding, has been subservient to powerful Communist parties in foreign countries. At first, it was subordinated to the Russian Communist Party through its connection with the Comintern. After the signing of the Partial Nuclear Test Ban Treaty of 1963, it clearly assumed the role of a fifth column for the Chinese Communist Party. This, together with the absence of popular support, has rendered the Marxism of the Japanese Communist Party highly dependent on foreign direction and influence. But since early 1966, the Party is becoming more and more independent from Peking.

c.

Conditioned by the above three factors, the Marxian ideology of the Japanese Communist Party was after an era of "Fukumotoism" brought to a basic completion in the "1932 Thesis" and the theory of the "Kôza" faction which substantiated this general thesis by specific examination of Japanese capitalism. (The "Kôza" faction derived its name from the seven-volume *Courses on the Development of Japanese Capitalism* published in 1932–1933 under joint authorship.) The ideas in the new platform adopted by the Japanese Communist Party in July, 1961, may be said to be essentially an extension on "Kôza"-faction Marxism.

The so-called "Fukumotoism" made its debut as a critique of "Yamakawaism." Hitoshi Yamakawa in an essay on "New Direction for the Proletarian Class," published immediately after the founding of the Japanese Communist Party, had warned against the vanguard becoming isolated from the masses and urged the necessity of reorienting it toward them. The background of "Yamakawaism" was the rapid growth of Japanese capitalism after World War I and the rise of the labor union movement in Japan on a popular and nationwide basis. These developments had prepared conditions for the acceptance of Marxian Socialism by the laboring masses in Japan, as had been the case with the German Social Democratic Party in pre-World War I days.

The labor movement, however, was subjected to a far more ruthless suppression in Japan than it had been in Germany. Furthermore European labor movements had turned increasingly radical after the triumph of the Russian Revolution. For these reasons, Yamakawaism could never become the guiding theory of the Japanese Communist Party. Kazuo Fukumoto, who had studied in Germany from 1922 to 1924 and had fallen under the strong influence of Georg Lukács' *Geschichte und Klassenbewusstsein* (1923), attempted to apply Lenin's theory of the vanguard party to Japan in a highly dogmatic fashion. He encouraged sectarianism within the Japanese Communist Party and asserted that the proletarian movement, before it could be united, must first be divided along neat theoretical lines. His emphasis on theoretical disputes as a primary factor in the advancement of the labor movement and the Communist Party fostered the "cult of theory" so characteristic of the Japanese Communist Party.

Whereas Fukumotoism provided the Japanese Communist Party with a theoretical framework, its substance was filled in by the "1932 thesis" of the Comintern and by "Kôza"-faction Marxism. The distinctive feature of the "Kôza"-faction type of Marxism was the theory of two-stage revolution. This theory which stressed the semifeudalistic character of Japanese capitalism set as an immediate goal a bourgeois revolution aimed at the downfall of the "Emperor-system Absolutism," leaving to the future the socialist revolution that was to overthrow capitalism. The theory of two-stage revolution was, in short, Marx's theory of revolution in backward countries, imported to Japan by way of Russia. According to this theory, all efforts must be concentrated on the immediate objective of a democratic revolution, and the hard fact that Japan was a highly advanced capitalist country was evaded as much as possible. In this theory, the Emperor system was equated with Czarism and Japanese "parasitic landownership" with Russian landed aristocracy.

Even after the land reform had been enforced during the American occupation following World War II, the Japanese Communist Party did not discard "Kôza"-faction Marxism. The current party platform (published in 1961) declares: "Today, Japan is basically controlled by American Imperialism and Japanese monopolistic capital which is allied to it. Although Japan is a highly developed capitalist nation, she is a de facto dependency in a state of semi-occupation by American Imperialism." The Japanese Communist Party still continues to regard national liberation and democratic revolution as its immediate objectives and concentrates all its forces on the anti-American struggle. This policy is also in line with the Party's role as a satellite of the Chinese Communist Party.

Today thirty-four years after the announcement of the "1932 Thesis," "Kôza"-faction Marxism is far removed from the reality existing within Japan; however this brand of Marxism has acquired a new role: it postulates a theory of anti-American struggle with its center in the Chinese Communist Party. Therefore the dominant characteristic of Marxism developed by the Japanese Communist Party lies in its tortuous attempt to apply to Japan, a highly developed capitalist nation, that aspect of Marxism which relates to a theory of revolution in backward countries.

D.

In contrast, the Marxism of the Japan Socialist Party represents the other aspect of Marxism—a theory of socialist revolution in advanced capitalist nations. The Japanese Socialist Party is a coalition party and its spectrum ranges from the non-Communist left to the revisionism of the Bernstein school. The Marxian ideology of the Socialist Party may be roughly divided into the theory advanced by the Worker-Peasant faction and the theory of structural reform. The former centered in Hitoshi Yamakawa, who was expelled from the Communist Party, and remained the dominant theory of left-wing Social Democracy until the Miike coal dispute of 1960. The Worker-Peasant faction, in opposition to the "Kôza"-faction, advocated a socialist revolution that would overthrow monopolistic capitalism, and for this reason it was closer to Otto Bauer's Austrian Marxism than to any other school of European Marxism.

The Labor-Peasant faction differed from Otto Bauer in its emphasis on the inevitability of the downfall of capitalism and in its lack of a theory on transition from capitalism to socialism which Otto Bauer had developed in his Linz platform. In this sense, the Marxism advocated by the Worker-Peasant faction resembled Kautskyanism of the Erfurt platform.

The theory of structural reform, represented by Saburô Eda in the area of practical politics and led by Noboru Sato and Ichiji Nagasu on the theoretical side, was, needless to say, imported from the Italian Communist Party. In Italy and Japan, where capitalism has reached an advanced stage and where political democracy has taken root to a considerable extent, it would be manifestly impossible to stage a revolution in the form of an armed uprising or a civil war. The Communist Party in Italy and the Socialist Party in Japan—the second largest parties in their countries—would, therefore, achieve a socialist revolution through accumulation of structural reform.

While the Marxist ideology of the Japanese Communist Party represents that aspect of Marxism relating to a theory of revolution in backward countries, the Marxist ideology of the Japanese Socialist Party is closely linked to Kautskyanism and the theories of Otto Bauer and structural reform. What is common to both parties is an almost total lack of any theory of human alienation. Although during the 1920's and 1930's Hegel's works were studied in some depth and the works of G. Lukács, Karl Korsch and Herbert Marcuse on early Marxism were being slowly introduced to Japan, surprisingly little interest was shown in Marx's theory of human alienation. One reason why Japanese Marxists were contented with such an unsophisticated "philosophy" as Lenin's *Materialism and Empiriocriticism* or Stalin's *Dialectical Materialism and Historical Materialism* may be that there was in Japan no tradition of Western philosophy and its religious source, Christian theology. Moreover there is no monotheistic religion in Japan; neither militant atheism nor materialism was understood in Japan as anything more than a scientific method, and the only fruit was the cult of theory—worship of the Marxian dogma.

It is interesting to note that since the 1920's until quite recently, Japanese Marxism, despite all these limitations, continued to exert a powerful influence over her intelligentsia. Since Japan did not develop any social science discipline until after the Meiji Restoration, Marxism may be said to have served as a substitute for the social sciences. The special attraction which the Japanese intellectuals have felt toward the deductive philosophy of the Hegel-Marx type as well as toward its monistic views of the world and history may be explained by their early training in deductive reasoning through their study of the Confucianism of Chu Hsi, the state ideology of Japan during the Tokugawa period (1603–1866).

III. MARXIAN SOCIALISM IN CHINA
A.

Whereas in Japan neither the Communist Party nor the Socialist Party—representing the two elements of Marxism—has produced much results, in China, Marxism as a theory of revolution in backward countries, has achieved a great success in the form of Maoism and is now contending with Soviet Marxism for the leadership of international Communism. On the other hand, Marxism as a theory of human alienation and Communist revolution could not amount to anything in China, for China, forced into a semicolonial status by Western and Japanese imperialism, could never develop indigenous capitalism to any advanced degree.

It was primarily among the intellectuals that Marxism first took root in China. This process was conditioned by two important events: the Twenty-One Demands forced by Japan on China in 1915 during World War I, which made the Chinese intellectuals keenly aware of the need of internal reforms in order to protect China's independence; and the Russian Revolution of November, 1917, which keenly inspired them. In the spring of 1918 the Society for the Study of Marxism was organized under the leadership of Ch'en Tu-hsiu, Dean of Literature at Peking University. Li Ta-chao, Professor and Head Librarian at that University, was the central figure of this Society which became the guiding force of the May Fourth Movement of 1919. In April, 1920, three members of the Bolshevik Party—G. N. Voitinsky, Yang Ming-chai and I. K. Mamaev—were dispatched to China as representatives of the Comintern and had interviews with Li Ta-chao in Peking and with Ch'en Tu-hsiu in Shanghai. In July, 1921, the Chinese Communist Party was founded with Ch'en Tu-hsiu as the head; it became a Comintern member party in the following year.

Chinese Communism from the founding of the Party to the breakup of the first Kuomintang-Communist Coalition in 1927 was almost completely under the control of the Comintern and was not endowed with any national peculiarity of China. It was during the so-called Chingkangshan period in 1928 that Mao Tse-tung gave Chinese Communism a uniquely national shape. Until he finally cemented his control over the Chinese Communist Party during the Long March from Juichin to Shensi in 1935, Mao had been forced to struggle with both the Comintern which was ignorant of the actual condition in

China and with the leaders of the Chinese Communist Party who were under the influence of the Comintern. Since 1935 Mao Tse-tung's leadership over the Chinese Communist Party—demonstrated by his accurate judgments concerning the anti-Japanese war, brilliant victory over Chiang Kai-shek's Nationalist Regime in the Civil War, effective conduct of the Korean War, and the success of economic build-up until 1958—has been heightened into a kind of charisma. The agricultural crisis of 1959–1961 and the Sino-Soviet split which began to intensify roughly about this time have not yet shaken Mao Tse-tung's prestige and influence.

B.

Maoism draws a great deal on Leninism-Stalinism. I have pointed out elsewhere[1] that Mao's theory of "people's democratic dictatorship" and Lenin's theory of "dictatorship of the proletariat and the peasants" have much in common with each other and that there is perfect agreement between Maoism and Leninism-Stalinism concerning "guidance by a vanguard party and by its party organs" and the so-called "socialist primitive accumulation." In this sense, Maoism is a theory of revolution in backward countries, imported from Soviet Russia in the form of Leninism-Stalinism. The clearest expression of this feature of Maoism is found in Mao Tse-tung's characterization of the Chinese Revolution as a neodemocratic revolution in his essay entitled *The Chinese Revolution and the Communist Party* written in 1939.[2] However Maoism has four major features that were absent in Leninism-Stalinism.

In the first place, Mao Tse-tung regarded the peasant movement as the primary driving force of the Chinese Revolution. Although Lenin, too, had advocated an alliance between the proletariat and the peasants and had stressed the importance of the peasant movement, he by no means considered it to be the chief force of the Russian Revolution. In his *Report on an Investigation of the Peasant Movement in Hunan*, Mao Tse-tung stated:

[1] Masamichi Inoki, "Leninism and Mao Tse-tung's Ideology," *Unity and Contradiction*, ed. by Kurt London, New York 1962, pp. 103–121.

[2] *Ibid.*, p. 107.

... the present upsurge of the peasant movement is a colossal event. In a very short time, in China's central, southern and northern provinces, several hundred million peasants will rise like a mighty storm, like a hurricane, a force so swift and violent that no power, however great, will be able to hold it back. They will smash all the trammels that bind them and rush forward along the road to liberation. They will sweep all the imperialists, warlords, corrupt officials, local tyrants and evil gentry into their graves. Every revolutionary party and every revolutionary comrade will be put to the test, to be accepted or rejected as they decide. There are three alternatives. To march at their head and lead them? To trail behind them, gesticulating and criticizing? Or to stand in their way and oppose them? Every Chinese is free to choose, but events will force you to make the choice quickly.[3]

Mao Tse-tung made evident his choice and underscored the historical mission of the peasant movement in the Chinese Revolution in "Down with the Local Tyrants and Evil Gentry: All Power to the Peasant Association!"

... the fact is that the great peasant masses have risen to fulfill their historic mission and that the forces of rural feudalism, . . . the patriarchal-feudal class of local tyrants, evil gentry and lawless landlords has formed the basis of autocratic government for thousands of years and is the cornerstone of imperialism, warlordism and corrupt officialdom. To overthrow these feudal forces is the real objective of the national revolution. In a few months the peasants have accomplished what Dr. Sun Yat-sen wanted, but failed, to accomplish in the forty years he devoted to the national revolution. This is a marvellous feat never before achieved, not just in forty, but in thousands of years. It's fine. It is not "terrible" at all. It is anything but "terrible."[4]

Similarly Mao asserted that there was no need to fear "going too far" and that, on the contrary, it would be necessary to "create fear":

There is revolutionary significance in all the actions which were labeled as "going too far" in this period. To put it bluntly, it is necessary to create terror for a while in every rural area, or otherwise it would be impossible to suppress the activities of the counter-revolutionaries in the countryside or overthrow the authority of the gentry. Proper limits have to be exceeded in order to right a wrong, or else the wrong cannot be righted. Those who talk about the peasants "going too far" seem at first sight to be different from those who say "It's terrible!" as mentioned earlier, but in essence they proceed from the same standpoint and likewise voice a landlord theory that upholds the interests of the priv-

[3] Selected Works of Mao Tse-tung, Peking 1965, vol. I, pp. 23–24.
[4] Ibid., p. 27.

ileged classes. Since this theory impedes the rise of the peasant movement and so disrupts the revolution, we must firmly oppose it.[5]

The second distinctive feature of Maoism is the theory of the people's war. Mao had armed the peasants and had fought in the forefront of the land revolution war, but as the counterrevolutionary forces gained an ascendancy throughout China, he entrenched himself in the mountainous area of Chingkangshan in Kiangsi Province to prepare his forces for a future comeback. In October, 1928, he stated five reasons why the Red regime in China could hold out amidst the encirclement of the counterrevolutionary forces. Among these, the following was of particular importance:

First, it cannot occur in any imperialist country or in any colony under direct imperialist rule, but can only occur in China which is economically backward, and which is semi-colonial and under indirect imperialist rule. For this unusual phenomenon can occur only in conjunction with another unusual phenomenon, namely, war within the White regime. It is a feature of semi-colonial China that, since the first year of the Republic (1912), the various cliques of old and new warlords have waged incessant wars against one another, supported by imperialism from abroad and by the comprador and landlord classes at home. Such a phenomenon is to be found in none of the imperialist countries nor for that matter in any colony under direct imperialist rule, but only in a country like China which is under indirect imperialist rule. Two things account for its occurrence, namely, a localized agricultural economy (not a unified capitalist economy) and the imperialist policy of marking off spheres of influence in order to divide and exploit. The prolonged splits and wars within the White regime provide a condition for the emergence and persistence of one or more small Red areas under the leadership of the Communist Party amidst the encirclement of the White regime. The independent regime carved out on the borders of Hunan and Kiangsi Provinces is one of many such small areas. In difficult or critical times some comrades often have doubts about the survival of Red political power and become pessimistic. The reason is that they have not found the correct explanation for its emergence and survival. If only we realize that splits and wars will never cease within the White regime on China, we shall have no doubts about the emergence, survival and daily growth of Red political power.[6]

In December, 1936, Mao Tse-tung synthesized his experiences during the second revolutionary war in his "Problem of Strategy in

[5] *Ibid.*, p. 29.
[6] *Ibid.*, p. 65.

China's Revolutionary War" and formulated his famous four principles of guerrilla warfare:

> By May 1928, however, basic principles of guerrilla warfare, simple in nature and suited to the conditions of the time, had already been evolved, that is, the sixteen-character formula: "The enemy advances, we retreat; the enemy camps, we harass; the enemy tires, we attack; the enemy retreats, we pursue." This sixteen-character formulation of military principles was accepted by the Central Committee before the Li Li-san line. Later our operational principles were developed a step further. At the time of our first counter-campaign against "encirclement and suppression" in the Kiangsi base area, the principle of "luring the enemy in deep" was put forward and, moreover, successfully applied. By the time the enemy's third "encirclement and suppression" campaign was defeated, a complete set of operational principles for the Red Army had taken shape.[7]

Learning from his direct experience during the second revolutionary war, Mao enumerated the following six conditions for going over to the counteroffensive: 1) the population actively supports; 2) the terrain is favorable for operations; 3) all the main forces of the Red Army are concentrated; 4) the enemy's weak spots have been discovered; 5) the enemy has been reduced to a tired and demoralized state; and 6) the enemy has been induced to make mistakes.[8] The "Three Rules of Discipline" and the "Six Points for Attention,"[9] which Mao Tse-tung spelled out for the Red soldiers in 1928, show how anxious he was to secure the support of the population; for he stated such support was to a successful guerrilla war what water was to fish.

The third basic feature of Maoism is its heavy stress on self-reformation and "mind-training," which spring from China's intellectual tradition and its lack of emphasis on militant atheism. This tendency, which I have commented on in my paper mentioned above, is clearly revealed in a noteworthy speech on "The Mind-Training of Communists," made by Liu Shao-ch'i at the Marx-Lenin Institute in Yenan on August 7, 1939. In it, he stated:

> For revolutionaries to make personal efforts to train their minds and to study while engaged in revolutionary struggles is quite necessary and indispensable for their self-reformation and improvement.

[7] *Ibid.*, p. 213.
[8] *Ibid.*, pp. 215–216.
[9] *Selected Works of Mao Tse-tung*, vol. IV, p. 156.

A revolutionary trained through many years of revolutionary struggles does not always grow into a distinguished, skilled revolutionary. That depends chiefly on the effort and self-training of the revolutionary himself. A real, distinguished, skilled revolutionary is made through many years of training and mind-cultivation in the revolutionary struggle. Therefore, we Communists should train ourselves and cultivate our minds through various difficulties and hardships in the extensive popular revolutionary movement and at the same time keep ourselves sensitive to new things and improve our brains so that we can be revolutionaries with noble character and firm political conviction.

Confucius says: "I began my studying at fifteen, became independent at thirty, learned not to be troubled at forty, knew my Heaven-assigned mission at fifty, learned to listen to anything at sixty, and found myself acting at will without going to extremes at seventy." This is one course of self-training and mind-cultivation, and Confucius here does not profess himself to be a wise man.

Mencius says: "So, when Heaven is about to entrust a man with a vital mission, it always first tortures his heart, works his body hard, famishes his flesh, deprives him of his means, and frustrates his plans, all for the purpose of training his mind, strengthening his character and making him learn to do what he has been poor at doing." This also shows that one needs a course of training and mind-cultivation in order to be a great man. The Communists, entrusted with the "vital mission" of achieving a world reformation unprecedented in history, particularly need such training and mind-cultivation.[10]

The above statement shows a close connection between Maoism and Confucian thinking in China. In Christianity, which finds salvation in the grace given from above by a transcendental God, there is no such concept of mind-training as is contemplated in Confucianism. Atheism, as the antithesis or the negation of Christianity, considers human nature as inherently good and regards all evils as stemming from such external factors as state power or private ownership of property. In Leninism-Stalinism, reformation of man—self-criticism—as something given *from above* and *from outside* was considered necessary whereas in Maoism the Party head Mao Tse-tung himself must constantly *reform and train himself*.

It is true that ideological reformation, called "brain-washing," implies coercive persuasion through group pressure, and in this sense self-reformation resembles self-criticism in Leninism-Stalinism. However we must not ignore the fact that self-reformation and mind-training

[10] Liu Shao-chi, *Shuyô Chosaku Shû* [*Major Works*], Japanese edition, Kyoto 1959, vol. I, pp. 16–17.

in Maoism contain elements essentially different from self-criticism in Leninism-Stalinism. These elements clearly spring from China's intellectual climate, especially Confucianism. In his essay published in October, 1938, Mao Tse-tung stressed China's historical heritage:

> Our people have a history of thousands of years. We have distinct characteristics of our own and many other things of value. So far as these things are concerned, we are as yet mere school children. Present-day China is a phase of historical China. We believe in Marxian history. We should not cut up history. We should sum up all things between Confucius and Sun Wen and succeed to this priceless heritage, which contains much that would be useful to us in guiding the great movement now under way. Communists are international Marxists. But Marxism can be achieved here only in connection with the actual peculiarities of our country and in a manner well suited to our people. Marxism-Leninism is powerful because it finds itself in harmony with the actualities of a revolution in any country. As for the Chinese Communist Party, it must learn to apply the theories of Marxism-Leninism to the real environment in China. If any Chinese Communist, who is part of the Chinese people and their flesh and blood, talks about Marxism without regard to the peculiarities of China, his must be only academic, empty Marxism.[11]

The following statement by Liu Shao-chi in a report made to the Seventh Party Congress on May 14, 1945, may be said to show clearly the relationship between Maoism and Chinese tradition:

> Mao Tse-tung's ideology is one in which the theories of Marxism-Leninism and the actual experiences in the Chinese revolution are united. It is Chinese Communism, or Chinese Marxism.[12]

As the fourth feature of Maoism, not yet fully developed, we must mention the theory of "contradictions among the people themselves," which Mao Tse-tung elaborated in his speech of February 27, 1957:

> However, this does not mean that there are no longer any contradictions in our society. Such an idea is too simple and does not agree with objective facts. There are two kinds of social contradictions before us— those between enemies and those among the people, which are clearly distinguished from each other in nature. . . . Contradictions between enemies are antagonistic. Contradictions among the working people are

---

[11] Mao Tse-tung, Senahû [Selected Works], Japanese edition, Kyoto 1952, vol. IV, p. 31.
[12] Liu Shao-chi, Shuyô Chosaku Shû, vol. II, p. 40.

nonantagonistic, and differences between the exploiters and the exploited have both antagonistic and nonantagonistic aspects. Contradictions among the people, which have always existed, have characteristics in each stage of the revolution and socialist construction. Under the present conditions of our country, "contradictions among the people" include those within the proletariat; within the peasant class; within the intelligentsia; between workers and peasants; among workers, peasants, and intellectuals; between the proletariat and other working classes on one hand and the nationalist bourgeoisie on the other; and within the nationalist bourgeoisie. Our people's Government represents the true interest of the people and is the servant of the people. But even between this Government and the people at large there are contradictions, including those between national or collective interests and individual interests, between democracy and centralism, between the leaders and the guided, and between some Government-agency members with their bureaucratic ways and the public. . . . Generally speaking, different contradictions among the people grow from the ground of basic agreement in interest among the people.[13]

What is particularly noteworthy is that Mao Tse-tung in admitting that contradictions can arise between the people and the Government which represents their true interest as well as between the guided and the leaders implies the necessity and the possibility of patient persuasion and indoctrination instead of physical liquidation of opponents in the manner of Stalin. In other words, Mao's admission of contradictions among the people themselves and his emphasis on self-reformation and on mind-training are inseparably linked with each other.

The four features of Maoism we have described above show that it is a peculiarly Chinese brand of Marxism built on the pragmatic lesson learned from the unique experience of the Chinese Revolution. The core of Maoism lies in the creation of a peculiarly Chinese theory of revolution by drawing on Marxism as a theory of revolution in backward countries rather than by simply applying Marxism to China.

What is most significant is that Mao Tse-tung seems to have read hardly any of the original works of Marx and Engels and only a portion of Lenin's writings; he obtained his knowledge of Marxism from this narrow reading of Lenin's works as well as from *The Courses on Dialectic Materialism* written by the members of the Institute of Phi-

---

[13] Mao Tse-tung, *Sengo Chosaku Shû* [*Works Since World War II*], Japanese edition, Kyoto 1959, pp. 136–138.

losophy of the Leningrad branch of the Soviet Academy.[14] When we recall that Lenin had studied not only Marx's major writings but also Hegel's works, the contrast becomes markedly sharp.

Today Maoism exerts powerful influence over Korea and Viet Nam, which have had a strong tradition of Chinese civilization, and also over Japan. In these countries, where Confucianism and Mahâyâna Buddhism have been introduced from China, Maoist "mind-training" can easily take root. However it is only in Viet Nam that the theory of the people's war with its stronghold in the village is being put into practice. Reading the works of Ho Chi Minh[15] left me, naturally enough, with a strong impression of his emphatic harping on the inhumanness of colonialism. In view of the fact that Ho Chi Minh had originally been a member of the French Communist Party, it is hardly surprising that Western Humanism has had a far stronger impact on the Vietnamese Communist Party than on Maoism. The distinctive factor of Ho Chi Minh's Communism lies in its denunciation of the cruelty of Western colonialism and its attack on racial prejudices by use of the logic of Western Humanism.

[14] Mineo Nakajima has made a paragraph-to-paragraph comparison between Mao Tse-tung's On Practice and On Contradiction on the one hand, and The Courses on Dialectic Materialism on the other, demonstrating how he was influenced by the latter. According to this study, there occur in Mao Tse-tung's Collected Works 37 quotations from Lenin's works, 25 from Stalin's, 6 from Marx's, 2 from Engels' and 2 from the joint works of Marx and Engels. Most of his quotations from Lenin are from the latter's Philosophical Notebooks, and the quotations from Marx and Engels are familiar and widely known statements. Cf. Mineo Kakajima, Gendai Chûgoku Ron [On Contemporary China], Tokyo 1964, pp. 52–53; p. 59.

[15] Ho Chi Minh, Selected Works, Hanoi 1960, vol. I, pp. 11–24.

Part III:
Marx and Christianity

14: MARX'S ATTITUDE TOWARD RELIGION[1]

Nicholas Lobkowicz

It is often believed that the founder of "scientific Communism" was a militant atheist who considered the extermination of religion and, in particular, of Christianity one of his major tasks. This belief is, to say the least, inexact. Marx, of course, was an atheist. And we may add that his atheism is neither a purely methodological one (in the sense in which modern science, for example, might be called "methodologically atheist" insofar as it disregards God as a possible explanatory factor); nor is it merely a skeptical one (in the sense in which some modern philosophers maintained that they would have granted God's existence if only their philosophical reflection were to force them to do so). Nor does it seem correct to say, as M. Reding did in a much discussed book,[2] that Marx's atheism is a historical accident rather than an essential feature of the Marxian *Weltanschauung*. Marx's atheism is distinctly dogmatic, in the sense that Marx always denied decidedly and uncompromisingly the existence of a divine being, and this denial is one of the major cornerstones of Marx's outlook.

Marx, however, was far from ascribing to the antireligious fight the importance which it has, for example, in the eyes of contemporary communists. He looked on religion as a consequence of a more basic evil, the evil of a society in which man "has not yet found himself or has already lost himself again."[3] He was always somewhat surprised, indeed annoyed, by the persistent attacks on religion of such militant atheists as Feuerbach or the Bauer brothers. As he saw it, religion in general and Chrisitanity in particular were *in extremis*, if not already dead. No wonder, then, that the passionate atheists of the Hegelian

---

[1] This article originally was published in *The Review of Politics*, 1964 (26), pp. 319–352.

[2] M. Reding, *Der politische Atheismus*, Graz 1958.

[3] *MEW*, I, 378.

Left reminded him of Sancho Panza who, according to Cervantes' *Don Quixote*, mercilessly beat harmless attendants at a funeral procession.[4] One does not come to blows with a dying figure, especially if such a fight cannot hasten his decease.

This last point is of some importance. After all, one might be willing to finish a dying enemy by a final deathblow. But Marx did not believe that such a direct attack against religion would ever work. Since religion is only the symptom of a more basic discrepancy, the demise of religion cannot be hastened. Any direct struggle against religion, therefore, appeared to Marx as useless and misplaced: useless, because religion simply cannot be abolished as long as the world is not put straight; misplaced, because the real enemy is the perverted social order of which, as Marx put it, religion is only the "spiritual aroma."[5] Any efficient treatment has to be radical, that is, to reach the very roots of the evil.

It is in this sense that Marx accused his onetime friend, Bruno Bauer, of treating religion as if it were an independent being: "Mr. Bauer comprehends only the *religious* essence of Judaism, not the worldly and thus real foundation of this religious entity."[6] To criticize religion without criticizing its secular roots amounts to persisting in a standpoint which is not less "theological" than the religious standpoint itself. Aristotle and, more recently, Hegel, used to say that contraries belong to the same genus. Atheism which takes itself to be an end in itself, when it is only the negation of and the antithesis to religion, cannot radically succeed in transcending the "religious level":

> The question about an *alien* being, about a being above nature and man—a question which implies the admission of the inessentiality of nature and man—has become virtually impossible. *Atheism*, as the disavowal of this inessentiality, has no longer any meaning, for atheism is a *negation of God* and postulates the *existence of man* through this negation; but socialism *qua* socialism no longer stands in any need of such a mediation.[7]

Later it will be noted that this passage, though implicitly aimed at Ludwig Feuerbach, is modeled on Feuerbach's own conceptual scheme. Here it may suffice to state that whereas Feuerbach and the

[4] *MEW*, III, 216 ff.
[5] *MEW*, I, 378.
[6] *MEW*, II, 115.
[7] *MEGA*, I, 3, 125.

Left Hegelians viewed religion simply as a wrong ideology, that is, as a competing *Weltanschauung* which misinterprets the nature of man, Marx considered it as the reflection of a wrong world. In his "Theses on Feuerbach," Marx stated that Feuerbach saw religion as a sort of division of the world "into a religious, imaginary world, and a real one" and then proceeded to the "dissolution of the religious world into its secular basis." In short he unmasked religion as a self-illusion and opposed to it what he considered to be the true facts. But what he overlooked, as Marx pointed out, is the fact "that after completing this work, the chief thing still remains to be done. For the fact that the secular foundation detaches itself from itself and establishes itself in the clouds as an independent empire can only be explained by the self-cleavage and self-contradictoriness of this secular basis."[8]

There is even a sense in which Marx would seem to be prepared to admit that religion is "true." For though it is objectively false and thus cannot be defended against a scientific *Weltanschauung*, it adequately reflects a world which itself is wrong.[9] Religion is true in the sense of "true" intended in the possible reply to someone who, having lost himself to material pleasures, maintains that man does not differ from animals: "Of course, you made it true."

Feuerbach had shown that God is nothing more than a fictious agglomerate of everything which is admirable, good and beautiful in man; because he has yielded them to an "alien being," the religious believer views himself as stripped of all perfections. Marx, for his part, proceeds to show that the image which the believer has of himself is correct. Though God, of course, does not exist and all religion is simply nonsense, man is right in believing that he has no perfection of his own; indeed, this is the sole reason why he invents religion—to compensate for and to sublimate his real wretchedness. Just as the absolute monarch who despises his subjects and treats them as if they were not human beings is right, since there actually are no true men where the "monarchic principle" is not queried,[10] so too, the religious

---

[8] *MEW*, III, 6 .

[9] As I. Fetscher has pointed out in *Marxismusstudien* Tübingen 1957, vol. II, p. 33, Marx always described "ideologies" as false reflections of a false world; the same applies to religion. But precisely because they are *reflections*, both ideologies and religion are "true" in the sense described above. Cf. E. Weil, *Marxismusstudien*, Tübingen 1962, vol. IV, p. 47.

[10] *MEW*, I, 340.

believer with his "perverted world consciousness" is right, since he is the product of a perverted world of which religion is merely a reflection.[11]

Accordingly Marx's criticism of religion moves on two levels. There is, first, the unmasking of religion which, according to Marx, has been "in the main" completed by his predecessors, especially by Bruno Bauer and Feuerbach. But as this unmasking of religion reveals that religion is "true" in the sense just described, a second kind of criticism has to follow: religion has to be *made false*, that is, the secular world has to be changed in order to cease producing this pathological secretion. Once the secular world is discovered to be the source of religious ideas, it must be "annihilated in theory and in practice."[12] As Marx put it in his famous introduction to the never completed *Critique of the Hegelian Philosophy of Right*, the criticism of heaven has to turn into a criticism of earth.[13] *This* kind of criticism cannot be limited to words. Feuerbach's analysis of religion resulted in no more than the correction of an error; Marx's more radical analysis inevitably leads to revolutionary action.

This idea that religion is merely an epiphenomenon which, if properly analyzed, reveals the nature of a fundamentally wrong world explains Marx's reserve with respect to all doctrinal and aggressive atheism, not to speak of any violent coming to grips with the churches. The atheism of Feuerbach and of all the Left Hegelians looked almost like a "last stage of theism, a negative recognition of God";[14] they simply ascribed "much too great an importance" to the fight against religious illusions.[15] The French Revolution itself showed that terrorism, instead of exterminating religion, only succeeds in converting it from a public into a private affair.[16]

The few references to religion made by Marx in his later years indicate that, in spite of his lack of interest in this kind of problem, his view on religion and atheism did not change as the years passed. Thus, for instance, in his critique of the Gotha Program of 1875, though stressing that bourgeois "freedom of conscience" is nothing but the

[11] *MEW*, I, 378.
[12] *MEW*, III, 6. In Engels' edition of the "Theses on Feuerbach," the passage runs: "criticized in theory and revolutionized in practice." Cf. *ibid.*, 534.
[13] *MEW*, I, 379.
[14] *MEW*, II, 116.
[15] *MEW*, III, 218.
[16] *MEW*, II, 118, cf. I, 357.

toleration of all possible kinds of religious freedom of conscience, Marx argues that "everyone should be able to relieve religious and bodily nature without the police sticking their noses in."[17] In 1874, Engels even went so far as to claim that "the only service which one can still render to God is to declare atheism a compulsory article of faith."[18]

How, then, did it come about that advocates of communism have been among the most violent persecutors of religion? E. Weil a few years ago provided an answer which, as is the case with most good answers, is so obvious that it is easily overlooked.[19] As the proletarian revolution did not take place, Marx's pupils sought to explain the apparent failure of the master's predictions. These explanations thus enabled the Marxists to continue their adherence to their creed in spite of the inadequacy of its predictions. The explanations also provided prerequisites for future revolutionary actions.

At this point the Marxists discovered the power of ideas which to Marx had been only afterthoughts to real events. They discovered that religion, being basically antirevolutionary, for it invites men to accept this vale of tears, was a powerful brake restraining history from taking the course predicted by Marx. Thus Christianity and Christian Churches again became a true enemy as the representatives of competing social and political doctrines. They were also powerful supranational organizations which opposed the interest of the proletarian class in general and the proletarian revolution in particular. As Weil put it, Marx believed that only a transformation of the circumstances could succeed in making religion superfluous; his followers, in an odd but quite understandable return to Feuerbach, reached the conclusion that the fight against religion is a precondition of the transformation of circumstances.

Marx's original attitude toward religion, however, is far more shock-

---

[17] *MEW*, XIX, 31.

[18] *MEW*, XVIII, 532. In the same text which criticized the Blanquists and Bakuninists for their militant atheism, Engels wrote: "Of the German social-democrat workers one can say that atheism is something obsolete among them; this purely negative expression does no longer apply. . . ." (This passage was written in 1874; in a later edition (1894) Engels amended the passage: "Of the great majority of German social-democrat workers, etc."). See also Engels' letter to W. Liebknecht, December 15, 1871, cf. K. Marx-F. Engels, *Briefe an A. Bebel, W. Liebknecht, K. Kautsky und andere*, Moscow-Leningrad 1933, vol. I, p. 41 ff.

[19] E. Weil, *Marxismusstudien*, Tübingen 1962, vol. IV, p. 159.

ing than that of his followers. Religion, especially Christianity, always had its enemies and almost every religion has been criticized, attacked or persecuted at one time or another. But seldom if ever has Christianity been so radically "taken unseriously" as in Marx. What could be more humiliating to a Christian than to be told that he is not an enemy worth fighting, since he is done for anyway?[20]

In the *Communist Manifesto* Marx and Engels defended themselves against "bourgeois objections to Communism." This defense follows a peculiar pattern: whenever accused of wanting to abolish this or to establish that, the authors of the *Manifesto*,[21] instead of clearly stating that they do or do not want to do it, reply: "There is no need to do it. History already has done it for us." Thus, for instance, when accused of trying to introduce community of women, they reply: "The Communists have no need to introduce it; it has existed almost from time immemorial." The authors then proceed to show how and why. Similarly when accused of trying to abolish Christianity and to establish atheism, they reply (after having duly emphasized that such charges do not deserve serious examination): "When the ancient world was in its last throes, the ancient religions were overcome by Christianity. When in the eighteenth century Christian ideas succumbed to the ideas of the Enlightenment, feudal society fought its death battle with the then revolutionary bourgeoisie."[22] That is to say, Christianity gave up the ghost on the eve of the French Revolution, just when the class now to be replaced by the proletariat was coming into power.

In a book review written about two years after the *Manifesto*, Marx explained that all conceptions and ideas are transformed with each great transformation of social circumstances. Different social circumstances generate different religions. Presently people have at last discovered the secret of this historical process and are no longer willing to deify this process in the exuberant form of a new religion.

[20] This has been well emphasized by H. Gollwitzer in *Marxismusstudien* IV. See my review in *Natural Law Forum*, 1963 (8), p. 137 ff.

[21] It is comparatively seldom noticed that the final version of the *Manifesto* must have been written by Marx alone. Marx completed the manuscript in January, 1848, while Engels was away in Paris; he used Engels' sketch "Principles of Communism," of 1847. For an interesting comparison between Engels' original sketch and the *Manifesto*, see H. Bollnow, *Marxismusstudien*, Tübingen 1954, vol. I, p. 76 ff.

[22] *MEW*, IV, 480.

They simply "strip off all religion."[23]

In the presence of such an almost flippant attitude toward religion it would seem proper to ask: what made Marx think that Christianity is dead and that all religion is in its last agonies? Indeed, to maintain that "all religion is nothing but the fantastic reflection of the exterior powers which dominate man's everyday life"[24] is one thing; to say that all religion has been played out as a historical phenomenon is quite another thing. Yet it is, let us repeat this, precisely this last point which permits Marx to desist from all pugnacious attitudes toward religion.

If I am not mistaken, neither Marx nor Engels ever stated why they believed Christianity to be dead; indeed, they never put it literally this way. But they occasionally speak of an eventual "withering away" of religion; and as to why religion sooner or later will disappear, they seem to offer two kinds of answer.

The first type of answer is found mainly in Engels. It amounts to saying that, as religion is only a "fantastic reflection" of those powers of nature and society which man does not understand and thus is unable to master, religion will disappear with the progress of science, somewhat as alchemy and other "occult sciences" disappeared with the advent of modern science. A passage from Engels' drafts for *Anti-Dühring* illustrates this argument:

> To primitive man, the forces of nature were something alien, mysterious, superior. At a definite stage through which *all* civilizations pass he assimilates such forces by personifying them. This inclination to personify produced gods everywhere—and the *consensus gentium* which is used to prove God's existence proves nothing more than the universality of this inclination, and thus also of religion, as a necessary, but transitory stage of civilization. It is not till the forces of nature are really understood that the gods and God are expelled from their positions one by one. At present, this development has reached a point which permits one to say that it is virtually completed.[25]

This argument, of course, is not peculiar to Marxism. It is common to all rationalism with an atheist tinge. Accordingly whenever developing this argument, Engels tends to deviate from the original Marxian conception according to which all "theoretical products and forms

---

[23] *MEW*, VII, 201. The passage is translated in the selection: Marx-Engels, *On Religion*, Moscow 1963, p. 90 ff.

[24] *MEW*, XX, 294.

[25] *MEW*, XX, 582 ff.

of consciousness such as religion, philosophy, morals and the like" have to be explained exclusively in terms of the "material process of production."[26] Thus, for example, after having emphasized that religion is based upon what today we would call nonsense, Engels admits that religion and similar wrong conceptions of nature and of the human condition "in most cases, have only a negative economic foundation."[27]

Apart from this rationalist argument, there is a specifically Marxian argument for the withering away of religion. It is an argument that cannot really be separated from the first argument and that has not been explicitly stated. It amounts to saying that, as religion is the pus of a sick world, it will disappear as soon as the world is restored to health again. Whereas the former argument assumed that religion originates from man's impotence in the presence of "blind forces," the latter is based upon the assumption that religion is both an expression of, and a protest against, "economic alienation." In religion, man's own activities "operate on man as an alien, divine, or diabolic activity" as though they were operating independently of the individual, just as, and because, in his material life man has lost himself to another.[28] Consequently the abolition of the ultimate roots of this self-alienation (which, in 1844, Marx saw as involved in the very act of labor) in restoring man's true nature also destroys religious alienation. "The positive transcendence of *private property* as the appropriation of *human* life *is, therefore,* the positive transcendence of all alienation—that is to say, the return of man from religion, family, state, etc., to his *human,* i.e., *social* mode of existence."[29]

In short, once man has found his way back to himself in the "material" order, he has no need to delude himself. Religion as an expression of his distress will disappear exactly as morbid delusions vanish with the body's restoration to health. Insofar as it is a protest against this distress, the sigh of an oppressed nature, it will become superflu-

[26] *MEW,* III, 37 ff.

[27] Engels to C. Schmidt, October 27, 1890, cf. *On Religion,* p. 284. Engels says that religion "stands furthest away from material life, and seems to be most alien to it," *MEW,* XXI, 303. Cf. also the following passage in Marx: "It is indeed far easier to discover by analysis the earthly kernel of religious formations than to develop the deified forms out of the particular situations of real life. And yet the latter method is the only scientific one." *MEW,* XXIII, 393.

[28] *MEGA,* I, 3, 86.

[29] *MEGA,* I, 3, 115.

ous. The illusory happiness which the religious opiate offers will be replaced by "real happiness."[30]

Although this argument cannot truly be separated from the one mentioned earlier, the difference between the two arguments may be stated. The first does seem to allow for the abolition of religion independently of the social revolution, simply in terms of the progress of science; the second, on the contrary, considers the final restoration of man, that is, the social revolution, a necessary condition of the ultimate downfall of religion.

As the progress of man's mastery over nature and the social world finally enables man to destroy the coercion of social circumstances, it might be argued that science will overcome religion exactly when the progress we make in the means of production effectuates man's final shedding of everything asocial. The two processes are perfectly parallel, as it were. The progress of man's mastery over nature is the ultimate principle of history;[31] Marx's claim that man is living in a state of alienation, in the end, amounts to saying that he is governed by physical, biological, economical, in short, preconscious and thus subhuman, powers instead of governing them. But the progress of man's mastery over nature finds its adequate expression in science and is in turn furthered by science, the history of which is the history of the gradual clearing away of all ideological nonsense, "or rather the history of its replacement by fresh, but always less absurd nonsense."[32]

Whereas Engels' more rationalist argument views the withering away of religion mainly as the gradual destruction of an ideology by science, the second argument, found principally in Marx's early writings, is based upon the assumption that the economic and social restoration of man entails a dissolution of all ideological superstructures into spontaneous and, as it were, "earth-based" attitudes of man.

Yet it is precisely at this point that the second argument cannot do without the first one.[33] Indeed, Marx has to explain why, for example,

---

[30] *MEW*, I, 379.

[31] In the end, the principle of development and thus of history is the dialectics of need and satisfaction as described in the *German Ideology*. Means of production develop only because each new means generates new needs and thus asks for new instruments. Cf. *MEW*, III, 28.

[32] Engels to C. Schmidt, cf. *On Religion*, p. 284.

[33] This point is of some relevance to the discussion as to whether Engels' "dialectical materialism" is compatible with Marx's philosophical conception.

morals, philosophy and arts are not simply liquidated but rather freed from a false "ideological" consciousness, that is, integrated in man's real life, whereas religion just disappears. This, it seems, can be done only by showing that religion, contrary to all other ideological forms, has no proper foundation at all in man's material life. To this end, then, scientific research must solve the pseudo-problems of religion. Even the state, though it, like religion, will wither away, has a real foundation; in future society, the state will die by losing its legitimate function, whereas religion will wither away by losing its entirely illegitimate function.[34]

Marx's own interpretation goes to this point. But we must add that Marx "knew" about the imminent death of religion and, in particular, of Christianity a long time before he developed his "materialist conception of history." His system presents as a conclusion what is in fact one of his major premises. Thus re-emerges the question raised earlier as to why Marx believed that religion is virtually dead.

Without pretending to completeness, I should like here to discuss briefly three causes of Marx's atheism which in their interplay may help to explain his premise about religion's end: the complete lack of what one might call "religious experience" which, by and large, can be explained in terms of his youthful education; the influence of Hegel and of the Left Hegelians; and, last but not least, Marx's secular messianism which, emerging long before Marx developed his mature doctrine, has its ultimate roots in Marx's struggle with Hegel.

Contrary to most Young Hegelians,[35] Marx never went through a period of "religiousness." Feuerbach and Bruno Bauer, to mention only those who most influenced the young Marx, began as students of Protestant theology, like most representatives of German Idealism;[36] they came from middle-class Protestant families which tried to

[34] Cf. Gollwitzer, vol. IV, p. 34.

[35] For a recent and concise discussion about the difference between "Young Hegelians" and "Left Hegelians," cf. H. Stuke, *Philosophie der Tat*, Stuttgart 1963, p. 32 ff.

[36] Feuerbach studied theology at Heidelberg, where his teachers were the Hegelian Daub and the exegetist Paulus; Bauer studied theology at Berlin, where his teachers were Schleiermacher, Hegel and the editor of Hegel's *Philosophy of Religion*, Marheineke. For Feuerbach, cf. L. Feuerbach, *Sämtliche Werke*, Stuttgart 1959, vol. I, p. 359. Hereafter cited as *FSW*, followed by volume and page. For Bauer, cf. D. Hertz-Eichenrode, *Der Junghegelianer Bruno Bauer im Vormärz*, Berlin 1959.

educate their children as good Christians. Even Engels grew up in a staunchly Pietist family and, at the age of nineteen, still prayed "every day, indeed, almost all day," and "with tears welling up as I write," to find his way back to the faith of his childhood.[37] In other words, all these figures grew up as believing and often devout Christians. Their later unbelief and atheism always had the connotation of an overcoming of their past, of a breach with a tradition which once was their own. Some of them, in spite of their all the more militant atheism, never really were able to free themselves from this past. The most striking example is Feuerbach, who at the age of thirty, wrote that God was his first thought, reason his second and man his third and last thought,[38] but up to his old age never was able to put aside the fight against his "first thought."

Marx, on the contrary, grew up among men to whom religion never was more than a question of propriety, indeed, of expediency. His father, though a descendant of a respected family of rabbis, seems to have been converted to Protestantism mainly in order to conform to the Prussian State in general and to Frederick the Great in particular; he was a lifelong and ardent admirer of both. According to the memoirs of Marx's daughter, Eleanor, he was imbued with the "French ideas of the eighteenth century on religion, science, and arts";[39] his belief in God restricted itself to an acknowledgment of a supreme moral value.[40] Marx's mother, to judge from the few surviving letters to her son, was completely engrossed in her household and, in any case, never bestowed upon her son anything comparable to a religious education. With his father, the young Marx used to read Voltaire, Racine and Rousseau; at the home of his first patron and later father-in-law, Baron von Westphalen, he learned to appreciate Homer and Shakespeare. The only place where he might have come into contact with living Christians was the grammar school in Trier which Marx attended for six years. At Trier his final essay in religion (the subject assigned was the union of the believers with Christ according to St. John, XV, 1–4), indicates that even at that time he was unable to

[37] MEGA, I, 2, 531.

[38] FSW, II, 388.

[39] Karl Marx als Denker, Mensch und Revolutionär, ed. by D. Rjazanov, Berlin 1928, p. 27.

[40] See, for example, his letter to Karl Marx of Nov. 18, 1835, cf. MEGA, I, 1/2, 186.

approach religion otherwise than as an invitation to self-improvement. As the evaluating teacher remarked, Marx had in no way indicated the nature of the union in question and had proved its necessity only inadequately.[41]

It is not astonishing, then, that nothing in Marx's early writings and letters indicates that he would have lost his faith or been "converted" to atheism.[42] In his early poems, he never spoke of God, but always of "the gods";[43] and even these "gods" are little more to him than abstract values. When writing a philosophical dialogue "Kleanthes, or the starting-point and the necessary proceeding of philosophy," he struggled with a "philosophical and dialectical development of divinity"; but this "divinity" interested him only insofar as it manifested itself as religion, nature and history.[44] In short the passage from his purely conventional and extremely cerebral "Christianity" to the atheism of the Young Hegelians was perfectly smooth—so smooth that it would be inconceivable if Marx had ever undergone anything like a religious experience.[45]

This utter lack of a genuine *Erlebnis* largely explains why Marx's antagonism to religion always remained completely impersonal. Unlike Feuerbach, for example, he never came to know religion as an "object of practice" before he began to theorize about it.[46] He only knew it as something which he could observe in others, as a historical phenomenon.

But in Marx's view religion as a historical phenomenon had been *aufgehoben* by Hegel. To understand this, Hegel's outlook on religion must be considered, for, in spite of all their criticism of Hegel, the Left Hegelians were never able to see religion with other than Hegel's eyes.[47]

---

[41] *MEGA*, I, 1/2, 171 ff.

[42] This is also stressed by G. M.-M. Cottier, *L'athéisme du jeune Marx, ses origines hégéliennes*, Paris 1959, p. 145 ff.

[43] See, for example, his poem "The Prayer of Prometheus," *MEGA*, I, 1/2, 30 f.

[44] Cf. the only surviving letter of Marx to his father, *MEGA*, I, 1/2, 213 ff.

[45] Even the pseudo-religious experience yielded by Hegel's pantheism seems to be missing in Marx. Cf. J. Gebhardt, *Politik und Eschatologie*, Munich 1963, especially p. 49 ff.

[46] Cf. *FSW*, II, 381.

[47] Besides the works by Gebhardt and Stuke, cf. K. Löwith, *Von Hegel zu Nietzsche*, Stuttgart 1958, p. 350 ff.

Hegel, far from aiming at atheism, considered himself a Christian, more precisely, a Lutheran. Whether Hegel's philosophy is compatible with the basic tenets of Christianity has been a much discussed question.[48] Nevertheless Hegel believed himself a Christian. Indeed, his whole philosophy aims to show that Christianity is meaningful even in modern times. His speculation "ends in a gigantic effort to overcome the contemporary debacle of the Christian epoch by a conquest of the Logos representative of the world."[49] As to his own philosophy, he considered it as a perfect expression of Christianity's most intimate truth, indeed, as the fulfillment of the one Truth which had been sown by Christ, had sprouted at Pentecost, and matured in the course of history.

For Hegel, Christianity is religion in its completion, the "absolute religion."[50] And as the content of religion does not differ from that of philosophy, as the object of both philosophy and religion is "*eternal truth in its very objectivity*—God, and nothing but God, and the explication of God,"[51] his own philosophy, together with Christianity, is "divine service which renounces all subjective brain-waves and opinions while engaging with God."[52] Hegel went so far as explicitly to deny that he ever intended to subordinate religion to philosophy:

> Philosophy has been accused of placing itself above religion. This is objectively false. For philosophy has the same content as religion and no other. Of course, it gives to religion the form of thought; but in doing so it merely places itself above *the form of faith*, the content remaining the same.[53]

According to Hegel, all great theologians have recognized philosophy in its form as superior to religion. Did not the Fathers of the Church try to conceptualize their faith? Did they not assume that

---

[48] The best formula is probably that of I. Iljin, *Die Philosophie Hegels als kontemplative Gotteslehre*, Bern 1946, p. 418: "Hegel learned his best in Christ's gospel; but what he taught was not Christianity." For a thorough treatment, see Cottier, *op. cit.*; for the young Hegel, P. Asveld, *La pensée religieuse du jeune Hegel*, Paris-Louvain 1953. From the Protestant point of view see K. Barth, *Die protestantische Theologie im 19. Jahrhundert*, Zürich 1952, p. 343 ff.

[49] Cf. Gebhardt, *op. cit.*, p. 45.

[50] Hegel, *Sämtliche Werke*, ed. by H. Glockner, Stuttgart 1959, vol. XVI, p. 193; cf. vol. XV, p. 99. Hereafter cited as *HSW*, followed by volume and page.

[51] *HSW*, XV, 37.

[52] *Ibid.*

[53] *HSW*, XVI, 353.

theology is "consciously understood religion"? Did not all mediaeval theologians, far from viewing it as detrimental, consider the rationalization of faith as absolutely essential to its maintenance and development?[54] Was it not St. Anselm who said: *negligentiae mihi videtur si, postquam confirmati sumus in fide, non studemus, quod credimus, intelligere?*[55]

Hegel obviously considered his own work as a continuation and completion of this Christian tradition. To him, all the "difficulties" involving the relation between philosophy and religion, "difficulties" which seem so great as to make people believe that philosophy is opposed to religion, stem from the simple fact that, though both are concerned with the same subject, each grasps the Absolute in its own way.[56] Homer tells us that some stars have two names, one in the language of the gods, another in the language of mortals. This is true about the Absolute, too: the language of religion describes it in terms of feelings, of symbols, of finite categories and one-sided abstractions; the language of philosophy, on the contrary, gives to the same content its most adequate expression—the form of pure thought.[57]

Accordingly Hegel emphasized that philosophy does not seek to overthrow religion; it even does not maintain that the content of religion is not truth. "Religion is indeed the true content. . . . Philosophy is not required in order to bring forth the substantial truth. Nor did humanity have to wait for philosophy to receive the awareness of truth." In the end, philosophy does nothing more than to add to religion's truth the "determination of the form"; it translates religion's symbolism into the "form of thought."[58]

Sometimes, it is true, Hegel criticized orthodox Christians. But his criticism never deliberately aimed at the essentials of faith. He opposed the narrow-mindedness of his Protestant brethren who, busying themselves with a "vast number of accidentals," scorned all rational development of their doctrine. They forgot that even the Holy Scripture states that faith becomes Truth only by the advent of the Spirit, in terms of a "spiritual expansion."[59] Insofar as it is a "trans-

[54] *HSW*, XV, 38 f.
[55] *HSW*, VIII, 183.
[56] *HSW*, XV, 38.
[57] *HSW*, VIII, 17.
[58] *HSW*, XV, 166.
[59] *HSW*, VIII, 27.

figuration of faith into philosophy,"[60] Hegel viewed his own system as the ultimate realization of the Spirit whom, according to St. John, VII, 37–39, "they who believe in Christ shall receive."[61]

Still there can be no doubt that Hegel in fact dissolved religion into autonomous philosophical thought. His claim that he was doing nothing more than what all great theologians had done since time immemorial is misleading. For whereas a genuine theologian submits his reason to the very letter of the Holy Scripture and tries to understand what the Gospel, *as it stands*, has to say, Hegel in fact knocked Christian faith into shape until it fitted his own ideas. Philosophy expresses the Absolute in a way superior to all religion. This amounts to saying, first, that philosophy, though preserving everything which is valuable in religion, transcends the latter; philosophy and, one must add, Hegel's own philosophy, is *the end of all historical religions*, including Christianity, just as, in a sense at least, it is the consummation of history. Secondly as philosophy transcends religion, philosophy, and philosophy alone, will decide what the "true content" of religion is. "Philosophy, by explicating religion, does nothing else than to explicate itself; and by explicating itself, it explicates religion."[62] In other words, by analyzing and comprehending religious statements, philosophy discovers in religion its own superior truth. And as its own truth, being more rational, is the superior one, it tells religion where the line separating imagery and symbols from truth proper ought to be drawn.

Hegel did not mean to say that man's finite understanding should presume on willfully deciding which of the tenets of "positive religion" is true and which is not. He was perfectly willing to admit that religion and, in particular, Christianity is a "product of the divine spirit, the work of the divine action and production in man, not man's invention." But so is philosophy, for, as Hegel explained in his *Lectures on Philosophy of Religion*:

[60] *HSW*, XVI, 316.

[61] To anyone who has studied Hegel, it becomes obvious that he views his own endeavor as a continuation of the Paraclete's work. Of course, Hegel does not want to say that his private insights are revelations of the Holy Spirit. Rather he considers his philosophy as a creative development of Christian theology which, in turn, he views as a continuation of the wonder of Pentecost. This pneumatological aspect of Hegel's philosophy is somewhat concealed by the usual English translation of 'Geist' by 'Mind.'

[62] *HSW*, XV, 37.

there cannot exist *two different kinds of Reason* and *two different kinds of Spirit.* There cannot be a divine reason *completely different* from that of man, as there cannot be a divine spirit *completely different* from the human one. Human reason, man's consciousness of his own nature is Reason *tout court;* it is the divine in man. And Spirit, in so far as it is God's spirit, is nothing beyond the stars, beyond the world. God is present, omnipresent, he is Spirit in all spirits.[63]

God as reason, which includes both religion and philosophy, rules the world. But "God is God only if he knows himself; and His knowledge of himself is His self-consciousness in man and man's knowledge of God";[64] religion and philosophy, being man's knowledge of the Absolute, are the element in which God "comes to his senses." Accordingly God, Reason, Spirit are essentially process; the Absolute is "essentially result, it is only at the end that which it truly is."[65] The history of religion, then, just as the history of philosophy, is the path which the Absolute covers, the path on which the Absolute reaches its self-realization. As far as religion is concerned, this self-realization of the Absolute is reached in Christianity which has for its content absolute truth. Philosophy cannot transcend this content. But it still can, and must transcend the finite form in which this absolute content is given in religion. "All forms such as feeling and pictorial thought can have truth as their content; but they are not the true form which alone makes the true content necessary. Thought is the absolute judge in the presence of which all content has to stand the test and prove good."[66]

It has been argued that Hegelianism actually is nothing more than "esoteric Christianity."[67] This is as true and as misleading as if one were to say that Christianity is esoteric Judaism. Hegel believed that with his philosophy Christianity had been *aufgehoben,* that is, that Hegelianism had absorbed Christianity in so radical a way that, as a distinct *Weltanschauung,* Christianity had become an antiquated holdover of a venerable but irrevocably departed past. Christianity was the consummation of all religion, and Hegelianism is the consummation of Christianity. Accordingly Christianity by itself had become

[63] *HSW,* XV, 50.
[64] *HSW,* X, 454.
[65] *HSW,* II, 24.
[66] *HSW,* XVI, 353.
[67] W. T. Stace, *The Philosophy of Hegel,* New York 1955, p. 509

superfluous, indeed, reactionary—just as the advent of Christ had made Judaism superfluous and reactionary. To a Christian, there is a perfectly legitimate sense in which he may say that Judaism is dead, though, as an anachronism, it survives. Without really being aware of it, Hegel declared Christianity dead in this very sense; only Reason, as an eternal phoenix of which Christianity was but a finite form, survives. Hegel's pupils will hasten to spell this out explicitly a few years after their master's death.

We may add that Hegel was only interested in "justifying" basic Christian *dogmas*, not the Christian *way of life*. Precisely because he aimed to reconcile Christianity with the self-consciousness of modern man, Hegel can only abandon the basic Christian idea that this world is provisional, that man's life on earth is only a period of trial. K. Barth is correct in saying that Hegelianism is a philosophy of self-confidence;[68] its enormous, though short-lived, success is due to the fact that Hegel dared to put into practice the secular self-confidence which since the Renaissance had been the motive power of history. How far Hegel is from acknowledging the Christian way of life appears particularly in his criticism of the Catholic ideal of saintliness. By inviting Christians to abstain from marriage and issue, Hegel claimed that the Catholic Church questioned the reverence of family which is the "first condition of moral propriety and decency." By making poverty a condition of saintliness, it "devaluates the diligence and integrity in the care for, and in the maintenance of, human property." By demanding blind obedience, it questions the greatest value of all, freedom.[69]

How little, in the end, Hegel thought of religion may be illustrated by his conception of the relation between religion and the state. It is sometimes argued that the state, to Hegel, is the supreme value and, thus, that the state has an absolute authority in all realms, including that of religion. This is not altogether true.[70] In several passages Hegel did describe the state as "divine"; but he often uses the same epithet

[68] K. Barth, op. cit., p. 349 ff.

[69] Cf. Hegel's Latin speech on the occasion of the tricentennial of the Augsburg Confession, translated in *Die protestantische Staatsidee*, ed. by W. van der Bleek, Leipzig 1919; also *HSW*, X, 438 ff., where Hegel explicitly opposes saintliness to *Sittlichkeit im Staate*. See also the section on reformation, *HSW*, XI, 519 ff.

[70] For a sympathetic exposition of Hegel's philosophy of state, see E. Weil, *Hegel et l'Etat*, Paris 1950.

when speaking of the family, of the individual, of philosophy. In the whole of Hegel's system, the state appears merely as the culmination of the antithetic realm of "objective Spirit" which, in turn, is transcended by the realm of "absolute Spirit" (art, religion, philosophy). In short the supreme value in Hegel's system is rational thought which finds its ultimate expression in philosophy, not in the state.

Nor did Hegel mean to say that the state has absolute authority over all realms, including religion. To him, absolute authority is conceivable only where an insoluble conflict requires authoritarian intervention. But there can be no such conflict between the Rational State and Absolute Religion, for there can be no conflict between reason and reason. There have been times in which "everything spiritual had its seat in the Church"; times in which the state virtually was without rationality and represented a "rule of violence, arbitrariness, and passion."[71] But this was not the case with the modern state the idea of which Hegel analyzed. For the modern state is the objectivization of perfect freedom which knows and wills itself; "and this, at the same time, is the elementary concept of Reason."[72] Between *this* state and a religion such as Lutheran Christianity which is built upon free Spirit knowing itself in its rationality and truth,[73] there can be no conflict. Here as everywhere, Hegel's Reason is the great reconciler.

On the other hand, it is not difficult to show that Hegel's conception of the relation between Church and State is perfectly analogous to his view on the relation between religion and philosophy. Though the "content" of the state, objectified self-conscious freedom which Hegel terms *Sittlichkeit*, is inferior to that of religion (the Absolute), the state possesses its content in a form clearly superior to that of religion, that is, in the medium of rational thought.

Accordingly Hegel cannot agree with those who would like to make of religion the ultimate principle of the state. The formal aspect of religion makes it unsuited for this purpose. Religion is a relation to the Absolute in terms of feelings, pictorial thought and mere belief. If it were the reason of the state, all laws ultimately would be based upon the principle "Be pious and then you may do whatever you wish"—and the whole complex organism of the state would be aban-

[71] *HSW*, VII, 357 ff.
[72] *HSW*, XI, 82.
[73] *HSW*, X, 444.

doned to "staggering insecurity and disorganization."[74] There is, of course, a perfectly legitimate sense in which religion is the foundation even of the most perfect state; in Hegel's queer terminology, religion is the "substantiality" of *Sittlichkeit* which, in turn, is the "substantial core" of the state.[75] But it merely is a foundation, a building-stone integrated in the higher unity of the state. For the state is "divine will as present—Spirit which unfolds into the real form and organization of a world."[76]

Therefore whenever religious faith leaves the realm of *Innerlichkeit*, that is, whenever it encroaches upon the objective domain, upon the domain of ethics, right, law, institutions and so on, the state knows better. This should be emphasized: it *knows* better. Its authority is based upon superior *knowledge*, not upon power. "As opposed to religion's *subjective conviction*, the state is indeed the Knowing One (*das Wissende*); for in the principle upon which it is based, the content does not remain in the form of feeling and belief but belongs to the realm of definite thought."[77]

In short Hegel's Rational State is the True Church, exactly as Philosophy is the Ultimate Theology. Hegel, of course, carefully avoided such slogans. He even explicitly rejected the idea of a unity of State and Church which, as he said, "has been much discussed and set up as ideal recently." Yet the reason why Hegel opposed this idea is revealing: only by disengaging from particular churches is the state able to live up to its very nature, to "universality of thought."[78] In short Hegel opposed the unity of State and Church for the sake of the State, not for the sake of, and the protection of, religion. It is beneath the dignity of a rational state to engage in particular, that is, one-sided doctrines.[79]

The consequence of all this should be obvious. Christianity, as a historical phenomenon, has been consummated, and thus also consumed, by the modern state, exactly as the Christian *Weltanschauung* has been transcended and superseded by Hegelian philosophy. Taken

[74] *HSW*, VII, 358.
[75] *HSW*, X, 434 ff.
[76] *HSW*, VII, 350.
[77] *HSW*, VII, 359.
[78] *Ibid.*, 362.
[79] *Ibid.*, 353.

by itself, as opposed to the state and to philosophy, Christianity is of the past, dead.

This, at least, would seem to be the objective outcome of Hegel's philosophy. It is the *objective* outcome, for Hegel himself never spelled it out and even in his old age he probably would have been quite dismayed to discover that many of his pupils interpreted him in such a fashion. After all, his whole philosophical endeavor had been undertaken in order to reconcile the modern *Kulturbewusstsein* with Christian faith. But unfortunately he tackled his justification of Christianity in such a way as to make it sound as a condemnation rather than a justification.

Such was not the conclusion drawn by those among his pupils who had been mature and well-balanced Christians before they came under the spell of Hegelianism. Indeed, these disciples were so far from feeling compelled to turn against Christianity that they always thought of Hegel's philosophy as making possible a modern Christian theology. This applies, in particular, to the leading spokesman for Hegelianism after the master's death, C. F. Göschel, whose *Aphorisms on Ignorance and Absolute Knowledge* had been highly praised by Hegel, and to the later editor of Hegel's *Philosophy of Religion*, P. F. K. Marheineke.[80] Both were mature Lutheran Christians when they first came to know Hegel; Marheineke, for example, already had published a textbook of dogmatic theology of which only the second edition was written from a properly Hegelian point of view.

The situation of the younger generation was quite different.[81] They had all come to know Hegelianism at a comparatively youthful age. From the very beginning of their academic careers, they approached Christianity as Hegelians. Instead of viewing Hegelianism as an "expansion" trying to justify religion before the court of the modern mind, they were Christians insofar as, and because, they were Hegelians. The theology they had been taught was "Hegelian theology."

---

[80] On Göschel, cf. Gebhardt, *op. cit.*, p. 54 ff., cf. p. 76 ff.; on Marheineke, K. Barth, *op. cit.*, p. 442 ff.

[81] This is probably the main reason why all Young Hegelians are often described as Left Hegelians. It has to be emphasized, however, that the equation was not perfect, in particular, if the criterion for Left Hegelianism is politics. Thus, for example, the Old Hegelian E. Gans clearly was a Left Hegelian; and Kierkegaard whom Löwith describes as a Young Hegelian, clearly was not a Left Hegelian. Cf. Stuke, *op. cit.*, p. 33.

Feuerbach, for example, studied theology under C. Daub who had been one of the first to reinterpret Lutheran theology in Hegelian terms; moreover Strauss and B. Bauer, not to speak of Stirner, Marx and many others, came to know Hegelianism only after Hegel's death.

The discussion initiated a few years after Hegel's death and deriving from purely theological problems eventually resulted in political radicalism.[82] But it is not my purpose here to offer even a rough sketch of the development of the Hegelian school. Nevertheless an understanding of Marx calls for some account of Feuerbach's attitude toward religion. After all, it was Feuerbach who had shown to Marx that religion and Hegelianism were but two variants of one and the same "alienation of man's essence."[83]

Feuerbach's atheism and materialism are usually viewed as a reaction against Hegel's extreme spiritualism. Exactly as German Idealism, it is argued, was rooted in a profound distrust of the immediately intuited and sensible (and, consequently, of the material world), post-Hegelian anti-idealism feeds on an even more profound mistrust of everything which cannot be grasped except by abstract thought (and so of everything transcendent and spiritual). As if surfeited with abstractions and spiritual realities, the more radical among Hegel's pupils enthusiastically turned toward the concrete, the immediately lived and experienced, the sensible, indeed the sensual.[84] It is pointed out that Feuerbach, for example, never got weary of repeating that only the objects of sense, of intuition, of perception, are "indubitable and immediately certain."[85] In short it is argued that because German Idealism still shared the conviction of classical philosophy that the "really real" is Spirit, Reason, Idea, and indeed precisely because German Idealism had exaggerated this claim, the post-Hegelian generation looked for "true reality" in those realms in which spirituality and rationality appear only as epiphenomena: in the realm of matter, of the bodily sensible, of economy.[86] Feuerbach may serve as an illustration, for it was he who first emphasized that the "mystery of being"

[82] Cf. Gebhardt, op. cit. As for the political aspect, see G. Mayer, "Die Anfänge des politischen Radikalismus im vormärzlichen Preussen," Zeitschrift für Politik, 1913, pp. 1–114.

[83] Cf. MEGA, I, 3, 152.

[84] Cf. Löwith, op. cit., p. 93.

[85] FSW, II, 217.

[86] See, for example, Löwith, op. cit., p. 156 ff., and Gollwitzer, p. 39.

reveals itself only to life in being lived, to sensible intuition, indeed to passion.[87] "Only that which is object of passion truly is."[88]

If Feuerbach's "materialism" is viewed exclusively as a mere antithesis to idealist "spiritualism," the centering of his interest around man, not around matter, becomes unintelligible. Both the French materialists of the eighteenth century (Lamettrie, Holbach, Helvetius and so on) and the German materialists of the second half of the nineteenth century (Vogt, Moleschott, Büchner and Engels) were almost exclusively interested in matter. Feuerbach's "materialism," on the contrary, is little more than a corollary to his anthropology and the same is true of the young Marx. Some may want to argue that Feuerbach did not manage to free himself completely from the idealist heritage. But, then, who did? In this light, it becomes perfectly unintelligible to say that Marx, who, it is true, was a more radical materialist than Feuerbach, reverted from Feuerbach to Hegel (a claim often intimated by those defending the above interpretation).

To understand Feuerbach's "anthropotheism" (so he describes his position) it is necessary to look beyond his quite obvious sensualism and "materialism." It is necessary to consider those passages in which Feuerbach claims that Hegelian philosophy is lacking "immediacy," "*immediate* unity, *immediate* certainty, *immediate* truth,"[89] as well as those in which he stresses that such an "immediacy" is present only in concrete life and sensible intuition.

Hegel's philosophy aims at showing that history is the process both of the "humanization of the Divine Being"[90] and of the deification of man. Christ is thus a central figure in Hegel's thought: "*Christ has appeared*—a Man who is God—God who is Man; and thereby peace and reconciliation have accrued to the World."[91] In Christ, the unity of God and Man appeared for the first time and afterwards history became the gradual expansion and universal realization of this fundamental "*reconciliation* that heals the pain and inward suffering of man." In this process, just as Christ died and was transfigured into "universal"[92] Spirit, and as the originally individual Incarnation of the

[87] *FSW*, II, 297 ff., 287 ff.
[88] *FSW*, II, 297 ff.
[89] *FSW*, II, 27.
[90] *HSW*, II, 569.
[91] *HSW*, XI, 416.
[92] *HSW*, II, 596 ff.

Logos is realized with ever increasing universality, so God abandons His transcendence and man transcends his finiteness. God becomes Man and Man becomes God.

"But this unity must not be superficially conceived, as if God were only Man, and Man, without further condition, were God."[93] Though it may become true that God is Man and Man is God, this unity never will be simple identity. It will always remain a dialectical identity of two totally different things. It will always remain a *unity achieved in terms of innumerable mediations*. These mediating steps, instead of dissolving into nothing, will forever remain an inextinguishable seal both of the Humanity of God and of the Divinity of Man. To the revolutionary impatience of those who claim that Man *is* God without further ado, Hegel opposes the patience of someone who knows the secret both of the Absolute and of History: "impatience asks for the impossible, namely, the achievement of the end without the corresponding means. . . . Even the World Spirit had the patience to cross its forms through the long extension of time."[94]

Feuerbach is no longer able to summon up this kind of patience. He denied Hegel's claim that the Divinity of Man is different from natural man, that it is something *to be achieved*, that it is mediated by a lengthy and laborious process. Whereas Hegel had insisted that man is God only insofar as he "annuls the merely Natural and Limited in his Spirit and elevates himself to God,"[95] Feuerbach reduced Hegel's dialectics of self-aggrandizement to a perfectly undialectical idolatry of natural man.

In short to claim that Feuerbach's philosophy, although it dispenses with the notion of a transmundane God and sets up the human race as the supreme being, nevertheless "contains elements of a critique of pride,"[96] is completely to misunderstand Feuerbach's intention. Far from initiating a "critique of pride," he is interested in an "*ensarcosis* or incarnation of the Logos"[97] which would make possible the elimina-

---

[93] *HSW*, XI, 416.

[94] *HSW*, II, 31 ff.

[95] *HSW*, XI, 416.

[96] R. Tucker, *Philosophy and Myth in Karl Marx*, Cambridge, Mass. 1961, p. 93 ff.

[97] Feuerbach's letter to Hegel, *Briefe von und an Hegel*, ed. by J. Hoffmeister, Hamburg 1952, vol. III, p. 245. On this important letter, cf. Löwith, *op. cit.*, p. 85 ff.; Stuke, *op. cit.*, p. 52 ff.

tion of complicated process of self-elevation, and the achievement of the unity of God and Man by a simple return to natural man. Hegel may have been a gnostic in the sense that he tried to break man's natural condition, but what Feuerbach is doing resembles a gnostic "short circuit." Instead of trying to transcend man's finite condition, he simply declares man's finite condition infinite. The task of philosophy, then, consists of "putting the infinite into the finite,"[98] that is, of rediscovering the original infiniteness of natural finite man.

Accordingly Feuerbach's sensualism and "materialism" are far from simply being an antithetic reaction to Hegel's rationalism and "spiritualism." Feuerbach sought the "really real" in matter as opposed to spirit, in the senses as opposed to reason, in intuition as opposed to abstraction, the living of life as opposed to philosophy, because he claimed Hegel's speculative reconciliation and deification of man for man's primitive, prespeculative nature. Hegel conceived the self-realization of man as the transcendence of the limited and natural biological level, but Feuerbach viewed all such transcendence as "alienation." In this sense, he is a precursor of all "philosophers of life" such as Nietzsche and Klages.

It is easy to see the consequences of these ideas for religion. Both religion and Hegelian philosophy have deprived man of his natural absoluteness. Actually Hegelianism is only religion brought to reason. Claiming that God is different from man and, accordingly, that man's divinity is something to be achieved, both religion and Hegelian philosophy have "alienated" man from his very essence. They ascribe man's own highest perfections to a being different from man, to someone who does not even so much as exist. Therefore the more they exalt the Absolute, the more they degrade man. "To empty the real world and to enrich God is one and the same act—only a poor man has a rich God," as Feuerbach put it in *The Essence of Christianity*.[99]

Eventually, it is true, religion and speculative philosophy will try to reunite what they had separated. Religion, after it has ascribed all of man's perfections to God, will allow for a reunion in terms of grace, of mystical union, of beatific vision. Similarly Hegel reunited man with the Absolute in terms of a series of "mediations," both speculative and historical. But as the separation was artificial to begin with, the reconciliation never really succeeds.

[98] *FSW*, II, 230.
[99] *FSW*, VI, 89 ff.

Consequently Feuerbach's criticism of Christianity and of Hegelianism is an attempt to show that, in order to reach Divinity, man does not need either Incarnation or a wearisome historical process. He or rather the human species is divine by his very nature.

Whereas most other Hegelians (including, as we shall see below, Marx) took it for granted that man cannot escape his finite condition except by reaching a new level, either in his speculative or his material existence, Feuerbach claimed that man simply has to recover that which was always his—his very nature. This, incidentally, is the reason why Feuerbach was so utterly ahistorical a thinker, and why he was comparatively little interested in revolutionary, world-transforming, action. In order that the all-embracing reconciliation be achieved, Hegel needed History; Feuerbach only needed Nature. Since man is divine by his very nature, there is no need to transform the world. As soon as he has realized that religion and Hegelianism are nothing but a "belief in ghosts,"[100] all alienated characters are returned to man as to their rightful owner. Thereafter man simply has to give way to his divinity.[101]

In a sense Feuerbach is right in asserting that this "anthropotheism" is the "secret" of all theology since Luther's time. Even K. Barth does not shrink from acknowledging it.[102] In his exuberant way Luther claimed that the deity has to be sought on earth rather than in heaven. Granted that, when he said this, he had Jesus Christ in mind: he was urging not so much a search for God as He is in Himself but that we ought to look at God as He has appeared to us. Though Luther was far from questioning Christ's Divinity, he had Christ the Man primarily in mind; for Luther, Christ's humanity is more than merely human nature assumed by God—it is humanity become divine. In the sixteenth and seventeenth centuries, many Lutheran theologians began to treat the *communicatio idiomatum* accordingly: thus the sharing of Christ's humanity in all the predicates of the Divine

[100] FSW, II, 227.

[101] Gollwitzer, p. 38 points to FSW, II, 219, and tries to prove that Feuerbach was not so apolitical a thinker after all. Of course Feuerbach was well aware that, after man has overcome his state of "alienation," he will be obliged to reorganize society, to build up a new kind of state and the like. But "politics," here, does not mean the building up of something radically new (as most politically minded Left Hegelians understood it); it simply means to organize life according to the ever present Divinity of Man.

[102] K. Barth, *op. cit.*, p. 487 ff.

Logos meant to them that God had abandoned His transcendence and had *turned into* man (as opposed to only *assuming* a human nature).[103] Hegel seems to have thought along the lines of this development of Lutheran theology.[104] Eventually under the influence of Hegel's exaltation of man in general, what Lutheran faith claimed for Jesus Christ alone was extended to all men. In short Feuerbach's reduction of theology to anthropology is a consequence of the Lutheran tendency to describe Incarnation as an act in which God depletes himself and gives himself up to man. More generally it is a consequence of the Lutheran tendency to consider God only in his relation to man as opposed to worshipping a God who is *semper maior*, essentially beyond the grasp of man.

In any case, Feuerbach treated orthodox Christian faith as a dead relict of the past because his own "anthropotheism" is the outcome and logical consequence of an increasingly anthropocentric theology. A theology centering around a God different from man no longer corresponds to the "needs of our time and of humanity." The history of theology points to this conclusion: first Luther, then Hegel and the Hegelians, Schleiermacher, and others.

> Today, Christianity corresponds neither to the man who theorizes nor to the man who acts; no more does it satisfy the mind, nor does it satisfy the heart. . . . Christianity is negated, negated in the mind and in the heart, in science and in life, in art and in industry. It is negated radically, irremediably, irrevocably.[105]

To Feuerbach, as to Hegel and almost all their contemporaries, Christianity is meaningful only insofar as it corresponds to the "needs of our mind and heart." Heart, mind, reason, in short, man, has become the measure of Christianity. Hegel still had tried to show that Christianity corresponds to the requirements of Reason, but he had to dissolve faith into autonomous human thought. Feuerbach, taking Hegel at his word, characterized religion as a relict of the past—and eventually attacked Hegel himself as the Last Theologian. He spelled out explicitly what Hegel had suggested only tacitly: phi-

---

[103] Cf. the article "Théologie de la Kénose," by Henry, *Supplément au Dictionnaire de la Bible,* V (Paris, 1957), col. 138 ff. Henry goes so far as to describe Luther's position as "monophysism."

[104] Cf. Cottier, *op. cit.,* p. 27 ff.

[105] *FSW,* II, 217.

losophy supersedes religion[106] and the state is the true reality "but also the practical refutation" of all religious faith.[107] Hereafter all that remains of religion is man, and man alone.

One might ask how far Marx agreed with Feuerbach and in which sense he may be said to have reverted from Feuerbach to Hegel. In brief the answer is this: Marx agreed with Feuerbach's claim that both religion and speculative philosophy are forms of the "alienation of man's essence," but he disagreed with Feuerbach's claim that the human nature underlying this alienation is fully developed, indeed, untainted and divine. On the other hand, though rejecting Hegel's idealism, Marx agreed with Hegel that history had not yet become the "*real* history of man as of a given subject, but only man's *act of procreation*, the *story* of man's *coming to be*";[108] in short that the Divinity, or rather the Humanity, of man is something still to be achieved and always to be the result of an achievement. All in all, Marx's philosophy of man is a "materialist" interpretation of Hegel's *Phenomenology* rather than a pendant of Feuerbach's anthropotheistic pseudo-materialism.

Marx never joined in Feuerbach's rather primitive idolatry of *natural* man. In his *Critique of the Hegelian Philosophy of Right* in which the influence of Feuerbach for the first time became really tangible, he simply took over Feuerbach's scheme for criticizing Hegel and applied it to Hegel's political theory.

Moreover he applied the Feuerbachian scheme in a way which indicates that his ideas radically differ from those of Feuerbach. In the course of his analysis of Hegel's *Philosophy of Right*, instead of showing that only man, family, civil society and the like are primary realities and the state only a secondary reality,[109] Marx more and more tended to say that the state is a hypostatized abstraction comparable to Feuerbach's "God" and that the whole realm of politics actually is a realm of alienation comparable to that of religion. It has seldom been noticed that this extension of Feuerbach's notion of *alienation* to politics is thoroughly incompatible with Feuerbach's "anthropotheism." For the Feuerbachian "alienation," being after all only a misguided evaluation of an otherwise sound reality, required merely

---

[106] *Ibid.*, 218.
[107] *Ibid.*, 220.
[108] *MEGA*, I, 3, 153.
[109] For Feuerbach's scheme, cf. *FSW*, II, 224.

an adjustment in knowledge. Though by his very nature divine, man had a wrong idea of himself; as soon as this idea was corrected, his divinity would be restored. In fact his underlying divinity never had been challenged.

But a reality such as the state cannot be abrogated by revealing its unsound character. As the state is alienation become reality, it can only abolished by transforming the "real world." Yet if the *real* world has to be transformed, if human *reality*, not only human thought, needs to be corrected, then it cannot be true that the humanity underlying the political alienation is divine. Almost without being aware of it, Marx reverted from Feuerbach to Hegel: by being a more radical "materialist," that is, realist, than Feuerbach, by reducing thought-alienation to *real* alienation, Marx was forced to admit that the "divinity" of Man is still something to be achieved.

This development of Marx's thought may contribute to explain why, many years later, Marx, contrasting Feuerbach and Hegel, found the former a "very poor" figure.[110] Feuerbach never grasped that Hegel's exaltation of man did not concern the rational *animal* but only the free and rational being which this animal can make of itself. To Feuerbach, the Absolute, though sometimes hidden, is always present; for Hegel and Marx it is "essentially result." As Marx put it: "The outstanding thing in Hegel's *Phenomenology* and its final outcome . . . is that Hegel conceives the self-procreation (*Selbsterzeugung*) of man as a process."[111]

Actually Feuerbach's rejection of all "mediation," his claim that the biological animal, man, is something ultimate, was unique even as compared to the ideas of other Left Hegelians; most other Hegelians shared Hegel's conviction that the Divinity or "true Humanity" of man, the emergence of the *homo divinus seu realiter humanus*, is the result of a long and wearisome process in which "biological" man transforms himself into a superior being. Hegel himself believed that, with the emergence of modern society, of constitutional monarchy and, last but not least, of his own speculative "reconciliation," this process was about to draw to a close. Within a few years after Hegel's death, his pupils made the disenchanting discovery that the reconciliation offered by Hegelianism was only a speculative one—that, as the

---

[110] Letter to Schweitzer of January 24, 1865.
[111] *MEGA*, I, 3, 156.

philosophy restricted itself to a reconciliation of consciousness alone, it had left the *real* world "unreconciled." Thus Hegelianism which its author had conceived as a speculative analysis of the world *as it is* became a picture of the world *as it ought* to be. In this, but only in this, sense, *all* Left Hegelians, instead of really overcoming the Hegelian speculative synthesis, reverted from Hegel to pre-Hegelian ideas: Feuerbach to French materialism about which he published several studies; Cieszkowski, Bruno Bauer, Moses Hess, and others, to Fichte's, and ultimately to Kant's, philosophy of *Sollen*.

In 1833, the first critic of speculative Hegelianism, Friedrich Richter, criticized Hegelian speculation for its one-sidedness inasmuch as its limits are placed at the very point at which true reconciliation begins—in the realm of *praxis*. In 1838, the Polish Count August Cieszkowski (who, incidentally, always remained faithful to his Catholic faith) spelled out the same idea by claiming that philosophy will have "to descend from the heights of theory to the open country of *praxis*."[112] Thereafter all radical Hegelians tried to discover exactly whereof this prolongation of Hegelianism into *praxis* consists. Cieszkowski himself described it as "social life" and, after a bashful reference to the "system of Fourier" and a recommendation of it to the attention of speculative thinkers,[113] left it at that. A few years later, Bruno Bauer developed his method of "critique," a sort of literary criticism supposed to bring about a transformation of the world in terms of ideas alone—as he put it, a "perfect realization of the (Hegelian) system" and thus the "last deed" of Hegelianism.[114] In his *Hallische Jahrbücher*, Arnold Ruge carried on a similar, though more realistic, critique which he described as "scientific journalism."[115] In 1843, Moses Hess formulated his "philosophy of action": "The task of the philosophy of spirit is to become a philosophy of action. Not only human thought, but all of human activity has to be raised to a level at which all contradiction disappears."[116] Even Feuerbach joined in

[112] A. v. Cieszkowski, *Prolegomena zur Historiosophie*, Berlin 1838, p. 129.

[113] *Ibid.*, p. 126.

[114] B. Bauer, *Kritik der evangelischen Geschichte der Synoptiker*, Leipzig 1841, vol. I, p. xxi.

[115] For the origin and meaning of this expression, cf. A. Ruge, *Aus früherer Zeit*, Berlin 1863, vol. IV, p. 446 ff.

[116] *Einundzwanzig Bogen aus der Schweiz*, ed. by G. Herwegh, Zürich-Winterthur 1843, p. 321.

this chorus. In an article which was not published until after his death, he argued that philosophy had to become a principle of action, a guide to human life within this world. "Politics has to become our religion."[117]

In this paper I cannot discuss the sense in which Marx's philosophy of the revolutionary proletariat is superior to all these feverish attempts to go beyond and to overcome Hegel's speculative "reconciliation." It may suffice to say that this superiority is mainly due to the fact that Marx succeeded in penetrating Hegel's *Phenomenology* more deeply than any of his contemporaries. The point I wish to make here is that the philosophy of the young Marx has to be viewed along the lines of the development sketched in the preceding paragraph rather than along the lines of Feuerbach's undialectical and ahistorical "anthropotheism." It is true that Marx owed to Feuerbach the insight that "the Hegelian philosophical fantasy is not simply a fantasy, but a fantastic reflection of reality."[118] But where Feuerbach used his transformist criticism only for castrating Hegel, Marx used it as a shield to enable him to enter the magic circle of Hegelian ideas without ever becoming a Hegelian. In the end, Marx owed to Feuerbach little more than precisely this shield, that is an extremely handy scheme for criticizing both religion and Hegelianism, and the idea that man is and forever will remain a being rooted in the material world rather than one able to develop into a pure self-consciousness. This last idea, of course, was important enough. It permitted Marx to translate the merely mental dialectics of self-aggrandizement which Hegel had developed in his *Phenomenology* into a dialectics of "self-production" in terms of material labor.[119]

It is in connection with this "activist" or, rather, "revolutionary" dimension of Marx's thought that the third and last, and possibly the most important, root of Marx's atheism becomes visible: the Promethean attitude of someone who is about to serve as an active midwife of History at the imminent birth of True Man.[120] In Hegel, who first

[117] *FSW*, II, 219.

[118] R. Tucker, *op. cit.*, p. 96.

[119] For an interpretation of Hegel's *Phenomenology* from Marx's point of view, cf. A. Kojève, *Introduction à la lecture de Hegel*, Paris 1947, especially the section "En guise d'introduction."

[120] Cf. the quotation from Aeschylus' *Prometheus*, verse 966–969, in the introduction to Marx's doctoral dissertation, *MEGA*, I, 1/1, 10.

conceived the idea that the humanity of man is the result of man's own effort, this Promethean attitude never was very explicit; he always saw behind man's self-creation the *Weltgeist* which "has given to Time the word of command to advance" and now irresistibly advances in spite of all obstacles laid by man.[121] In Feuerbach, though he was the first of Hegel's pupils radically to free himself of the burden of the Hegelian "advancing ogre,"[122] this Promethean attitude was not very explicit either; the only Promethean deed he was able to conceive was the abrogation of the *mental* alienation represented by religion. In short to make possible the Promethean attitude characteristic of Marx, a combination of Hegel's dialectics of self-aggrandizement and of Feuerbach's radical immanentism was necessary.

It is obvious that someone who wants to create a "new man," and who believes that this "new man" will emerge in terms of man's effort alone, cannot tolerate religion. Even if religion were only a symptom of a more basic evil, it is also the most radical expression of an attitude which has up to now prevented man from prevailing against this evil.[123] As long as man has the possibility of feeding himself with hopes of a better future beyond life and history, he never will be able to summon up the energy and determination required by Promethean deeds.

Accordingly, for Marx, the criticism of religion has the function of forcing man to give up all illusions. To some extent, this is true of Feuerbach's antireligious critique as well. For example, Feuerbach explicitly commented upon the connection between a vigorous interest in politics, on the one hand, and the emancipation from religion, on the other hand.[124] Man, as Feuerbach viewed him, immediately upon recovering from religious and philosophic alienation, would relax in the serene light of his own Divinity. Thus there would be almost no need to set man's Promethean energies free. Accordingly Feuerbach hardly had to urge the renunciation of *all* illusion. Man, as Feuerbach viewed him, has to give up only his faith in a *transcendent*

---

[121] Cf. Hegel's famous letter (1816) to Niethammer, *Briefe von und an Hegel*, vol. II, p. 88 ff.

[122] J. Weiss, *Moses Hess, Utopian Socialist*, Detroit 1960, p. 33, has a very suggestive passage on Feuerbach's role in this respect.

[123] Cf. *MEW*, I, 378 ff.

[124] *FSW*, II, 220 ff.

God and in a beyond, not his faith in the existence of an eternally present divinity.[125]

Marx's man, on the contrary, is never less God than at the moment when he abandons his religious and pseudo-religious beliefs. Instead of being able to revel in his Divinity, he is forced to realize how wretched a being he is—and consequently to revolt and to act with the force of a desperate man who has nothing to lose and everything to win. As Marx puts it: "The criticism of religion disillusions man, to make him think and act and shape his reality like a man who has lost his hope and come to reason."[126]

Earlier in this essay, I distinguished three causes of Marx's peculiar atheism: the complete lack of religious experience; the influence of Hegel and his pupils; and Marx's secular messianism. The first two features largely explain why Marx never became a militant atheist; the last feature, on the contrary, seems to explain why Marxist atheism always remained *latently* militant and, more generally, why atheism is an integral element of Marx's *Weltanschauung*. Perhaps it may be put this way: an eschatological philosophy such as that of Marx which, on the one hand, predicts with quasi-scientific certainty an ultimate salvation and, on the other hand, makes the predicted salvation completely dependent upon man's action, is bound to be atheist.[127] For only a man who gave up all his daydreams and illusions, who forgot once for all the hopes of a beyond, who knows that no divine intervention is possible, who considers all laws of nature, history and society, as perfectly knowable and therefore as manipulable —only such a man is determined enough to bring about the ultimate salvation, the "Communist revolution." In a word, a philosophy in action such as Marxism is in need of atheism as much as it needs materialist scientism: it has to exclude everything which would permit man to elude reality or to be resigned; it has to predict the *eschaton* as an event of secular history; and it has to rule out a priori everything beyond man which may hinder or help history's predicted and carefully planned course.

[125] Cf. *FSW*, II, 237, where anthropotheism is described as "religion conscious of itself"; or VI, 26, where Feuerbach argues that "a true atheist is one who denies the predicates of the divine being . . . not the one to whom the subject of these predicates is nothing."

[126] *MEW*, I, 379.

[127] For a further elaboration of this point, cf. Gollwitzer, p. 80 ff.

It is easy to see why an atheism based upon these premises became militant[128] as soon as its advocates discovered that religion was slower in dying than expected. Curiously enough, however, Marx seems to have been opposed to militant atheism on the ground of the very same premises: to fight against the Divine entailed taking it seriously. And it entailed, too, the danger that atheism would become a pseudo-religion; Feuerbach and all Left Hegelians were here a warning example.

[128] In order to avoid misunderstandings, I have to add that even contemporary Marxism-Leninism clings to the Marxian theory of a non-militant atheism; yet it is significant enough that, *in practice*, Communists often felt obliged to act contrary to this theory. As far as *theory* goes, Lenin, for example, is in perfect agreement with Marx. Cf. "Ob otnoshenii rabochey partii k religii" (1909), *Sochineniya*, 5th ed., Moscow 1958, vol. XVII, p. 415 ff.

15: IS MARX'S THOUGHT RELEVANT TO THE CHRISTIAN? A CATHOLIC VIEW

Gaston Fessard, S.J.

Is Marx's thought relevant to the Christian? Yes, without any doubt. Moreover I do not hesitate to add: it is of such tremendous importance for him that his first duty is to understand all the strength of Marxism as well as its extreme weakness. For Marx initiated Communism in a conception of the world that is in radical opposition to all religion, particularly to Christianity of which it claims, nevertheless, to "realize the human foundations by secular means."[1]

After nearly one-half century of changes that its conquests have brought about in the world, Communism is a historical phenomenon whose importance sufficiently indicates the effectiveness of Marx's thought, so that Christians more than anyone else should wish to penetrate its secret. Even the relentless or dissimulated persecutions, which its atheism provokes and maintains everywhere that it dominates, should make them reflect and should prompt them to examine their consciences. For it could well be that the explosions of hatred are in part the effect of resentment, the manifestation of a disappointed love resulting from our own inability to incarnate the ideal we profess. From this point of view, the Marxist ambition to take the place of Christianity in order to free man better than any church has done should appear to us as the finest homage that its irreligion can pay to our faith. We shall try to envisage the thought of Marx with complete objectivity and impartiality, even with a profound sympathy, without undertaking, however, to draw from it a criticism of the conduct of Christians and of their churches. For, however legitimate this task may be, it is secondary to the one proposed to us here: to understand, first of all, this thought in itself according to the whole histori-

[1] MEGA, I, 1/1, 587; cf. K. Marx, *Early Writings*, ed. by T. B. Bottomore, London 1963, p. 16.

cal dimension in which it appeared and revealed its effectiveness.

To enter immediately into this dimension and to evaluate its significance, let us go back by stages toward the past. Today it is well worth noting that young Marx's claim, "to realize the human foundations of Christianity" is no longer put forth to justify the reality and the end of Communism. It is scarcely mentioned even by some of his good apostles who have some difficulty in obtaining, as in France and Italy for example, the collaboration of Christians naive enough to believe that through Communism's progressivism they will find themselves in the avant-garde movement of history. We also must remember that, at other times and in the same countries, Nazism exercised an analogous seduction over no less credulous minds by inviting them also to "collaborate" for an apparently no less seductive end: "to save Christian civilization from Communism."

Personally the fact of having known and lived through this twofold temptation has helped me considerably to see clearly amidst the interplay of ideologies of our time that have, like the gods of Homer's time, dominated the struggles of us poor mortals and that continue to confront each other in our Empyrean. Let no one be shocked to see me compare Communism and Nazism in this way. Even Raymond Aron, as well known in America as in Europe, as early as 1944 made this comparison by calling them both "secular religions." The expression has become trite he noted in 1955,[2] so much so, for the truth of it is obvious.

For my own part I twice had the occasion to denounce the close relationship of these two ideologies precisely as "secular religions." First, in 1941 during the Nazi occupation when Russia had just been thrown onto the Allied side by Hitler's attack and the United States had not yet taken sides in the world struggle, I wrote a short book *France, prends garde de perdre ton âme (France, Beware of Losing Your Soul)*, the first underground booklet of *Témoignage chrétien* in which I showed Nazism to be an anti-Christian, antinational, antihuman doctrine and in which I described the three phases of its insidious propaganda: "seduce-compromise-pervert or destroy."[3] Four

[2] *L'opium des intellectuels*, 1955, p. 274. "I believe," R. Aron notes in this connection, "it was I who used this expression for the first time in two articles which appeared in *France Libre*, June–July, 1944."

[3] Text reproduced in *Cahiers clandestins du Témoignage Chrétien*, Editions du Témoignage Chrétien 1946, vol. I, pp. 13–45.

years later in October, 1945, just after our liberation and at the time
that the French Communists boasted of their newly found patriotism,
an off and on patriotism seemingly on the verge of seizing power, I
wrote a second booklet *France, prends garde de perdre ta liberté*
(*France, Beware of Losing Your Liberty*) in which I showed that
Communism was an anti-Christian, antinational, antihuman mys-
tique which used the same tactics: "seduce-compromise-pervert or
destroy."[4]

On both occasions Marx's thought was doubly precious to me: first
of all, because by taking it just as he formulated it, I was able to use
it to refuse all collaboration with Nazism; then since I had recognized
at the same time that Hitler, a proletarian educated by the Marxist
trade unions of Vienna, had taken up the same doctrine while inverting it, I could by the same token reject any collusion with Communism. Like many other Frenchmen, I undoubtedly owe my safety and
sanity today to the Russian and American armies; I express my thanks
to them. But my personal thanks go to Marx in a special way, for his
philosophy helped me to understand that the mutual hatred of Communism and Nazism does not exclude that they both derive from the
decomposition of the rationalist Liberalism which dominated the
Western world from 1789 to 1914. Hence it was this fraternity that
permitted these two ideologies to ally against liberalism and to unleash
World War II after the Russian-German Pact of August, 1939; and
hence also there exist numerous resemblances between their governmental procedures—one party system, a tyrannical police state, concentration camps and so on, not to mention the anti-Semitism which,
from time to time and *mutatis mutandis*, was common to them in
fact, if not in principle.[5]

When in 1945 I developed this parallelism for the first time, many
who then took Communist ideals at their face value were scandalized.
How could one put on the same level as racist particularism this universalist humanism? Without denying this difference which is the
more dangerous because it is the more seductive in the Communist

[4] First edition, 152 pp. (Oct., 1945), second edition, 318 pp. (1946), Edit.
du Tém. Chr. In *L'Étoile contre la Croix*, Paris 1954, p. 82 ff., Father Dufay, a
witness of the Communist invasion of China, describes the implementation of
the same tactics.

[5] See my article: "Antisémitisme en U.R.S.S., Faits et Réflexions," *Études*,
Sept., 1960, pp. 215–232.

ideology, all the events which have occurred since then, particularly the revelations on the period called the "cult of personality," have simply confirmed the basic truth of this parallel to the extent that many of those who live beyond the Iron Curtain have become aware of and even familiar with it. It would be easy to find many instances of this.[6]

It would be useless to linger over these ancient souvenirs already more than one-quarter of a century old. Since we have recalled, thanks to them, the period of triumphant Liberalism, let us try rather to understand how the thought of Marx, well before it brought forth Communism, and then its most fierce enemy, Nazism, could between 1840 and 1850 give birth to a fundamentally anti-Christian ideology. If we succeed we shall have thereby explained why the first duty of the Christian is to discover its strength and its weakness.

My analysis will start from an expression used by Nicholas Berdiaev. This Russian philosopher knew Siberia during the tsarist regime, because of his Marxist ideas and his revolutionary tendencies and then spent five years under the bolshevik regime before being expelled from Russia. Now this impartial witness of the beginnings of the Communist revolution immediately denounced it as a "theocracy in reverse."[7] Since contraries are of the same species, an *atheocracy* must, like any theocracy, rest on theological foundations but turned upside down by the atheistic negation. I shall try to show how we can discover these foundations and understand this inversion, for this should be of primary interest for every Christian.

To do this we must remember that the whole thought of Marx was worked out under the influence of Hegel and against him, so much so that in his later years it seemed to Marx that he had simply uncovered "the rational kernel" of Hegelian dialectic "under its mystical dress," by putting it back on its feet.[8] But at heart and in principle, Hegel was

[6] For example, the *New Class* by Djilas is an undeniable proof of it, not to mention the reflections one can glean in the speeches of Tito and, more recently still from the pen of Mihaijlov, author of the Report *Un Été à Moscou* (Cf. *Est et Ouest*, no. 341, May 1–15, 1965). We shall quote only one sentence from this latter, drawn from his letter of protest of March 1, 1965, addressed to the Editor of the Yugoslav weekly *Nin* who had attacked him: "I am deeply convinced that any revival of Stalinism would be the equivalent of Neo-Nazism" (*ibid.*, p. 32). Cf. also Tito's words comparing Stalin to Hitler, *ibid.*, p. 5.

[7] *Les Sources et le Sens du Communisme russe*, Gallimard 1934, p. 194.

[8] *MEW*, XXIII, 27; cf. K. Marx, *Capital*, Moscow 1954, vol. I, p. 19.

a theologian whose ambition was to "understand history" by means of the fundamental mysteries of Christianity. A Protestant, he interpreted them freely without worrying about any ecclesiastical *Magisterium*; and when he had finished his *Phenomenology of the Mind*, he did not doubt that he had acquired a purely rational intelligence of these mysteries, thanks to Absolute Knowledge and the "movement of the Concept," which "annuls time." Based on this dialectical movement, his logic primarily and then the System of the *Encyclopedia* permitted him to unite Being and Thought as theory and practice and thereby to identify himself with the absolute Spirit. Marx rejected this identification which to his mind was mystifying because it left the philosopher, even if he has understood all the past, in an unchanged social world remaining always open to an indeterminate future. But apart from the conclusion of the system, Marx admits the truth of the process which builds it and wants precisely "to actualize the philosophy" of Hegel in the history to come and to make it "become the world."[9] Hence he asks the dialectics, the "movement of the Concept," not to be content with "interpreting the world" but "to transform it"[10] by becoming the principle which directs the movement of history and leads it to its fulfillment.

In this way, although Marx was little concerned with Christianity except to deny it any value, he was nonetheless led to adopt its essential structures because of his opposition to the speculative mysticism of Hegel. Failing to distinguish any better than Hegel between idealism and religion, his all-out atheism that rejects both outright, prevents him from seeing that he is keeping the same schemas of thought and of representation but in a negative form. Unconscious though it was, this adoption of Christian structures is nonetheless so real that it contains in principle the wherewithal to remedy precisely the very defects of Hegel's interpretation of them. Hegel, indeed, understood very well the rational link between the three mysteries: Trinity, Incarnation, Redemption; but giving free rein to his speculative genius in virtue of free thought, he conceived the first in such an idealist manner that, by a rebound, it practically destroyed and suppressed the existential and historical foundations of the two others. Marx, on the other hand, retains of Hegel's speculation on the Trinity only the dia-

[9] *MEGA*, I, 1/1, 64.
[10] Cf. eleventh thesis on Feuerbach, *MEGA*, I, 5, 535; cf. K. Marx-F. Engels, *Selected Works*, Moscow 1955, vol. II, p. 404.

lectical aspect while his materialism leads him to re-establish the foundation of the Incarnation and of the Redemption by linking them to the carnal and sensible presence of a community which assures their effectiveness. Thus opposing both the idealism and the Protestantism of Hegel, Marx, without realizing it, comes so close to the realist and Catholic conception of human existence that he lays the foundation on which a "secular religion" could be established, or better, a Church whose *Magisterium* shall have to guide its members infallibly in the way of salvation, while its social body will make present to the eyes of all this very salvation, the End of History. Thanks to Lenin, the Communist Party of Russia will begin to represent the atheocratic Church which Berdiaev saw come to life, and soon it will be so much alive that enriched by "the spirit of Marxist-Leninism," it will give birth to a specific "cult" corresponding to its theory and practice.

However we must examine more closely the process which we have just skimmed over. We shall group the analysis of the theological structure adopted by Marxism under three headings: first, Marx presupposes a unity of Man and of Nature which corresponds exactly to the unity of Man and God revealed by the Incarnate Word; secondly, anxious to explain why modern man is nevertheless enslaved and alienated, Marx throws the blame on the "original sin" of private property; finally, to diminish the different human alienations and to re-establish the primitive unity of Man and of Nature, he counsels workers to form groups and to entrust to the proletariat, thus "formed into a single class," the mission of achieving universal redemption by means of the "class struggle." By way of conclusion we shall examine the destiny of the atheocratic Church founded by Lenin in this threefold structure, which Marx, thanks to Hegel, inherited from Christianity.

I

"The objective man, true because real, is the result of his own labor";[11] this is the first truth which Marx learned from the *Phenomenology* of Hegel. From this he immediately draws this conclusion:

For socialist man, the *entire so-called universal history* is nothing else than the procreation of man by human labor, the becoming of nature

[11] *MEGA*, I, 3, 156; cf. K. Marx, *Early Writings*, p. 202.

for man; he therefore has the obvious and irrefutable proof of his generation through himself, of his *process of his coming-to-be* . . . [so that] the question about an alien being, of a being above nature and man has become impossible in practice.[12]

Inspired by Hegel, this reflection on the historicity of Man and of Nature ought therefore to lay the foundation for atheism which proclaims: "*man is for Man the Supreme Being.*"[13] However since at the same time Marx rejects Hegelian idealism in order to adopt the "*true materialism*" of Feuerbach, he goes to the point of affirming that atheism is so little a problem that "the denial of God no longer makes sense," neither for positing the existence of man nor for "socialism as socialism."[14] From this new point of view, positive Humanism and Communism posit themselves so firmly, without any need of proof, that the atheism implied by them becomes an intuitive evidence, a sense-certainty.

Since the materialism of Feuerbach has the fault of not being historical,[15] Marx, without fear of contradiction, must return to Hegel to seek, for the historical process whence his atheism came, a *metaphysical* basis, or, to speak like Heidegger, an onto-atheological basis, resembling a sense-intuition as much as possible. He finds it in "the essential unity of man and of Nature [which has] become a concrete and evident fact" for "*the theoretically and practically sensuous consciousness.*" In view of this Marx will go even to the point of giving as an object of intuition "*the substantiality* [*Wesenhaftigkeit*] of Man and nature, in virtue of which man is for man the existence of nature, as nature is for man the existence of man."[16] Let us admire the precision of a phrase that designates the Supreme Being of Marxist atheism. For it implies not only a perfect equality of Man and Nature but also entails that Man and Nature mutually engender each other, so that their "substantiality" is, properly speaking, a consubstantial unity in

[12] *MEGA*, I, 3, 125; cf. *Early Writings*, p. 166 ff.

[13] "Zur Kritik der Hegelschen Rechtsphilosophie. Einleitung," *MEGA*, I, 1/1, 615; cf. *Early Writings*, p. 52.

[14] *MEGA*, I, 3, 125; cf. *Early Writings*, p. 167.

[15] *MEGA*, I, 5, 34: "To the extent that Feuerbach is a materialist, we do not find history in him, and to the extent that he takes history into consideration he is not a materialist. With him, materialism and history are completely separate," cf. K. Marx, *The German Ideology*, trans. by R. Pascal, New York 1960, p. 37 ff.

[16] *MEGA*, I, 3, 125; cf. *Early Writings*, p. 167.

the precise sense in which this theological expression defines, in the Trinity, the unity of the persons with the Divine Nature.

Of course, Marx does not suspect that the intuition upon which his atheism is based can owe anything to the Christian mysteries or even derive from them directly. But to grasp this derivation more clearly, one has only to examine how much he disagrees with Hegel on this point. For the latter, the unity Man-Nature rests first of all on the fact that finite spirit is the bond of Nature and Logic and, in last analysis, on the splitting of the Idea into Spirit and Nature. Disdaining such abstract speculations, Marx portrays, in opposition, the unity Man-Nature on the model of "the relation of Man and Woman" in which he sees "the unequivocal, decisive, manifest expression which reveals the secret" of the unity of the twofold relationship of man to man and of man to nature:

> The immediate, natural and necessary relationship of human being to human being is the *relation* of *man* to *woman*. In this natural species-relationship, the relation of man to nature is immediately his relationship to man, just as his relation to man is immediately his relation to nature, his own *natural* determination. In this relationship, therefore, is *sensuously manifested*, reduced to an observable fact, the extent to which the human essence has become nature to man or nature has become the human essence of man. From this relationship, therefore, judge man's whole level of development.[17]

This is a marvelous analysis. Indeed, there occurs in conjugal union the "immediate, natural, necessary" joining of two human beings who are as humans identical, while at the same time they differ in the natural order by their sex. Identity and difference are properly dialectical, and what is more, basically historical, so that Marx is justified in saying that his Naturalism—or the unity Man-Nature thus conceived—goes beyond idealism and materialism, unites their truth and is alone capable of understanding the *Act of Universal History*.[18] As

---

[17] MEGA, I, 3, 113; cf. *Early Writings*, p. 154.

[18] In fact, according to Marx, in the course of history Man as a "species being" and Nature ("the non-organic body of man") engender each other through labor, as Man and Woman do by Love. For, on the one hand "history," especially that of *industry* (history's "concretely present and most accessible part," *MEGA*, I, 3, 122; cf. *Early Writings*, p. 163) is a "*real* part of *natural history* of the transformation of Nature into man" (*ibid.*, 123). On the other hand, "Man is a part of Nature" in whom Nature is "indissolubly linked with itself" because in virtue of

this last formula indicates, Marx intends to take up and realize the project of Hegel: "to understand history" (not only past history but that to come) by understanding the Act of Universal History. By his conception of the unity Man-Nature on the type of the relationship Man-Woman, he goes so far beyond Hegel that he gives his humanistic atheism a specifically Christian foundation, relative now to the Incarnation of the Word in which the unity of Man with God is manifest.

We must insist on this surpassing of Hegel because it characterizes Marx's atheism, explains its virulent power and determines its whole evolution.

When, while reflecting on Christianity as "manifest religion," Hegel meets the relationships Father-Mother and Father-Son, in connection with the Incarnation and with the Church and then with the Trinity, he says that they have no value for speculation, because they are "relationships borrowed from natural generation" and consequently simple "natural relations." This was a major error of his idealism that did not recognize the symbolizing value of language. Indeed, although paternity and maternity obviously exist among animals, in mankind these two relationships are not simply natural; they are also, and above all, historical. The proof is, first of all, in the prohibition against incest, a specific universal law among humans, and then especially in brotherhood which, unknown in the animal world, is not only a synthesis of paternity and maternity but also the condition of their development on the ethnic or national level into the paternity and maternity of the fatherland which, in turn, gives birth to a national brotherhood trying

---

his "species being, he treats himself as a *universal* and consequently free being," whose universality appears in vague practice precisely in the universality which makes of all Nature his "an organic body" (*Ibid.*, 87; cf. *Early Writings*, p. 126). "Man creates, posits objects—[objects in which "nature is engendered by history," *ibid.* 156 ff.; *Early Writings*, p. 202 ff.] only because he is himself posited by objects, because he is basically *Nature*." In other words, since his "pure activity" is not, as Hegel imagined, "*a creation of the object*," man is, with all that he does, a product of Nature in the same way as Nature is for its part destined to become Man, thanks to human labor and to industry. From this reciprocal generation Marx draws a consequence in adding: "We see here that fully-developed Naturalism, or Humanism, differs both from Idealism and from Materialism and at the same time is their truth which unites them. We see also that Naturalism alone is capable of comprehending the Act of World History" (*ibid.*, 160; cf. *Early Writings*, p. 206).

to extend itself to the human race and therefore to become universal.[19] If only Hegel, when recalling his own analyses of marriage, had put paternity and maternity in relationship with these analyses of marriage, he could easily have avoided his error. But when he reflected on Christian dogmas, he completely failed to ask himself about the role of the Husband-Wife relationship. This, on the contrary, captivates Marx's attention so much that his materialism spontaneously restores to the difference and union of the sexes the primary and universal value they have for the Christian. According to the Bible "man was created male and female in the image of God" (Gen. 1:27); moreover prepared by all the symbolism of the Covenant and of the Law in the Old Testament, it is as a conjugal union of the divine Nature and human nature that the New Testament presents the Incarnation of the Son in Christ, so that subsequently the historical relations of God with Humanity can no longer be symbolized other than by the Man-Woman relationship.

No doubt, when young Marx adopts the same symbol for his unity Man-Nature, he hardly thinks of Hegel nor even of Christianity,[20] although he discerns very clearly, as we have seen, the promise of *becoming like God* for Communist humanity. No doubt also, his short explanation of the Man-Woman relationship is a veritable *hapax* in all his works. Moreover one finds many passages that refer to it and confirm the importance of this intuition for his very thinking.[21] The

---

[19] On this see my "Esquisse du Mystère de la Société et de l'Histoire," *De l'Actualité historique*, vol. I, Paris 1960, pp. 121–211.

[20] Judging by the context it is Plato who seems to have suggested to him the choice of such a symbol. In fact, in opposition to "marriage, a form of *exclusive private property*," Marx has just evoked the community of women in which the woman becomes a "common and collective property" and recognized that this idea forms the "revealed secret" of a Communism, still very crude and ill-thought out, which universalizes in an abstract way the relationship of private property. As against the "general envy" and the "thirst of riches" that are in his eyes the principle of such a universalization, Marx has recourse then to the Man-Woman relationship to give Communism, as he understands it, a definition which we shall soon comment upon. It is worth noting that the essential part of this analysis of the Man-Woman relationship—the last three sentences of the text we have quoted—is found (as *MEGA*, I, 3, 113, indicates) in the margin of the original text and represents therefore a later reflection intended to clarify and to develop the first draft.

[21] For example, Marx notes in *The German Ideology* that "division of labor was originally nothing but the division of labor in the sexual act" and that "the

importance of this is never emphasized by his Communist commentators, nor even noticed by Marxists, although some of them go so much to the heart of the Man-Woman relationship that their analyses, continuing those of Marx, reveal the religious root of the marriage and "what makes a sacred mystery of it for all social thought."[22]

Such blindness or negligence is easily explained. For to stress the depth of a symbolic comparison, apparently fortuitous and without value, would be to call attention to the fact that Marxism borrows the best of its truth from a Christian structure and thereby to risk making the falsity of its atheism too apparent. Such is, on the contrary, the point of view we must insist upon. For, thanks to this symbol, the more Communist consciousness approaches Christian consciousness, the more it also draws away from it—its denial of God condemns it immediately to insurmountable contradictions.

On the one hand, because the unity Man-Nature presents itself to the Communist's "positive consciousness of self" on the model of the Man-Woman relationship, it is the exact counterpart of the unity

distribution, and indeed the unequal distribution, in quantity and in quality of labor and its products, hence property, has its nucleus, the first form in the family where wife and children are the slaves of the husband" (*MEGA*, I, 5, 22; cf. *The German Ideology*, p. 21). And further on, in contrasting "the theoretical weapons inherited from Hegel" and thus Hegel's speculative philosophy with "the material, empirical attitude" of the emerging historical materialism, he uses this contrast in order to define them each in relation to the other: "Philosophy and the study of the real world are like Onanism and sexual love" (*ibid.*, 216). Finally in *Das Kapital*, Marx takes for his own the expression of William Petty in order to define the role of human labor in the creation of "material wealth": "The worker is its father and the land its mother," *MEW*, XXIII, 58; cf. *Capital*, p. 43.

[22] Thus in his dissertation on *Les Structures élémentaires de la Parenté*, Paris 1949, in which he explains the prohibition of incest as universal law which conditions the passage of Nature (of animality) to Culture (to humanity), Claude Levi-Strauss writes: "What *makes a sacred mystery of marriage for all social thought*" is that "at the moment of marriage, if one considers it isolated from all the others," Nature and Culture, or "parental love and conjugal love, meet and fuse . . . in order to take each other's place and do a sort of exchange" (*op. cit.* 607; italics are mine). This is to take up the idea of Marx and to go into it more deeply by pointing out the role played by the word in the union of man and woman, since the coincidence of the Nature-Man relation (or culture) occurs in this "isolated moment" in which the "yeses" of the conjugal alliance are exchanged (cf. our article "Symbole, Surnaturel, Dialogue," *Demitizzazione e Morale*, Actes du Colloque de Rome, Jan. 7–12, 1965, published in *Archivio di Filosofia*, no. 1–2, 105–141).

Man-God of Christian consciousness. The Christian believes in the original alliance of God and Humanity in Christ and his faith in the Incarnate Word makes already present to him the Mystical Body in which, at the end of time, men will be reconciled among themselves and with Nature as with God. It is the same for the Communist, and the proof that the unity Man-Nature is for him truly a theological structure is precisely that it projects itself also in his eyes under the same eschatological form. This is evident in Marx's definition of Communism, the best because the most pregnant, which he gives just after his analysis of the relationship Man-Woman and by way of conclusion:

> [Communism is the] *positive* abolition of *private property* (as *human self-alienation*) and consequently as real *appropriation of the human essence* through and for man. . . . Communism as fully developed Naturalism equals Humanism, and as fully developed Humanism equals Naturalism; it is the genuine resolution of the conflict between man and nature and between man and man, the true resolution of the strife between existence and essence, between objectification and self-affirmation, between freedom and necessity, between the individual and the species. It is the riddle of history solved and it knows itself to be this solution.[23]

Between the Communist who believes in the classless society and the *true end* of History, and the Christian who, thanks to his faith in the Mystical Body, lives in loving expectation of the *Parousia*, there is then perfect similarity. Only one difference separates them: atheism. This is a fundamental difference because it introduces into the Communist conscience a negation from which comes a threefold formal contradiction, bearing first of all on the end of History, then on its beginning and consequently on its totality and finally on atheism itself which, having indeed no more meaning, is nonetheless required to give one to Marxism but can do no more than communicate, by making it universal, what it is itself, namely pure nonsense.

Moreover these three contradictions are linked together. Six pages after having announced that Communism is the true end of History, Marx happens to affirm justly that "atheism makes no more sense," because "Communism establishes the positive without needing to abolish either religion or private property" and concludes his entire development with this final sentence:

[23] *MEGA*, I, 3, 114; cf. *Early Writings*, p. 155.

> Communism is the necessary form and the dynamic principle of the immediate future, but it is not as such the goal of human development —the form of human society.[24]

Is this absent-mindedness or an error due to youth? Certainly not. For when he was a mature man Marx again asserts that the establishment of Communism ought to "accomplish the end of the prehistory of human society."[25] A radical contradiction indeed, for what could a History be in which there would no longer be a place for the slightest antagonism between man and man, nor between man and nature, and therefore neither suffering nor error nor even death? Since atheism prevents the Communist from identifying such a history with the transcendent Heaven of the Christians, the classless society is an "end of history" which does not end it, a limit which limits nothing, in short, an imaginary paradise that belies the unity Man-Nature conceived as end of History and is soon going to destroy it even more fundamentally.

For here is the second contradiction which this time destroys historical materialism at both ends. In 1860 Marx reads *The Origin of Species* by Darwin and accepts its evolutionism as the foundation of the history of Nature. He therefore has to admit a "history [of nature] anterior to man" and independent of man's work; precisely what he has hitherto denied.[26] Hence the contradiction no longer builds only

---

[24] *Ibid.*, 126; cf. *Early Writings*, p. 167.

[25] Cf. *MEW*, XIII, 8; cf. K. Marx, *A Contribution to the Critique of Political Economy*, Chicago 1904, p. 13.

[26] Darwin's *Origin of Species*, published in 1859, was immediately discovered by Engels, who described it to his friend as "very famous" (letter of December 12, 1859). A year later Marx who had meanwhile read the work wrote to Engels: "It is the book which contains, from the point of view of natural history, the foundation of our theory" (December 19, 1860). Without being cognizant of this fact, it seems, Marx thus gave up the conception of history he had had at the time historical materialism was born. Faithful on this point to Hegel for whom "organic nature has no history," he admits the becoming of nature only in dependence on human work. Among dozens of texts in the *Manuscrits de 1844*, several of which we have already quoted, let us cite these few more: "Nature as it develops in human history—the act of genesis of human society—is the actual nature of man; thus nature, as it develops through industry, though in an alienated form, is truly *anthropological* nature" (*MEGA*, I, 3, 122–123; cf. *Early Writings*, p. 164). "The creation of the *earth* has been seriously shaken by *geogeny*; that is, by the science which sees the formation and development of the earth as a process, a self-engendering. *Generatio aequivoca* is the only practical refutation of the theory

on the end of history but just as much on its beginning. This was so true that his friend Engels, in his Introduction to the *Dialectic of Nature*, came to admit, in the name of "the logic of thought," the "eternal return" and to write: "what has happened once can happen again," only to cross out this too flagrant admission in order to replace it with an obscure sentence but still its exact equivalent.[27] This was to deny history as such and consequently the very foundation of the materialism as conceived by young Marx.

Let us admit that evolution legitimately replaced the "spontaneous generation" in which young Marx had believed and that it is a better "refutation of the idea of creation," which is anything but sure, for no evolutionist has yet been able to explain even the appearance of language. Still the Marxist must ask himself about the "*true* end of the antagonism between man and man as between man and nature" affirmed by Marx. As atheism prevents him from admitting a transcendent end and as an immanent and terrestrial end is not one, he must believe either in Engel's "eternal return" or trust in the indefinite progress of the sciences and of technology. However what a

of creation" (*ibid.*, 124; cf. *Early Writings*, p. 165). In *The German Ideology*, Marx remains faithful to this conception and ridicules Feuerbach "who does not see that the sensuous world around him is, not a thing which is given immediately from all eternity, ever the same, but the product of industry and of the state of Society and, in truth, in the sense that it is a historical product, the result of the activity of a whole succession of generations. . . . This nature, prior to human history, is not the nature in which Feuerbach lives, nor the nature which today no longer exists anywhere (except perhaps on a few Australian coral-islands of recent origin) and which, therefore, does not exist for Feuerbach . . ." (*MEGA*, I, 5, 32–34; cf. *The German Ideology*, pp. 35–37). In all Communist and even Marxist literature I have not encountered a commentator who noticed the change of meaning of *Naturgeschichte* which occurred in Marx's works between 1844 and 1860. Although I pointed out this problem at the Vienna Congress on Hegel in 1960 (cf. my article, "Attitude ambivalente de Hegel en face de l'Histoire" in *Hegel-Jahrbuch*, 1961, I, 25–60; reprinted in the *Archives de Philosophie*, Apr.–June, 1961, pp. 207–241), I do not know of any Marxist who has tried to resolve the contradictions resulting from it for historical materialism and particularly with respect to its conception of the unity Man-Nature.

[27] *MEGA*, Sonderausgabe, 1935, p. 497. Only the edition of V. Adoratskij points out the erasure of Engels; the French translations of P. Naville and, more recently, that of E. Bottigelli not only do not say a word about it, but the Communist edition of the Dietz Verlag in Berlin (*MEW*), while claiming to be better than *MEGA*, is modestly silent about this "slip" of Engels which is incidentally not the only one in these pages. See my article mentioned in footnote 26.

Communist, if he has read anything of Hegel's *Logic* without which, Lenin says, "one cannot understand *Das Kapital*"[28] should know but cannot admit is that such an infinite progress is "the *contradiction* expressed as without solution and always present."[29]

We must not expect the Communists to tell us first what they choose, end of history, eternal return or infinite progress and secondly to justify that choice. We would have to wait until the *Parousia*. To complete the picture of the ravages produced by the denial of God in the theological structure which founds the unity Man-Nature, we still have to see the contradiction which destroys this very denial.

For humanism or for "the Communism which posits itself in the true way,"[30] that is, "directly and without mediation, [as] the positive self-grounded affirmation founded on sense-certainty . . . atheism no longer has any meaning."[31] Directed against the "false positivism"[32] of Hegel and his negation of the negation, an "abstract, logical, speculative expression of the movement of history,"[33] this affirmation is repeated by Marx still more strongly at the end of his critique of the *Phenomenology*.

> Atheism and Communism are not a flight, an abstraction, . . . but rather the first actual coming-to-be, the actualization become effective for man of his essence and of his essence as become actual.

Let us admit this, but let us read the middle of the paragraph which precedes this:

> Atheism is humanism mediated to itself by the annulment of religion, while Communism is humanism mediated to itself by the annulment of private property.

Will Marx add that atheism and Communism have no need for

---

[28] "It is impossible completely to understand Marx's *Das Kapital,* and particularly its first chapter, without having thoroughly studied and understood *all the Logic* of Hegel. Therefore, half a century later not a single Marxist understood Marx." *Philosophical Notebooks;* cf. *Collected Works,* vol. 38 (Moscow 1961), p. 180.

[29] "Dieser Progress ist daher der *Widerspruch,* der nicht aufgelöst ist, sondern immer nur als *vorhanden* ausgesprochen wird," *Wissenschaft der Logik,* ed. by Lasson, vol. I, p. 131.

[30] *MEGA,* I, 3, 114; cf. *Early Writings,* p. 155.

[31] *Ibid.,* 152; cf. *Early Writings,* p. 198.

[32] Cf. *ibid.*

[33] *Ibid.,* 153–154; cf. *Early Writings,* p. 200.

this double suppression in order that positive humanism may be established and brought back to itself? No, he asserts exactly the contrary:

> Only through annulment of this mediation—which is itself, however, a necessary premise—does positively self-deriving humanism, *positive* humanism, come into being.

Thus far from "setting itself up on its own, immediately and without proof," atheistic humanism *can be born only by the suppression of God*. Obviously such a suppression would not be possible if there was not something to suppress. Hence it follows from Marx's very words that what establishes itself positively by itself is the existence of God, were it only by way of a "necessary premise" to the constitutive negation of atheistic humanism.

But let us go back to the beginning of the same paragraph we are commenting upon and we shall understand better the source and the meaning of such a contradiction: "As atheism, being the annulment of God, is the coming-to-be of theoretical humanism, . . . Communism, as the annulment of private property, is . . . the coming-to-be of practical humanism."[34] In other words, atheism alone can give meaning and theoretical truth to the positive humanism of Marx, as Communism alone can achieve it in practice. In fact, without the close relationship of theory and practice, atheism and Communism could not be, as Marx wishes, "the real becoming, the effective realization of the essence" which consists in the consubstantial unity Man-Nature and ought to make us "capable of understanding the act of world history." But how can we reconcile this perspective of a two-faced becoming with the other affirmation of Marx—"atheism makes no more sense" for positive humanism whose unity Man-Nature has become the object of a sensuous, evident, concrete intuition in the theoretical and practical conscience of the Communist? How can atheism, already become meaningless, give a meaning to the theoretical becoming of a humanism still to be accomplished? Such a becoming can only rest on a contradiction: as we have seen, the contradiction that namely, positive humanism, owes its existence to an atheism which necessarily presupposes the existence of God.

Let us not be surprised by this last contradiction in which all those preceding are summed up and which prepare for those which Marxism will run into later. In the main, it is not different from that which,

---

[34] *Ibid.*, 166–167; cf. *Early Writings*, p. 213.

according to the Bible, rises "in the heart of the fool who says: there is no God."[35] However in Marx, disciple of Hegel, who wishes better than he to unite theory and practice as dialectic and history, it takes on a sharpness which is worth bringing to light.

Indeed, where can this *praxis* be realized and where should it first manifest itself, this *praxis* that according to Marx ought to unite "the practical, real and objective activity of man with the sense-intuition" in order to be "rationally understood in so far as it is revolutionary *praxis*"?[36] It is not, as he sometimes says, in labor, nor even in struggle. It is above all in *language* in which all the pairs of contraries that constitute human existence and its activity are found both distinct and indissolubly united: sense and intellect, necessity and freedom, individuality and sociality, and the like. Also the *word* is, in truth, the first historical fact, the first tool, both material and practical as well as simultaneously being theoretical and intellectual; it is the initial *praxis* by which man, acquiring the mastery of his organic body, can communicate with the social world, understand rationally his own language and that of others, and afterwards devote himself with them to the work capable of transforming Nature, his inorganic body, in order to make it become Man. Although his revolutionary *praxis* and his work have hardly consisted of anything more than using words and the pen, Marx completely omits reflecting on *language* and the *conditions it imposes on the unity of theory and practice as of dialectic and history.*

In particular, when he claimed that atheistic humanism presents itself without proof and is the object of a sensuous intuition as evident and concrete as the unity Man-Woman, he forgot the teaching given by Hegel at the beginning of his *Phenomenology* on the subject of sense-certainty: far from being stable, solid, immediate, Hegel says, sense-certainty is a "dialectic which is nothing else than the simple history of its movement."[37] And whoever believes he can stop its mobility and retain the immediate by recourse to words, exposes himself to a dialectical vengeance. Indeed, Hegel adds, "the divine nature of language" immediately reverses my opinion and makes something

---

[35] Ps. 13; S and L II, 1.

[36] Theses on Feuerbach.

[37] Hegel, *Sämtliche Werke* (Jubiläumsausg.), vol. II, p. 89; cf. *Phenomenology of Mind*, trans. by T. B. Baillie, London 1964, p. 158.

else of it,[38] a universal which no longer has anything immediate. Marx was the victim of such a vengeance: his "opinion" on atheism, as an "evident and concrete fact," was immediately divided according to a Before and an After, becoming, on the one hand, that which already "no longer makes any sense," and on the other, that which should still and always give one to the "becoming of humanism." In the same way and as a consequence, his sense-certainty of the unity Man-Nature immediately reversed itself and transformed itself into a theory which, contradictory in itself, belies the practice which it must found and direct.

It was necessary for us to point out this knot of contradictions amidst which is born the materialism of Marx because they determine the whole becoming of the Humanism founded on them. If only, while reflecting on the unity Man-Woman, Marx had asked himself how, under the circumstances, dialectics and history and also theory and practice can join together in the exchange of the conjugal "yes," which must be for each a *praxis* and "revolutionary" *praxis*, perhaps he could have found the means of escaping the contradictions which were to strangle his materialism. But atheism barred once and for all the way to such an answer.

Nevertheless let us pay homage to Marx, to the power and the truth of an intuition, not at all sensible, but rather philosophical—in the Bergsonian sense of the term—which caused him to see in the labor uniting Man and Nature an analogy of the love which binds Man and Woman, an intuition of a richness and depth he himself scarcely suspected and which his disciples do not even notice. For it binds, or more exactly, invites us to seek the link which ought to unite *love, work and language* in the least of our acts as in the universe and history.[39] However in pretending to make himself God and to divinize

[38] *Ibid.*, p. 92; cf. *Phenomenology*, p. 160.

[39] Among the reflections interspersed by Marx in the extracts from economists, such as Ricardo and James Mill, which he read in 1843 (*MEGA*, I, 3, 437–583), just before writing his *Manuscripts of 1844*, one sees very clearly his search for a *work* the production of which would have as result, on the economic and social level, a universal mutual "recognition" similar to that of love between Man and Woman, as Hegel in his introduction to the Master-Slave dialectic defined it, without, however, any clear allusion to this latter relationship. It is characteristic that the analysis of Marx develops under the form of a *dialogue between me and you* and consequently in agreement with the definition of Feuerbach: "the *true* dialectic is *not* a monologue of a solitary thinker with himself, it is a *dialogue*

Humanity starting from a structure which is properly that of the Incarnate Word, Marx was to become inevitably the victim of his own words. For the divine Word on which he wanted to lay his hand could only condemn him by his very omnipresence to every word to the multiple and fundamental contradictions which ruin the theory of the so-called dialectical materialism before perverting its practice in history.

II

Due to his conception of the unity Man-Nature, Marx was persuaded he had solidly founded atheistic humanism and Communism. Yet how can one explain that? In spite of a basis as profound and as universal as the mutual love of man and woman one nonetheless meets, everywhere in history and in the world, religions and societies where private property prevails. Marx's answer is well known: private property constitutes "the original sin" of humanity. This is the perfectly logical reply of his atheism; if the facts belie a fundamental theological structure one can explain it only by having recourse to another of the same nature.

However before making his analysis of capitalism, Marx devoted himself to a critique of religion; consequently he declared that the doctrine which proclaims that "Man is for man the Supreme Being" should "take as its starting point the decidedly *positive* suppression of religion."[40] Here let us follow the same historical order which is, incidentally, in perfect agreement with the primacy of the atheistic denial in its atheology.

One quotation will suffice to recall the essence of such a criticism:

> Man makes religion, religion does not make man. Religion is indeed the self-consciousness and the self-awareness of a man who has not yet

between me and you" (*Werke* II, 345). The use of such a form leads him to take up the problem of *language*, which to his mind has been completely perverted by the capitalistic mode of production and of exchange. If we take his analyses on this subject literally we notice that his own definitions of the unity Man-Nature, of labor and of Communist society cannot be made in "truly human language" and are, therefore, condemned to reflect the alienation of the capitalist world in which they were drawn up. The fact remains that the effort of the young Marx to link work, love and language attests the depth of his reflection and the unconscious influence of Christianity on his thought.

[40] *MEGA*, I, 1/1, 614 ff.; cf. *Early Writings*, p. 52.

found himself, or has already lost himself again. But man is not an abstract being squatting outside the world. Man is the *world of man*, the State, Society. This State, this Society, produces religion, an *inverted conscience of the world*, because they are an *inverted world*. . . . The *religious* misery is at the same time the *expression* of real misery and the *protest* against real misery. . . . Religion is . . . the *opium* of the people.[41]

In other words, religion is a purely imaginary superstructure, produced by a social state which is not what it should be, through the fault of private property, the source of all evil.

Before returning to this last point, note right away that to define religion as a "consciousness which has *not yet* found itself, or is *already lost* again" and as an "*expression* of the real misery and a *protest* against it" conceals a two-edged ambiguity. Indeed, "not yet" and "no longer" are existential determinations that refer to "the positive consciousness of self" of the unity Man-Nature, the basis of atheism for the Communist; in like manner, "the expression of misery" and the "*protest* against it" concern, through these same determinations, a theoretical or practical deficit which can also be met in the Communist consciousness since its faith in a classless society is exactly analogous, as we have seen, to that of the Christian with regard to the Mystical Body of Christ.

The ambiguity which results from this works at first in favor of the Communists who, profiting from this analogy, can, on the one hand, "hold out the hand" to the Christians and invite them to a dialogue; they can impress upon them that on the social and earthly level Communists are pursuing the same ends as Christians: a more just and more fraternal society, and so to invite them to a "collaboration without compromise of doctrine" in which their faith will be respected completely—provided that, remaining a "matter of private conscience," as Lenin says, it does not prevent them from following the practical directives of the Party; while, on the other hand, the Party will employ all its power, "not to refute [as Marx says] but to destroy its enemy,"[42] religion. Today, for example, in France and in Italy, we see Communists being delicate to the point of explaining to Christians that the persecution from which they suffer in Russia or in the People's Democracies has no other purpose than to purify or to make

[41] MEGA, I, 1/1, 607; cf. *Early Writings*, p. 43 ff.
[42] *Ibid.*, p. 609; cf. *Early Writings*, p. 46.

their religious consciousness more dynamic by making impossible the compromises their Church makes with bourgeois states and the propertied classes.[43]

The illusion of the progressist Christians who accept such explanations and invitations to dialogue stems precisely from the fact that they do not discern the atheism working in a dialectical, that is, deceitful way through the theological structure which makes the unity Man-Nature of the Communist consciousness similar to the unity Man-God for the Christian consciousness.[44]

However the same ambiguity can also work against the Communists. For how could they prevent their own ideology from playing the same role for them as religion does for others, namely, to bridge the distance opened by a "not yet" and a "no longer" between their "positive consciousness" and their ideal unity Man-Nature and afterwards to serve as "theoretical expression of their real misery" and the "practical protest against it"?

Marx scarcely bothered to protect his disciples against such consequences and we shall show in the conclusion how they became real. It was more important for him to explain the social state which has given birth to the imaginary superstructures of religion. In his eyes, the evil cannot come from labor, "the first historical act,"[45] where man becomes natural, that is, universalizes himself, at the same time as he humanizes nature. A true conjugal union of Man and of Nature, this first fact, as the love of a Man for a Woman, can by itself result only in a beneficial action: the mutual creation of one by the other. If, on the contrary, there does not result a reciprocal loving recognition extending to all society, the fault can be due only to private property which disassociates the process of work. Normally the latter appropriates the inhuman nature to the needs of the producer who maintains his way of life by consuming the fruits of his labor. It is no

[43] Roger Garaudy, De l'Anathème au Dialogue, p. 53 ff.

[44] In De l'actualité historique, Paris 1960, particularly in the second volume, Progressisme chrétien et Apostolat ouvrier, I analyzed at length, and with numerous specific examples, the mechanism of this dialectical action of atheism. It rests essentially, as Madeleine Delbrel saw and spelled out in Ville Marxiste Terre de Mission (Collection Encontres, no. 50, Edition du Cerf, 1957) on the "pitfalls of vocabulary," all the words which Communists use, for example, "poverty," "justice," "history" which never have the meaning that the Christians or even the man whose honesty is not subjected to the Party give to them.

[45] MEGA, I, 5, 18; cf. The German Ideology, p. 17.

longer the same if there is a split between the producer and the consumer, a split such that the latter appropriates the results obtained
by the former and, in this way, despoils him. Fruit of the division of
labor and of exchange, private property provokes precisely such a division, whence comes the servitude of the worker dominated and exploited by the owner.

Let us not quarrel with this analysis, but let us note at least that it
squares badly with Marx's analysis of the family where Marx finds, in
the difference of the sexes and of the tasks of Man and Woman, first,
the origin of the division of labor, then of private property and finally
of the subordination of the children and of woman to man. Since this
triple difference, far from harming the cohesion of the first and "at the
beginning unique relationship at once social and natural,"[46] is on the
contrary the condition of its development, Marx should, it seems,
have looked for some profounder cause of human divisions. But he
does not take the time for this and is satisfied with observing that in
the economy, in which exchanges have created a world market, private property has extended itself to the means of production, bringing about the appearance of capital, its accumulation in the hands of
a small number and finally all the injustices from which the great mass
of exploited workers suffer. He concludes from it:

> The primitive accumulation plays in Political Economy about the
> same role as original sin in theology. Adam bit the apple and thereupon
> sin fell on the human race.
> Original sin is at work everywhere. As capitalist mode of production,
> accumulation and wealth develop, the capitalist ceases to be the mere
> incarnation of capital. He has "fellow-feeling" for his own Adam, his
> flesh. . . .[47]

Such is the second theological structure that Marx uses to analyze
the diverse "alienations" which private property produces in the world
of men: first of all, economic alienation, the most fundamental because it reduces man to the state of a beast of burden and of mer-
chandise; secondly, political alienation because the State, founded or
taken over by the holders of economic wealth, profits from its power
to enact laws that protect the privileges of the wealthy; thirdly, ideological alienation, since the rulers base their power on theories they

[46] Cf. ibid., 13–19.
[47] MEW, XXIII, 741 and 619 ff.; cf. Capital, vol. I, pp. 713 and 593.

impose as unquestionable truths even on their slaves; and finally a *religious* alienation which crowns with a sacred and supernatural halo the ideology of a ruling class and, thereby, its political and economic power. In the Prussian state, magnified by Hegel by reason of the mission that fell to it—to become the "incarnation of the Spirit"—Marx denounced, on the contrary, a "mediator" who, like Christ, separates real man from the citizen and prevents him from attaining true freedom.[48] For by maintaining him in the illusion of a political life as celestial and transcendent as the divine life of the Christian, the State condemns him to remain the needy member of an economic society dominated by "money, the god of practical need and self-interest."[49] While the atheistic state is alone capable of "realizing in a secular way the human foundation of Christianity . . . the so-called Christian state is the imperfect State" which uses religion as a "means of *completing* and *sacralizing* its imperfection: it is the state of hypocrisy."[50]

In 1844, Marx criticized "theology for explaining the origin of evil by original sin, that is, of supposing as a historical fact what it ought to explain." In opposition, he claimed "to start from an actual economic fact."[51] We should note that theologians, too, never have any other starting point than the very *actuality* of the human situation before their eyes. If not, their explanations could not even be related to it. In taking up the expression "original sin" in order to make private property responsible for all the evils of humanity, Marx followed their example and reasoned as a good theologian. He was logical in his atheism. But, in doing so, his explanation is less historical than a priori, to the greater harm of his later criticisms of a capitalistic economy, however true they may be. For the a priori, which serves as basis for these analyses, is belied by the universal historical fact of the family where, as even Marx admits, private property does not disassociate in any way the unity Man-Woman and parent-children nor consequently the unity Man-Nature, although the "*distribution* of the

---

[48] "The State is the mediator between man and the liberty of man. Just as Christ is the mediator to whom man imputes all his divinity, all his religious dependence, so the State is the mediator on which he transfers all his non-divinity, all his *human independence*," "Zur Judenfrage," *MEGA*, I, 1/1, 587; cf. *Early Writings*, p. 11.
[49] *Ibid.*, 603; cf. *Early Writings*, p. 37.
[50] *Ibid.*, 587; cf. *Early Writings*, p. 17.
[51] *MEGA*, I, 3, 82; cf. *Early Writings*, p. 121.

fruits of labor" takes place, as he is careful to note, "unequally in quality as in quantity."[52]

III

Let us see now how the same logic led Marx to adopt a third Christian structure. How, he wonders, can we abolish private property and the disastrous consequences for humanity of this original sin in order to restore the original blessed unity of Man and of Nature and to attain "the true end" of History promised by Communism? Nothing less is needed than a Redemption. Marx, we know, entrusted to the proletariat a universal redemptive mission: thanks to the "class struggle" led by the slave workers against their bourgeois or capitalist masters, all the antagonisms of men among themselves and with nature will be suppressed in order to make way for the classless society and classless state.

Such is the third theological structure which, according to Marx, ought to link the two others dialectically, since by denying the original negation of private property, it must reunite Man and Nature on the model of the loving relationship Man-Woman. More directly still than the two preceding ones, it is borrowed from Christianity by the intermediary of Hegel.

In fact, Marx originally found the first inspiration for it in the Master-Slave-dialectic which Hegel himself conceived while meditating on the situation and the destiny of the Jewish people in the Old Testament. The proof of this, among many others, is the verse of Scripture which Hegel invokes and cites in the Phenomenology of Mind to explain the fecundity of servile work carried out in the anguish of death: "Fear of the Lord is the beginning of Wisdom."[53] Only, for Hegel, this dialectic is only one of the numerous moments which consciousness meets on the road to absolute Knowledge. While, for Marx, it becomes historical so that it must embrace and

---

[52] Cf. text quoted above note 21.

[53] Eccl. 1:16 and Ps. 110:10, quoted in Phenomenology (German text, 156; English trans., 237). It is well known how much the young Hegel was preoccupied at Tübingen with the relationship of Abraham and of his descendants with Jahveh (see the Early Theological Writings) and later the central place which "the unhappy consciousness"—that of Israel in the first place—occupies in the Phenomenology of Mind as does in his Philosophy of History the destiny of the Jewish people.

enlighten the total becoming of human societies. Moreover Marx had to reverse the moments: for Hegel, indeed, the first is the struggle to the death having as issue the unequal and nonreciprocal recognition of the Master by the Slave, and the second moment is servile labor which humanizes and universalizes. For Marx, on the contrary, labor becomes the "first historical fact" of a becoming which can only be terminated by the victorious struggle to the death of the proletariat.

Let us not insist on the ruinous contradictions which such inversion fatally brings to the Marxist dialectic.[54] However we should note this: the dialectic takes on meaning and becomes intelligible only if we interpret the struggle to the death of the proletariat according to the model of the struggle which Christ, Son of God, appearing in the form of slave, led against sin by sacrificing himself on the cross. This is a new proof that the Redemptive mission of the proletariat constitutes a theological stucture of Marxist atheism. But here is another proof which completes that one and is still more manifest. By reversing the Master-Slave dialectic in order to make the proletariat the mover of History, Marx found, without noticing it, another dialectic which Hegel had missed to the detriment of his system: that which, according to St. Paul, distinguishes and unites the two peoples, the Pagans and the Jews, whom "Christ, our peace, reconciles by his sacrifice and fuses in himself in a single new man in order to make a single body with God."[55] There is every reason to believe that the destiny of the Jewish people, thus fulfilled in Christ, was at the horizon of the thought of Marx and unconsciously directed the genesis of it.[56] It is enough here to indicate one reason. There is an identical type of

[54] On this subject see my De l'Actualité historique, vol. I, p. 149 ff.

[55] Eph. 2:14–16 and all of Romans but especially 1:18–32 and 11:25–33. For an exposition of the dialectic of the Pagan and the Jew see my book Pax Nostra, Examen de conscience international, Paris 1936.

[56] In the first place, the influence exercised on Marx and Engels by Moses Hess, the "old Communist rabbi" and author of Die Heilige Geschichte des Menschheit, 1837, cf. Charles Wackenheim, La faillite de la religion d'après K. Marx, Paris 1963, pp. 163–164; and A. Cornu, Moses Hess et la gauche Hégélienne, Paris 1934. But also some sentences of Marx himself who refers piously to the destiny of the Jewish people. Let us quote only this one: "The present generation resembles the Jews whom Moses leads through the desert. It has not only to conquer a new world, it must disappear in order to give way to men who will meet the demands of a new world." MEW, VII, 79; cf. Marx-Engels, Selected Works, New York 1955, vol. I, p. 212.

dialectical opposition which, on the one hand, distinguishes and unites Pagans and Jews in St. Paul, and on the other, bourgeois and proletarian in Marx: indeed, in comparison to the *particularity* of the idolatrous Gentiles, the Jews are the monotheistic people, and as such bearers of the promise of a *universal* salvation; likewise the proletarians are a "class of individuals *dependent on universal history* and empirically universal facing the world market"[57] in comparison to the *particularism* of the bourgeois interests and nationalisms. Moreover if such an identity did not exist, how could the proletariat assume the very mission of the Church and pretend to "realize the foundation of Christianity in truly human creations"?

Thus when the masses of exploited workers group themselves into a class, thanks to the intellectual bourgeois (which is, as Lenin emphasized, what Marx and Engels were[58]) and when the proletariat thus "formed" becomes conscious of a destiny it will not be able to fulfill without the help of the Communist Party, its Vanguard and guide, at that very moment it is invested with a *universal and transcendent redemptive mission* which corresponds, feature for feature, to that of the Church, since it must, like her, reunify definitively humanity and nature by destroying the consequences of "original sin."

Such are the theological structures by which Marx, heir of Hegel, explicated in an atheistic mode the three essential dogmas of Christianity: Incarnation, Original Sin, Redemption. They explain the influence of its materialism, its historical and dialectical appearance, its mystical and ecclesial character and finally its power of seduction among "progressist Christians." But though a source of the expansion of Communism, they are also the cause of its weakness and of its essential impotence.

---

[57] MEGA, I, 5, 24; cf. *The German Ideology*, p. 25.

[58] *What is to be done?*, cf. V. I. Lenin, *Selected Works*, New York 1943, vol. II, p. 53. The passage is quoted and analyzed in *De l'Actualité historique*, II, 451 ff., to show what the slogan is worth; it was invented by a certain left-wing Christian philosopher, then repeated endlessly during the years when the experiment of the priest workers was being tried: "*Marxism is the immanent philosophy of the proletariat.*" The impetus of the bourgeois intellectuals, necessary for the creation of the Party, proves on the contrary that the *proletariat as such is a transcendent creation of Marxism.* The difference between the two formulas makes clear the error of those who were content with the first one. For failing to discern "the spirit" which hides behind the theological structures of Marxism, they have been the unconscious victims of its atheism. Cf. *op. cit.*, p. 156 ff.

Thus in concluding, we must state briefly how, because of them, the lie of atheism is effectively becoming clear in the eyes of all, even to the Communists, on a threefold level: economic, political and religious.

Let us admit that the successes of the Soviet economy are, as its partisans say, as brilliant as those of the sputniks, and not, as the contrary propaganda claims, that the success of the latter are a veil for the failures of the former. There still remains to be explained the *Iron or Bamboo Curtains*, the Berlin Wall and especially the constant reshuffling of the planning methods which, since the revelations of Khrushchev in 1956, the industrial and agricultural councils of the Party regularly envisage. Supposing the production of the Socialist States surpassed that of capitalist countries, would Soviet man thereby be nearer the unity Man-Nature than the citizens of bourgeois nations; or, in other words, freer from suffering, from moral faults and finally from death?

On the political level, the bourgeois State has been replaced by the "dictatorship of the Proletariat," which has employed all its strength to destroy capitalism and to suppress classes. According to Marx, Engels and Lenin this "lower phase" of Communism had to be followed by a "higher phase" during which "the state would wither away." Although the dictatorship of the proletariat has already been transformed, according to Khrushchev, into a "State of all the people," it has remained, in fact and even for its own citizens, the most arbitrary police state which has ever existed. Nothing permits us to foresee that it can ever "wither away."

On the religious level, not only has the Church of Russia not disappeared despite all the persecutions and all the attacks made by antireligious propaganda, but atheistic ideology has itself given birth to a veritable Church by a supreme contradiction. It is an atheocratic Church, which in full twentieth century has taken up and carried to the extreme all the defects and abuses that the Catholic Church has been guilty of during its nearly two thousand years of existence but that it has shed a long time since: for example, the inquisition and torture of heretics, the claim to legislate on artistic and scientific matters and so on.

That the Communist Party deserves the name of Church and rests on the theological structures we have analyzed has been irrefutably proved by the famous secret report of Mr. Khrushchev which, in February, 1955, unveiled the existence of the "cult of personality," recognized its absolute grip on Russia for a long time and enumerated, though only in part, the ravages caused by it. No doubt the purpose of this report was to liberate Russia from Stalinist tyranny and idolatry, but without his knowing it, Khrushchev was also signing the death warrant of the Communist ideology by defining very exactly, from the first lines, the religious, supernatural character of the "cult" engendered by the Party. Let us note these lines:

> It was intolerable and foreign to the spirit of Marxist-Leninism to exalt a person and to make of him a superman endowed with supernatural qualities and the equal of a God. Such a man is supposed to know everything, to think for everybody, to do everything and to be infallible.[59]

For Communists, I know, the cult of Stalin represents, in the history of Russia, a temporary deviation, a simple "sore on a perfectly healthy organism," as Ilyitchev said. And even if this were so, one would still have to explain the genesis of such an evil. This is a problem over which the historians of Russia ponder in vain today,[60] and

[59] Text published in *Est-Ouest*, February 16/18, 1957, no. 168, pp. 89–120.

[60] On this subject we must read the report of the "Debate between Historians" which took place on June 17–18, 1964, at the Academy of Sciences at Moscow a propos the ninth volume of the *History of the U.S.S.R.* for the years 1934–1941. First published in the Polish review *Kultura*, no. 5, May, 1965, pp. 122–128, the text published from notes taken by students present at these sessions, was translated and published in *Est et Ouest*, no. 346, July 16–31, 1965, pp. 20–24. Let me quote only a few extracts:

"The cult constituted a definite period in the history of the U.S.S.R.; the ninth volume should explain it by indicating likewise why and to what extent the nation believed in Stalin. . . . How could the Party accept this for thirty years? . . . the half-truth which hovers over the evocation of this period in the ninth volume represents great progress over the complete lies of the former historians. . . . But this volume should indicate, a propos the "cult," what the opposition to Stalin was at that time. It was probably non-existent. How can one explain the genesis of the "cult"? I must frankly admit [an old Bolshevik declares] that I do not know how to explain the genesis of the cult. . . ."

A member of the editorial committee justified the imperfections of the ninth volume by saying: "It was only after the 'cult' was condemned that it was possible to take up the study of this period. During the 'cult' we were obliged to consider every fact as either exceptionally good or exceptionally bad. There was never any middle position. We still have the tendency to do the same thing. In this regard we continue to feel the influence of Stalin. Have we succeeded in

one can be sure that it will remain an insoluble enigma for their materialism, for the origin of it is *basically spiritual.*[61]

In fact, this "cult" is so little foreign to the spirit of Marxian-Leninism, that it represents, on the contrary, the immediate natural and necessary product, as Marx said, of the union of Man and of Woman. How can we doubt it, if we recall that it was inaugurated on the morrow of the death of Lenin, by a canonization of the dead one that all his collaborators approved, for once unanimously, and which they announced to the country in terms paralleling very closely the Pauline

establishing an objective study of a personality by speaking of his qualities and of his shortcomings [the attendance agreed that this was not done]? Now, no one is God or the Devil. That cannot go on like that; today it is no longer possible to write like that. We should write in such a way that in ten years, we shall not be ashamed of what we have written. Likewise, in order to fight the 'cult' we cannot use Stalin-like methods. We must be objective. . . ."

Finally the academician Kime, president of the debate, took up an idea already expressed: "numerous questions should be studied in depth before the genesis of the 'cult' can be explained." But he did not forget to conclude by saying: "I take my stand for the truth and the truth is precisely this: That under Stalin and with Stalin we built socialism. . . . The problem of the 'cult' should not make us overlook the real progress accomplished. . . ."

[61] To convince oneself even better than with the extracts quoted in the preceding note that the problem of the "cult" is *spiritual* in nature, one must read the report of the meeting between Bukharin and Dan, a propos of Stalin, published by the friends of Lydia Dan, first of all in *Novy Journal* (no. 75, Mar., 1964), then translated from the Russian in *Contrat Social*, vol. VIII, No. 4, July-Aug., 1964, pp. 196–201.

In 1935 Bukharin came to Paris with a delegation sent by Stalin to negotiate with the German and Russian socialists the eventual purchase of the archives of Marx and Engels, which had been evacuated from Berlin after the accession of Hitler to power. . . . He profited by this occasion to pay a visit, alone and without being invited or even announcing his coming, to an exiled Menschevik, T. Il'ich Dan. It was an unusual visit but "his heart," he said, "urged him to it." During a long conversation he expressed himself on Stalin to Dan and his wife in these words: "You do not know him as I do, as we have learned to know him. He is unhappy because he is unable to persuade everybody, including himself, that he is the greatest of all, and this is his misfortune, perhaps the most human trait in him, perhaps the only human trait in him; but what is no longer human in him, but properly diabolical is that he cannot prevent himself from avenging his misfortune on men, and especially on those who are in some ways greater and better than he is. . . . If someone speaks better than Stalin he is lost: Stalin will not let him live . . . for this man always remembers that he, Stalin, is not the first, nor the best; if someone writes better than Stalin, woe to him, because it is he, Stalin,

doctrine of the Body of Christ?[62] After this it was in the very name of Leninism that Stalin could, without much difficulty, "make himself the equal of a god" and profit by it to impose, for thirty years, a regime of terror over all of Russia, and first of all over the Party, especially the former companions of Lenin, who were in the end all "liquidated." Moreover the revelations of Mr. Khrushchev did so little to suppress the "cult" that he himself shortly afterwards was deposed for having been in his turn the object of such a cult. Finally and especially, it is impossible for this "cult" to disappear, so necessary is it to the Communist Church and so much is it the logical fruit of its atheistic ideology.

Indeed, to denounce the "past errors" for which the cult was responsible does not suffice to extirpate its root. It is rather the means of protecting it and the occasion to give it a new vigor by affirming, as Mr. Khrushchev did, that "the Leninist principles of the Party are sacred."[63] Since they are sacred, it is impossible to disown them or to suppress the cult which is its necessary fruit. But "the spirit of Marxism-Leninism" is dialectical enough to dissimulate such a consequence

and he alone, who must be the first Russian writer. Marx obviously has nothing to fear from him except perhaps to be presented to the Russian workers as inferior to the great Stalin. . . . No, no, Theodor Il'ich, he is a petty and mean individual; no, he is not a man, he is the devil."

And, as Theodor Dan, overwhelmed by such language, asked Bukharin how he and the other Communists could so blindly believe this Devil and in his destiny and in the destiny of the Party and the country, Bukharin was moved and immediately changed his expression, and said: "You do not understand that it is quite different; it is not himself who is trusted; it is the man whom the Party has invested; henceforth it so happens that he is like the symbol of the party; the humble, the workers, the people believe in him; perhaps it is our fault, but still it is a fact, and that is why we all rush into his clutches, though we know for certain that he will devour us. He knows it too and is content to choose the favorable moment" (art. cit., p. 200).

This is an extraordinary witness of a mind, at once clear-sighted and fascinated, on the process whereby Stalin was deified as "symbol of the Party." One should note that, for the essential, the explanation of Bukharin agrees with that which would be supplied twenty years later in the Report of Mr. Khrushchev.

[62] "Lenin is dead, but he lives in the soul of each one of the members of the Party. Each member of the Party is a portion of Lenin. Our whole Communist family is the collective incarnation of Lenin." Appeal launched by the leadership of the Party, January 22, 1924. Cf. Pierre Chasles, Vie de Lenine, Paris 1929, p. 229.

[63] Ibid., p. 95.

under an apparent denial. Indeed Marxists know as well as, if not better than, Hegel that the notion of personality is susceptible, like every other concept, of a threefold determination, so that one can apply it not only to the individual, but to the particular and to the universal just as well. Written under the influence of this "spirit," the Report of Mr. Khrushchev blasts the "cult of the *individual*" Stalin only to magnify the more that of the Party, "vanguard and guide of the people in so far as it is creator of the history of humanity."[64] Placing itself between the individual and the universal in this way, the Party can therefore at will and according to circumstances lean to one side or the other, thanks to a dialectical balancing which hides its failures and deceives its faithful. But it cannot, under pain of suicide, abandon a "cult" that expresses the ideology which justifies its power. In fact, similar in every way to the religion of "the so-called Christian State" denounced by Marx, the ideology of the Party plays, thanks to its "sacred" principles, exactly the same role as regards the so-called socialist state, and is just as indispensable. For in the Soviet consciousness, a split has developed between "the higher phase of Communism" with its unity Man-Nature "not yet" attained and the golden age of Lenin already lost again; thus do the people need a "[theoretical] expression of their real misery" as well as a "[practical] protest against it" which takes the place of "opium." In short, the Socialist State is also "imperfect . . ." and the more "imperfect" since it should not be, or at least should "wither-away." It cannot then do without an ideological "cult" which, as religion of the so-called Christian State, is the "*complement and the sacralization* of its imperfection." Thus it is, as Marx added, "the State of hypocrisy."

However such a universal *hypocrisy* began to reveal itself to the eyes of the world through the quarrel which has occurred between the two socialist states, or more exactly, between the two Church-Parties, namely, Russia and the China of Mao-Tse-tung. The occasion, if not its deepest motive, was precisely the revelations of Mr. Khrushchev on the "cult of personality." From that day on the rulers of these Churches have not ceased to mutually denounce their lies which are less theirs than those of their common ideology. No doubt they regret the loss of unity of the world Communist movement, so that each Party seeks from the Brother-Parties, the assurance of a major-

[64] *Ibid.*, p. 120.

ity in planning the future assembly of the Communist world which should remedy the split that has occurred in the heart of proletarian ecumenism, as Vatican II tried to do it for the division of the Christian world. But the arguments exchanged up to now and the very means employed by the two Church-Parties have simply revealed more clearly "the State of hypocrisy" created by the ideology and ought to bring despair for a reunion which is anything more than a superficial and provisional patching up.

After all we have said, it is easy to understand the reason for this. Marx appropriated so well the structures of the Incarnate Word, and his atheism so completely reversed and perverted them that the very bases of the human word, and, therefore, of our common language, have been destroyed by it. Is that exaggeration or pure a priori deduction? Not at all. For, on the very morrow of World War I, this destruction was first noted as a fact by a Russian diplomat and then justified in law by the jurists of Moscow. Indeed Litvinov, representing Russia at the Hague, refused the obligatory arbitration then proposed by the permanent Court of Justice and gave the following reasons: "It is impossible to find in the whole world an impartial judge, because there is not one world, but two worlds: the Soviet world and the non-Soviet world." After this, in his Le Droit international à l'Epoque de Transition, published in Moscow in 1924, the jurist Korovin notes that Soviet Russia, abandoning the tradition of the Tsarist regime, has become "the systematic enemy of arbitration" and he justifies this abandon by adding:

> The necessary minimum for the fundamental preliminary condition, for any arbitration, is the community of juridical conceptions and of normative criteria; if this community is lacking, every attempt to find a third authority between the two halves of humanity which speak different languages is a priori without hope.

By evoking "the different languages of the two halves of humanity," the author sees so clearly that the unity of human language is thereby destroyed that he finally concludes:

> To find a common language in the sphere of political, social and economic relations between the League of Nations of Versailles and the Russia of today—U.S.S.R.—is an obviously insoluble task.[65]

[65] We take these various quotations from Jean-Yves Calvez, Droit international et souveraineté en U.R.S.S., Paris 1953, pp. 43–53.

In 1924 when Lenin still lived, the atheocratic Church was founded, but it had not yet had the time to deploy its virtualities by establishing the "cult of personality." Since then, the years have passed: the "cult" has grown and prospered so well that it was necessary to denounce its most crying misdeeds. But its principles remain "sacred": the unity Man-Nature, original sin of private property, universal redemption by the proletariat. Thanks to these theological structures, "the spirit of Marxism-Leninism" continues unrelentingly a work the first result of which is—supreme irony—to destroy the *material* basis of language in the name of materialism and thus to make impossible in the name of Communism, the minimum of communication indispensable for men, for their nations as for individuals.[66]

From then on, who can be surprised that the division that first occurred "between the two halves of humanity" and has been obvious since 1924 should appear forty years later, no less visible, between the two halves of Communist humanity? How can we not recognize by this sign alone the true nature of the Spirit which, well before "endowing Stalin with supernatural qualities" in order to "make him the equal of a God," inspired in the young Marx the ambition to "understand the act of universal history"? This spirit was suggesting taking up for himself the old project of those who wished to build a City which reaches Heaven. . . ; however has not the story of Babel taught us a long time ago about the fatal issue of such ambition: division and confusion of tongues?

Is it too much to ask of the lucidity and good will of the disciples of Marx to urge them to ask themselves about the events they are living through, particularly on the intrinsic perversion of the language, bitter fruit of the spirit of atheism whose proper name is "Father of

[66] The problem is the same one whether it is a question of a simple dialogue between individuals or of an agreement on the international level. As for myself, I noticed this identity when I first made an attempt at contact to Paul Vaillant-Couturier at the time Thorez offered the "outstretched hand." And I pointed out at the time in a book *Le Dialogue catholique-communiste est-il possible?* (Grasset, 1937) the *perversion of language* which, as Paul VI was to say later, makes "dialogue with Communists very difficult, not to say impossible." Anxious precisely not to affirm an impossibility, I examined the difficulty and raised the problem in the form of a question: If the question so raised has not since then received the slightest sign of reply; quite the contrary, international events of the past thirty years have fully confirmed the value and the legitimacy of the position taken.

the Lie"? In proportion as they refuse to render a cult to this spirit and to participate in these deceits by being the first victims of it, the truths contained in the thought of Marx will only appear more fruitful, and the good which their nations seek, particularly a peace in justice, will be able, instead of remaining a decoy, to take some consistency and to become reality for all Humanity.

16: IS MARX'S THOUGHT RELEVANT TO THE CHRISTIAN? A PROTESTANT VIEW

James L. Adams

When one uses the term Christianity the question immediately arises: What branch of Christianity is presupposed? The same sort of question arises if we speak of Protestantism. In the present discussion it will be impossible to take into account the full spectrum of Protestantism. Therefore in view of the fact that Protestantism has characteristically appealed to the Bible, I shall center attention upon biblical perspectives in order to assess certain features of Marx's thought and in terms of these perspectives to indicate the relevance of his thought to a Protestant. In addition I shall focus my exposition on Calvinism, the left wing of the Reformation from which many Protestant groups have descended.

According to Ernst Troeltsch, two comprehensive systems of effective social doctrine have appeared in Western Christianity, namely, Thomism and Calvinism. Both of these systems have been concerned with the full range of the problems of social order. Calvinism in certain respects arose in protest against the ecclesiastically controlled civilization of the Middle Ages (symbolized by historic Thomism). In Calvinism there were contrary motifs, and this fact has given to Calvinism its strength and viability. One of these motifs we may call *theocracy*, the concern for a new order of society; the other motif appeared in Neo-Calvinism and in certain sections of the left wing of the Reformation, namely, the concern for *democratic freedom*. Lord Acton has asserted that the origin of modern democracy as we know it is to be found in the small independent churches of the seventeenth century in England. Economic liberalism also received some impetus or enhancement from this source.

If Thomism and Calvinism are the two major social philosophies of

the Christian era, we may say that Marxism is the major social philosophy, particularly in terms of its influence, which has emerged in
the era of post-Christian secularism. The first two systems, Thomism
and Calvinism, found their ultimate sanctions in a theological orientation. Karl Marx apparently attributed such power to the theological
sanctions of the Protestant and Catholic Establishments that he was
convinced that these traditions could not be radically altered without
coming to terms with theology, and this he did by appealing to
antitheology, i.e., to atheism. For him the beginning of all criticism is
the criticism of religion.

It is obvious that in important respects Marx cannot be understood
without taking into account the religious tradition, the Judeo-Christian background. Likewise contemporary Christianity, the particularly prophetic Christianity, cannot today be understood without
recognizing the stimulus and challenge it has received at the hands
of Marx and the Marxists. Because of these relationships, the question
of the *relevance* of Marx for Christianity is a question that is closely
bound up with a consideration of the similarities and dissimilarities
between Christianity and Marxism.

The similarity and dissimilarity have been given cryptic formulation in the familiar assertion that Marxism is a Christian heresy. This
is only a way of saying that the one cannot be properly understood
apart from the other. Still another way of saying this is to observe
that Marx himself promoted a humanism that had some of its
roots in previous Judeo-Christian outlooks. Marx's humanism—his
intention to promote the full realization of the potentialities of man
—cannot be viewed as something completely unique and as something bearing no positive relation to the previous Judeo-Christian
humanism.

Certainly it is misleading if one speaks of Marx as a materialist if
one thereby assumes that his materialism is the direct contrary of
everything that belongs to Judeo-Christianity. In face of this false
assumption the late Archbishop William Temple was inclined to say:

> Christianity . . . is the most avowedly materialist of all the great re-
> ligions. . . . Its own most central saying is: "The Word was made
> flesh," where the last term was, no doubt, chosen because of its specially
> materialistic associations. By the very nature of its central doctrine
> Christianity is committed to a belief in the ultimate significance of the

historical process, and in the reality of matter and its place in the divine process.[1]

We do not need here to survey the familiar delineation of the different meanings of the word 'materialism.' Rather it is more to my purpose to point to one of the most significant similarities between Christianity and Marxism, and in this connection to take note of one of the most fundamental of the differences between them.

This similarity and this difference involve the biblical doctrine of creation. Here one must distinguish between the original mythological formulation of the doctrine of creation—the narrative about the creation of the world in six days—and the implications of the doctrine which have been scrutinized again and again in the myth-research of cultural anthropology. In its cultural implications the biblical doctrine of creation is presupposed by Marxism as well as by most forms of secularism in the West. In the biblical view, creation (nature and human nature) is essentially good. According to Genesis, God looked upon his creation and saw that it is good. *Esse est bonum qua esse.* The evil in man or in nature does not issue from their materiality. The true destiny of man is not to escape from flesh and time. No matter how evil he may become through the abuse of his freedom, his restoration or his fulfilment is held to be a realization that fulfils creation.

The ancient doctrine of the resurrection of the body is a mythological expression of this view as is also the doctrine that "the Word became flesh." That this positive evaluation of the material order is not something that one may simply take for granted is obvious. It had to be fought for in the earlier centuries, as against dualistic conceptions emanating from Greece and from the Orient. Even after the mythological formulations of the Book of Genesis have been abandoned or "broken," this positive evaluation has remained. In this respect we may say that modern secularism is a Judeo-Christian secularism and this is also true for Marx.

Another aspect of the Genesis myth is worth mentioning here. From of old, the doctrine of creation has borne the implication that man is not only to subdue but also to care for, or to love, the creatures of earth. Nature is not merely to be used, to be exploited, by man. This Judeo-Christian view of creation appears by implication in

[1] William Temple, *Nature, Man and God*, London 1935, p. 346.

the view of the Yugoslav Marxist philosopher Gajo Petrović who rejects the idea that nature is "only a possible object of subjection and exploitation" and who asserts that true humanity requires that man shall "participate in the blessings (of nature) in a human way."[2] This view from a Christian perspective is a form of Judeo-Christian secularism.

Bearing all of these things in mind, we may say that Marx presupposes the cultural implications of the Judeo-Christian doctrine of creation. But in this connection we encounter also the most significant difference between Christianity and Marxism. The Christian doctrine of creation asserts that man and nature are creatures—they depend upon a divine Creator. Not only man's body but also his freedom and the very possibility of meaning are gifts of God's grace. If we use here a category of philosophy of religion, we may say that man is oriented ultimately to the transcendent. The modern Protestant does not accept literally the Old Testament myth of creation, for it is a broken myth. Nor does he view God the Creator as a divine being who as a separate entity brings creation into existence. The formulations of the transcendent reference of man and creation have varied greatly. Indeed, one must concede that a clear and readily plausible conception of transcendence is not easy to formulate. Since the time of Kant as well as of Feuerbach, the popular, traditional conception of God and of transcendence has been increasingly brought into radical question by Christians themselves. This skepticism has been in part the consequence of Marx's critique of religion as ideology. By now, however, the sophisticated Marxist is aware of the fact that something more than "ideology" is in question here.

Two rather obvious considerations must come into play with respect to the relations between Christianity and Marxism. On the one hand, the Christian cannot accept the secularism, the self-sufficient finitude (as Tillich called it), of Marx. On the other hand, the Marxist offers a vigorous challenge to the Christian, the challenge to give a cogent restatement of the "ground" or "object" of his faith. The issues at stake are relevant for the discussion of every major dimension of the confrontation between Christianity and Marxism, although varying

[2] Gajo Petrović, "Man and Freedom," Socialist Humanism, ed. by E. Fromm, New York 1965, p. 252.

formulations of the issues can be found in different branches of Judeo-Christianity.

One may give historical reasons for the atheism of Marx. For example, one may say that atheism is an understandable and rationally or psychologically justifiable response to the *Realpolitik* of ecclesiastical powers in collusion with economic and political privilege, in short, that atheism not only in Marxism but also in much of secularism is a reaction that is passionately promoted for the sake of human values. In face of this situation, prophetically minded theologians have felt constrained to give positive theological significance to atheism; for example, the German pastor Christoph Blumhardt in the 1890's asserted that the kingdom of God was being promoted better by the Marxist atheists than by the churches.

A similar transvaluation may in the end accrue to atheism within the context of Marxism itself, particularly if Marxism should live to be as old as Protestantism. The atheism of Marx may not be an inextricable element in Marxism. Atheism may be viewed simply as a *Kampfbegriff* contrived by Marx in order to promote revolution in face of entrenched ecclesiastical powers. The intrinsic merit of this atheism may be distinguished from its utility in a revolutionary movement at a given moment in history. There is a profound difference between utility and truth. One is reminded here of the statement of Nietzsche that some things have to be loved for more than they are worth if they are to make an impact on history. What I am saying is that, given time, reflection upon the fundamental presuppositions of Marx may discern ultimate resources that are not of human origin and that are not subject to human manipulation. I have spoken of the disposition of the Protestant theologian to revise his own theology and even to discover positive theological significance in atheism. Marxism has not been immune to change and to revaluation at the hands of Marxists themselves.

In this connection we should recall the fact that the Marxist system of ideas, like the ideas of religious groups, almost inevitably change somehow in the course of the success of the movement. When Marxism was struggling to get a toe-hold in history, its system of ideas, including its atheism, assumed the stance of a *Kampfbegriff* promoting revolution. But in the course of time and after the revolution was successful and a new order of society was being established, the Marxist ideas had to perform a new function. They figured more as a sanction for the ruling powers and for hope than as a sanction for radical criticism. This kind of shift is thoroughly familiar in the history of religion. It is usually referred to as the shift from a sect-type to a church-type of religious association (Troeltsch). The shift is somewhat analogous to the sort of change that Weber characterized as the routinization of charisma in the direction of bureaucracy. Thus in Marxism, as in other social movements, the function of ideas may change from serving as a means of protest to becoming a means of domination. The reverse trend is also possible, as for example in the current use of the Marxist concept of alienation as a basis for criticism of the Communist bureaucracy in Hungary. The Marxist can readily appreciate these observations because of his conception of the relation between theory and practice. Ernst Topitsch, the Heidelberg social philosopher, has pointed out that change in the social situation can bring about the transformation of a revolutionary idea into "empty formulas" (*Leerformeln*).[3] With the change of situation it becomes more and more difficult to connect these formulas with specific norms and with decrees being promulgated.

Not only this process of change occurs but also we encounter the introduction of ideas previously overlooked or suppressed. The new concern with the concept of freedom, as is evident in the writings of Garaudy, Schaff, Petrović, Rubel, Supek and others, illustrate this trend. Moreover one can observe in certain Marxist circles an increasing concern with metaphysics. Given freedom of discussion, one can conceive of the eventual development of concern for a revision, or deepening, of the concept of immanence which has characterized Marxist thought.

Already in the writings of Adam Schaff, one encounters the recognition that an economic interpretation of history is incapable of adequately interpreting the meaning of death or even of human life as a whole. Here we see the emergence of a new humanism in Marxism. Likewise a Marxist might appear who would raise the radical question as to whether atheism is self-evident or is scientifically demonstrable. Science is capable of re-examining its presuppositions insofar as its method is that of freedom of inquiry. Thus Marxists might be

---

[3] Ernst Topitsch, *Vom Ursprung und Ende der Metaphysik. Eine Studie zur Weltanschauungskritik.* Wien 1958, p. 221.

expected eventually to raise the radical question as to whether atheism is an indispensable and integral ingredient of Marxism. Accordingly we must take account of the possibility that atheism will not remain a category, or a dogma, in Marxist thought. A new and transitional crypto-metaphysics might take the form of a revised articulation of atheism issuing in what might be called neo-atheism.

Every Marxist today will perhaps view the prognostications just set forth to be utterly ludicrous. But a Protestant theologian cannot properly take a rigid view of Marxist antitheological concepts any more than he can do so with respect to Christian theological concepts. The modern Protestant theologian recognizes, even with gratitude, that certain fundamental concepts of Christian theology have been subjected to radical criticism and transformation, such as the idea of revelation, of miracle, of divine providence. Many Protestant theologians would insist, with the modern scientist, that for empirical scientific investigation no attempt should be made to identify the specific action of divine agency in natural and social processes. Among some of these theologians, the doctrine of special providence has practically disappeared. More than that, in certain quarters Protestant philosophical theology does not view theism as an acceptable solution of the problem of transcendence. Paul Tillich, for example, interprets the concept of the infinite as referring not to a being called God (alongside other beings) but rather to the infinitely inexhaustible resources in the depth of Being which are both a support and a threat to man. This disposition of some theologians to reinterpret the doctrine of transcendence contained in the doctrine of creation may be taken as an earnest of their willingness to enter into dialogue with the Marxist at the most fundamental level of presuppositions and implications.

Here we must in part reject the view of the Polish Marxist philosopher Leszek Kołakowski who seems to define the proponent of religion ("the priest") as the "guardian of the absolute who upholds the cult of the final and the obvious contained in the tradition." Greater discrimination than this is required to achieve empirical acquaintance with the theologians. There are priests and priests. On the other hand, Kolakowski has defined a philosophical stance which the radically Protestant theologian could in part accept. In his characterization of "the jester" (whom he sees in contrast to "the priest" defined above), he desiderates the inquirer who, "although an habitué of good society, does not belong to it and makes it the object of his inquisitive impertinence; he who questions what appears to be self-evident . . . one who detects the non-obvious behind the obvious and the non-final behind what appears to be final." Kołakowski does not appear to recognize that a radically Protestant theologian views the transcendent as precisely that which stands beyond and against human self-projection into the absolute. Moreover he lamentably gives to his "jester" a Faustian flavor. This jester comes short of displaying ulti-mate seriousness if he retains the Kołakowski principle of promoting a philosophy that "has no foundations and desires, no roof." Apart from this limitation, the spirit of the jester, as characterized by Koła-kowski, is the spirit that should inform the dialogue between Chris-tians and Marxists who are willing to forego the security of absolutes and are willing to question the allegedly self-evident. "The philoso-phy of the jester," he says, "is a philosophy which in every epoch denounces as doubtful what appears as unshakable; it points out the contradictions in what seems evident and incontestable; it ridicules common sense and reads sense into the absurd."[4] This spirit might tease us into admitting that our discourse whether it be Christian or Marxist is *human* discourse, never final in its findings, never exempt from criticism, never absolutely unified. I would say that the chal-lenge of the jester is relevant for both the Christian and the Marxist. At the same time, the Christian must concede the view expressed by Lucian Gruppi, one of the Marxist philosophers who in April, 1965, participated in the international conference on Christianity and Marxism in Salzburg, Austria, that Marxists have the right to their philosophy and no one is justified in expecting them to abandon their positions.[5] This view, however, does not preclude the possibility of open-ended dialogue between Christians and Marxists.

In such a dialogue, Marxism will make itself peculiarly relevant by insisting that crucial consideration be given to the question of the practical significance of any theory of transcendence for the struggle for justice and for the fulfillment of man.

[4] Leszek Kołakowski, "The Priest and the Jester," *The Modern Polish Mind*, ed. by M. Kuncewicz, Boston 1965, p. 323 ff.

[5] Cited by Walter Hollitscher, "Dialogue between Marxists and Catholics," *World Marxist Review*, Toronto 1965 (8), p. 57. This article gives an extensive report of the conference on Christianity and Marxism held in Salzburg, Austria. April 29 to May 2, 1965.

Before turning now to consider other aspects of the dialogue let me summarize: The Marxist and the Christian share a common presupposition which is rooted in the Judeo-Christian doctrine of creation, namely, the view that materiality in its essence is good. Neither Christianity nor Marxism are fundamentally ascetic in their evaluation of nature and human nature. On the other hand, the Christian and the Marxist differ with respect to another aspect of the doctrine of creation: the Christian emphasizes a doctrine of grace or of transcendence—man is a creature—and the Marxist is oriented to a philosophy of radical immanence. Neither of these views is subject to scientific demonstration.

The remaining portion of the present discussion will focus attention upon three additional *Anknüpfungspunkte*, namely, certain structural analogies between Christianity and Marxism. These connecting points are to be observed in the doctrine that man is a historical being, that man is a fallen creature and that man is a social, associating being.

In a letter by Karl Marx, which I have been unable to locate again, Marx speaks of the annoyance he suffered from the fact that his wife and daughters were in the habit on Sunday mornings of dressing up in their Sunday clothes and attending church. He reports that one Sunday morning he reproached them for going to church by telling them that for the sake of their religion they should stay at home and read the Old Testament prophets.

The Marxist interpretation of history presupposes in important ways the Old Testament prophetic conception of history. In a fashion comparable to what we have already indicated regarding the Judeo-Christian doctrine of creation, there is a structural analogy between Marx's conception and the prophetic view of history.

Permit me to recall here the principal features of the Old Testament prophetic conception. The Old Testament prophets rejected both a naturistic view and mystical view. As the late Paul Tillich was inclined to say, the Old Testament prophetic view provides a historical rather than a nonhistorical interpretation of history. Nature is understood in subordination to history, and history is oriented to time rather than to space. Moreover history consists of group formations and not merely of the aggregate of individual experiences, although the individual in later prophetism assumes an intrinsic status and significance. The driving force of history is the struggle between ethical monotheism and polytheism (naturism)—the struggle between justice and injustice. God makes a covenant with a people who promise to be faithful in the pursuit of righteousness, justice and mercy. This covenant involves collective responsibility before God. The people are responsible for the character of their society and especially for the poor and the neglected. When the nation is unfaithful, God has a controversy with his people as a people. Thus their responsibility is for institutional as well as for individual behavior. This ethos, however, is not a purely externalized, institutionalized one. It is rooted in inward commitment of the individual as a party to the covenant. The Ten Commandments are couched in the second person singular.

The reference to the covenant gives us occasion to emphasize that the dominant metaphors of the Bible are political metaphors. The idea of covenant was drawn from the realm of international relations (treaties). Along with king, kingship, kingdom and messiah, the concept of covenant permeates the whole of the Bible. These political metaphors suggest that God is sovereign over the whole of life, inner and outer.

Political metaphor in the Bible possesses cosmic scope and it also includes the sphere of the family. But it prevents the scope of responsibility from escaping out of the institutional or collective sphere in the name of the cosmic. In addition it aims at preventing any escape into a mystical sphere that is beyond time and history. Finally political metaphor aims at preventing the reduction of the social-ethical sphere to the exclusive realm of the individual, to the inner life alone, and to the sphere of merely interpersonal relations. The domestic metaphors—father and child, bridegroom and bride, brother and brother—are essentially political in the sense of being broadly institutional and in the sense of being subordinate to the wider sovereignty of God. In the New Testament, political metaphor reappears in the ideas of the kingdom of God and the kingship of Christ.

The historical interpretation of history does not view history and responsibility in merely abstract, timeless fashion. It presupposes that historical events possess a certain singularity. Faithfulness and unfaithfulness to the covenant become manifest in particular events and in institutional malpractices. The Old Testament prophets constantly specify the sins of the people, manifest in the social distance between the monarch and the people, in the callousness of the ruling and propertied powers, in the special privileges of the elite, in the grinding of the poor.

The historical interpretation of history in its emphasis on the particularity of the historical situation becomes especially evident in theories of periodization that articulate the various stages of the past and that epitomize the particularities of the present. Biblical thinking about history exemplifies what Karl Jaspers has called epochal thinking. The levels of discourse with regard to this periodizing combines the mythological, the legendary and the genuinely historical. The embracing periodization includes a period in which man is whole and innocent, a period of fall into contradiction and of partial loss of essence and a period of fulfillment. The first period is in the Garden of Eden and comes to an end when man is expelled because of his disobedience, his misuse of a God-given freedom and responsibility. In the first period man and nature enjoyed an original innocence or wholeness, but man, created in the image of God, occupies a special position in relation to nature. Moreover mankind is envisaged as a whole and in unity. However in the second period differentiation appears and eventually the perspective tends to be that of one nation that in a later period is subjected to slavery in Egypt and then is delivered from slavery. Thereupon ensues a new covenant. However throughout the people are enjoined to adhere to a law of righteousness in history, in the here and now. God does not offer escape from history but rather demands righteousness in the present historical situation.

Not only the creation and the fall are understood structurally in terms of periodization but also the drive toward the future. Eschatology thus becomes a crucial ingredient of this historical interpretation of history. Indeed, one might say that a historical interpretation of history is one that by definition requires an eschatology. On the one hand, the divine promise is to be realized in the messianic period; but, on the other hand, the human voluntary response and responsibility of obedience is a condition of human fulfillment that is viewed at the same time as the work of God and as something for which social-ethical striving is a preparation. With the appearance of apocalypticism, however, the work of God is emphasized to the detriment of human responsibility. Moreover the End or the fulfillment is projected more and more beyond history. In the New Testament a paradoxical view comes sharply to the fore—the kingdom is future and present, is immanent and transcendent. But even here the doctrine of the kingship of Christ expresses the conviction that fulfillment is not merely for the individual but is also for the political and economic institutions. Here the universal dimension reappears, for the fulfillment hoped for is intended for humanity. Indeed, nature is to enjoy the redemption since it has also suffered in the fall.

This expectation of the kingdom is not to be realized without dust and heat, for the divine power demands a response that is fit for struggle. Indeed, the response entails a severe struggle with pervasive demonic powers, the principalities and powers that seduce and enslave men. Time does not permit our dealing here with the special kind of social responsibilities, somewhat truncated, which characterize the early Christian community. Rather special historical considerations have to be taken into account here. These truncated conceptions that appear in peculiar circumstances, unfortunately, have been accepted as normative by some Christians.

Looking forward in history, we may observe that the eschatological tension and the dynamic theory of periodization reappears in Christian history, most conspicuously (for example) in the three-period theory of Joachim of Fiore which in the twelfth century arises against the Augustinian conservative periodization. Here it appears in a revolutionary proclamation of a coming, new era, when there will be a new social structure and even a new church and a new art. Of special interest to the Marxist is Thomas Münzer, the most violent of the revolutionaries with his demand that economic transformation must be accomplished by force, indeed that this economic revolution must be achieved first if the religious reformation is to have validity. Here the special place assigned to suffering (depicted in the paintings of Grünewald) is peculiarly significant. According to this view, the new era can emerge out of despair and suffering and out of a daring resort to violence. The book on Münzer by Engels makes it unnecessary to dwell any further upon this figure and his significance for Marxism. Much new light has been shed upon Münzer which of course makes the Engels volume of limited value today.

Dynamic theories of periodization emerge in great variety in the century following upon Münzer. New eschatologies accompany and motivate the struggles of the seventeenth century, struggles that anticipate the democratic, political revolution. Here the rational and systematic use of propaganda and agitation appears for the first time. In this many-pronged movement one can see many of the features of a historical interpretation of history that have been already noted above.

Now it must be recognized that a considerable variety of interpretation obtains among Protestants with regard to the framework which has been adumbrated here. Some scholars, for example, would insist upon a greater degree of discontinuity between the Old Testament and the New. On the other hand, there are many aspects of this framework with which Marxists would disagree. We have already noted the most obvious difference involved here, the difference of attitude regarding the transcendent powers. The Marxist would charge the Christian with mystification; he would also claim that this framework as presented is scarcely the basis for revolutionary action, and the Christian for his part would find the Marxist lacking in an awesome and reverent sense of the gift of life. But the Marxist and the Protestant Christian should find some degree of agreement. They could agree, for example, that the historical interpretation of history is decisive, that the meaning of history is to be seen in the struggle between justice and injustice, that these are universal values, that the fulfillment of human life requires active criticism and participation in transformation of social institutions. They would also agree that a tripartite periodization is pertinent—the Christian interpreting individual and institutional behavior in terms of creation, fall and redemption and the Marxist positing a sociological and perhaps also a philosophical conception of an original wholeness, a subsequent rise above nature and a "fall" into division of labor or private property and a development toward a fulfillment of human nature. The modern Protestant and the Marxist would agree that scientific investigation should be the basis for the determination of historical origins (the question, for example, of primordial communism). And what shall we say of the end of man? When stated in the broadest terms, the ideal of human fulfillment would find Marx and the Christian in significant agreement. Because of Feuerbach, Marx adopted the idea that God the Creator is really man whose essence is creativity. The means of fulfillment through violence is of course radically rejected by the Christian.

But when it comes to the discussion of the nature and cause of alienation profound differences appear. From the Christian perspective alienation can never receive adequate explanation in terms of sociological structures alone and certainly not in terms of property alone. So long as freedom is possible for man, he will abuse it no matter what social system obtains. Moreover even if property is held in

common, the administration of it and of other resources will provide
the opportunity for the abuse of power. If class struggle comes to
an end in the classless society, new struggle will ensue unless monolithic power prevents it, and monolithic power requires unyielding
violence, a requirement that itself violates the fulfillment of human
nature. From a Christian perspective, such a perduring violence
would be a demonic power of enslavement. We do not need here to
examine Marx's own ideal of complete spontaneity and of the dissolution of the division of labor. There are two crucial deficiencies in traditional Marxism: first, that it presupposes that there is one, and only
one, system of society that accords with the essence of human nature;
and, secondly, that it assumes that when the prehistory of mankind is
finished, there will be no conflict of powers, and real communism will
be identical with ideal communism. However before such a state of
affairs could exist for the test, the transitional stage of the dictatorship
of the proletariat would have to show that it is not a permanent stage,
in short, to show that the promise of ideal communism is not simply
another ideology protecting entrenched power. For all these reasons
the merely sociological concept of alienation promoted by Marxism
must be abandoned, and in addition the vision of the future entertained by Marxism must be rejected as largely utopian.

At the same time the Protestant who accepts the conception of the
sovereignty of God over the whole of life must assess Marxism as presenting a valid challenge to those types of Christianity that interpret salvation in purely individualistic terms. The criticism directed
against Kierkegaard by Georg Lukács may be accepted as a valid challenge here. Lukács, in Die Zerstörung der Vernunft, is correct in his
claim that Kierkegaard in the name of Innerlichkeit both desocializes
and dehistoricizes man and that he shows himself to be an apostle of
monarchist elitism. In its maintenance of the historical interpretation
of history as demanding responsibility for the criticism and transformation of institutions, in its concern for the poor and the neglected
and the exploited, in its claim that the criticism of religion is the
beginning of all criticism, Marxism (perhaps even in its atheism) is
an ally of an authentically Christian interpretation of history.

At this point I would like to interject a challenge of this sort to the
Marxist. In some quarters one can observe the disposition of certain
Marxists to enter into dialogue with Western philosophy. It is surpris-
ing to note that the philosophy of Heidegger is attracting attention.

But Heidegger seems in effect to reject the historical interpretation of history and thus to be indifferent to social structures and social responsibility. One might hope that the Marxists would also attempt to enter into dialogue with philosophies and theologies that are concerned with institutional analysis and criticism and transformation. I recall recently hearing an account of a conference with Heidegger in Switzerland. One of the members of the group ventured to ask Heidegger why he does not concern himself with a broader scope of problems than that of the individual in relation to ontology. In response Heidegger said, "You are quite right. I am not concerned with institutional problems. If you are interested in that sort of thing, you should not be reading my works. I recommend that you turn to the writings of Martin Buber." It is significant that Buber was a man who was oriented to the historical and prophetic interpretation of history found in the Old Testament.

I turn now to a final, brief discussion of the concept of freedom. Marxism has viewed prehistory, the period of the fall, as a period in which men are torn asunder in consequence of class struggle, and it looks toward the *eschaton* of a classless society where such cleavage will no longer obtain. In other words, it seems to look for a time when contrasting powers will no longer exist. It assumes that if private property is abolished, alienation will disappear. From a Christian perspective, pride of prestige, individual good before common good, will obtain regardless of the nature of social institutions. This romantic notion that man becomes evil simply as a consequence of institutional arrangements smacks of Rousseauistic illusion. In Weberian terms it is a victim of a monocausal theory. From a Protestant perspective the hope for the disappearance of contrasting powers is a hope for the end of freedom. It is the hope for a completely integrated society, in short, for an overintegrated society. This kind of hope raises the question as to the rights of minorities.

The issue comes to the fore in a special way today. One encounters Russian Communists who insist that one can enjoy freedom of speech in Russia today. But freedom of utterance is not yet an effective freedom. It requires freedom of association.

Here a major perspective of one type of Protestantism deserves mention. Neo-Calvinism, along with Spiritualist groups, fought for and established a high degree of freedom of association in English and American society. This is an aspect of left-wing Puritanism that was overlooked by Max Weber in his stress merely upon this-worldly asceticism and individualism. This is by no means the whole story.

Left-wing Protestantism emerged in the modern world in protest against the concept of Christendom, the late-medieval and the right-wing Protestant view that the authenticity and stability of a Christian society require uniformity of faith. From the magisterial (right-wing) Reformation as well as from Roman Catholicism in the sixteenth century came the reassertion of "the principle of Christendom" in the promulgation of the policy. The religion of the prince is the religion of the territory.

The Radical Reformation looked upon this policy as a policy of holy compulsion. The proponents of the Radical Reformation would have remained unmolested if they had been willing to nourish their own faith in silence, or if they had been content with occasional freedom of utterance. But they insisted upon the freedom to form independent religious associations. They "organized" their freedom and in return they were given punishment at the hands of both the church and the state. But the issue of freedom did not remain there. The question arose also as to the freedom to be permitted within the newly formed sects.

Out of many formulations of the issues let me mention one principal articulation of the concept of freedom. In certain quarters the question was posed: How can the Holy Spirit blow where it listeth if the new sect formed in the name of freedom does not permit freedom within the sect itself? In face of this question certain sects asserted that the group should itself make room for free utterance under the impulse of the Spirit. They even asserted that new truth can emerge only if the group is willing to listen patiently to a minority view and to alter policy under persuasion. It was entirely likely, they said, that new insight would come precisely from the minority. As a consequence they institutionalized freedom of utterance. They asserted that it is the right and the duty of every member of a church to participate in the determination of policy—the principle of radical laicism. By virtue of this principle a dispersion of power ensued in these small churches, that is, the dispersion of the capacity to participate in making social decisions. It has been claimed that by analogy this conception of the free church led to the idea of the democratic state. From it also came to birth the system of plural political parties in the commonwealth. Considering the proto-democratic church's respect for the minority and its permission for the minority to organize, A. D. Lindsay, the late Principal of Balliol College, Oxford, has asserted that the principle of Loyal Opposition in the House of Commons was born in the Church.

The history of effective freedom in the West is the history of the organization of freedom. Effective freedom requires freedom of association. To be sure, if such freedom is not to issue in anarchism, there must be an overarching loyalty or covenant under the roof of which freedom of association is exercised. Moreover freedom of association may become an ideology that tries to prevent the total community from remedying pervasive social or economic maladjustment. On the other hand, the practice of gradual revolution, or even of sudden revolution, is possibly only where freedom of association obtains. Marxism as a movement could not have succeeded at all if such freedom of association had been completely suppressed. Freedom of association, we may say, is the institutionalization of evolution and revolution.

However there is a profounder justification for freedom of association. The strength of a society does not depend upon universal conformity, but universal conformity produces deformity, a pernicious form of alienation. The strength of a society depends upon the capacity of its members to be heard and to exercise an influence. It depends upon the capacity of the members of the society to participate and to make their several contributions. Without some such conception of the theory and practice of freedom, any society is monolithic. It produces Hobbes' *Leviathan* in which free associations are considered to be "worms in the entrails" of the sovereign, and only an entrenched elite (afflicted with ankylosis) will be responsible for the character of the society. By this means, humanism, whether Marxist or Christian, is provided with organized frustration and suppression. It may be that Marx had in mind some such freedom of association when he expressed preference for the commune, for the localized microcosm.

Today among the Marxists in certain countries, we can observe an increasing concern for freedom of utterance. It will perhaps be a long time before they can enjoy freedom of association. One swallow does not make a summer.

For both Marxism and Christianity the fundamental social problem is the combining of a radical concern for a just society and the freedom to organize differentiation. The fundamental problem, in short, is to devise an effective federalism.

If justice and freedom are to be achieved, we shall require a new birth of federalism. It is the hope of the present speaker that such conferences as the present one may in a modest way contribute to this new birth. In this way Marxism can be relevant to the Christian, and Protestant experience may become relevant for the Marxist.

Part IV:
Marx and the Western World

17: FROM THE MARXIST-LENINIST
POINT OF VIEW
E. V. Il'enkov

I

I think that the organizers of the Symposium were quite correct in suggesting that we consider the ideas of Marx in their original form and completely abstract them from all their later interpretations and practical-political consequences.

This is not easy, particularly if one considers the enormous role these ideas play in the tense spiritual situation of the present time. However as a first step in the dialogue between Marxists and non-Marxists, it is necessary to make such an abstraction; otherwise the Symposium would immediately turn into a heated polemic on present-day issues, become something in the nature of a general assembly committee or subcommittee, and ultimately fail to carry out its task.

But this amounts to saying that if my paper were planned as a direct polemical antithesis* to contemporary Western European and American interpretations of Marx, it would contradict the basic intention of the proposed discussion. I am therefore obliged, if not in essence, then in form, to deviate somewhat from the topic directly suggested for this paper.

I shall not present a straight polemic with these or other objections to Marx's ideas or with these or other specific counterarguments. I think that the best mode of polemic refutation is to state clearly that position which has been subjected to doubt. If it is true that every negation is an affirmation, then it is also true that to affirm an idea means to repudiate its antithesis.

---

* The title originally suggested to the author was "Marxist-Leninist Objections to the Current West European and American Interpretation of Marx." [Editor]

II

I fully agree with the premise from which the organizers of this symposium proceed, namely, that Marx is indeed a "son of the West" as are Plato and Aristotle, Descartes and Spinoza, Rousseau and Hegel, and Goethe and Beethoven. In other words, the system of ideas called "Marxism" is a natural outgrowth of the development of the tradition of "Western Culture," or more precisely, Western Europe civilization.

It is an outgrowth of that very civilization which for various reasons and circumstances during the last centuries (roughly from the fifteenth-sixteenth century) was undeniably in the vanguard of all earthly civilization and of all technological and scientific culture of the entire globe. Consequently the repudiation of Marx by "Western Curlture" is, in our view, a repudiation of the most progressive traditions of its own past.

III

First of all we must define this concept, "Western World." It is, of course, in no way a geographical concept. Cuba, it is true, lies to the east of the United States, but the Soviet Union is situated "more to the West" than Japan, and North Korea is not a bit closer to the "East" than South Korea. The world is presently divided into "West" and "East" according to a different criterion, and this criterion is the form of ownership.

In this sense the terms 'West' and 'East'—in all their confused inexactness—can be used. However we must keep in mind that the "Western World" is the part of the world based on private property while the other part which is on the road to collectivization, that is, on the road to socialism and communism, is the "Eastern World."

In fact the contrast which we are discussing does not involve opposition between the "Western" and the "Eastern" world with their respective traditions at all. Rather it is an organic, internal divergence within the "Western World" itself, that is, strictly speaking, within that part of the world which in the course of the last centuries has developed its culture on the basis of private property. (Or, to use a more flattering though less exact term, on the basis of "free enterprise.")

Marxism was born out of the soil and the culture of this world as one means of solving its social problems and it can be described as a theoretically founded way out of its antinomies.

IV

Why were Marx's ideas first realized in practice in the "East"? The answer is not that they conformed more to "Eastern psychology." As far as Russia is concerned, we must remember that Lenin's more conservative political adversaries upbraided him for his stubborn "Westernism." They viewed socialism as a system of ideas organically foreign to the "Russian character." Moreover the more vulgar and evil among them even called Lenin a "German saboteur" and an "agent of Wilhelm"; for them, Marx and the Prussian Emperor were the same "Germans."

The adversaries of Marxism clung to the so-called national Russian traditions for "specific characteristics," but the backwardness of Russia's economic and cultural development not only failed to provide victory for the ideas of Marxism on Russian soil but, on the contrary, because of Russia's greater sluggishness, hindered them in every way. Not "easiness," but rather laboriousness in the realization of these ideas in economics and in the consciousness of the people was historically tied to the backwardness of Russia.

The victory of the ideas of Marx in Russia in 1917 was a direct result of the fact that Russia, with all its backwardness, was drawn into the orbit of the sharpest contradictions of general European development. The world slaughter of 1914–1918 was indeed the direct stimulus for the revolutionary outburst. The Revolution of 1917 was necessary to decide a typically "Western" problem and not a "specifically Eastern one." It appears both in theory and practice to have been the only possible way out of the condition of national crisis. However this crisis was not precipitated by specific "Eastern" and national-Russian causes but rather by reasons rooted in general European conditions of Russia's development.

And if, at that time, the revolution occurred on the geographical "periphery of the Western World," this happened not because Russia was located on that periphery but because there, on the periphery of the Western World, Russia was lying in the grip of those same antinomies in which the development of Western-European capitalism was also gripped. These antinomies then precipitated the revolution.

Thus we may justly quote the Russian proverb: "The chain is no stronger than its weakest link." Not external "Eastern" forces, but centrifugal forces of development of private property destroyed private (private-capitalistic) property in Russia.

If Lenin, the theoretical and practical political leader of the 1917 revolution, was "a son of the West," then certainly Marx was a "son of the West" also. It goes without saying that as Marxism, an ideological-theoretical extract of "Western Culture," was first actualized on the "periphery of the Western World," that is, in countries least prepared for it in terms of technological and cultural development, so also a peculiar coloring was superimposed on the practical-empirical forms of the implementation of these ideas, the ideas of Marx and Lenin, the ideas of scientific communism.

Directly connected with this fact are those negative phenomena, those specific difficulties in our development, which anticommunist propaganda so zealously exploited and still exploits. These phenomena to which we, as communists, relate no less critically than any intelligent "Western" humanist in no way offer an argument against the ideas of Marx. With these ideas, with the program we are effecting, these phenomena had nothing in common (nor do they now). Furthermore these phenomena are wholly explained, not as due to the influence of the ideas of Marx and Lenin, but on the contrary as a kind of bigoted and sometimes perfidious resistance of that material in which these ideas had to be realized.

These are not the results of the ideas of scientific communism but the results of how these ideas were altered according to the "specific character" and traditions inherited by us from prerevolutionary Russia—in accordance with the remnants of the past, as this phenomenon is sometimes called.

(In parenthesis we note that these are remnants, not only, and not even as much, of the commercial capitalistic forms of the organization of life as of the prebourgeois, precapitalistic forms of the development of private property. If you like, this can be called specifically an "Eastern" legacy, which did not and does not bear any relationship to the ideas of scientific communism. This legacy with its traditions hindered the affirmation of the ideas of Marx and Lenin. In a number of instances it led to the distortions with which communism can and has come into conflict in countries possessing an insufficiently developed economy and culture. But communism has successfully overcome phenomena of a similar nature, and the farther we go along the path of economic and cultural development, the less and less fodder for anticommunist critics will there be.)

However since we have agreed not to speak about the latest historical fate and latest "interpretations" of the original ideas of Marx, let us return to the topic, to the question concerning the relationship of these ideas to that culture in the soil of which they arose and were formed.

V

That all "Western Culture" developed and flowered in the soil of "private property" is a historically acknowledged fact. "The Declaration of Independence" and the "Declaration of the Rights of Man and Citizen of 1789" that legally settled this form of property as the basic principle of all legislation were documents of greatest revolutionary significance. They freed the tremendous resources of human potentialities from the surveillance of bureaucratic regimentation and established wider limits for the realization of these potentialities and for personal initiative. In this sense the whole technological and scientific culture of Europe and North America owes its very existence to private property as an indispensable condition sine qua non.

No sensible Marxist has denied or denies this. On the contrary, the theory of Marxism has, in all fairness, always valued the historically progressive role of private property and has stressed its advantages in comparison with the prebourgeois, feudal type-class forms of the social organization of human activities.

Both Marx and Engels began their careers precisely as the most radical theoreticians of bourgeois democracy, as the most determined defenders of the principle of private property, which in their eyes at that time coincided with the principle of full and unconditional freedom of personal initiative in any sphere of life, whether material or spiritual.

In his capacity as leader of revolutionary democracy, the young Marx even opposed the idea of a socialization of property. His *Rheinische Zeitung* did not, as he wrote in 1842, acknowledge the theoretical reality of Communist ideas and consequently could even less desire or consider possible their practical implementation; it only could promise to subject these ideas to a thorough "criticism."[1]

Marx rejected communism as a theoretical doctrine, for to him it seemed to be a reactionary attempt to galvanize the "corporate principle," the ideal of Plato. However he viewed the dissemination of communist ideas as a symptom, as a theoretically naive expression of a strictly practical conflict—a pressing point among the social organisms of the progressive countries of Europe. In this sense, he assessed communism as "the most serious contemporary question for France and England."[2]

That this conflict undeniably existed is attested to by the fact that the Augsburger Zeitung used the word, "communism," as a swear word, as a kind of bugaboo. Marx characterized the position of this newspaper thus:

> It takes to its heels when it confronts the tricky phenomena of today, and it thinks that the dust thus raised as well as the dirty words it fearfully mutters through its teeth while running away suffices to blind and confuse both the embarrassing contemporary phenomenon and the complacent reader.[3]

The following declaration is also quite typical of Marx's position:

> We are firmly convinced, that it is not practical experiments which are dangerous but the theoretical articulation of communist ideas; true practical experiments (and be they carried out en masse) can be answered by cannon as soon as they become dangerous; ideas, however, which control our thoughts, subordinate our convictions to them, and to which reason rivets our conscience—these are bonds impossible to break without tearing into pieces one's heart, these are demons which a man can conquer only by subjecting himself to them.[4]

In a word, it is impossible to deal with ideas either by cannon or dirty words; on the other hand, unsuccessful practical attempts at actualizing ideas are in no way an argument against them.

Moreover if some ideas displease you, then you should analyze the soil from which they spring and disseminate, i.e., find a theoretical solution to the real conflict, to that actual conflict from which they arise. Expose them; only in this way is it possible to fulfill that tense

[1] MEW, I, 108.
[2] Ibid., 105.
[3] Ibid., 106.
[4] Ibid., 108.

social demand that expresses itself at the sight of these ideas. Then, and no sooner, will unpleasant ideas disappear.

In this, essentially, is the position of the young Marx. This is not the position of a communist nor of a Marxist in the modern meaning of the word. It is simply the position of a sensible and honorable theoretician. It is precisely for this reason that Marx in 1842 did not turn to a formal analysis of contemporary communist ideas (they were indeed quite naive), nor to a criticism of the practical attempts to implement them (they were quite feeble), but rather he contemplated a theoretical analysis of the conflict within the social organism which spawned these ideas and the elucidation of that real demand which expressed itself in the form of ideas such as Utopian socialism and communism.

The question for Marx arose in the following form: Is it possible (and if so, precisely how) to resolve the conflicts in the development of private property in the soil of that private property itself? "Peacefully?" This again is not the position of a communist. But it is the position of a theoretician and it retains within itself the possibility of transferring to the communist position.

This position employed a wholly objective, fearless, ruthless and critical analysis of the social situation that was developing in the world of private property, especially in those countries where private initiative had secured the utmost freedom from any external, legal kind of regulation, namely, in England and France. And so the criticism of communist ideas, so far as Marx considered it a serious-theoretical matter and not a demagogical-idealistic one, became a criticism of the actual conditions of life that gave birth to these ideas and aided their dissemination.

The opinion that the wide dissemination of these or other ideas could be explained by the activity of evil agitators had been alien to Marx from the very beginning, even when the ideas themselves were distasteful to him. Marx believed (and I think his opinion can be justified today) that only those ideas that correspond to reality win sympathy and a growing audience and that these ideas must arise from the social demands of a more or less wide category of the population. Otherwise the most beautiful and alluring idea will never get a hearing in the consciousness of the masses, for the masses will remain deaf to it.

It is this very point concerning the dissemination of communist

ideas in France and England that Marx assessed as a symptom of the
real conflict ripening in the bosoms of those countries where private
property had received maximum freedom of development in all its
facets and all legal restraints had been removed from it.

Therefore communism was even viewed by the young Marx as an
ideological current arising out of private property itself. Thus the
criticism of communism finally became a criticism of private property
as the foundation of communist ideas.

This plan of critical analysis became central for Marx and served as
the basic theme for the *Philosophical-Economic Manuscripts*. This
work led him to the conclusion that those actual-empirical conflicts,
in the soil of which sympathy arises for the ideas of communism, were
not accidental phenomena, characteristic only of the England and
France of that time but inevitable outcomes of private property seen
as an international and general principle for the organization of all
social life. Marx became convinced in the course of this analysis that
the conflicts actually observable in France and England were, in
essence, necessary consequences of private property; they were already
present implicitly in the very principle of this private, individual kind
of property.

And if this were so, then further developments of this principle,
its dissemination into new spheres of activity and into new countries,
inevitably would lead to much sharper conflicts, and through these,
to an expansion of the "empirical basis of communism"—to an
increase in the number of people willing to go along with communist
ideas and in the number of those seeing in such ideas the only way
out of the gloomy antinomy of private property. For this reason, then,
Marx accepted communistic ideas as a necessary phenomenon in the
development of private property, notwithstanding the fact that these
ideas remained for him as unacceptable as previously, so far as representing a "positive program."

This actual (crude, as he called it) communism, which appeared as
a prime product of the movement of "private property," Marx considered lacking in appreciation of its own goals and problems and void of
a genuine theoretical self-awareness. Born out of its direct antithesis,
the principle of private property, this elemental popular communism
could only oppose private property and could possess only a sign of
negation to distinguish it. It simply brought to fulfillment all private
property's inherent tendencies.

Therefore in this "crude communism," in this elemental frame of mind called forth by the pressure of the antinomies of private property, Marx saw first of all an enlarged and unique mirror reflecting to the world of private property its own tendencies carried to their final, ultimate expression. "Communism is in its first form only a *generalization* and *consummation* of . . . [the] relationship [of private property]. . . . Initially it comes out as common private property."[5]

Nonetheless even with all the "crudeness and unreasonableness" of this initial form of communism and despite the extreme abstractness of its positive program, Marx assessed it as the only possible first step toward removing that "alienation" which had been created by the movement of private property. Marx's way out is this: Although "communism as such is not a goal of human development, is not the form of human society," nonetheless, this very communism is the "next stage of historical development in the process of human emancipation and recovery. Communism is the necessary form and the dynamic principle of the immediate future."[6]

Marx, the theoretician, found it necessary to reach this conclusion in spite of all his antipathies to communism's "positive program" and to the ideals of a "crude and unreasonable communism." Therefore in 1844, Marx came out openly for the communist position, for a position of a "negation of private property" and as a theoretician— began to ponder the special problem of providing the real communist movement with a genuine theoretical self-awareness, that is, with a basis not only for its immediate, short-term goals and problems but with a clear understanding of its final goals and its obligations to all human civilization.

His basic thesis, which is still being developed in abstract-philosophical phraseology (that of Hegel and Feuerbach), consists in the following, it seems to me: a simple, *formally-legal* "negation of private property," and the establishment of social property by the wealth that society has already created, is in fact a necessary first step, a first stage on the road to social progress. To take this step, this political legal action, people are pushed and compelled by the antinomy of this very world of "private property." And the breadth and keenness of this

---

[5] MEGA, I, 3, 111; cf. K. Marx, *Economic and Philosophic Manuscripts of 1844*, trans. by M. Milligan, Moscow 1961, p. 99.

[6] MEGA, I, 3, 126; cf. *Manuscripts*, p. 114.

antinomy increases in the same degree as material and spiritual life develops.

"Crude and unreasonable communism" represents a movement that arose quite naturally from the pressures of the antinomies of private property; it is a frame of mind, unilluminated by the light of theory; consequently it has neither achieved a genuine world-historical role nor realized the immensity of the problems objectively arising before it. It has been provoked by the rather blind but genuine power of "alienation" and spurred on by the development of private property into personal-capitalistic property and subsequently into monopolistic, capitalistic property.

But this genuine, theoretically unenlightened "communism" has, in fact, realized its immediate goal, always combined with a mass of illusions, the revolutionary abolition of the principle of "private enterprise." We say "combined with a mass of illusion" because a political revolution that has established "social property" as a means of production and as a socially significant boon to culture has been interpreted as decisive for the whole problem as if this purely negative action were a final "positive resolution of the problem."

According to Marx, or rather, according to his understanding of the total complexity of the problem, which can be sharply contrasted to the outlook of theoreticians of Utopian socialism, the business of political revolution is only a start, and the whole problem will be visible to the communist movement only after this act.

The real problem, which the communist movement must solve after performing its immediate task, is directly dictated by the antinomies of private property. After the revolutionary conversion of private property, as a means of production and a boon to culture, into "social property," this social property must then, in turn, be converted into the property of each person, of each separate individual.

In the social context, this question coincides with the abolition of the *division* of labor among individuals, a concept inherited from the world of "private property." In regard to the individual, the problem of his all-around development and his conversion into a "totally" developed individuality must be confronted.

The political revolution is viewed here as a condition to be fulfilled whereby society will then find itself with the power to face itself, and moreover, to really accomplish the gigantic task of creating a society without government, without currency and without any other external mediators for relationships among men.

Society in representing voluntary cooperation for the all-around development of the individual will, in this capacity, no longer need "External Mediators." On the other hand, only the all-around development of the individual has the strength to establish such a cooperation.

VI

In this connection I must touch upon one important current phenomenon. I have in mind the phenomenon, which in Western literature is often considered as somewhat of a "renaissance," of a "return" of a number of Marxists from the ideas of the "mature Marx" to the ideas of the "young Marx," from Marx's *Das Kapital* to the *Philosophical and Economic Manuscripts*.

In this trend one occasionally may observe (a few Marxists are included in this observation) a tendency toward a "supplementation," toward "filling up" the ideas of the mature Marx with humanistic ideas and toward exclusions, as if what was done by Marx himself in the course of his development as a theoretician was likewise done by the whole communist movement. I cannot agree with this interpretation although the very phenomenon that has served as its basis undoubtedly does exist.

It is indisputable that in the Marxist literature of the last ten years one can observe a heightened interest in the problems of personality and individuality, in the problem of a human being as the subject of the historical process, in the problem of "reification" and "de-reification," and in general, in that entire gamut of questions connected in one way or another with an analysis of human activity and its conditions; this latter includes the problem of "alienation," and of the reappropriation of alienated wealth and so on.

This may be explainable in part by the fact that in Marxist literature the themes as well as the phraseology of *The Philosophical and Economic Manuscripts* of 1844, of the various extracts from the economists and other earlier works have played a larger role than formerly. This is a fact—a fact which I also personally approve, since I see in it a healthy and fruitful tendency in Marxist theoretical thought.

However in this phenomenon I do not see any "return" of Marxist theoretical thought from the ideas of "mature Marxism" to the ideas of an "immature Marxism." Rather I see in it, first of all, an exceptional tendency toward a deeper and more truthful understanding of the *mature* Marx as the author of *Das Kapital* and the writings affiliated with it.

I allow myself to assert that the highly diffused interpretations in "the West" of the development of Marx's views as contained in *The Philosophical and Economic Manuscripts* in opposition to those developed in *Das Kapital*, an interpretation according to which this development was connected with Marx's loss of interest in problematical humanism, represents the most complete misunderstanding. If anything has been lost in this process, it is only that some parts of the specifically philosophical phraseology of the *Manuscripts* have been replaced by a more concrete phraseology, and in this sense, a more exact and stronger one. What occurs here is not a loss of concepts but only the loss of a few terms connected with these concepts.

To prove this fact is not difficult; it is purely a formal procedure, a procedure of extensive quoting with which I do not wish to weary the reader. Of course, the mature Marx no longer used such terms as the 'essential powers of man,' preferring instead the more exact expression 'the energetic ways of man,' and in place of 'Entäusserung' he chose to use 'Vergegenständlichung,' or more simply, 'the *Aufhebung* of activity in the product of that activity' and so forth. There is no doubt that the mature Marx uses the term 'alienation' (*Entfremdung*) more sparingly (and more accurately), as the strongest way to distinguish this concept from reification and "objectification" and other similar phenomena.

For me this is so unquestionable that all the problems of the early works are actually rendered more fully later, and moreover, in a more definitive form. It is quite obvious that the process of the "human alienation" under the conditions of an unhindered development of "private property" (in the course of its becoming private-capitalistic) is viewed here more concretely and in more detail. The problem of the "*Aufhebung* of alienation" and of "reappropriation" is shown much more concretely, as a person "alienated" from his wealth by the movement of private property. It is easy to demonstrate that the mature Marx maintained, and defined more exactly, his critical relationship toward that "crude and thoughtless communism," which still bore the marks of its violent origin out of the movement of private property and because of this was still, to a large degree, contaminated by moral and theoretical prejudices (see, for example, documents that describe Marx's fight against Proudhonism, against the "barracks communism" of Bakunin and Nechaev and so on). It is also obvious that the mature Marx, and after him Lenin, never, even in a single phase of his theoretical writings, viewed the act of turning private-capitalistic property into "state" property as the highest and final goal of the communist movement but only as a first, although necessary, step toward creating a society, without government, without currency, without forcible-legal forms for regulating man's vital activity, and without any "alienated" forms of human collaboration. It is these very forms that the communist movement, because it is not in a position to overcome them immediately by decree or by force, preserves during the first (socialist) phase of its maturity; however they are preserved only as signs of the movement's historical *immaturity*.

In this way the fourth question of the Symposium is answered: "Western" criticism of present day communism, so far as a grain of rationality is to found in it, is in its entirety, even though only implicitly, *self-criticism*. It is justified in so far as it objects to those tendencies and phenomena which still have not been overcome by communist society—tendencies which were inherited by this society from the world of "private property."

However the essence of the problem is that these "wrong" tendencies of a socialistic society are, in fact, surmountable; they can be overcome even while certain elements of a commodity-capitalistic society, and especially of a monopolistic one, are being inescapably strengthened.

Therefore let us make clear that the nightmares of Aldous Huxley and George Orwell—aside from the authors' illusions in these Utopian works—do not at all picture the evolution of socialist society but rather the development of private-capitalistic forms of property. While, according to external acceptances and signs, these authors are painting a picture of "contemporary communism," they are actually depicting a tendency in the commodity-capitalistic system of life. In this way these nightmares frighten even the humanistic intelligentsia of the "Western World." They do not frighten us. We understand these tendencies as a part of our heritage that is almost but not completely past.

After all has been said, I can assert that no problem of "editing the mature Marx" in the spirit of the "immature" Marx has ever arisen as far as scientific communism is concerned. We were and are speaking only about the fact that the ideas of the "mature" Marx have been converted into personal property, the "personal" property of each participant of a real communist movement, and in this way, of the entire communist movement and that these ideas must be set against the actual philosophical-legal and moral-humanistic context in which they are framed.

We are speaking, however, of more than those immediate practical-political deductions and slogans of war which are assimilated by a genuine movement and which rise in the bosoms of the private-property portion of the world more easily and quickly than in any other and which, in any case, are easier to grasp than the philosophical-theoretical basis and context of the mature Marx's ideas. So far as we are speaking about the "appropriation" of these ideas by every participant of a communistic movement, about their conversion to an actual theoretical "awareness" of the whole movement, the *Manuscripts of 1844* can and should play an important role.

These manuscripts were the first approach, from the standpoint of theoretical thought nurtured in the soil of a classical Western-European culture, toward understanding the true rationale and true goals of the communist movement. They represented the first awareness of the existence of a "real" transitory stage from the still indefinite position of "humanism" and "formal democracy" to the ideas of a practical-effective, concrete understanding of how humanism and democracy must fare in the world of private property.

From accepting the *Manuscripts*, one can proceed to a genuine understanding of *Das Kapital* where nothing of substance is lost except abstract philosophical phraseology. But the *Manuscripts* can be a help in the text of *Das Kapital* itself in scrutinizing those passages that could otherwise be overlooked. If such passages are overlooked, *Das Kapital* easily appears as an "economic work" only, and in a very narrow meaning of the term. *Das Kapital* is then seen as a dryly objective economic scheme free from any trace of "humanism" —but this is not *Das Kapital*, it is only a coarsely shallow interpretation. It is essentially true that a humanistic orientation of thought encompasses the theoretical thinking of the mature Marx, by its very method, in its interpretation of the dialectic, as a method of critical analysis of the life conditions of man and not simply as an "objectification" of an alien being.

Moreover this example of the method of Marx that is basically different from the revealingly "scientific" version of Hegel's dialectic can be viewed more readily through the *Manuscripts*. For in them is found precisely this process of humanistic-humane interpretation of the Hegelian *Logic*—as an "alienated form of thought alienated (from humanity)"—a process of a "reappropriation" of the *Logic*, alienated from man and his activity in the guise of a scheme-structure of an Absolute, Suprapersonal and Impersonal "Spirit."

V. I. Lenin was quite correct when he noted that "it is impossible to fully understand *Das Kapital*, and especially its first chapter, without having studied and mastered Hegel's *Logic*." Without this condition, the understanding of *Das Kapital* remains formal, i.e., tendentiously dogmatic.

To achieve a critical mastery of the actual content of Hegel's *Science of Logic*, that is, to discover therein the "alienated form," the *Manuscripts* have one other important aspect. This has in no way arisen from the desire of individuals to "humanize" Marxism as existentialist authors have suggested. The desires of individuals can be significant in the scales of the historical process only if they coincide with a need that has grown out of a wide, objective mass movement. No one will attend to these desires if such is not the case.

The fact is that the problems connected with "reappropriations," with the "*Aufhebung* of alienation" and with similar such categories have sprung up and confronted the communist movement itself. The necessity for reaching a practical solution to these problems is dictated not for reasons of the "prestige doctrine" but by the pressure of real needs that have become urgent in the organism of socialized production. The fact of the matter is that industrial production of present-day proportions represents an objective, the realization of which can only be effected by a democratically organized collective that would include in its number all interested individuals. It is precisely from this point of view that the problem of drawing all individuals into the direction of social affairs and into the business of directing "property" arises. Therefore the basic goal of the development of a socialist society consists in the gradual and consistent transmission of all the functions of directing collective affairs from a government apparatus to those individuals immediately banded together about a common business. In other words, the goal is the conversion of formally collective property into genuinely collective property. This tendency will no doubt pave the way for a further expansion of the scales of production.

But the solution to this question demands that each and every individual—and not merely a chosen few—be capable of really participating in the business of directing "collective property," possess the necessary theoretical competence and skills and the appropriate culture for this.

From this viewpoint, the question of building a communist society amounts to the converting of each individual from a one-sided professional—from a slave of the division of labor system—into an all-around personality, a real master (proprietor) of the material and spiritual culture created by all mankind.

This point is even expressed in the Marxian formula, according to which communist society liquidates "the division of labor" and replaces it with a rational "distribution of the kinds of activity" among equally widely and thoroughly developed individuals. These people, among others, will be able to carry out the directive role within the individual collective, within the national economy and within all human society.

Under these conditions, social property, as a modern form of production, is not a Utopian perspective, but a real need. It does not depend on the will or awareness of indivduals, but is dictated by the interests of a rational, functioning organism of present day industrial production—"the stuff of property."

Under the conditions of private property the opposite tendency is stronger; it moves toward a governmental, monopolistic form of "collectivization" of property and the duties of directing it. The forces of market elements inescapably doom individualism to one-sided professional specialization, to professional "cretinism," as Marx expressed it. Therefore to counteract this tendency, a monopoly of leadership of socially important affairs is given over to professionals. This, taking place independently of the will and desires of individuals, represents a tendency toward "total government." Thus the ultimate goals of these two movements for the organization of social life turn out to be directly contradictory.

The system that is based on the principle of socialized property will necessarily evolve toward a democratic direction of socially significant affairs and toward the withering away of government as an apparatus opposing the majority of individuals, for all will be called on to direct social (collective) affairs and all will be required to grow in social consciousness.

The world of private property will undoubtedly drift toward the opposite goal. Therefore in summary it seems that Marxist communism in the twentieth century is the only rationally based doctrine that is strong enough to offer people a real earthly ideal. There is no rational doctrine opposed to communism but only an absence of one. Therefore reasonable people must choose now between Marxism, some form of social pessimism or salvation in the form of a transcendental religion. I, personally, prefer communism which opens to humanity a real, albeit difficult, road to a future here on earth.

18: THE OBSOLESCENCE OF MARXISM

Herbert Marcuse

I feel that I have to begin by objecting to the title given to my paper. A most important thing was omitted—the question mark. For me, this question mark is the most condensed symbol of the dialectic in Marxian theory, but specifically it is symbolic of the fact that it is obsolete precisely to the degree to which this obsolescence validates the basic concepts of the theory. In somewhat plainer English: the factors which have led to the passing and obsolescence of some decisive concepts of Marx are anticipated in Marxian theory itself as alternatives and tendencies of the capitalist system. Therefore a re-examination and even reformulation of Marxian theory cannot simply mean adjusting this theory to new facts but must proceed as an internal development and critique of Marxian concepts. In my presentation I do not make the distinction that some of my colleagues make, between Marx and Engels themselves and later Marxian theory. Rather I consider for example Rosa Luxemburg's, Hilferding's and Lenin's theory of imperialism as genuine developments of the original Marxian theory. A third and last *caveat*: since I was introduced as a philosopher I should like to apologize for taking up very concrete and immediate political problems and conditions.

The title of my paper is not supposed to suggest that Marx's analysis of the capitalist system is outdated; on the contrary I think that the most fundamental notions of this analysis have been validated, and they can be summarized in the following propositions.

1) In capitalism the social relationships among men are governed by the exchange value rather than use value of the goods and services they produce, that is to say their position is governed by their marketability.

2) In this exchange society, the satisfaction of human needs occurs only as a by-product of profitable production.

3) In the progress of capitalism, a twofold contradiction develops:

between a) the growing productivity of labor and the ever growing social wealth on the one side, and their repressive and destructive use on the other; and b) between the social character of the means of production (no longer individual but collective instruments of labor) and their private ownership and control.

4) Capitalism can solve this contradiction only temporarily through increasing waste, luxury and destruction of productive forces. The competitive drive for armament production profit leads to a vast concentration of economic power, aggressive expansion abroad, conflicts with other imperialist powers and finally to a recurrent cycle of war and depression.

5) This cycle can be broken only if the laboring classes, who bear the brunt of exploitation, seize the productive apparatus and bring it under the collective control of the producers themselves.

I submit that all these propositions with the exception of the last one seem to be corroborated by the factual development. The last proposition refers to the advanced industrial countries where the transition to socialism was to take place, and precisely in these countries, the laboring classes are in no sense a revolutionary potential. This falsification of one of the basic Marxian concepts calls for an analysis of the international situation in which the advanced industrial societies develop.

The Marxian concept of the transition from capitalism to socialism can be meaningfully discussed only within the international, global framework in which the system of advanced capitalism actually operates. Within this framework, the following conditions can be ascertained. The continually rising standard of living in the developed industrial countries is due not only to "surface" phenomena but to the overflowing productivity of labor and to the new means of profitable waste open to the advanced industrial system.

Another factor which promotes the unification and integration of the society is a highly effective scientific management of needs, demand and satisfaction. This scientific management, which operates most forcefully in the publicity and entertainment industry, has long since ceased to be merely a part of the superstructure; it has become part of the basic productive process and of the necessary costs of production. Vast quantities of goods would not be purchased were it not for the systematic, scientific management of needs and scientific stimulation of demand.

These factors have made possible the continued growth of capitalism, and the vital need for revolution no longer prevails among those classes that as the "immediate producers" would be capable of stopping the capitalist production. Marx's conception of revolution was based on the existence of a class which is not only impoverished and dehumanized but which is also free from any vested interest in the capitalistic system and therefore represents a new historical force with qualitatively different needs and aspirations. In Hegelian terminology, this class is the "definite negation" of the capitalist system and the established needs and satisfaction. But the emergence of such an *internal* negative force whose existence and action would demonstrate the historical necessity of the transition from capitalism to socialism is blocked in advanced industrial countries—not by violent suppression or by terroristic modes of government but by a rather comfortable and scientific coordination and administration. The internal historical link between capitalism and socialism thus seems to be severed, not only ideologically but also practically as a result of changes in the very basis of the system.

I would like to mention briefly two attempts to save this endangered Marxian conception of the transition to socialism. There is first the theory of the labor aristocracy, which maintains that the integration of labor into the capitalist system actually affects only some privileged groups of workers, those in the trade union bureaucracy and those who control the party machines whereas the rank and file are not subject to this integration. I consider this theory outdated; the integration is by no means confined to the small minority of a labor bureaucracy but extends to the rank and file. The underprivileged groups that bear the brunt of exploitation remain outside organized labor. Secondly, there is the theory of the "temporary stimulization" of capitalism and of "relative impoverishment." In regard to the notion of a temporary stimulization, one can only remark that, as far as is known, everything in history is temporary; moreover from a semantic point of view the concept does not make much sense—for how long is "temporary"? "Relative impoverishment" is a meaningful concept both logically and sociologically but is insignificant in the context of the revolutionary preconditions for the transition to socialism. If one can still speak of impoverishment when the laborer has not only one automobile but two automobiles, not only one television set but three television sets, this may still be impoverishment,

but I do not think anybody can maintain that this kind of impoverishment activates the vital need for radical thought and action.

Has Marxian theory been invalidated by this breakdown of the
classical conception of the transition from capitalism to socialism? In
answering this question I shall begin by referring to a passage in the
Grundrisse der Kritik der politischen Ökonomie (1857). The importance of this passage consists in the fact that Marx apparently attempts
to "abstract" from the revolutionary proletariat and to focus entirely
on the internal technological-economic tendencies in capitalism that
would provide the disintegrating tendencies of the capitalistic system.

> As large scale industry advances, the creation of real wealth depends
> less on the labor time and the quantity of labor expended than on the
> power of the instruments set in motion during the labor time. These
> instruments, and their powerful effectiveness, are in no proportion to
> the immediate labor time which the production requires; rather their
> effectiveness depends on the attained level of science and technological
> progress or the application of science to production. . . . Human labor
> then no longer appears as enclosed in the process of production; rather
> man relates himself to this process merely as supervisor and regulator.
> He stands outside of the process of production instead of being its
> principal agent. . . . In this transformation the great pillar of production
> and wealth is no longer the immediate labor performed by man him-
> self, nor his labor time, but the appropriation of his own universal
> productivity (creative power), that is, knowledge and his mastery of
> nature through his social existence, in one world: the development of
> the social (all-round) individual. *The theft of another man's labor time
> on which the social wealth still rests today* then appears as a miserable
> basis compared with the new basis which large scale industry itself has
> created. As soon as human labor, in its immediate form, has ceased to
> be the great source of wealth, labor time will cease, and must of neces-
> sity cease, to be the measure of wealth; and exchange value must of
> necessity cease to be the measure of use value. The *surplus labor of the
> mass* [of the population] has then ceased to be the condition for the
> development of social wealth, and the leisure of the few has ceased to
> be the condition for the development of the universal intellectual facul-
> ties of men. The mode of production which rests on exchange value
> then collapses.[1]

Nothing is said here about class struggle or impoverishment; the
analysis of the collapse of capitalism is focused entirely on the internal

[1] K. Marx, *Grundrisse der Kritik der politischen Ökonomie*, (East-) Berlin
1953, p. 592 ff.

"technical" dynamic of the system, in a word, on the basic tendency of advanced capitalism toward automation. In the images and notions of this passage (man no longer enclosed in the process of production, standing outside, relating himself to the process of production), Marx has expressed his most progressive and most radical vision of socialism.

What are the implications of this passage? The technical development of the productive forces within the capitalist system attains a level at which the use of physical human labor as instrument of production becomes all but unnecessary. However techniques by themselves accomplish nothing; the transformation of the capitalist into the socialist operators of production would still require a revolution. But the level of capitalist development on the eve of the revolution would be such that it would call for a different ideal and reality of socialism. In other words, it appears that Marx's own idea of socialism was not radical enough and not utopian enough. He underrated the level which the productivity of labor under the capitalist system itself could attain and the possibilities suggested by the attainment of this level. The technical achievements of capitalism would make possible a socialist development which would surpass the Marxian distinction between socially necessary labor and creative work, between alienated labor and nonalienated work, between the realm of necessity and the realm of freedom. In Marx's time, this vision was indeed premature and unrealistic, and therefore his basic concept for the transition to socialism remained that of the development and rationalization of productive forces; their liberation from repressive and destructive controls was to be the first task of socialism. But in spite of all qualitative differences this concept of a "development of the productive forces" establishes a technological continuity between capitalism and socialism. By virtue of this continuity, the transition from capitalism to socialism would at first be a *quantitative* change, greater productivity. Then the passage from quantity to quality, the determinate negation, was to be the redirecting of the productive apparatus toward the all-round development and satisfaction of human needs and faculties.

It seems to me that this conception corresponds to a stage in the development of the productive forces that is already being surpassed by the advanced industrial societies. In these societies what is gradually reduced is: a) physical labor power as producing commodities; b) machines as mere instruments of individual or group labor; c) scarcity due to a low degree of productivity and to the drive for maximization of profit; and d) the need for abolishing exploitation of organized labor.

These are the possibilities of the advanced industrial society and especially of the "affluent society" (I shall use the term in an ironical sense). The affluent society indicates the passing of the stage of the development of the productive forces that Marx considered as the inner limit of capitalism. It has surpassed these conditions in spite of the poverty prevailing in this society. For the Marxian concept implies the identity of the impoverished classes with the basic immediate producers, that is, with industrial labor. Such is hardly the case in the affluent society, for this society has surpassed the conditions of classical capitalism in spite of the destructive and wasteful use of the productive forces which, according to Marx, was one of the unmanageable contradictions leading to the final crisis of capitalism. Moreover the affluent society seems to have mastered this contradiction because the destructive and wasteful use of the productive forces proves to be profitable and promotes prosperity. Has the affluent society indeed succeeded in the containment of radical social change? Or, has it succeded in containing the revolutionary potential?

This question calls for a re-examination of the transition theory in view of the prevailing historical factors. I would like to offer some suggestions for such a re-evaluation by distinguishing between the advanced industrial countries, the less advanced industrial countries and the backward countries and by indicating very briefly the situation in these three categories with respect to the socialist potential. To phrase it differently: can we today identify in these three types of societies the forces (political, economic and cultural) which, in terms of the Marxian conception, may be explosive by operating in the direction envisaged by Marxian theory?

I should like to start with the relation between the less advanced and the advanced industrial countries. The question here is: can we say that the affluent society, that is, contemporary American society, will provide the model for the development in the still more backward capitalist societies such as France and Italy and even Germany? Those arguing against this assumption usually emphasize the existence of a still powerful political labor movement in France and Italy and its new strategy, "autogestion," that combines Marxist and traditional syndicalist elements. This movement aims at gaining, within the capitalist system, extended influence and power for labor in the management of the key industrial and other establishments and is supposed to lead to gradual control by the workers themselves.

In my view this new strategy can be effective only after the revolution, but not before it. Prior to the revolution, and carried out within the framework of a still healthy capitalist system, this strategy would in all likelihood promote the creation of vested interests on the part of labor in the capitalist system itself. The argument for the assumption that the American society will provide the model for the more backward capitalist societies finds support in the Marxian notion that the most advanced and most productive modes of labor will sooner or later have a "model effect" on less advanced countries.

Let me now comment, equally briefly, on the situation in the backward countries. I think that in the militant underdeveloped countries today at least one series of objective prerequisites for socialism prevails.

1) The majority of the "immediate producers" live in conditions of misery and intolerable exploitation, and the abolition of these conditions would involve the abolition of the established social system.

2) The small ruling classes are evidently incapable of developing under their own direction the productive forces; indigenous exploitation is thus protected and perpetuated by foreign powers, and the social revolution would coincide with national liberation.

3) An advanced militant leadership is active in the work of organizing the underlying population and developing its consciousness. To be sure, the ruled classes are not an industrial but an agrarian proletariat; however as such they are the "immediate producers" who, by virtue of their function in the productive process, constitute the social basis of the established system, and it is on these grounds that, according to Marxian theory, the proletariat becomes the historical agent of revolution.

Moreover in these countries there is the possibility of skipping the stage of repressive capitalist industrialization, an industrialization that has led to increasingly more powerful domination of the productive and distributive apparatus over the underlying population. Instead the backward countries may have the chance for a technological development which keeps the industrial apparatus in line with the vital needs and freely developing faculties of human beings. However this historical chance of skipping preceding stages of repressive development seems to be overshadowed by the fact that these countries depend, for the capital requirements of primary accumulation, on the advanced industrial societies and their imperial interests.

Thirdly, and lastly, there is the situation in the affluent society itself. I repeat that in my view the affluent society corroborates rather than refutes the internal contradictions which Marx attributed to capitalist development. It is true that these contradictions (which I have outlined in the beginning) are suspended and "managed," but they are not solved by the welfare or warfare state. For this state is faced with the increasing difficulty of absorbing the rising economic surplus, which is itself a result of the rising productivity of labor. Temporarily this difficulty is overcome by the intensified productivity of labor, by the reproduction of a huge military establishment, by planned obsolescence and by scientific stimulation of needs and of demand. But these integrating and cohesive tendencies are counteracted by the progress of automation which tends toward technological unemployment, a trend which can be arrested only by producing more and more unnecessary goods and parasitarian services.

Within the system of repressive affluence, a conspicuous radicalization of the youth and of the intelligentsia takes place. This is far more than a mere ideological phenomenon; it is a movement which, in spite of all its limitations, tends toward a fundamental transvaluation of values. It is part of the human or social forces which, on a global scale, resist the oppressive power of the affluent society.

I submit, in concluding, a summary identification of these forces within the international and global framework. For only within this framework can we discuss the question, whether the advanced capitalist system is facing a "final crisis" as Marxian theory maintains. What happens in Asia or Africa is not external to the system but has become an integral part of the system itself. Taking this into consideration, one may sketch the following syndrome of a revolutionary potential: first, the national liberation movements in the backward countries; secondly, the "new strategy" labor movement in Europe; thirdly, the underprivileged strata of the population in the affluent society itself; and fourthly, the oppositional intelligentsia. To these four categories may be added one which I shall not discuss here, namely, the established Communist societies as powers which may sooner or later clash with the capitalist societies. Are these established Communist societies active opponents, are they neutral observers or are they physicians at the sick bed of capitalism (that is to say does the very existence of Communism stimulate the growth and cohesion of capitalism)?

Among the four tendencies which I have called the syndrome of a revolutionary potential, the major catalyst seems to be the first: the national liberation movements. In fighting against the wars of liberation, the affluent society fights for its future, for its potential of raw materials, cheap labor and investment. To be sure, the classical concept of imperialism is outdated; there are certainly no basic United States economic interests that would explain the war in Viet Nam. However Viet Nam has to be seen in the global context: a triumph of the national liberation movement there may well be the signal for the activation of such movements in other areas of the world—areas far closer to home where basic economic interests are indeed involved. Compared with this threat, the radicalization of the intelligentsia, especially among the youth, seems to be a very minor event. However I suggest a broader aspect. The historical dialectic here affects dialectical materialism itself. To the degree to which critical consciousness has been absorbed and coordinated by the affluent society, the liberation of consciousness from the manipulation and indoctrinations imposed upon it by capitalism becomes a primary task and prerequisite. The development not of class consciousness but of consciousness as such, freed from the distortions imposed upon it, appears to be the basic prerequisite for radical change. And as repression is flattened out and extended to the entire underlying population, the intellectual task, the task of education and discussion, the task of tearing, not only the technological veil but also the other veils behind which domination and repression operate,—all these "ideological" factors become very material factors of radical transformation.

19: SOME CRITICAL COMMENTS
ON MARX'S PHILOSOPHY
George L. Kline

I. INTRODUCTION

I do not accept the fashionable view that whatever is of philosophical interest in Marx is to be found in his early (pre-1848) writings. The works of Marx's maturity show a comparable interest in philosophical categories, a comparable concern with philosophical issues, a comparable addiction to philosophical punning, a comparable carelessness in the use of key terms. The main difference is that the early works contain larger and more indigestible chunks of philosophical argument and that they are, in a relevant sense, more systematic (philosophically speaking) and more "Hegelian" in both language and doctrine. At the same time, they are infected with a Fichtean or Feuerbachian —and quite un-Hegelian—romanticism and given to manipulation of large abstractions like "man" (*der Mensch*), "essence" (*das Wesen*), "nature" (*die Natur*), "reality" (*die Wirklichkeit*) and the notorious *Gattungswessen* ("species being" or "generic essence") and even *Gattungsbewusstsein* ("species" or "generic" consciousness) as descriptions of "Man"—which may be one of the reasons why Marx, in a long lifetime, never saw fit to publish the Paris Manuscripts or to republish the other pre-1848 essays (nor did Engels, Marx's literary executor, during the dozen years by which he survived Marx).

Marx's early writings are ingenious adaptations of, and variations on, Hegelian themes; but what is philosophically original in them is not profound, and what is philosophically profound is not original— because it is so clearly derivative from Hegel. As a sociologist and economist, however, Marx was, on occasion, both original and profound.

The Paris Manuscripts, for example, tend to truncate or water down what in Hegel was, comparatively, more comprehensive and adequate. Many of you will reject this evaluation. But most of you, I suspect, will agree that even the youngest possible Marx was neither a Zen Buddhist nor an existentialist nor a "naturalist" in the current Deweyan sense—although he has been identified as all three. Marx called his early position *Naturalismus* in a quite different sense and (in contrast to Engels and Lenin later) deliberately refused to extend the historical dialectic to nonhuman nature.

Marx is often grouped with Kierkegaard and Nietzsche as a "rebel against Hegel's system in the name of the existing individual." The extent of this nineteenth-century "revolt against Hegel" has been much exaggerated.

Nietzsche rejected Hegel's (and everyone else's) God, but his philosophy remained culture-centered, not man-centered. For Nietzsche no individual has value or dignity except as a creator and transvaluator of cultural values whose creativity serves future history and enriches a cumulative public culture. In other words, individuals for Nietzsche have only instrumental value, but their function is important since they, and not committees or collectivities, create historical culture.

Kierkegaard rejected both society and culture, but his philosophy in the end was not man-centered but God-centered. Only in the "ethical stage" does the existing individual stand at the center of Kierkegaard's value-universe (cf., e.g., *Either/Or*, Vol. II, and the early chapters of Part II of the *Concluding Unscientific Postscript*), but in the "higher" religious stage the central reality is God and the individual's "God-relationship."

Similarly Marx, in rejecting the Hegelian Absolute and the Christian God, assigns primary value not to individuals but to societies. His philosophy is, in this clear sense, society-centered. Like the culture-centered Nietzsche and the God-centered Kierkegaard, the society-centered Marx remains close to Hegel's position. None of the three revolts effectively against Hegel's system since culture, God and society are all decisive *Momente*—dialectical components—in that system. What each of the "rebels" does is to pare away one or two essential elements, and consequently retains a philosophically truncated Hegelianism.

Nietzsche's culture-centeredness and Kierkegaard's God-centeredness apply both to the present and to the future. But the society-centeredness defended by Marx is to give way to genuine man-centeredness in the historical future. Maximilien Rubel has said that Marx could not respect the freedom and dignity of the individual because at the present (precommunist) stage of history "there are no individuals." Marx not only refused to ascribe to existing human individuals any intrinsic value, inviolable rights or inherent dignity, but he also explicitly repudiated all "so-called human rights" as expressions of a bourgeois ideology that was egoistic and antisocial; furthermore he insisted that intrinsic value will accrue only to the unalienated, creative individuals of the communist future. Until that time individuals have only historically instrumental value: those who work to bring about a communist society are to be respected as persons; those who refuse or fail to do so are to be treated as mere obstacles on the path of historical progress.

Since individuals must subordinate themselves to the social groupings of which they are members (classes, trade unions, political parties) in order to participate in the "building of communism," Marx's position with respect to the present, as well as to the immediate future, remains in a clear sense society-centered. Only with respect to the remote future may it be called "man-centered." To put the point differently, Marx offers a humanist *ideal*, but he does not accept humanist *principles*. Thus, strictly speaking, he is not an ethical humanist. (He is, of course, a "humanist" in the loose sense of the term which makes it roughly equivalent to "secularist," just as he is a "naturalist" in the equally loose sense of that term which makes it equivalent to "anti-supernaturalist.")

On this point Marx is closer to Nietzsche, and both of them are farther from Kierkegaard, than is generally acknowledged. Both thinkers regard present, uncreative and conformist individuals as having only instrumental value, as being valuable only in so far as they serve to bring closer a future in which it will be possible for individuals to be nonconformist and truly creative. However two points should be noted. First in Marx's view, beyond a certain future date (i.e., at the end of what he sometimes called "prehistory," after the transition to communism), *all* individuals will be nonconformist and creative—and presumably, although Marx does not say so explicitly, will have intrinsic, noninstrumental value. In contrast for Nietzsche, even in the remote future, only *some* individuals—the few *freie Geister* ("free spirits") and ultimately *Übermenschen* (overmen) —will be nonconformist and creative while the many will remain, as before, conformist and uncreative. Secondly on my reading of Nietzsche, even his ultimate *Übermenschen* will not, as individuals, be ends in themselves but only, or primarily, instrumentalities for the enrichment of a high historical culture.

On this question Kierkegaard differed from both Marx and Nietzsche. He did not regard present individuals as instrumental to the creation of a future culture or as liberators of a future mankind. To be sure, he saw the existing individual as—in one sense—subordinate to and dependent upon God, but he insisted that at the level of human history intrinsic value resides uniquely in existing individuals. In this refusal to instrumentalize living men for the sake of an anticipated "mankind," Kierkegaard was in (unknowing) agreement with two of his Russian contemporaries, Alexander Herzen (1812–1870) and Visarion Belinski (1811–1848). Herzen spoke of the "individual person [lichnost']" as the "summit" of history and declared: "The subordination of the individual to society, to nation [narod], humanity, or Idea is a continuation of the practice of human sacrifice." But, inconsistently, Herzen anticipating Nietzsche sometimes referred to living men as "building a bridge," across which "the unknown man of the future will walk."[1]

A more consistent "rebel against Hegel" was Belinski. Less systematic than the Western three, not so much of a Hegel-Kenner as Marx, less sophisticated about culture than Nietzsche, less sensitive to religion than Kierkegaard, Belinski in his letters to Botkin of 1840 and 1841 passionately rejected the Hegelian system in the name of the intrinsic, noninstrumental value of the human individual (lichnost'). "The human individual," he then wrote, "has become the point upon which I fear I shall go mad." Individuality for Belinski is a "great and dreadful mystery," more precious than "history, society, mankind." In Hegel's philosophy the "subject is not an end in itself but a means for the ephemeral expression of the universal. . . ." Belinski declares: ". . . the fate of the subject, the individual personality is more important than the fate of the whole world . . . including Hegel's Allgemeinheit."[2]

---

[1] A. I. Herzen, Sobraniye sochinenii (Collected Works), Moscow 1955, VI, 125, 7; English translation in I. Berlin, ed., From the Other Shore, London and New York, 1956, pp. 134 ff., 3.

[2] Letter to V. P. Botkin, March 1, 1841: in V. G. Belinski, Pis'ma (Letters), vol. II, p. 212 ff.; English translation by Philip Rahv in Russian Philosophy, ed. by James M. Edie, James P. Scanlan, Mary-Barbara Zeldin and George L. Kline, Chicago 1965, vol. I, p. 304.

The individuality-centered young Belinski in his later works shifted his focus somewhat toward society, although in general he viewed social solidarity—*sotsialnost'*—as an instrumental value, a support for individual freedom and dignity. How such support could be made effective without eroding individuality he never made wholly clear, but he spoke of his own "wild, furious, fanatical love for the freedom and independence of the individual person, possible only in a society based upon truth-justice [*pravda*] and heroic virtue."[3]

II. "MATERIALISM" AND ECONOMICS

For three quite unrelated reasons I shall not, in this paper, consider in any detail Marx's doctrine of alienation (*Entfremdung*): a) because it has been overexposed in recent Marx literature; b) because it is receiving separate treatment in this volume; c) because Marx's early conception of alienation is so closely derivative from Hegel, while his variations on Hegel's theme are mainly economic and sociological.

Hegel's theory of alienation is commonly, but mistakenly, identified with the theory of "the self-alienation of Absolute Spirit."[4] But in Hegel's *Phänomenologie des Geistes* the relevant section is entitled "*Der sich entfremdete Geist; die Bildung*" ("Spirit Alienated from Itself. Culture—[or Education, Formation, "Shaping"]"). The "phenomenological" reference is not to *absoluter Geist* but rather to *dasciender Geist* (existing, finite spirit); the historical reference is to the highly formalized and sophisticated French culture which flourished under Louis XIV.

The individual can become *wirklich*—culturally and historically "actual" and effective—only by renouncing his natural selfhood. He can actualize his unique *individual* potentiality only by appropriating the *universal* forms of culture—of language, etiquette, mores and so on. These forms are not his creation; indeed, they are alien to him. Yet historical culture is a wholly human product. Thus men's own

---

[3] Letter to V. P. Botkin, June 27–28, 1841: *Pis'ma*, II, 246; *Russian Philosophy*, vol. I, p. 306.

[4] See the remarks by Petrović and Wartofsky in this volume pp. 137–138, 154.

collective creations stand massively over against, and alienated from, individual men.[5] Marx in 1844 adds to this account of cultural alienation motifs from Hegel's own theory of work (in the Master-Slave dialectic). But he simplifies and distorts Hegel's account by omitting the cultural, literary and linguistic dimensions of alienation and concentrates exclusively upon the economic, social and—to a degree— psychological aspects of "alienated labor" (die entfremdete Arbeit).

In the next section (Section III) of this paper I shall say something about Marx's related doctrine of "objectification" (Vergegenständlichung) in which his philosophical position departs clearly from Hegel's.

However I would first like to raise a question about Marx's "materialism." In my judgment neither young nor old Marx was an ontological materialist.[6] One reason why he has so often been considered such is the loose, popularly "materialistic" coloring of his terminology. From his earliest statements (e.g., in 1842) to his latest (in the various volumes of Das Kapital), Marx refers to "brain" (Hirn or Gehirn) or "head" (Kopf), when he means "mind" or "intelligence." He likes to describe men as "self-conscious things" (selbst-bewusste Dinge) or as having "thinking brains" (denkende Hirne). Thus he writes that "the same spirit [a secularized Hegelian Welt- or Zeitgeist] which builds railroads with the workers' hands builds philosophical systems in the brain of the philosophers."[7] Many years later Marx added that, in contrast to Hegel, he considered the "ideal" as only the "material, inverted and translated in the human head."[8]

---

[5] For a somewhat fuller account of Hegel's theory of alienation see my essay "The Existentialist Rediscovery of Hegel and Marx" in Phenomenology and Existentialism, ed. by Edward Lee and Maurice Mandelbaum, Baltimore 1967.

[6] Alfred Schmidt has convincingly refuted the view that Marx is an ontological materialist. However he makes his point in a misleading way and asserts that Marx, though not an ontologist, was a materialist, that Marx's materialism was non-ontological. (Cf. his book, Der Begriff der Natur in der Lehre von Marx, Frankfurt 1962, pp. 26, 45 ff., 70). Schmidt also perpetuates the terminological confusion of 'material' and 'economic,' which I shall discuss below.

[7] "Derselbe Geist baut die philosophischen Systeme in dem Hirn der Philosophen, der die Eisenbahnen mit den Händen der Gewerke baut," MEW, I, 97; cf. Marx's comment, referring to the absolute idealist, about the Einfall seines Gehirns, MEW, II, 148.

[8] "Bei mir ist umgekehrt das Ideelle nichts anderes als das im Menschenkopf umgesetzte und übersetzte Materielle," MEW, XXIII, 27; cf. Capital, Moscow 1954, vol. I, p. 19.

I submit that such expressions do not entail an ontological materialism, but insofar as they have any doctrinal implications, entail only a generalized reductivism. Such modes of speech derive from Holbach, Feuerbach and Büchner as well as from the nineteenth-century "man in the (German) street." Similarly in English, ontological materialists and nonmaterialists alike speak of people as having, or lacking, "brains," as having good "heads" and so on when they mean to refer only to people's intelligence or lack of it. The same is true of the ugly English expressions "to pick one's brain" and "to have such an open mind that one's brains fall out." In German there is the rather less unpleasant metaphor, which Marx used frequently, of the *Hirngespenst* (cf. English "cobweb in the brain"). The "materialism" implied by such usages is at most "colloquial," "idiomatic" or—if you will—"dialectological," not dialectical or ontological.

However the main reason why Marx has been considered by both his disciples and his critics as an ontological materialist is that he so regularly, in both early and late works, uses the term 'material' or 'materialist' as a synonym for 'economic.' Thus he speaks of "material process," "material relations," "material activity," "grossly-material production," "material life," "material conditions," "material forces of production." In all such expressions the term 'material' means 'economic.' This usage is highly misleading since there is nothing peculiarly "material" or "materialistic"—in the ontological sense—about the forces and relations of economic production.[9] Rather economic activities and institutions are a product of human energy and inventiveness, and economic relations are shaped by human attitudes and modes of response. Marx himself implicitly admits as much when he says that human *praxis* and production are accompanied by, or permeated with, consciousness (*Bewusstsein*).

Engels and Lenin, but not Marx himself, were committed to the view that the "base" and "superstructure" of society are of distinct ontological types. The base is a material entity, the superstructure a nonmaterial ("ideological") entity. And changes in the former produce changes in the latter. The superstructure is strictly epiphenome-

---

[9] This was recognized at least as early as 1896–1897 by the Russian intellectual historian, Paul Milyukov, who called the alleged "materiality" of economic relations "merely apparent." Cf. his *Ocherki po istorii russkoi kul'tury*, as cited by Thomas G. Masaryk, *Die philosophischen und soziologischen Grundlagen des Marxismus*, Vienna 1899, p. 153.

nal, as the mind is epiphenomenal to the body generally and to the brain in particular. (Marxist-Leninists quite explicitly assume that base is related to superstructure as body to mind; Marx was not so crude. He would have said that the relations were parallel only in being equally causal, where the primary causal pressure is of base upon superstructure and of body upon mind.) I do not intend to enter here into detailed criticism of the theory of superstructures. But I will say that it seems to me more sensible to classify both "basal" or "substructural," i.e., economic, and "superstructural," e.g., legal or religious, institutions as essentially *social*. One is no more material than the other, because neither is material at all—although, of course, *both* presuppose the biological existence of human beings and the physical existence of various artifacts.

Marx, both early and late but perhaps most uncritically in his early writings, confused two distinct senses of 'materialism'—a) selfishness or acquisitiveness and b) the ontological doctrine that only matter is "real." Marx's early critique of *die bürgerliche Gesellschaft* rests on the implicit identification of economic motivation with self-seeking. The later superposition upon this critique of a "materialist" (i.e., economic) interpretation of history and a materialist ontology—the last mainly by Engels—deepened a confusion which has become canonical for Marxist-Leninists.

Let me probe for a moment into the origins of this terminological and conceptual confusion. The term 'material need' (*materielles Bedürfnis*) is used by Feuerbach, and even occasionally by Hegel, in the sense of "vital need" or "biological need" (e.g., for food, drink, shelter). The contrasting term is *geistiges Bedürfnis*—"spiritual," "cultural" or "moral" need (e.g., for truth, beauty, dignity).

A less misleading term for 'material' would be 'bodily' or 'physiological.' Neither of these terms is equivalent to "acquisitive." More important, however, neither exhausts the range of economics. The "material goods" produced by the economic process may answer to "spiritual," "cultural" or "moral" needs as well as to "material needs." Consider the production of musical instruments, books, sheet music, record players, records, art reproductions and so on. It makes absolutely no sense to call such production "material." It might be called, loosely, a production of *things*, as opposed to the "production"—i.e., rendering—of services. But clearly not all things or goods serve biological or physiological needs. I think that Marx's strong emphasis upon the production of economic goods and his virtual neglect of economic services is related to his misuse of the term 'material'—which brings me to my next point.

III. NEGLECT OF ECONOMIC SERVICES AND THE THEORY OF *VERGEGENSTÄNDLICHUNG*

Marx's paradigm of economic activity is the bringing into being of shoes and ships and sealing-wax, not the polishing of shoes, the piloting of ships, or the packaging of sealing-wax. Similarly if he were to speak about those "goods" which serve "spiritual-cultural" needs—which he hardly ever does explicitly—Marx would refer to the making of violins rather than the repairing, tuning, or selling of violins. (There is a helpful ambiguity in the plain English verb 'make' as applied to beds: it means, on the one hand, to produce, on the other, to neaten and arrange.)

Parenthetically I might add that the Marxist-Leninist emphasis on the production of things seems to me not unrelated to the pervasive inefficiency and slovenliness of services in the Soviet Union. The editors of *Izvestia* have recently found it politic to assert that, although "people who work in restaurants, laundries, barber-shops, and stores do not produce material values [*material 'nye tsennosti*]"—i.e., commodities—still "their work is no less important and responsible than that of workers who make steel, mine coal, grow grain, and build ships" (editorial for November 17, 1964). I doubt that Marx would have concurred.

There seems a special irony in Marx's systematic neglect of economic services since most of his own activity could be interpreted as a form of teaching, the rendering of an economic service (even though Marx's economic reward for this service was negligible). I suggest two reasons for this neglect.

a) The pervasive influence of Hegel's Master-Slave Dialectic. The slave's "service" (*Dienst*) is a placing at the master's disposal of objects which are fitted by nature for consumption or use. The slave begins to work, i.e., to combine and reshape natural objects, only when his service proves inadequate to meet the master's desires. In a broad sense, of course, even such service is a kind of work, but it is neither "productive" nor "world-transforming." Marx and his followers have, understandably, shown little interest in it.

Marx neglects *Dienst*, and economic services generally, because they are *dialectically* inferior, are abstract$_H$.[10] *Dienst* is only a one-sided, abstract$_H$ Hegelian *Moment* in *Arbeit*. Secondarily, Marx neglects services, I suspect, because he regards the rendering of service as *morally* inferior to the producing of goods—as somehow submissive, humiliating. Compare the connection of 'service' with 'servant' and 'servitude.' (One might add that, in Hegel's account, work is also submissive and humiliating at the beginning of the Master-Slave Dialectic; the slave becomes self-sufficient and "independent" only as he continues to work, to impose shape on given materials and so on.)

b) Equally important is the theory of "objectification" (*Vergegenständlichung*) to which I have already alluded. Marx in the Paris Manuscripts of 1844 had charged that Hegel confused alienation (*Entfremdung* or *Entäusserung*) with "objectification" (*Vergegenständlichung*) and, while praising Hegel's attempt to overcome human alienation, had rejected his parallel effort to overcome objectification in knowledge, action and production. The contrast between Marx and Hegel might be expressed in Aristotelian terms by saying that for Hegel knowing is superior to both doing and making and that (absolute) knowledge involves the *Aufhebung* of both alienation and (externalizing) objectification. For Marx (social) making is higher than (individual) doing or knowing; every significant action or production must leave its permanent, external, objective mark on nature and history. Only under capitalism, with its private ownership of the means of production, is productive objectification an alienation. Beyond capitalism, alienation will disappear, but objectification will remain as a necessary and permanent aspect of all production.

Unlike Hegel, Marx refuses to recognize any self-sufficient Aristotelian *noēsis noēseōs*, any self-contained, unexternalized artistic creation, any purely "inward" action. For Marx, a poet who kept his poem to himself, like a painter who destroyed his painting as soon as it was completed, would not count as a producer. Self-contained creativity, like self-centered enjoyment, is for Marx—as it was for Hegel—"abstract$_H$."[11] and antihistorical. A *fortiori*, existential inwardness, decision, passion—so long as they lack objective expression, so long as they remain unobjectified (*unvergegenständlicht*), are of no interest

---

[10] See Sec. V below for explanation of this term.
[11] See Sec. V below.

or value in Marx's eyes. To exist, for Marx—even young Marx—is not enough. To be human, or rather to become human, one must make, must produce—which means, one must objectify, impose an enduring human shape on what is nonhuman.

To put the point differently, in more conceptual terms: Marx shares the substantialist assumption that "actualization" as process (*Verwirklichung*) must issue in a "product" (*Werk*). In particular *Arbeit* involves *Werke*; work involves works. Hegel's terms *Werk* and *Verwirklichung* deliberately echo the relation of *ergon* to *energeia* in Aristotle,[12] but there is an ambiguity in the term *ergon* which is only faintly reproduced in *Werk*: *ergon* can mean either *product* (as "law is the *ergon* of legislation" or "the statue is the *ergon* of sculpting") or *function* (as "seeing or sight is the *ergon* of the eye" or "cutting is the *ergon* of the knife"). "Function" is conceptually close to "service."

There is a passage in *Das Kapital*, formulated in very Hegelian language, that nicely sums up Marx's bias toward objectification as the production of objects rather than services: "During the work-process, work continually changes from the form of restlessness to that of being, from the form of motion to that of thinghood or objectivity."[13]

IV. THE MORALITY OF THE PRODUCER

Closely related to Marx's stress on *Vergegenständlichung* is his orientation toward a "producer's morality" as opposed to a "consumer's morality." He sees unalienated, liberated man as a producer rather than consumer. His concern, at least in the pre-*Manifesto* period, is with the quality of human life typical of the producer—i.e., maker—as opposed to that of the consumer—i.e., enjoyer.

Here Marx's inspiration is clearly Hegelian: under capitalism the worker—like the slave in Hegel's *Phenomenology*—is a pure producer;

---

[12] Marx follows Hegel in rejecting the Aristotelian claim that an activity (*energeia*) which has its product (*ergon*) within itself—e.g., dancing, or the acquiring of good moral habits—is superior to one which has an external *ergon*—e.g., painting, or the imparting of good moral habits.

[13] "Während des Arbeitsprozesses setzt sich die Arbeit beständig aus der Form der Unruhe in die des Seins, aus der Form der Bewegung in die der Gegenständlichkeit um," *MEW*, XXIII, 204.

the nonworker—like Hegel's master—is a pure consumer. The life of the nonworker, or capitalist, is characterized by passive *enjoyment* without active work, that of the worker by active *work* without passive enjoyment. Marx sees the dialectical overcoming of this opposition in the *enjoyment* of *active* work in the unalienated communist society of the future.

Of course, Marx admits that under capitalism most workers share the capitalist's passion for security but only because their work is alienated, because they work not for the pleasure of producing but from the necessity for making a living. In this sense the alienated worker, like Hegel's slave, defines himself in choosing the security of a less-than-human existence, rather than manfully resisting enslavement at the risk of death. But under communism producers will seek risk, spurn security.

Marx sides with Nietzsche against every form of utilitarianism: the *summum bonum* is not the security-oriented life of passive enjoyment but the freedom-oriented life of active creation. To produce is to risk, even to court, pain and loss. What must be eliminated is not suffering as such but only the suffering which degrades.[14] The suffering of the producer exalts.[15]

V. 'ABSTRACT' AND 'CONCRETE'

I referred earlier to Marx's terminological carelessness. In this respect he is more Kantian than Hegelian: Kant was inconsistent and careless in his use of key terms; Hegel tended to be much more consistent and careful. We have already considered Marx's unfortunate use of the term 'material.' Now I want to say something about Marx's use of the terms 'abstract' and 'concrete.'

In the parlance of British empiricism, what is *concrete* is the sense-

[14] The expression ("suffering which degrades") does not, so far as I know, appear in Marx's own writings. It does appear in the writings of an early Russian "Nietzschean" Marxist, V. A. Bazarov. Cf. his *Na dva fronta* [On Two Fronts], St. Petersburg 1910, p. xiv.

[15] For a more detailed discussion of the "morality of the producer" see Eugene Kamenka, *The Ethical Foundation of Marxism*, London and New York, 1962, esp. pp. viii–ix, 102, 107f, 113f, 159, 195; also my article, "Marx, the *Manifesto*, and the Soviet Union Today," *The Ohio University Review*, vol. VI (1964), esp. pp. 71–73.

particular; general terms and universals are *abstract*. We may call these senses 'concrete$_E$' and 'abstract$_E$,' respectively. In "ordinary usage," 'concrete' tends to mean either "specific" as opposed to "vague and general" or else "down-to-earth" as opposed to "flighty and dreamy." We may designate these two related senses of the term as 'concrete$_O$.'

Hegel's usage differs sharply from *both* of these. For Hegel, 'concrete' means "many-sided, adequately related, complexly mediated" (we may call this sense 'concrete$_H$'), while 'abstract' means "one-sided, inadequately related, relatively unmediated" ('abstract$_H$'). A concept or universal can quite sensibly be characterized as concrete$_H$, and at the same time, without paradox, as abstract$_E$. Sense-particulars, or "sensuous immediacy," will necessarily be abstract$_H$ but at the same time, unparadoxically, concrete$_E$.[16]

These divergent senses of the terms 'abstract' and 'concrete' have created havoc for Hegel scholars, most of whom switch back and forth uncritically from 'concrete$_E$' to 'concrete$_H$' without noting, or marking, the transition or the difference.

This also applies to the various Hegelian revisionists, beginning with Feuerbach. Perhaps because of his empiricist bias, Feuerbach tended to use both terms in their empiricist sense, even when discussing Hegelian problems in generally Hegelian jargon. Marx followed Feuerbach's bad example,[17] and Marxists of every stripe have continued this terminological abuse. There appears to be some clustering in Marx's usage: he most often uses the terms in their Hegelian sense when he is discussing history and society, and he tends to use

---

[16] See my article, "Some Recent Reinterpretations of Hegel's Philosophy," *The Monist*, vol. 48 (1964), pp. 40–44.

[17] In one place Marx falls into a paradox as a result of failing to distinguish between the two distinct senses of 'concrete.' He says that the concrete is, on the one hand, the *outcome* of a process of thought, a synthesis of many determinations; but on the other hand, the concrete is the *point of departure* for sensation and representation. Clearly the outcome is concrete$_H$ (and also abstract$_E$), while the point of departure is concrete$_E$ (and also abstract$_H$). The following is Marx's text: "Das Konkrete ist konkret, weil es die Zusammenfassung vieler Bestimmungen ist, also Einheit des Mannigfaltigen. Im Denken erscheint es daher als Prozess der Zusammenfassung, als Resultat, nicht als Ausgangspunkt, obgleich es der wirkliche Ausgangspunkt und daher auch der Ausgangspunkt der Anschauung und Vorstellung ist" *MEW*, XIII, 632. I must add that Alfred Schmidt's useful book (cf. fn. 6 above) suffers from careless use of the terms 'abstract' and 'concrete,' which appear quite indiscriminately in all three senses.

them in the empiricist sense when he is discussing (as he seldom does) experience, perception or knowledge. But often he uses *both* senses in a single paragraph, without any apparent awareness of the opposed meanings of 'concrete$_H$' and 'concrete$_E$' or 'abstract$_H$' and 'abstract$_E$.' And Marx sometimes slips into the "ordinary" usage: 'concrete$_o$' and 'abstract$_o$.' Some future Marx scholar could make a significant contribution to *Marx-Deutung* by a careful conceptual sorting out of these disparate usages.

VI. CONCLUSION

I have criticized several prevalent misinterpretations of Marx's philosophical position. I deny that, even in his earliest writings, Marx was either an existentialist or an ethical humanist. He advanced a humanist *ideal* for the future, but he did not accept humanist *principles* for the present.

Marx's use of such key terms as 'material,' 'abstract,' and 'concrete' is systematically misleading. He is not an ontological materialist, but one reason why he has been regarded as such is his own misequation of the terms 'material' and 'economic.'

Marx's philosophical position might better be called "economic objectivism" or "objectivist economism." It is both historical and dialectical or, perhaps more accurately if less elegantly put, it is both a "dialectico-historical" and an "historico-dialectical" economic objectivism.

COMMENT

Louis Dupré

According to Professor Kline, "neither the young nor the old Marx was an ontological materialist." Marx used the term 'materialism' in two different senses: in the sense of "acquisitiveness" which he further identified with "economically determined" and accepted; and as referring to the ontological doctrine that only matter is real, which was never accepted by Marx.

Much as I agree with Professor Kline's position on the latter meaning, I am not convinced that "acquisitive" or "economically determined" are the main connotations of the materialism that was acceptable to Marx. These connotations are certainly present in the term 'material' as Marx often uses it, they may even be present in the term 'materialism' as Marx uses it in his later works (in which I am not competent), but the only materialism that Marx advocates in his early works is an anti-idealistic theory of man.

The earliest instance of this conception is found in the discussion of eighteenth-century French materialism in *The Holy Family*. Marx rejects Bauer's metaphysical interpretation and, instead, interprets this materialism as an antimetaphysical and antitheological humanism which, like Feuerbach's anthropology, was rooted in a new, practical view of man rather than in a particular speculation on the nature of the universe. According to Marx, French materialism was primarily a social philosophy based on the idea that man is basically good and headed for infinite progress whereas organized religion is opposed to this progress. An optimistic belief in man and a denial of any sort of superhuman transcendence are, according to Marx, the essential features of French materialism; the ontological speculations are accidental.

Explicitly the problem of materialism first appears in *The German Ideology*. To understand Marx's position correctly, one must never lose sight of the fact that the *historical materialism* here developed is intended to be a theory of action which consciously avoids becoming a theory of being. That products of the mind have no autonomous value for Marx is obvious enough. "The phantoms formed in the human brain are also, necessarily, sublimates of their material life process which is empirically verifiable and bound to material premises. Morality, religion, metaphysics, all the rest of ideology and their corresponding forms of consciousness thus no longer retain the semblance of independence."[1] Yet even in this strongly anti-spiritualist text, the *substance* of the mind is not discussed and the term 'material,' as Professor Kline indicates, means 'economic.' Of course, this usage of the term is most misleading in an author who considers human *praxis* (which is primarily economic) an active relationship between consciousness and nature.

This last point bears some explanation. It is true that for Marx mental production is determined by material production. But this is by no means the same as a determination of consciousness by matter. Material production presupposes an *active* relationship with nature in which man has as much initiative as nature. This presupposes that man is not a mere

[1] *MEGA*, I, 5, 15–16; cf. *The German Ideology*, tr. by R. Pascal, New York 1960, pp. 14–15.

product of nature. That man is made by his environment is true only if one adds that he himself makes his environment. It is precisely for forgetting this important addition that Marx rejects ordinary materialism. The *Third Thesis on Feuerbach* reads: "The materialistic doctrine concerning the changing of circumstances and education forgets that circumstances are changed by men."[2]

Ordinary materialism *reduces* man to nature. Marx's "materialism" *relates* man to nature. It leaves the proper character of consciousness intact and only excludes *ideology*, that is, any mental creation which claims to be independent of consciousness' active relation to nature. It is precisely for not having seen the dialectical character of the relationship between consciousness and nature that Feuerbach is dismissed as a "materialist." Marx's historical materialism is as far removed from materialism as it is from idealism. It consists in a refusal to carry on a philosophical speculation, for its own sake, beyond the dialectic of action. Any such speculation on what consciousness and nature are *in themselves*, independent of the other term of the dialectic, is an *ideology*. This is true even if the conclusion is that all being is material, for such a conclusion reduces one term of the dialectic to the other and thereby eliminates the possibility of a true, that is, an active dialectical *praxis*.

Historical materialism reflects upon *praxis in order to further praxis.* Unless theory is based upon action and can be reconverted into action, unless theory becomes a moment in the dialectic of *praxis*, it is *eo ipso* false, for *praxis* alone contains the truth of man. In that sense, but in that sense only, is historical materialism the abolition of philosophy: it refuses any speculation which is a priori with respect to *praxis.*

Of course, this creates a problem insofar as historical materialism itself is a philosophy. Is not the dialectical relation of man to nature a speculative a priori through which the Marxist *interprets* practice? The only alternative to this inconsistency is to posit that the dialectic is empirically discovered *within praxis.* But by which method? By an existential analysis? Or simply by generalizing empirical observations? To understand it in the latter way would in the final analysis be destructive of the dialectic itself. For a purely empiricist view of the dialectic would lack the universality and predictability which are essential for historical materialism. It also would reduce the dialectic to an object of positive science and replace its teleology by a naturalistic determinism.

The dialectic, therefore, must have an ideal character, but this ideal should not be conceived prior to or apart from the reality of *praxis.* It is the ideal aspect of *praxis* itself. There seems to be no other way left to understand the principle of dialectic than to conceive of it as man's pre-

[2] *Ibid.,* 534.

reflective activity, the living unity of nature and consciousness, which can be explicated but not initiated by reflective thought. Only dialectical *praxis* justifies a dialectical *theory*.

According to Sartre's *Critique de la raison dialectique*, later Marxism again divorces theory from *praxis* and, instead of discovering the dialectic *in praxis*, *dictates* its own speculative principles *to praxis*. Strangely enough, it claims to obtain these (dogmatic) principles in a purely empirical fashion: the dialectic is reduced to a "dialectic of nature" in which man is merely the conscious part of the one, univocal, material reality of nature. We know what Marx would have thought of this "monistic" dialectic: he has anticipated and rejected it in his critique of Feuerbach.

Yet, as I have pointed out elsewhere[3] it is Marx himself who is responsible for these materialistic deviations. His onesided description of *praxis* in terms of economic production reduces all action to *making*; as professor Kline puts it, and thus eliminates all nonproductive activity from the process of humanization. But if man's entire activity is directed toward the satisfaction of material needs, what makes him proceed from the first stage of history described in *The German Ideology*, the fulfilment of natural needs, to the second stage, the creation and satisfaction of artificial needs? If human activity were restricted to the material life process, it could never pass the first stage. How could the *homo oeconomicus*, exclusively intended upon the satisfaction of physical needs, ever transcend his *immediate* relation to nature and create cultural values which have no direct bearing upon his physical needs? And yet, this is what man actually does; the more human he becomes, the farther he gets away from all purely physical determinations. Man's cultural development takes place within a dialectical relationship to nature. But if human *praxis* is reduced to a mere response to physical needs, man becomes a part of nature and the dialectical opposition disappears. This kind of Pavlovian conditioned reflex has never existed in man, for even in his most primitive responses to natural needs man *transforms* nature by imposing upon it the mark of consciousness.

Marx's simplistic identification of *praxis* with economic production is the main cause of Marxism's later development toward materialism. If Marxism is to be an integral philosophy of man, it will have to abandon not only its gross materialism but also Marx's own economism.

[3] *The Philosophical Foundations of Marxism*, New York 1966, pp. 220–230.

INDEX *

Abe, I. 286
abstract
    and concrete 430–432
    in history 187
activity
    economic 427
Acton, Lord J. E. E. D. 371
Adler, M. 162
Adorno, T. 21
Afghani Djamal al din al 260, 261
Aflak, M. 279
Aini 266
alienation 27–29, 136–137, 138, 139,
    140, 141, 142, 144, 145, 146, 148,
    150, 151, 153–154, 156, 158,
    205–206, 399
    and economic life 152
    in Hegel 137
    as identical with class society 143–
    144
    kinds 358–359
    in Marx 66–67
    and objectification 146
    and philosophy 152–153
    and revolution 151
    social solution to 29–31
    sociological phenomenon of 147–150
anarchism
    in Marxism 127, 129–130
Anselm, St. 316
anthropotheism (Feuerbach) 324–327
Anti-Dühring (Engels) 6, 213, 309
"apocalypticism" 381
Arakawa, K. 286
Arcos, S. T. 230, 232
Aristotle 103, 160, 174–175, 304, 392,
    429, 430

Aron, R. 338
atheism 304
    in Marxism 312, 348–353, 353–354,
    375
    methodological 303
    skeptical 303
Augustine, St. 181, 203, 216
autonomy 190
Azô, H. 286

Babeuf, I. N. 201, 210
Bakunin, M. 128, 130, 212, 213, 214,
    403
Barreto, T. 236
Barth, K. 319, 327
basis 62
    economic 63
    and superstructure 61–62
Bauer, Bruno 304, 306, 312, 323, 331,
    433
Bauer, O. 290, 291
Bazard, St. A. 201
Beaumont, G. de 220
Bebel, A. 23, 120, 128, 212
Beethoven, L. v. 392
Begdash, Kh. 275, 276
Behbudi, M. 266
Belinski, V. G. 422, 423
Benjamin, W. 20
Berdiaev, N. 340, 342
Bergson, H. 7
Berlin, I. 170
Bernstein, E. 162, 282, 290
Betancourt, R. 239
Bible 346
Bilbaō, F. 230, 232
Bismarck, O. v. 91, 94, 95, 236

* Compiled by T. Gerald.